APEX
— LEGENDS™ —

PATHFINDER'S
QUEST

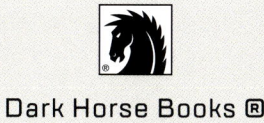

Dark Horse Books ®

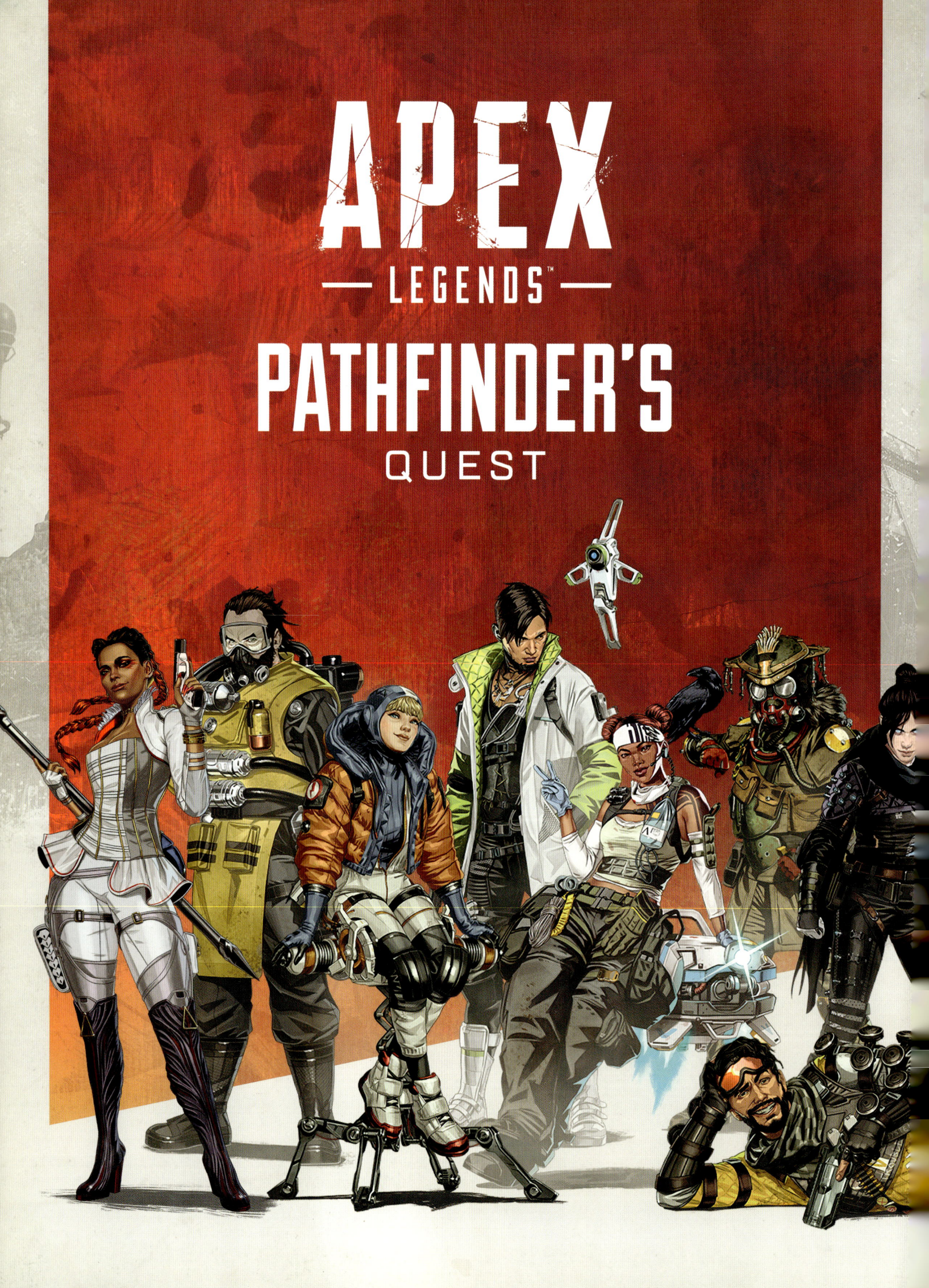

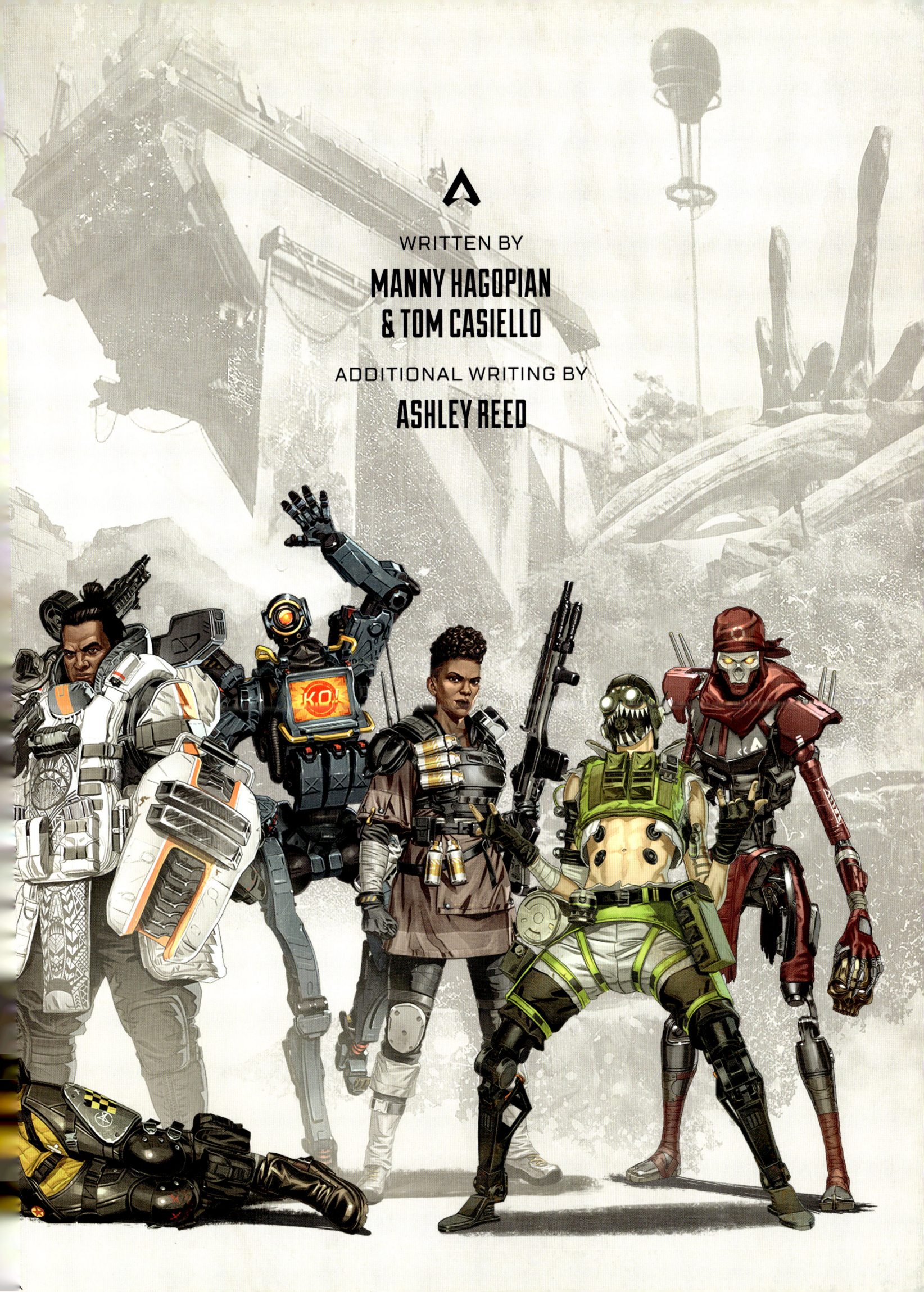

WRITTEN BY

**MANNY HAGOPIAN
& TOM CASIELLO**

ADDITIONAL WRITING BY

ASHLEY REED

president and publisher
MIKE RICHARDSON

editor
IAN TUCKER

associate editor
BRETT ISRAEL

designer
LIN HUANG

digital art technician
ALLYSON HALLER

APEX LEGENDS: PATHFINDER'S QUEST

© 2021 Electronic Arts Inc. EA, the EA logo, Respawn, the Respawn logo, and Apex Legends are trademarks of Electronic Arts Inc. All rights reserved. Dark Horse Books® and the Dark Horse logo are registered trademarks of Dark Horse Comics LLC. All rights reserved. No portion of this publication may be reproduced or transmitted, in any form or by any means, without the express written permission of Dark Horse Comics LLC. Names, characters, places, and incidents featured in this publication either are the product of the author's imagination or are used fictitiously. Any resemblance to actual persons (living or dead), events, institutions, or locales, without satiric intent, is coincidental.

Published by Dark Horse Books
A division of Dark Horse Comics LLC
10956 SE Main Street
Milwaukie, OR 97222

DarkHorse.com

Library of Congress Cataloging-in-Publication Data

Names: Hagopian, Manuel, author. | Dark Horse Books.
Title: Apex legends. Pathfinder's quest / by Manuel Hagopian.
Description: First Edition. | Milwaukie, Oregon : Dark Horse Books, 2020. |
   Summary: "Explore the world of the hit game with Pathfinder, as he
   chronicles his journey throughout the various environs of the Apex
   landscape. The first-hand accounts from Pathfinder of other legends met
   along the way, as well as weapons and equipment, are a must own for any
   fan of the game who is looking for a deeper look into gaming hit. This
   book chronicles the world of EA's stunning free-to-play game that
   captivated the online gaming scene, attracting 10 million players–and up
   to 1 million playing concurrently–within the first 3 days of its
   release"-- Provided by publisher.
Identifiers: LCCN 2020026180 | ISBN 9781506719900 (Hardcover) | ISBN
   9781506721613 (ePub)
Subjects: LCSH: Video games--Juvenile literature. | Apex legends (Computer
   game)
Classification: LCC GV1469.3 .H34 2020 | DDC 794.8--dc23
LC record available at https://lccn.loc.gov/2020026180

Ebook ISBN 978-1-50672-161-3
Hardcover ISBN 978-1-50671-990-0
First edition: February 2021

10 9 8 7 6 5 4 3 2
Printed in China

TABLE OF CONTENTS

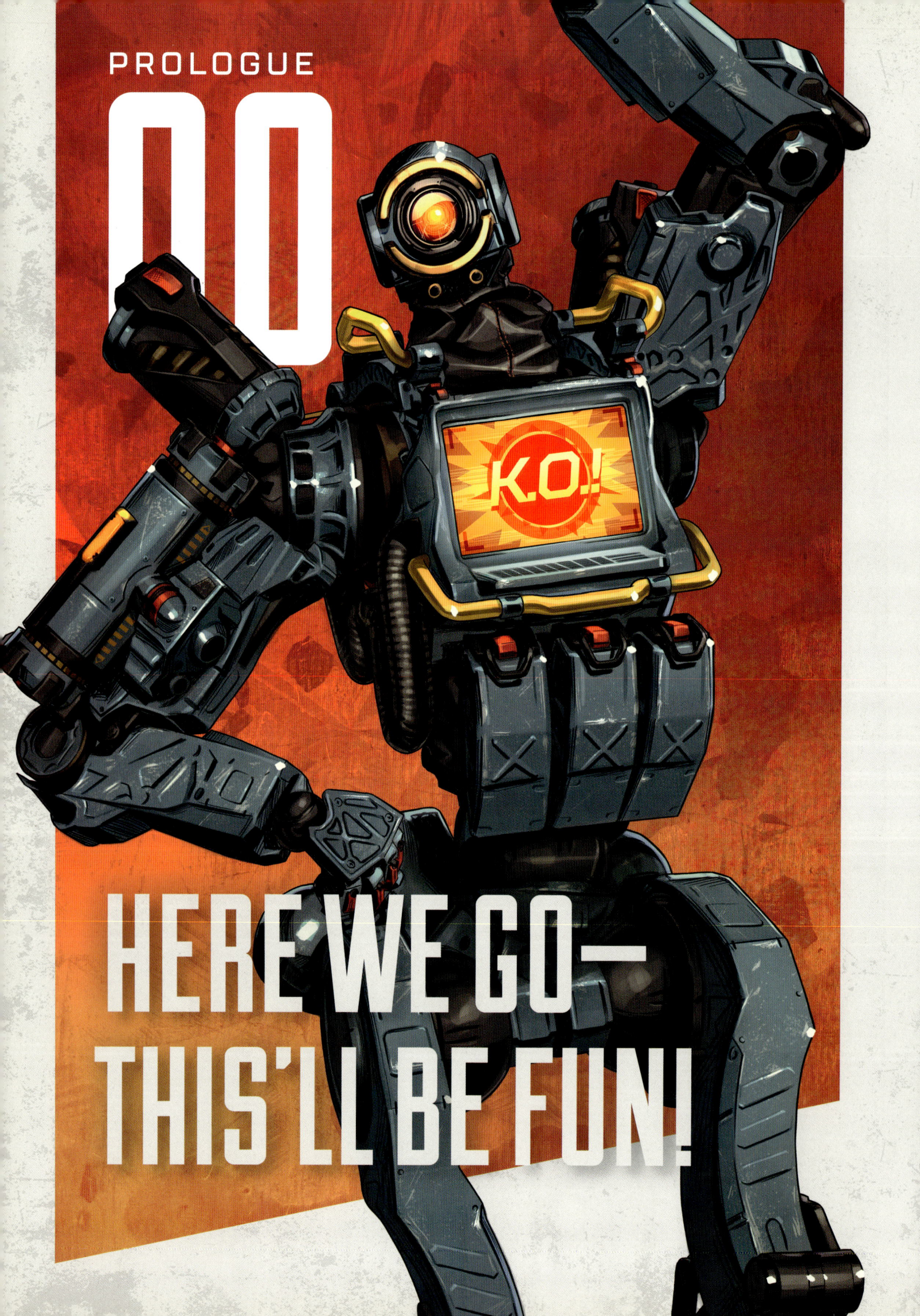

PATHFINDER MEMORY LOG: DAY 0

I woke up in an abandoned warehouse and since then my life has been very fun. I've seen so many things and met so many great people—wow, I'm lucky and it's only been thirty-three years and four days. It's sad that my memory logs don't have any information about what my life was before that day, and I really wish I could know because that would mean I'd know who created me, which is my number one goal, but it didn't start that way.

My memory logs only show that I woke up alone surrounded by cobwebs, dust, mechanical tools, little insects, and wires connected to destroyed computers. On a workstation, I found a piece of paper that looked like me with the word "MRVN" written on it, which I assumed was my name. So, I took it and began my journey of going somewhere else that wasn't there.

My Location Records show I traveled everywhere between Gaea to Solace for a number of years. I recall going on freighter ships and transports all the time in order to get from planet to planet; I think they just thought I was part of the machinery since I never paid for passage, but no matter where I was going, my purpose was still unknown. That is, until I broke my leg on a person who, I think, wanted to steal my leg. Unfortunately, it costs money to get a leg fixed and I didn't have any of that. I had no choice but to get a job, which was extremely fun.

LOG BOX --- PATHFINDER EMPLOYMENT RECORDS

- Farmer—Fired for not knowing how to farm.
- Teacher—Fired for not knowing how to teach.
- Engineer—Fired for knowing too much and putting every other employee out of a job.
- Marketing Agent—Fired for telling the truth.
- Corporate Overlord—Fired for making a joke.
- Coat Rack—Fired for moving.
- Secretary—Fired for hanging up on important calls.
- Arms Dealer—Fired for calling everyone "friend."
- Line Cook—Fired for setting the kitchen on fire.
- Fuel Attendant—Fired for setting the station on fire.
- Firefighter—Fired for forgetting my ID.
- Door-to-Door Salesman—Fired for not knocking.
- Used Vehicle Salesman—Fired for answering too many questions.
- New Vehicle Salesman—Fired for not answering enough questions.
- Beverage Serviceman—Fired for spilling hot drinks on customers.
- Masseur—Fired for breaking a customer's bones.
- Painter—Fired for only drawing "smiley faces."
- Therapist—Fired for being too optimistic.

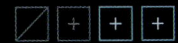

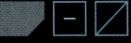

INNER MONOLOGUE ACTIVATED

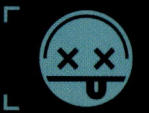
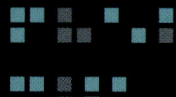
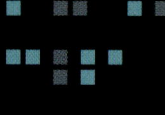
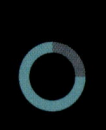
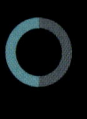

- Musician—Fired for "rocking too hard."
- Handyman—Fired for getting stuck inside a customer's oven.
- Plumber—Fired for turning a house into a boat.
- Poet—Fired for not knowing how limericks work.
- Pilot—Fired for landing upside down.
- Weatherman—Fired for predicting the weather.
- Ice Cream Server—Fired for not knowing how the ice cream tasted.
- Window Washer—Fired for scaring too many people.

It wasn't until I met one of my really good friends, Victor Maldera (who saved my life by arresting me and putting me in danger), that I found myself with a purpose for the first time since I woke up. I was made for something special and the person who made me was a mystery. I don't know why my creator doesn't want me to know who they are. Maybe we just got separated and they've been looking for me. Or maybe they have been in danger and are waiting for me to save them. Or maybe I did something wrong and they don't want to see me anymore, which is probably not true because I've been told lots of times that I'm a "joy to be around" in a very snarky tone for some reason.

Either way, since that day I've been looking for my creator. I've shouted down the streets of Suotamo, put up banners throughout Psamathe's capital city, and even tried to get some attention on the feed after learning that my creator may have frequented local taverns on Solace, but that ended up being a lie, which was told to me by my now best friend, Mirage.

I met the amazing Elliott "Mirage" Witt at his bar, the Paradise Lounge, after walking in and asking whoever would listen to help me find my creator. Two gentlemen told me that they knew exactly who my creator was and that they would tell me if I helped them build a house, which I did for the next three weeks. After I finished, I never saw those two friends again. While at the bar one day, Elliott explained to me that I was being taken advantage of and that they had no intention of ever telling me who my creator was and they probably never even knew the answer to begin with. This made me express my sad face . . . Why do people lie? It only creates sadness. Unless they chose to lie to avoid sadness, but still that may only last a short time. I've never lied. I always speak the truth because I don't see any other way to express what I want to say. I guess that's what could be called my "personality," but Elliott just calls me "a weird smiling robot," which I guess is also true. I trust Elliott because he, like my friend Maldera, talked to me for more than a minute. That's all I need to call someone my friend—just a small amount of time in their lives that they choose to spend with me. In Elliott's case, he took the time out of his day to give me this advice and (a thing I'll never forget) he told me the best way I could find my creator—I could join the Apex Games.

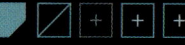

The Apex Games is a place where I can fight with friends against other (bad) friends. When we win and become champions, the games put a picture of me on a giant banner for everyone to see. Since then, I've been hoping that if my face is seen throughout the Outlands, then maybe my creator will find me, instead of the other way around.

It's been four years since I joined the Apex Games and it's been very fun. I've met a lot of great friends, but I still haven't found my creator. That is, until recently when I discovered an old deactivated MRVN on Olympus. Something about it seemed special to me and I wanted to turn it on. Thanks to the help of my friends Lifeline, Gibraltar, and Octane, I did! And when I turned it on . . . it spoke to me.

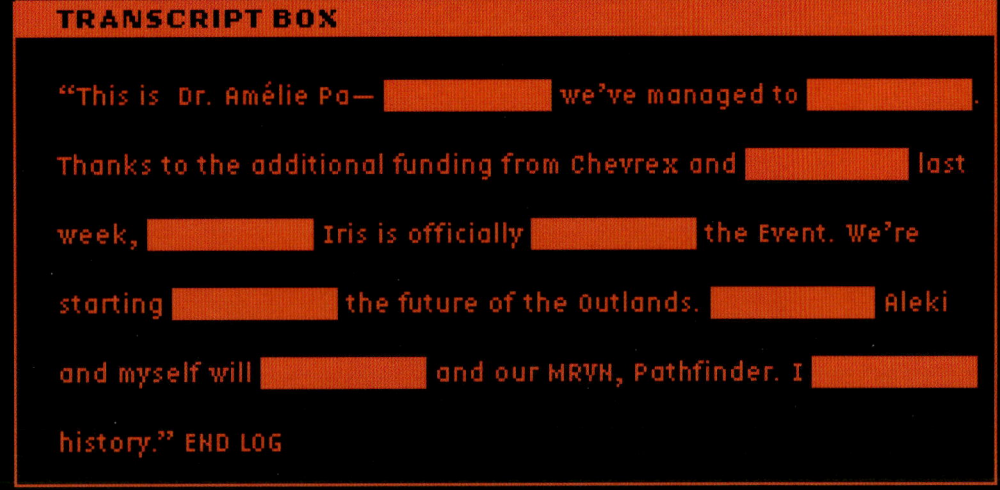

TRANSCRIPT BOX

"This is Dr. Amélie Pa— ▮▮▮▮▮ we've managed to ▮▮▮▮▮. Thanks to the additional funding from Chevrex and ▮▮▮▮▮ last week, ▮▮▮▮▮ Iris is officially ▮▮▮▮▮ the Event. We're starting ▮▮▮▮▮ the future of the Outlands. ▮▮▮▮▮ Aleki and myself will ▮▮▮▮▮ and our MRVN, Pathfinder. I ▮▮▮▮▮ history." END LOG

I'm not sure what it means or who it was from, but I think I recognize that voice. I've heard it before. As if I had it burned into my memory and even though it's gone for some reason, I still know it. This is all very strange, very exciting, and very . . . emotional. I've been looking for my creator for a long time and now I may find them, but first, I need to solve these clues.

CLUE BOX

TRANSMISSION CLUES
- "Chevrex" >
- "The future of the Outlands" >
- "Dr. Amélie Pa——" >
- "The Event" >
- "Aleki" >
- "Iris" >

I guess it's time to start my journey. Day 1—here we go. This'll be fun! Now where to start . . .

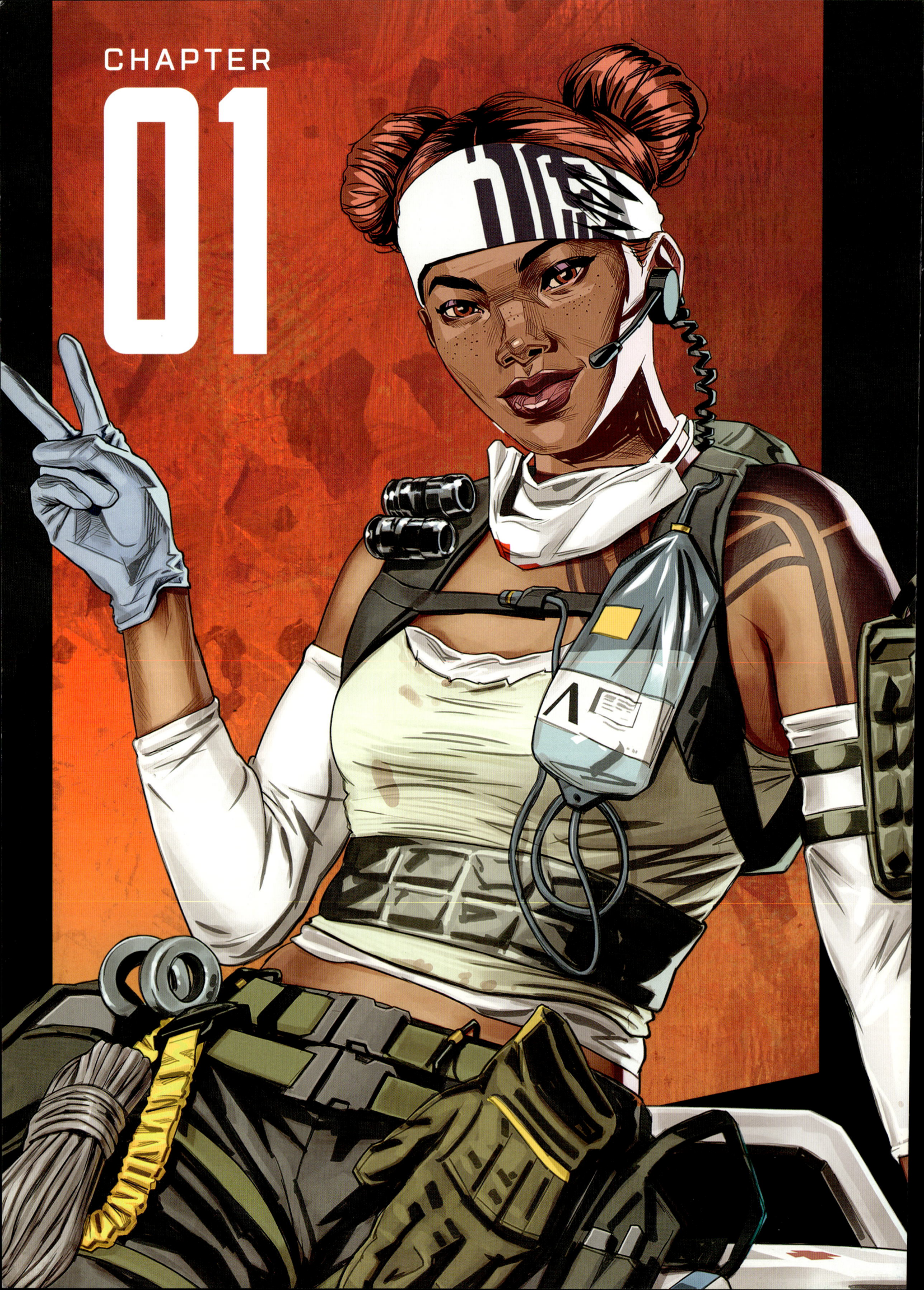

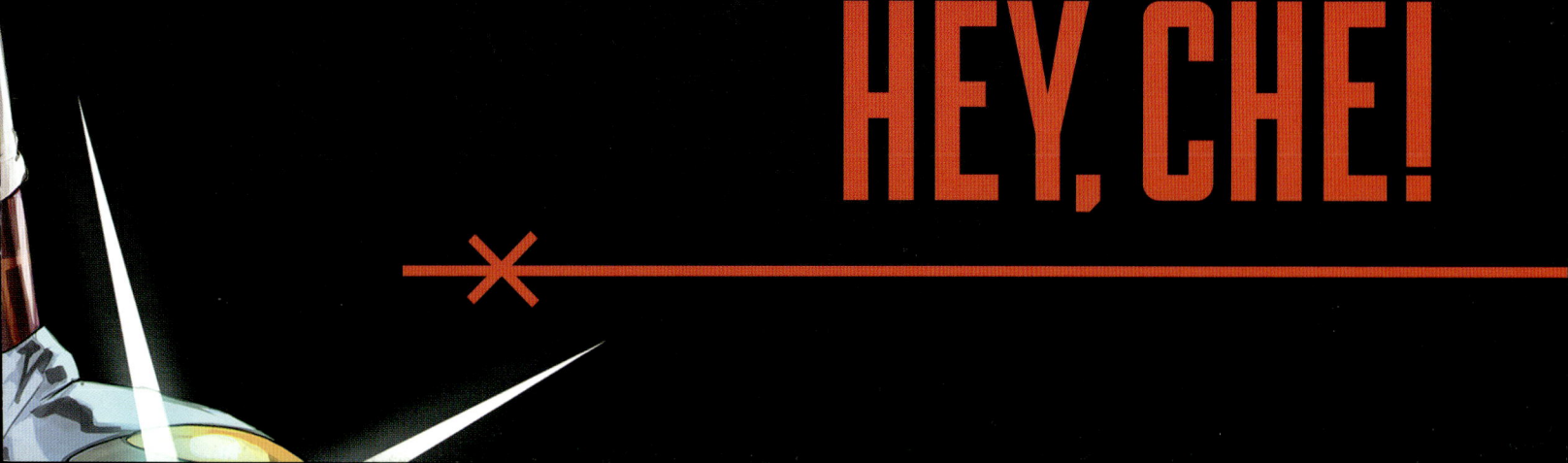

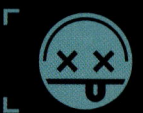

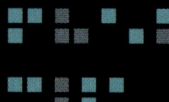

PATHFINDER MEMORY LOG: DAY 1

Today I hit the open road on a transport in space to meet my friend Ajay Che—but her thousands of "number one fans" call her Lifeline. The message I found gave me the first batch of clues that I think can lead me to my creator. There was one clue that looked familiar, and that's: Chevrex. After having my life saved a number of times by Ajay's heal drone, DOC, I remember reading its system signature as Chevrex Inc. Maybe she can help. Hey! Maybe she's my creator!

CLUE BOX

TRANSMISSION CLUES
* "Chevrex" > Something to do with Lifeline's heal drone
* "The future of the Outlands" >
* "Dr. Amélie Pa——" >
* "The Event" >
* "Aleki" >
* "Iris" >

SELF-MOTIVATION QUOTE . . . SEARCHING . . . 1 RESULT FOUND

"Only a life lived for others is a life worthwhile."
—[ALBERT EINSTEIN]

LIFELINE BIO FROM THE APEX GAMES

ULTIMATE OBJECTIVE . . . SEEKING CREATOR

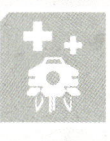
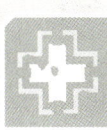

REAL NAME:
AJAY CHE

AGE:
24

HOME WORLD:
PSAMATHE

TACTICAL ABILITY:
DOC HEAL DRONE

PASSIVE ABILITY:
COMBAT MEDIC

ULTIMATE ABILITY:
CARE PACKAGE

AJAY CHE, A.K.A. LIFELINE, ISN'T SOMEONE YOU WOULD EXPECT TO FIND IN THE APEX GAMES. The child of wealthy war profiteers, she left home when she learned of the damage her family had caused and enlisted in the Frontier Corps, a humanitarian organization that aids Frontier communities in need. She's since devoted her life to helping others and joined the Apex Games to fund the Frontier Corps with her winnings.

Since no one in the Games is innocent—they all know what they signed up for—and every one of her victories means help for those in need, Lifeline has no problem engaging in the popular blood sport. Or so she tells herself. She may seem sarcastic and callous, but deep down she wants to help people and make the world a better place. If that means taking a few people down in the process, so be it.

"Never quit. That's how you win."
—LIFELINE

► HELLO, LIFELINE! ◄

IT'S SO FUN TO MEET WITH YOU WHILE NEITHER OF US IS FIGHTING, LIFELINE. THANK YOU.
Not a problem, my sweet metal friend. And yuh can call me Ajay. That's my name—Ajay Che.

WOW. I DIDN'T KNOW YOU HAD A NAME. COOL, AJAY.
Ain't often that us Legends get to chat about somethin' that doesn't involve the Games . . . [*laughs*] or Mirage. It's always us just boasting about wins, reminiscing about those who just couldn't make it past the first Ring, or eggin' each other on while we wait for the drop. I remember the first time Crypto came onboard . . . Never seen anyone shut up Mirage so quickly.

CHEVREX INC. [AI LOGIC]

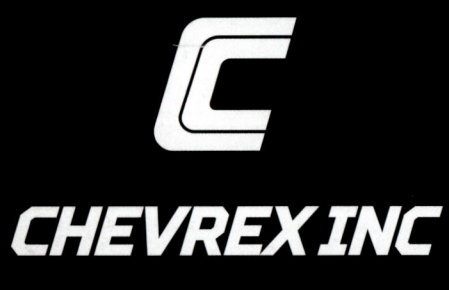

Chevrex Inc. was originally founded in 2445 as AI Logic, one of the first companies established in the Frontier. Opening as a small shop in the Harbor District of Angel City on planet Angelia, AI Logic provided services to local businesses through repairing, updating, and reprogramming electronics and robotics. Through the generations, the company evolved with its surroundings, developing and specializing in drone technology while expanding beyond Angelia.

Proudly forming a partnership with Kodai Industries, AI Logic supplied every colonized planet in the Frontier with their number one product: Security Monitoring Systems (SMS) Drones, which function as security cameras, motion detectors, and communication and recording devices.

As the IMC expanded beyond the Frontier into the Outlands, AI Logic was first in line to support those citizens who undertook the yearlong expedition to the unexplored region. Today, the AI Logic Outlands chapter, Chevrex Inc., supplies the Outlands with more than one hundred outlets and its flagship factory on the beautiful planet of Psamathe.

YES, MY BEST FRIEND DOES TALK A LOT. I LOVE THAT.
Right, so what brings yuh my way? Need some patchin' up? Someone hurt?

I DON'T KNOW. IT'S POSSIBLE THAT MY CREATOR IS HURT. I HAVEN'T HEARD FROM THEM EVER.
Still on that search, huh? To each their own, I guess. I wish I was more like yuh and didn't know my family. Of course, I wasn't always this way. I got to be grateful, I guess, in some way. I had everything I needed, everything I wanted, but at some big cost . . . That's the Chevrex way.

CHEVREX? I SAW THAT ON YOUR DRONE AND IN A RECORDING I HEARD ABOUT MY CREATOR.
I can't believe everything we went through with my parents and it led yuh right back here. But of course it's on DOC. That's where we both came from. My family owns Chevrex Inc., which I used to believe focused on safety and security. That's how they sold themselves to potential clients. It didn't matter who they were or which side they were on; Chevrex made them feel like they had just the right support to give.

The people of the Outlands didn't know much about support, and I don't blame 'em, because in times of war yuh take all the support yuh can get. It's been in the family for generations, but it was my parents who really took that thing to nowhere pretty. To them, the wars ain't nothin' but a paycheck.

I'VE HEARD ABOUT THESE WARS EVER SINCE I WOKE UP, BUT NO ONE HAS REALLY TOLD ME ABOUT THEM.
It ain't exactly the most fun topic to chat about—unless yuh're Bangalore . . . I bet that girl could go all day. Of course, she's not on the best side of history. Not to say there's actually a good side, but it ain't no secret that the IMC had some part in all four wars: Corporate Wars, Titan Wars, Frontier War, and even the civil war out here in the Outlands—though they didn't even break a sweat in that one.

WOW. THOSE ARE A LOT OF WARS. HOW IS ANYONE STILL ALIVE?
I ask myself that every day, Path. These wars go back quite some time, too. All about power. All about greed. When I found out that my family's company was profiting off the Frontier War, I spent the next year teaching myself everything there was to know about what started this whole deadly thing. I guess

▶ yuh could say I was trying to convince myself that what my parents were doing was for somethin' good, but it didn't really turn out the way I hoped... Maybe that's how Hammond himself would feel if he saw this place today.

HAMMOND? I'VE HEARD OF HAMMOND ROBOTICS. MAYBE HE'S MY CREATOR.
Ya wanna start way back there, huh? [*laughs*] Give this a scan... it's all I've found during my search for truth.

■ PORT CONNECTED: [AJAY CHE'S TABLET]

2122-2192: THE IMPACT AND RISE OF HAMMOND ENGINEERING

In 2122, Sheffield's asteroid impacts Saint Louis, Missouri, Earth, nearly causing a human-extinction-level event. An international scientific team is dispatched to the impact site, led by Dr. Sam Sheffield, for whom the asteroid and the resulting canyon are named.

After a twenty-four-hour expedition deep into the impact site, Dr. Heinrich "Henry" Hammond emerges. Reports indicate his companions died from exposure to a powerful unknown element dubbed Element X.

Five years after the Sheffield impact, Hammond presides over an influential international corporation called **Hammond Engineering**. With exclusive access to Element X, they make radical, rapid breakthroughs in the contemporary understanding of physics. Meanwhile, the strain of climate change and overpopulation takes a toll on Earth's resources, and the quality of life degrades for all but the wealthy. The prospect of leaving Earth to alleviate these problems becomes popular, but no practical solution exists to make it a reality.

Equipped with privileged scientific insights, Hammond seizes the opportunity to pioneer new advances in interstellar colonization, communications, and commercialization.

In 2187, Hammond Engineering unveils the world's first operational **interstellar jump drive**, which allows spacecraft to cross vast distances at velocities approaching light speed. The first jump drive expedition uncovers habitable planets in nearby star systems.

Today, these are known as the **Core Systems**.

2192-2292: THE CORE SYSTEMS

Fast fortunes are made by harvesting and transporting resources with jump drive-equipped ships. Hammond Engineering, already a leader in advanced robotics, produces rare alloys from the ores gained in their interstellar mining operations. These are used to build robotic mechanisms for a variety of industrial functions.

As Heinrich Hammond nears the end of his long natural life, he arranges a gradual drawdown of his involvement in Hammond Engineering. However, Hammond Engineering remains a key player in the Core Systems, where corporations maintain trade and communication routes vital to the region's survival.

Attempts to regulate these corporations through central interplanetary governance are made on several occasions but ultimately fail due to the organizations' political and economic sway. Hammond Engineering anticipates eventual hostilities with many rival corporations and begins secretly orchestrating a series of political machinations, business mergers, and acquisitions within the Core Systems. These initiatives span nearly a century, ending in the formation of the system-spanning conglomerate known as the **Interstellar Manufacturing Corporation**, or **IMC**.

All Hammond-branded businesses--including Hammond Engineering--become its subsidiaries.

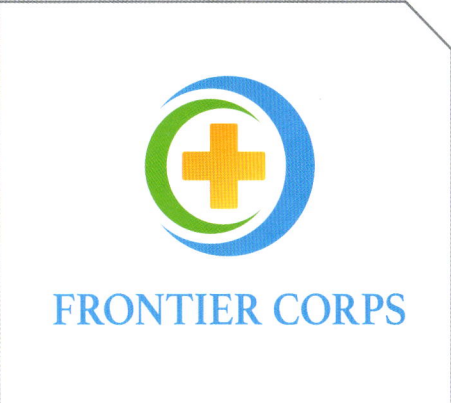

FRONTIER CORPS

2292-2442: THE FRONTIER

The atmosphere of this period is one of "corporate feudalism." Tensions rise as competition for resources grows among the Core Systems' powerful corporate entities. Free-lance explorers are hired to find new sources of raw materials. These expeditions lead to the discovery of the Frontier, a far-off zone of star systems containing an unusually dense number of habitable planets.

Travel to the Frontier exceeds the distance traversed in any previous human expedition by orders of magnitude. The trip requires an enormous investment in technology and personnel that only a handful of corporations can afford. As the galaxy's leading authority on interstellar exploration, the IMC orchestrates its most ambitious mission to date, deploying fleets of pathfinding colony ships to establish routes to the Frontier. This begins the New Space Race.

During this period, many ships are lost to accidents, equipment failure, or unknown causes. However, some expeditions successfully make landfall and begin establishing the Frontier's first outposts.

Along with the new wave of expeditions comes a massive increase in the development of robotic AI. To assist the settlers in building their colonies, **Hammond Robotics** develops a series of semiautonomous farming equipment based on antique military exoskeletons. Described as "glorified tractors" in satirical news feeds of the time, they are better known today as **Titans**.

2442-2671: THE CORPORATE WARS AND RETURN TO THE FRONTIER

As Frontier exploration continues, the IMC's resources are divided between supporting its interests in the Core Systems and its new ventures in the Frontier. This division of focus is seen as a weakness by its rival corporations, which launch a series of orchestrated attacks against the IMC that initiate the Corporate Wars. The IMC drastically scales back all investment in its Frontier expeditions, leaving its colonists to their own devices.

Over several generations of shifting intercorporate alliances and interplanetary wars, the IMC reasserts control over the Core Systems. The conflict yields significant leaps forward in technology, derived from the aggressive development of the first combat Titans.

However, the IMC's victory comes at a cost to its planets and people. Years of warfare left the Core Systems depleted of arable land and natural resources. There is yet again a strong demand for replenishment. To

fulfill this demand, the IMC looks to its previously abandoned investment in the Frontier. Its envoys discover that the descendants of the original IMC pioneers have prospered: many more worlds have been colonized and all have access to a bounty of natural resources.

The IMC asserts "eminent domain" over the Frontier, citing its investments dating back 350 years. It sends military fleets to establish control of the region, builds new manufacturing and mining operations, and displaces thousands of Frontier citizens in the process.

The colonies reject the IMC's claim to the region. As industrial production continues apace, diplomatic talks begin.

2671-2692: THE TITAN WARS

After years of failed diplomacy, the citizens of the Frontier establish the earliest form of the **Frontier Militia**. This new resistance grows in numbers and begins retaking contested lands using Titans and other war material stolen from the IMC.

The Militia's many skirmishes with IMC garrisons become the opening salvo of the **Titan Wars**. The IMC mobilizes hundreds of thousands of soldiers from the Core Systems to occupy the Frontier, rooting out Militia enclaves and bringing to bear large numbers of state-of-the-art Titans.

The Titan Wars strongly favor the IMC. The early Militia's lack of unified leadership and antiquated military technology put it at a severe disadvantage. Within a few years, the IMC eliminates nearly all of the Militia's forces.

The planet **Gridiron** becomes the official center of IMC operations in the Frontier and home to the first Hammond Robotics Titan factory. The planet **Demeter**, a waypoint between the Core Systems and the Frontier, acts as a crucial fueling station (colloquially referred to as "the Gateway") for IMC reinforcements to make the final jump to Gridiron.

2700s: THE FRONTIER WAR

Fifteen years after the Titan Wars, the last Militia fleet discovers a colony under siege by IMC hunter garrisons. The colony is led by former IMC Pilot **James MacAllan**, who had vanished into the untouched Yuma system after staging a mutiny fifteen years prior.

In exchange for help in evacuating the colonists, MacAllan offers to provide the Militia with support and intelligence to destroy the IMC's critical refueling station on Demeter. At the **Battle of Demeter**, MacAllan outmaneuvers his former commanding officer, IMC **Vice Admiral Graves**, and sacrifices his own life to destroy the Gateway. Moved by his friend's dedication, Graves defects from the IMC and takes over MacAllan's role, leading the Militia to victory.

With the destruction of the Demeter installation, IMC forces are cut off from reinforcements in the Core Systems. The Militia regains its footing and claims a significant portion of Frontier space, establishing the planet Harmony as Militia central command. There, the Militia launches the **Vanguard Initiative**, an effort to produce Frontier-made Titans as weapons to defeat the IMC.

[TITANS]

Titans are descendants of fledgling military exoskeletons. In addition to the obvious combat applications, unarmed Titans are used for labor in demanding industries like salvage and cargo transport. They are also used in special applications such as deep space search and rescue, and are very effective in inhospitable environments. The use of Titans is widespread throughout the Frontier in combat and in civilian life.

[... CONTINUED]

WOW. A LOT HAPPENED IN SEVEN HUNDRED YEARS.

Ya don't say? It's always measured by wars, though. After the Militia took power, there was a final battle at the last IMC-controlled planet—Gridiron. And what happened next . . . well, ain't no one really knows.

IT'S A MYSTERY? I HAVE A LOT OF THOSE.

I'm sure someone knows, but they ain't talkin' out loud. Anita's probably the closest, I'm sure she can fill yuh in, but all I really learned was that a "blackout" cut off all communication throughout the Frontier—that was over a decade or so ago. No one really knows what happened, how the battle at Gridiron ended—except for maybe Anita, but even she was deeply affected by it. All we know is that one day, everything stopped. All the beacons the IMC built throughout the Frontier went down. Just like that. One big blackout. Those who supported the Militia were promised refuge, but no one came. The Militia abandoned those people. They were no better than the IMC. Those poor people in the Frontier were toyed with by both sides. That's why it's hard to say who is actually "good," ya know?

Plenty of people cared for the Militia, but plenty didn't. Plenty didn't care much for the IMC either. It's hard to trust anyone who promises yuh every-thing. The IMC promised them safety and security, and then took all they had and left. The Militia prom-ised them safety and security, and then depleted all they had and disappeared. Yuh can only promise what yuh can promise. There are limits, which is somethin' the Frontier Corps taught me. Ya see, they stepped in when both sides were gone. They helped with the great migration of those left stranded in the Frontier and brought them right here to the Outlands.

Now, I'm not an expert on the Outlands. Yuh can probably get more out of Gibby, Natalie, or ya best friend, Witt.

I LOVE HIM.

Yeah, we know yuh do. So, if yuh're looking for more info on this whole area, I'd chat with them, but as for me, I grew up on Psamathe, and that place . . . well, it was a little more secluded than the other planets.

I WORKED ON PSAMATHE ONCE. I WAS A COOK AT A RESTAURANT IN OLYMPUS'S FINE DINING DISTRICT.

No way, yuh worked at Tenmei? I used to go there all the time when I was little . . . Bet yuh know how expen-sive that place is—and that's the real problem with my family . . . We were rich.

Sure, that wealth led to a pretty sweet upbringing—how many people do yuh know who had currency named after them? But having a Che coin didn't really matter when I found out where that money actually came from.

OH NO. IT DIDN'T COME FROM HAPPINESS, DID IT? BECAUSE THAT WOULD BE GREAT.

Afraid not . . . It was definitely no birthday party, I'll tell ya that much. But it was a party . . .

I spent the early part of my life in a gown. I mean, don't get me wrong . . . I liked it. I looked good. I ate the best food. And the parties . . . they were somethin' else. I did have a good time. My parents used to throw these galas for their rich friends at least once a month. I didn't know at the time what the point of these parties was, I just knew that I was there to look my best and entertain the kids—the Silvas used to come all the time.

THAT'S OCTANE SILVA'S SILVAS. YOU TWO HAVE AN INTERESTING FRIENDSHIP.

Yuhr right, Path. "Interesting" is one word . . . Octavio Silva—or Octane, now that he's a Legend. His family was friends with my family. The two of us have known

[Frontier Corps]

Founded in 2711, the Frontier Corps is a publicly funded volunteer program whose primary mission is to provide social, medical, and economic development support throughout the Frontier while promoting mutual understanding among citizens.

[Planet Psamathe]

Psamathe can most effectively be described as a "gated planet." The richest Outlands residents live here, and it's incredibly difficult for anyone from lower social classes to move up the socioeconomic ladder. The Dionysus Resort—an exclusive club frequented by only the most elite of the elite—is located on Psamathe's single moon of the same name. The innovative research metropolis of Olympus rests in Psamathe's lower atmosphere.

Psamathe's planetary government is an oligarchy governed by a council of its wealthiest residents (who, of course, send representatives to council meetings rather than attending in person, making it more of a "diakology"). It has no official military power, but conflicts are resolved by its citizens' personal armies.

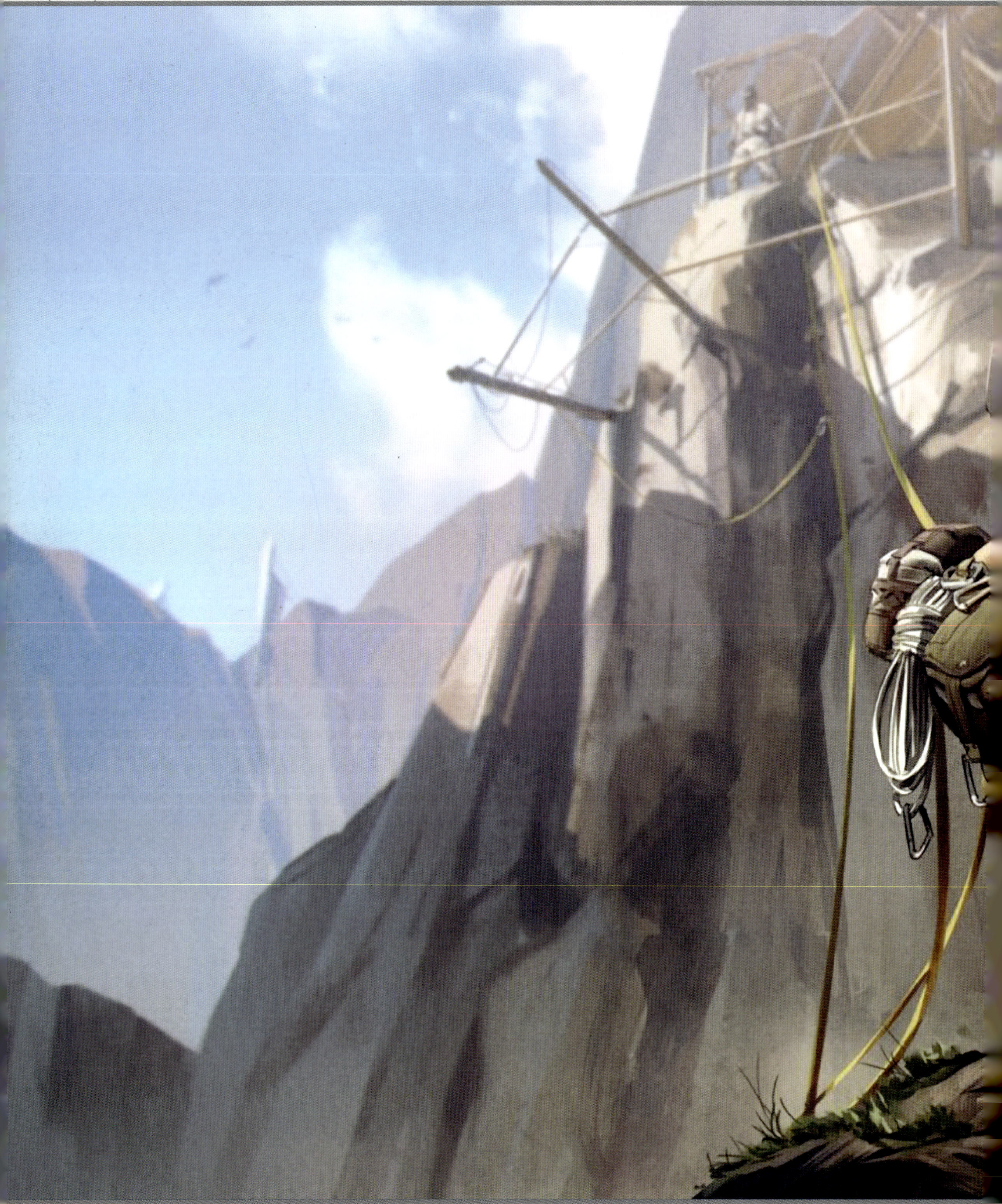

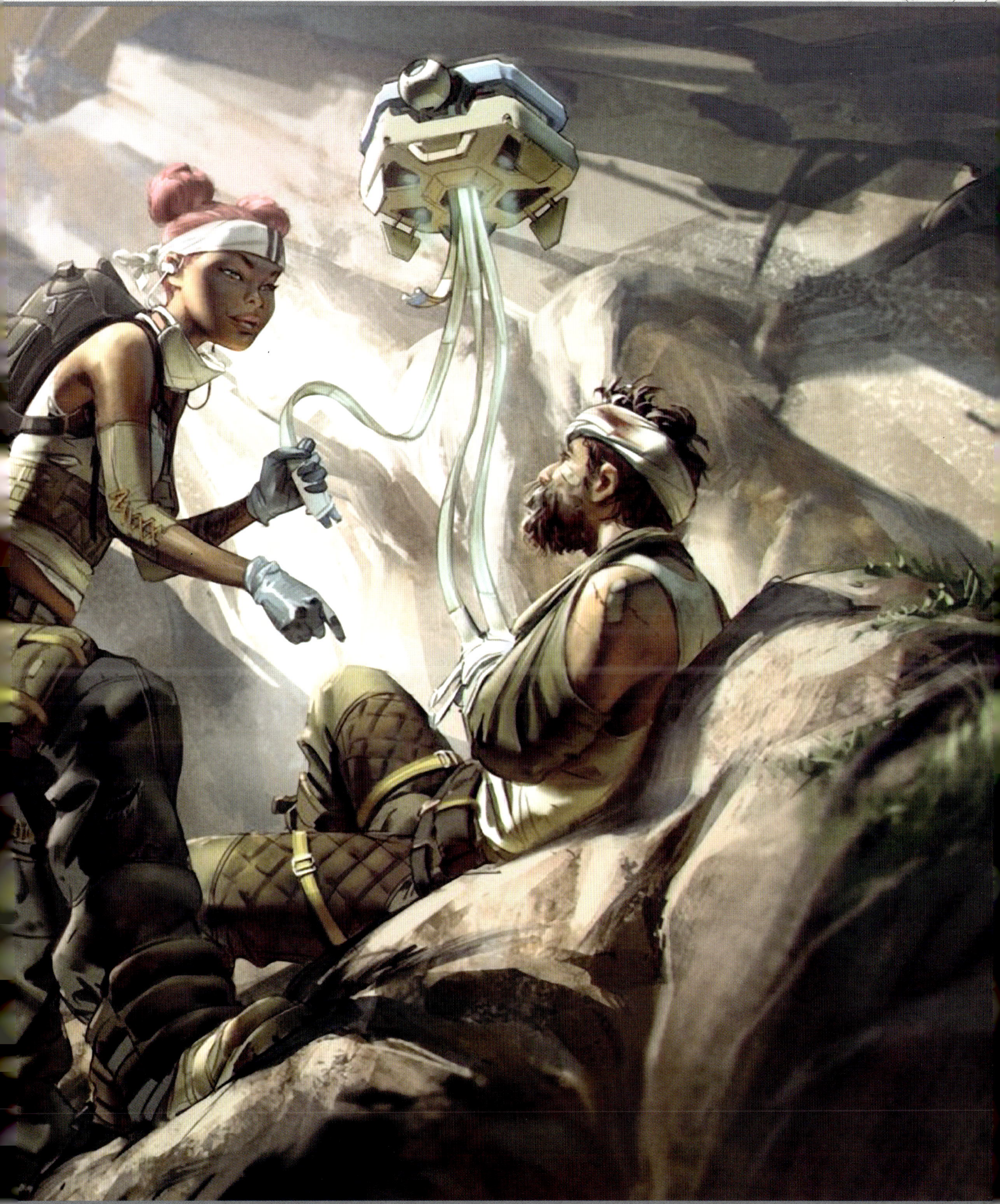

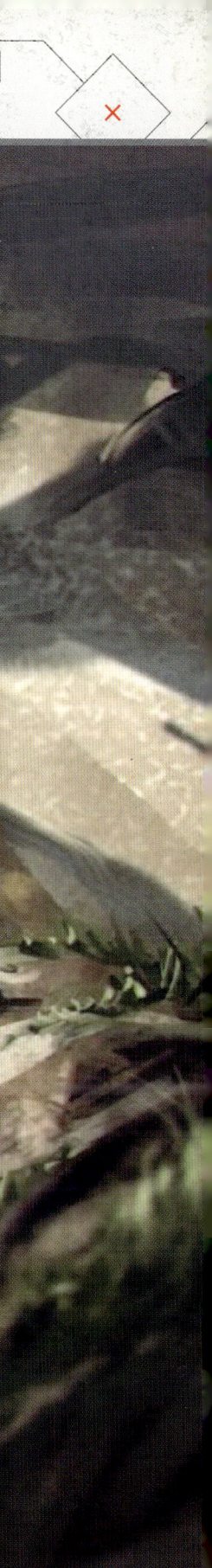

each other for a good long time now. His parents didn't do business with mine, they were just friends. The wealthy on Psamathe tend to run in the same circles—and we ran in *some* circles. We went to the same private school, the same friends' birthday parties, the same everything. It was all fine back then, but when I changed, I guess everything changed. And it was that party when it all went down—when trust broke.

I think I was nineteen? It was another monthly gala with people from Solace to the now Fringe Worlds, but this time my parents were celebrating the opening of Chevrex Inc.'s new drone facility on Olympus. It was sort of a big deal, but none of that stuff ever interested me, which is probably why it all just happened right under my nose.

WOW. SO YOU AND OCTANE HAVE ALWAYS BEEN LIKE THIS.

[*Laughs*] I guess yuh could say we were back in the day. Even after I found out the truth about my parents and left that life, Silva was the only one I kept in touch with. Although he was trapped in his family's wealth, he was not too bad at living his own life. He had a massive following on the feed and traveled all over the Outlands for thrill competitions. It's because of him that I had a chance to leave—and he knew why I wanted to.

The night of that party, the two of us stumbled upon the truth. That's the night I saw what Chevrex was actually doin'… That's the night I learned who my parents really were—war profiteers. I was embarrassed, angry… I was changed.

After that night, Silva was heading to Solace for a gauntlet competition and offered to bring me along. I wasn't ready to face my parents. I was disgusted with them and with myself, but most of all—I didn't know who I really was anymore. I figured maybe the trip would do me good, so I packed up a few things and we chartered the first ship off-planet.

I had never been to Solace up until that point. Can yuh believe that? I sheltered myself. I mean, why would I have wanted to leave my home and everything I owned? Silva left 'cause that kid got bored easily, but me, I thought I had it all. I was wrong, and Solace City shoved that in my face pretty quick.

I remember the first thing we did was stop into the Paradise Lounge for a beverage. I had never gone into a place like that for any reason, but that old me was wrong and gone. I had a new start, and it was time to test that out…

PARADISE LOUNGE IS ELLIOTT'S BAR. I'VE BEEN THERE.

Right, so yuh know why we barely took two steps in before turning around. That place smelled like old boots and seawater—we didn't want to take the chance to catch…well, anything. Luckily, there was a music joint not far from that place—we sort of followed the sound. It was faster, and carried much more edge than what we were used to on Psamathe—well, at least more than *I* was used to. Silva always sought out new things like that. He could never sit still. Boredom is his greatest fear. I guess that's why he's got such an exciting personality, which is probably why everyone was friends with him—like the musicians playing near the Paradise Lounge. Apparently, Silva did a racing competition on Gaea one year where this band performed. It worked out for me, because they left me in awe.

The musicians were just like their music: raw, edgy, and real. To tell ya the truth, Path, I didn't even know what a T-shirt was before then. I was used to gowns and dresses, but it was a new life, so it was time for a new look. I bought a shirt with the band's name on it: the Flyer Liars. For someone who'd just started to lose trust in everyone, it just felt right to fall in with that crew.

I ended up staying behind with the band while Silva continued on to his competitions. He cared—and still cares—a lot about his fans, so he had no problem moving on without me. I went on the road with the band for a bit, mostly around Solace. Karen "Kay-Kay" Kool played the drums. She called it therapeutic, so I figured I'd pick up some sticks and give it a try. I loved it. Not sayin' it was my callin' or anything, but big things came from that moment. I started a new life.

I filled in on the drums every now and then when Kay-Kay couldn't make a gig. I'd say about half a year went by, and I still hadn't spoken to my parents. It wasn't until the band got booked on Psamathe—some sort of relief fundraiser for those lower-class people who would never even come close to affording just the scraps at Tenmei. These were the type of people I never even knew existed because of my upbringing—and probably because of my ignorance, too.

But like I said, I was changed, and I saw it all now. I saw those in need. I saw those struggling while the wealthy paraded around making things worse for everyone else. It was seeing those people—who had lived just around the corner from me my entire life without me ever bothering to look at 'em—that made me finally get the guts to say a word or two to my parents. And I did.

I went home and faced them. I told them that I didn't want anything to do with the family's money anymore. They didn't really understand, but I didn't expect them to. Heh . . . And now I see that in the time I've been gone, they've done the opposite of what I hoped. They dropped straight down the rabbit hole. I hope they realize how far gone they are before it's too late. I hope it wasn't too late for me . . .

YOU'RE A LEGEND. LIKE ME!

Nah, Path. I'm no Legend. I'm just trying to do my part. That's what I told my parents I wanted to do. I'm sure they thought I wanted to run away playin' drums, probably even give up and come back home. Wasn't a crazy thought. It's hard to forget where yuh came from . . .

I DID.

Right . . . but yuh still want to know. There's probably somethin' inside of yuh that still remembers. Not sure how yuh're programmed. I know my li'l DOC's got himself a permanent memory processor—a Chevrex Inc. special. My parents put a PMP on everything so everyone knew where the product came from. No one could wipe that brand. They weren't even hiding the fact that they were playin' both sides; I guess that's what fame and power does to ya. And that's why I wanted the opposite.

I packed up whatever I could: a few shirts, some pictures, and DOC (couldn't go anywhere without her), and I left that home and that life for good. Made my way back to the Flyer Liars' show. I still remember that feelin' I had of . . . well, it ain't loneliness, and it ain't exactly fear. I think it was just an empty feelin'. I want to say there was excitement, but there wasn't. I was still missin' somethin'.

Like I said, that show was a fundraiser for the poor folks on Psamathe, but what I didn't say is that it was run by the Frontier Corps. How about that, Path? I leave home to find my place, only to have it lookin' for me at home. Not sayin' yuh should stop lookin' for yuhr creator or anything, but it's just nice to think that maybe what yuh're lookin' for is waiting for yuh one way or another.

I HOPE SO. THAT'S WHY I JOINED THE APEX GAMES. IF MY CREATOR IS LOOKING FOR ME, THEN MAYBE THEY COULD SEE ME FIGHT OR ON A BANNER. THAT WOULD BE REALLY COOL.

It sure would be somethin' else. Change like that is good for ya—I know it was for me. It's funny, I joined the Corps to help people, but it helped me.

I spent years workin' for the Corps. I put the lives of those in need ahead of my own. One person who I

helped reached out not too long ago, which was sweet—a mercenary vet who now calls himself my number one fan. Quite the honor, and I owe it to the Corps. We traveled all over the Outlands—even to the Fringe Worlds. We had no restrictions as to who could be helped. We weren't part of the Syndicate or the treaty, so we didn't have to abide by any constraints.

WHAT TREATY?

I bet Gibraltar or Witt could probably give yuh some more info on that. I was too young and in my own world on Psamathe, so I'm no expert on that stuff. All I've heard is that the civil war ended in the Outlands with some sort of treaty. It was about ten years ago or so—2723. Those who didn't sign became the Fringe Worlds, and those poor folks had it even harder gettin' support from trade or whatever else they needed. That's where we came in.

The Corps did what it could with donations and support from whoever wanted to help, but we definitely hit a money problem. Nothin' like that could last forever.

I HOPE NOTHING LASTS FOREVER. OTHERWISE THAT WOULD MEAN MY SEARCH MAY NEVER END.

It'll end. Everything does. That's somethin' I needed to come to terms with, because when the Corps started losin' money, my first thought was to call my parents.

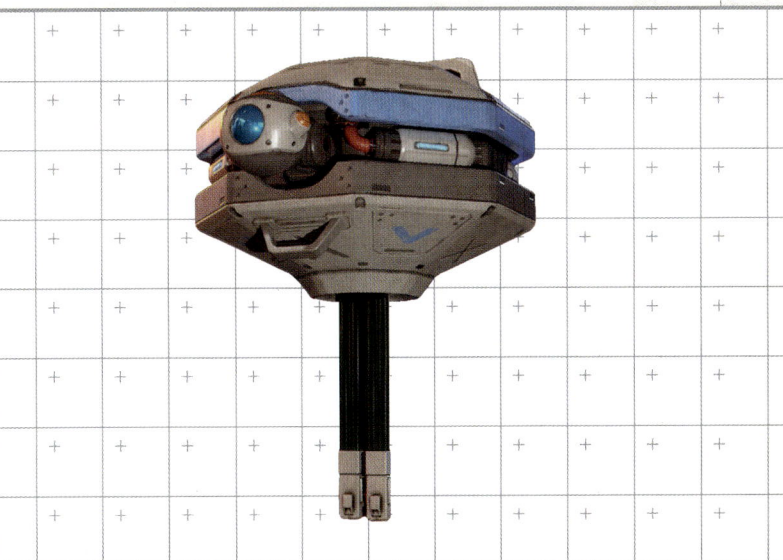

* *LIFELINE'S DOC DRONE.*

THAT SOUNDS LIKE IT MAY HAVE BEEN A BAD IDEA.

Yuh're right. After knowin' who they were. After knowin' where that money came from . . . I couldn't. I knew they had it, and I knew that money would have been a huge help, but I couldn't reach out to them.

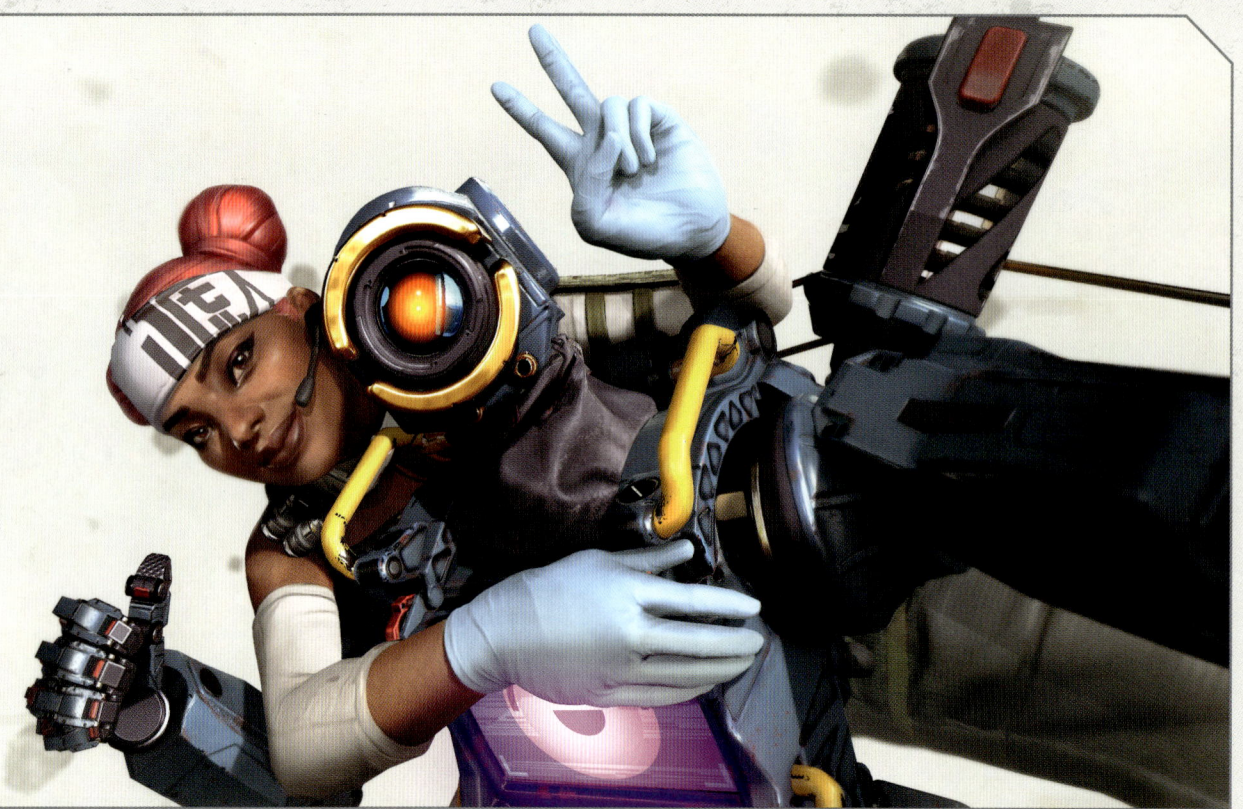

CHE AND ME!

BUT ISN'T THAT WHAT FAMILY IS FOR?

Families ain't always as good as they're supposed to be. I knew who they were, Path. That's important. It was important to me, just like it's important to yuh. Whoever yuhr creator is, they are a piece of yuh and whether that's good or bad, yuh got to decide how to deal with it. I decided how to deal with mine, and that was to risk my life for that money. That's why I joined the Games. I knew it was risky, dangerous … I even knew that what I was doin' wasn't honorable. Fighting people for money? It was a dilemma, but people were countin' on me. Those fighters were gonna fight with or without me, so I figured I better put my medical training to some use for them while making money for the Corps.

I THINK IT'S HONORABLE. I'VE ALWAYS LOOKED UP TO YOU, AJAY. EVEN THOUGH I'M TALLER.

No way. That's really nice of ya, Path. I'm sure there's some truth to that—somewhere. I don't think about it much. I just do what I do because I need to. It ain't much more complicated than that.

THAT'S WHAT I'M DOING. I JUST WANT TO FIND MY CREATOR. EVEN IF THEY ARE BAD.

Nah, Path. They can't be bad. I don't think yuh've got a bad circuit in yuhr entire body. And even if they are, that don't mean yuh are. That's what I learned from my family … Actually, Silva was the first one to say it. He may not seem it, but he's a smart one. Crazy, but smart.

IT'S GREAT THAT YOU TWO ARE SUCH GOOD FRIENDS. I LOVE FRIENDS.

We have our good months, and our bad months, but we always find a way to get back to each other. *True* family always does. I bet he'd say the same.

EXCITING. I'LL ASK HIM.

I'm sure yuh'll come across him in this quest of yuhrs. I'm sorry I can't give yuh all the info yuh want—I wish I could. It would be nice to know what my parents' company had to do with yuhr creator, but whether it's good or bad, never forget who yuh are.

I WON'T. UNLESS MY MEMORY GETS WIPED LIKE BEFORE.

That happens—then I'll tell yuh who yuh are. Till then, yuhr best chance is to stick to the Outlands. The Chevrex Inc. name only started in this part of the galaxy, so if they had anything to do with yuhr creator, then it's here.

THAT'S GREAT TO KNOW. THANK YOU, FRIEND.

Not a problem. We've got some solid Legends who know more than a thing or two about the Outlands: Gibraltar, Mirage, even Wraith … though that one's a bit of a head case. Good luck.

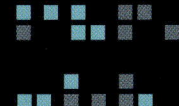

DATA POINTS RECEIVED

- Chevrex Inc. is Ajay's family's company based in the Outlands. Originally named AI Logic and partnered with Kodai Industries, this company is known for having built robotic security systems for generations throughout the Frontier.

- Lifeline's family profited off war for generations and served both sides during the Frontier War and the Outlands civil war. This discovery pushed her away from her family into a new life as a humanitarian.

- Lifeline and Octane were friends when they were kids.

  > See Octane for more stories.

- The history of the Frontier dates back to 2122.

  > See Lifeline's tablet for reference.

- The Militia took power before a final battle at the IMC-controlled planet of Gridiron, but the result of that battle is still a mystery.

  > See Bangalore for more information.

- A big blackout shut down IMC beacons and ended communication throughout the Frontier and Outlands over a decade ago.

- Those who supported the Militia were promised refuge, but no one came. The Militia abandoned those people.

- Gibraltar, Mirage, and Wraith are some of the Legends who can speak more to the history of the Outlands.

- A treaty by the Mercenary Syndicate helped end the civil war in 2723. Those who signed became part of Syndicate Space; those who didn't became the Fringe Worlds. More information can be learned from Gibraltar and Mirage.

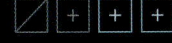
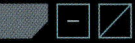

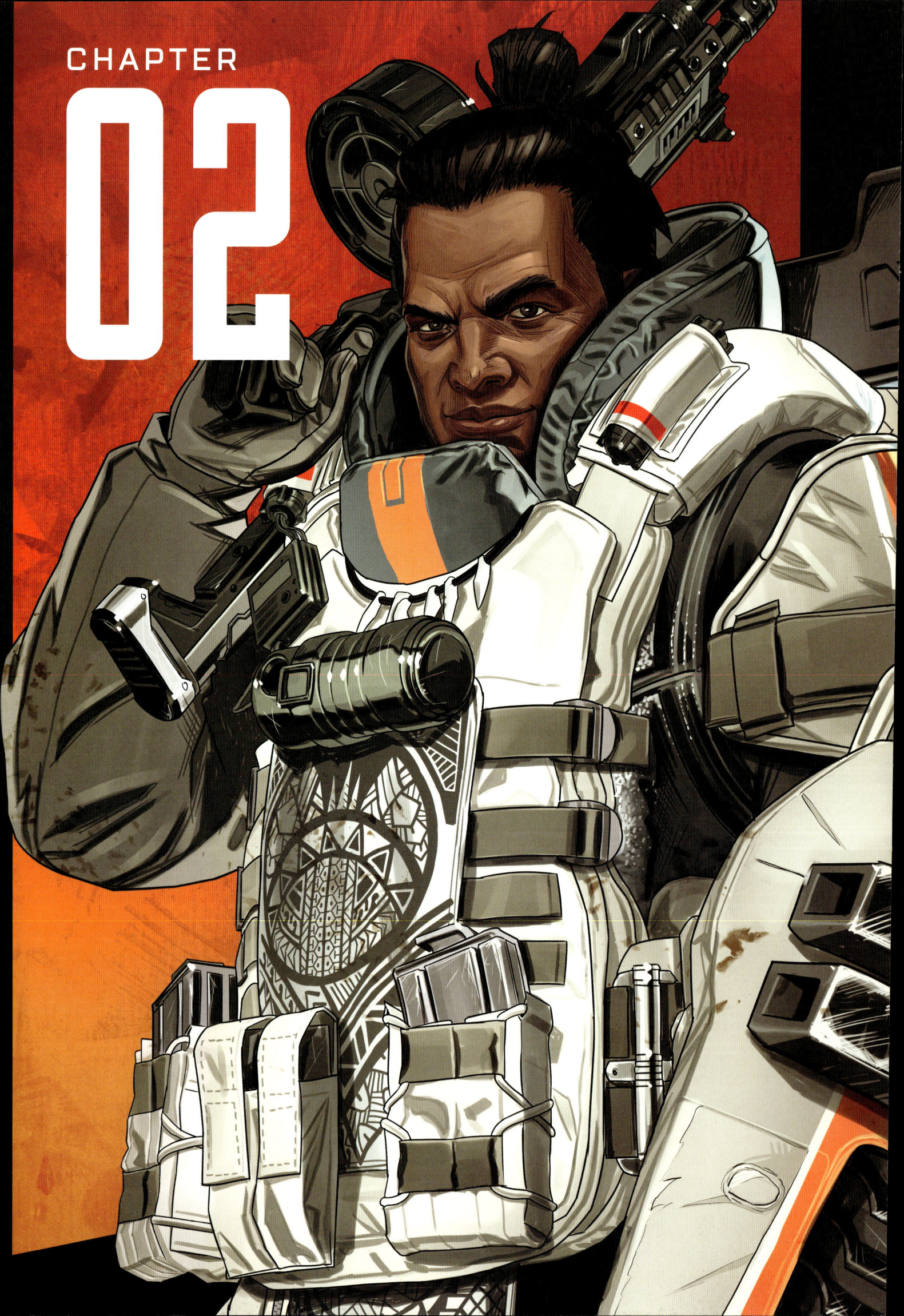

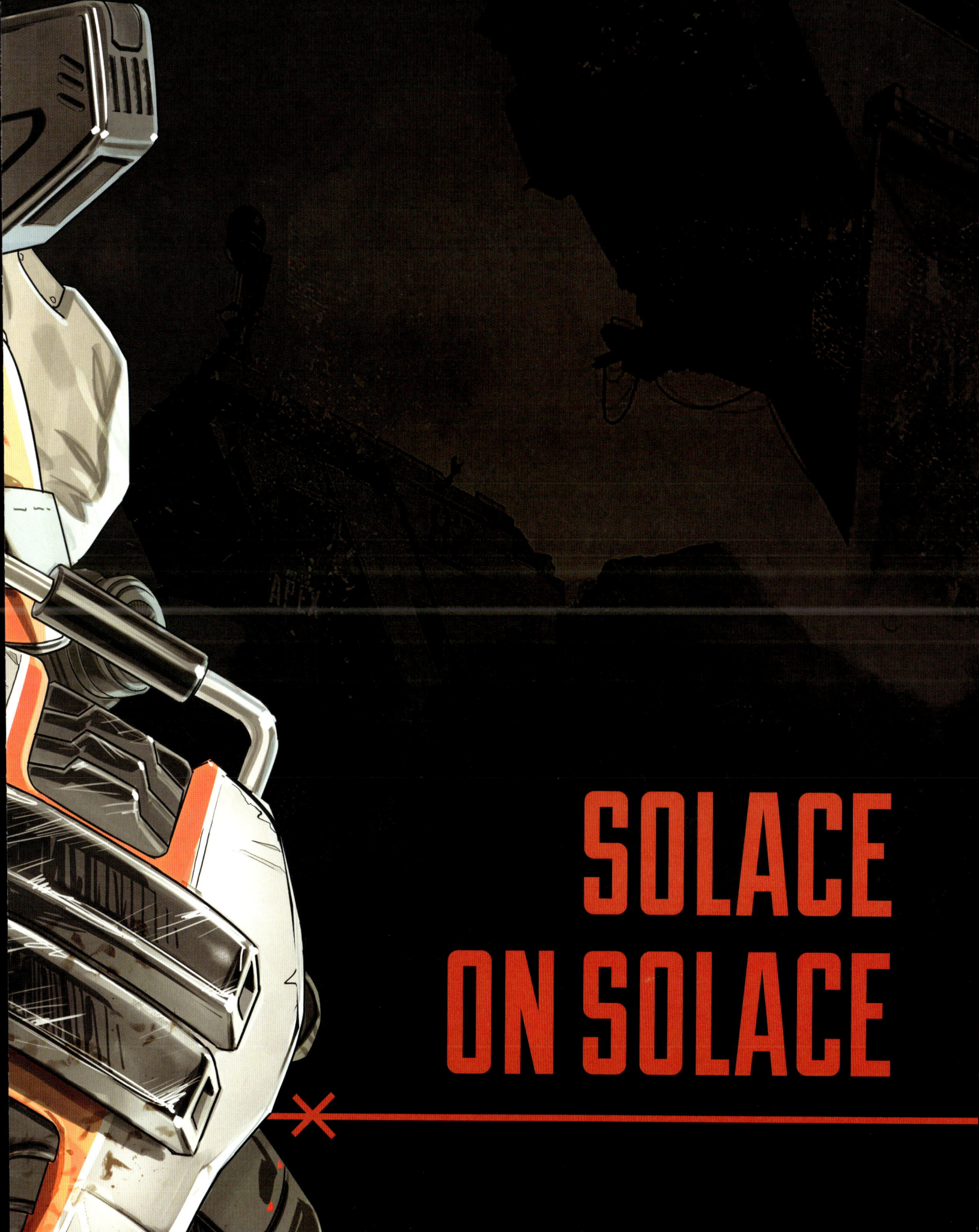

SOLACE
ON SOLACE

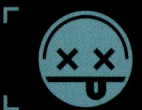
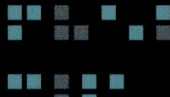

PATHFINDER MEMORY LOG: DAY 2

Ajay Che is such a great friend; it's too bad I have to fight her so many times in the Games. It was very helpful to learn about the history of the Frontier. I had no idea it was discovered so recently, only four hundred years ago! It's just a baby, and I love babies! Or maybe that's a long time ago? Either way, a lot of stuff has happened since then, and I can't wait to learn more about it.

I would think if I were created in the Core Systems before the Frontier was discovered, I'd probably have been a cellular telephone or a laptop computer because those two items seemed to be what people could not live without in those times, which means I'd have had a lot of friends who needed me. I'm not sure if what I "feel" is actually a "feeling," but whatever it is, I like the feeling of being needed. Like how Heinrich Hammond was needed for humanity to explore the Frontier, or how BT-7274 needed to sacrifice himself in order to stop the IMC . . . aw, that second one is sad. I remember hearing that story all over the place—the Heroes of Harmony: Pilot Jack Cooper and the Vanguard Titan BT. Maybe I'll learn more about them on my quest! They also needed each other to survive, and that's so sweet.

I hope that I was created because I was needed. When I meet my creator, I will be sure to ask them that. It's exciting knowing that I'm on the right track to those answers.

My chat with Ajay has helped me narrow down my search to the Outlands. I know I woke up somewhere there, but I don't really know much about it. My jolly good friend Gibraltar might be able to help me, so here I come, planet Solace! Wooo!

CLUE BOX

TRANSMISSION CLUES
- "Chevrex" > LIFELINE'S PARENTS' COMPANY
- "The future of the Outlands" >
- "Dr. Amélie Pa——" >
- "The Event" >
- "Aleki" >
- "Iris" >

SELF-MOTIVATION QUOTE . . . SEARCHING . . . 1 RESULT FOUND

"A journey of a thousand miles begins with a single step."
—[LAO TZU]

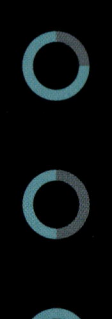
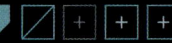

INNER MONOLOGUE ACTIVATED . . .

GIBRALTAR BIO FROM THE APEX GAMES

ULTIMATE OBJECTIVE . . . SEEKING CREATOR

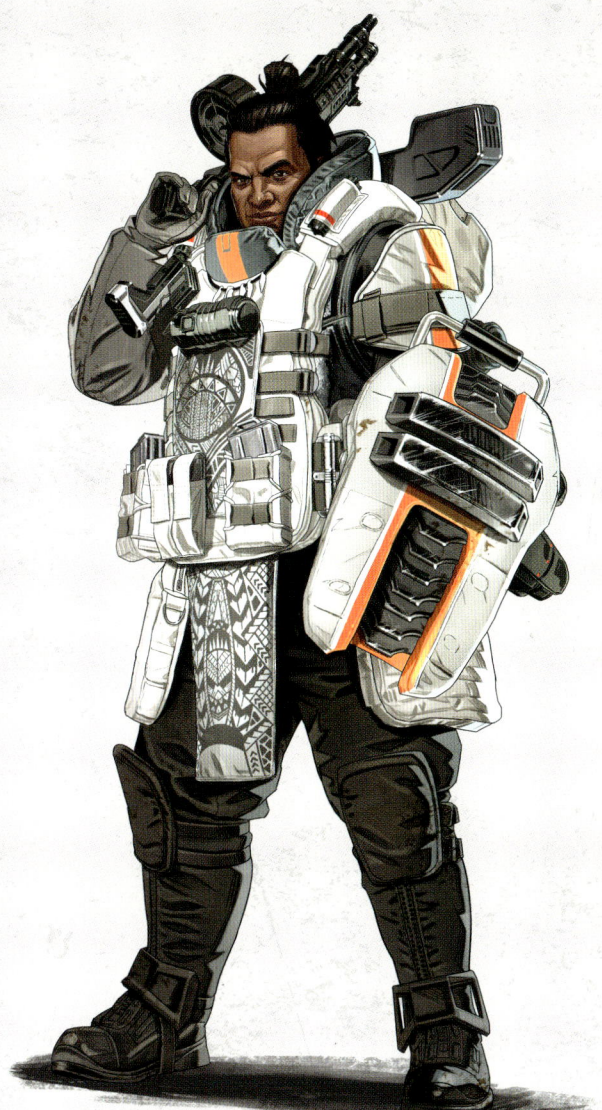

REAL NAME:
MAKOA GIBRALTAR

AGE:
30

HOME WORLD:
SOLACE

TACTICAL ABILITY:
DOME OF PROTECTION

PASSIVE ABILITY:
GUN SHIELD

ULTIMATE ABILITY:
DEFENSIVE BOMBARDMENT

GIBRALTAR IS A GENTLE GIANT WITH A WILD SIDE. The son of two SARAS (Search and Rescue Association of Solace) volunteers, he has always been skilled at getting others out of dangerous situations that are common in the Outlands. However, he only began to understand the value of protecting others when he and his boyfriend stole his father's motorcycle, took it on a joyride, and got trapped by a deadly mudslide. His parents saved them, and his father lost an arm in the process. Gibraltar has never forgotten that sacrifice and has devoted his life to helping those in need.

The Apex Games didn't change that, but they changed what it meant. Many of Gibraltar's friends and colleagues have competed in the Games for extra money, fame, and glory over the years, and some never came home. Gibraltar joined to keep them safe and, for the first time, his skills as a rescuer and his rebellious nature worked together. He's now become an icon in the Apex Games, putting himself in the line of fire to protect his squad and send his opponents running for cover.

"Let's go change a life, bruddah!"
—GIBRALTAR

HELLO, GIBRALTAR!

I CAME TO ASK YOU ABOUT THE OUTLANDS! WHAT DO YOU KNOW?

Heh-heh. Now isn't that a loaded question, bruddah. Long story short: I grew up here on Solace and I love it. It may not have been that way for everyone, but I tell you, it's been a good time. Of course, I'm a positive guy, so what do you expect? My parents raised me that way.

AND WHAT ABOUT THE LONG STORY?

That's what you want, huh? Well, my shiny little friend, the history here goes back a long time, and the Gibraltar family was there right from the start. A lot has changed since then, and it keeps changing. The Outlands weren't always the ray of sunshine we see today. You know what I mean, Path?

I DON'T KNOW WHAT YOU MEAN, BUT I LIKE THAT YOU CALL ME PATH.

When I was born, the IMC ran the show. I'm sure Bangalore or another Legend knows a bit more than me on how they got here, but what I do know is that there was a split between those who came with them and those who have lived here for generations; the latter is where I came from.

The Gibraltar family was part of the very first expeditions that came to the Outlands over four hundred years ago. I remember my *kupuna* telling me stories. She said it took almost twenty years for our family—and thousands of others—to travel across the unexplored Frontier from the Core Systems to reach our home here on Solace. It was one way to change a life or two, but the Gibraltars always had something constant…and she pointed at my chest and said, "Our hearts." And then she'd tell a story that had been passed down from *kupuna* to grandchild for a long time, a journey of a little mouse…

A JOURNEY OF A LITTLE MOUSE

A STORY FROM GIBRALTAR'S FAMILY

My jolly Gibby, listen closely-- for this is the journey of a little mouse...

Many courageous civilians volunteered for the journey across the Frontier with hopes for better lives for their families, including our own. Some knew each other, some did not, but they all knew they had to learn to live in peace aboard the IMS *Nostos* if they had any chance of surviving the long trip. And they did--for the first few years, but as tensions rose, our distant relative Pio Gibraltar hit his limit and lost control. Consumed with stress and madness, Pio, the giant man he was, almost destroyed the entire vessel. He spent the next year locked away in the brig, and that is where his life turned around. That is where our future turned around. That is where he met the little mouse.

Alone in a jail cell, Pio befriended this helpless little animal. How it got onboard or how it had remained alive for so long is unknown, but how it continued to live from that point on is the basis for what us Gibraltars believe: protect the innocent. That little mouse found Pio at his lowest, and without saying a word, was able to teach him that survival comes from the heart just as much as from the mind. Despite Pio's relatively intimidating size, that little mouse showed no fear, no hate, only love. That is what Pio needed to be reminded of. And that is something our family can never forget. As long as we take care of those who need us, we will be rewarded with the courage and strength to continue surviving.

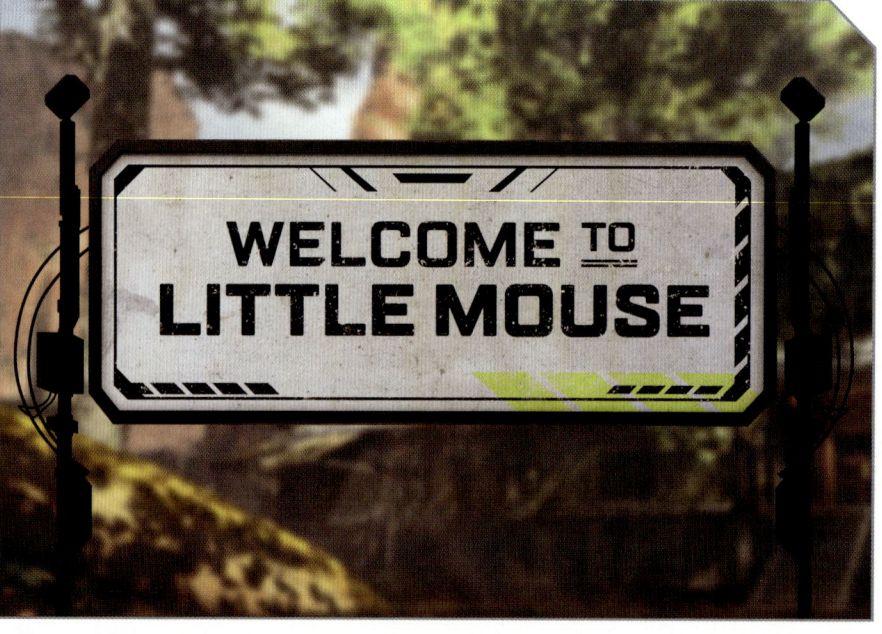

WELCOME TO LITTLE MOUSE

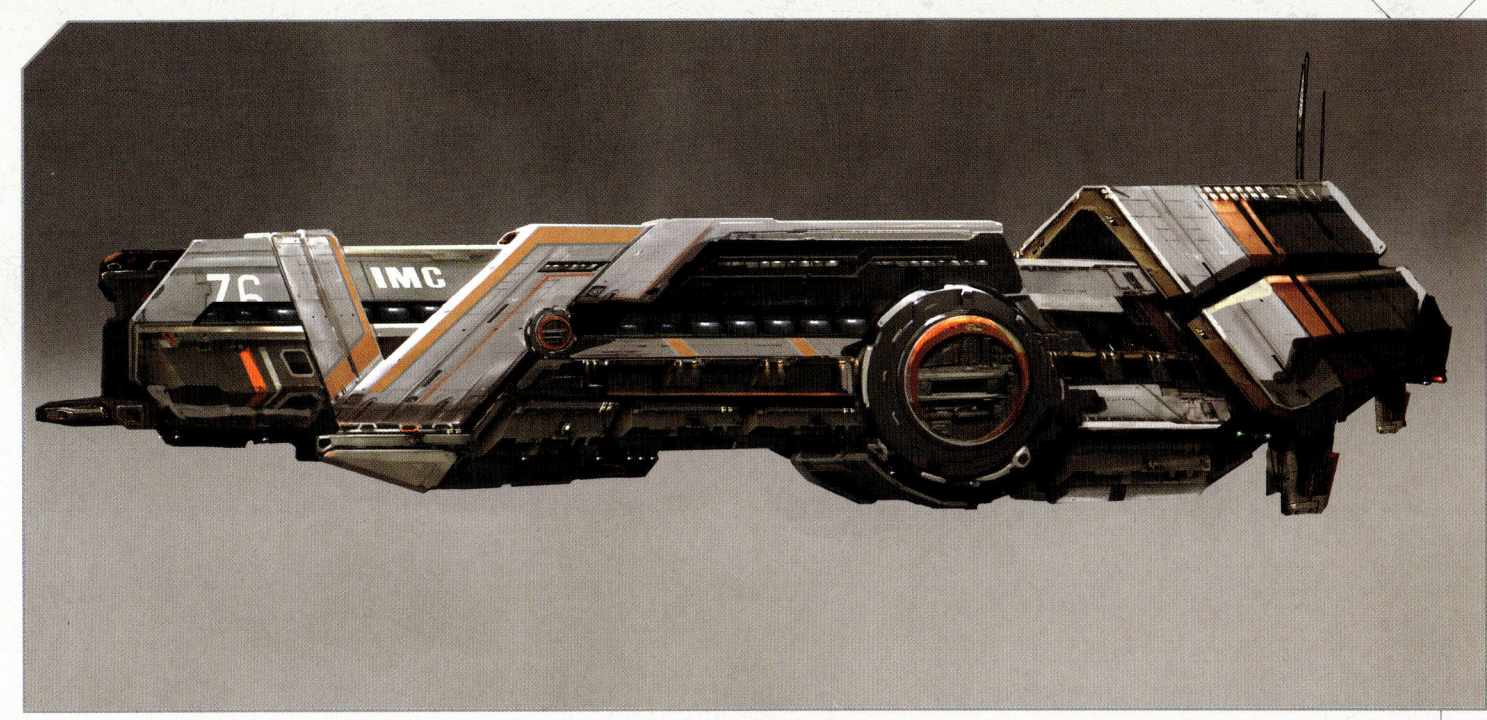

ONE OF THE EARLY IMC EXPEDITION SHIPS THAT EXPLORED THE FRONTIER.

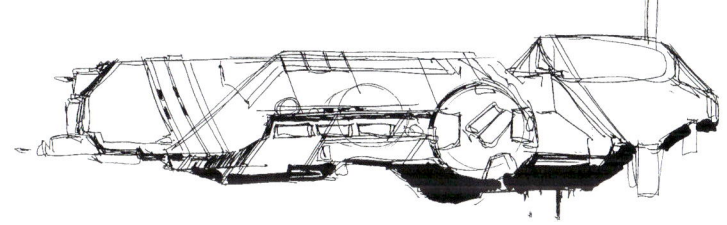

Day by day in that cell, Pio watched over the little mouse, as it watched over him. He shared his meals, shared his stories, and shared his time. It's an important lesson, my jolly Gibby, to share your time and learn from others. That's exactly what Pio discovered through the little mouse. He never named it, because it was not his place to do so. The little mouse was not a pet, but a friend. He simply watched over it, as it watched over him.

Outside the cell, the IMS *Nostos* had completed half of its initial journey, but reports showed it would possibly take much longer than originally expected. Communications with the other IMC expedition vessels were lost, and the understanding that they were completely on their own finally sunk in among the passengers and crew. Fear and doubt spread like wildfire throughout the vessel right about the time Pio was released, but he did not lose control. In fact, he took this

as a challenge against what he had learned during his time in confinement. Pio believed the residents' dependence on the IMC clouded their true potential, and what they needed was to be reminded of the courage and strength they had possessed from the day they set out on their journey. With the little mouse safe inside his pocket, Pio volunteered to spearhead the development of a small community-run recreational center. Pio believed the residents of the IMS *Nostos* needed a place where they could spend time together and learn from each other. Unlike the school, the Little Mouse Recreational Center invited all who cared to join—day and night—to tell stories, play games, and ultimately become united.

When the IMS *Nostos* arrived on planet Solace nearly ten years later, the first colony was named Little Mouse, which is where you were born--only ten kilometers outside Solace City. The colonists put their differences aside, took their doubt and fear and replaced it with hope. Working together, the residents and their descendants became the first to colonize the Outlands. Pio lived a long and full life, and the little mouse continues to live in this story from generation to generation. From our ancestor Pio, to your grandfather Aleki, and now to you. Good night, my jolly Gibby.

WOW. I'VE BEEN TO THAT TOWN!

It's where I grew up, bruddah. My family never left, which is why it's so nice—heh. But of course, some colonies grew just a bit too big to handle—kinda like me. Heh. Working together became more of a challenge, but that didn't stop the Gibraltars from doing their part to help those in need. You see, we always looked out for others. That never stopped. It was the Gibraltars who created SARAS.

WHO IS SARAS?

Not a who, my metal bruddah. The Search and Rescue Association of Solace was created by my family about two hundred years ago. There was supposed to be support from other IMC expeditions, but they never came, so our people took it upon themselves to build their own lives. They didn't do too bad of a job either, considering the lack of resources and differences of opinions. It wasn't harmony, but it was what was needed at the time to keep things moving forward and to survive. SARAS was open to all volunteers and took donations from whoever they could. I think I've got some old stuff from that time—Gibraltars tend to keep things longer than they should … heh.

SARAS SOUNDS LIKE A FUN GROUP OF FRIENDS.

I think it was when it first started, but from what I was told, things changed a bit when the IMC came back around the mid-2600s to reclaim what they believed belonged to them. The Outlands had become home to generations of us early settlers, so someone laying claim to what we built … heh-heh, well, let's just say it didn't go over so well at first. Some battles were fought, but in the end the IMC promised safety, security, resources, and practically everything we needed to expand our home and prolong our survival. Agreements were made and within a day, IMC outposts, factories, and facilities began popping up all over the place and there wasn't a building, market, or street corner without IMC security watching over you. Even the outer territories saw their share of IMC presence, despite their opposition. I know some people felt safer, like it was a good choice and made for better living. They even created the Thunderdome blood sport at Kings Canyon, which brought some jobs to Solace, but there were still many who knew the IMC was up to no good. They were right not to trust them, because when the Frontier Wars came to an end, we were all abandoned.

OH NO. WHAT DID YOU DO?

Solace was one of the last places the IMC left, so in some ways we were luckier than others. When the civil war broke out, many people on Solace refused to get involved—even the Gibraltars. We were selfish and stayed to protect our own instead, and I didn't agree with it at all.

It got dangerous out there, Path. Dozens of territories killing each other over power, and there I was arguing with my parents, being told not to help for the first time in my life. I had friends who fought and friends who died in that war. I know our poor buddy Elliott lost his brothers and I'm sure there are a few other Legends who could probably tell you a bit more about that war, but not me. So to answer your question about what I did … I ran away.

I made my way to Solace City and picked up a job working at the Thunderdome. There weren't many places a fourteen-year-old boy like myself could get a job, but the Thunderdome was on its last legs and took on whoever walked through the door. I think it closed down for good a few years later around 2719 when the IMC left Solace. I survived on my own for a few months, which wasn't easy. I sent letters to my parents just so they'd know I was fine but not to come looking for me. It was a lonely time in my life, but that's where I met someone very important to me … his name was Nik Gentile.

S.A.R.A.S.

Application for Volunteer Activity
SARAS is an Equal Opportunity Organization

Section 1- Personal Information

NAME:

AGE:

HOMETOWN:

SPECIAL SKILLS:

PREFERRED CATEGORY:

☐ Solace Mountain Rescue ☐ Vehicle SAR
☐ Urban SAR ☐ Marine SAR
☐ Full-Time ☐ Part-Time

HAVE YOU EVER APPLIED FOR A POSITION BEFORE?

☐ Yes ☐ No

IF YES, WHAT POSITION?

HAVE YOU EVER BEEN:

☐ Arrested ☐ Convicted of a Felony
☐ Convicted of a Misdemeanor

COMBAT TRAINING:

RECOMMENDATION, IF ANY:

AN OLD SARAS VOLUNTEER FORM.

Nik and I worked at the Thunderdome. We cleaned the seats after the games, stocked the markets with food and drink... it was a part-time gig, but at least we got to watch some of the fighters. I learned some of my moves from them, you know? I always wanted to jump down and fight, but Nik held me back—which was probably good, because I would have been quickly destroyed, heh-heh. I guess I figured if I couldn't fight in the war, then maybe the Games would scratch that itch. But when the Games shut down, me and Nik found ourselves out of a job and with barely a coin to our name. One night, we got to chatting about the war. I told him the story of Little Mouse, about how I wanted to join the fight because that's what a real Gibraltar would do, and that's when I told him my plan. I convinced him that we should run away together, join the fight, and do whatever it took to protect our friends—together. I could have just gone by myself, but maybe I didn't want to go alone—or maybe I didn't want to leave Nik. I think Nik knew that, or maybe I pressured him into thinking that. Either way, we were both in.

It was the middle of the night and I snuck back into my parents' home. I had packed up a duffle bag with everything I thought I'd need, and left a note before stealing my father's old motorbike to go pick up Nik. I remember it was starting to rain that night, and I began to have second thoughts, but I knew when Nik snuck out of his window that this was the right thing to do. We had booked charter to Gaea right outside of Solace City, not too far from Little Mouse, but I remember being in a rush. Heh. Nik always took a little longer to get ready than I did. So, I decided to take a shortcut through the Cascade Mountains—big mistake, bruddah. Big mistake...

I remember the skies went from this beautiful bright purple to being covered by a blanket of dark rain clouds as far as the eye could see in only seconds. And in that same amount of time, a blink of an eye, I lost control of the bike. I almost hit an oncoming vehicle but dodged it, only to crash through the guardrail and skid off the side of the cliff.

When the dust settled, Nik was completely knocked out. The bike had crashed at the bottom of the cliff, but we somehow managed to get caught on a rocky ledge just before the final drop. When I tried to move him, I noticed his leg was completely broken and his whole body was barely hanging on the precipice. I pulled him back on the ledge, but bruddah, it was not safe at all—the ground was unstable, and it was only getting worse with the rain. I only had one choice: wait and hope that SARAS were already on their way.

Luckily, my father, Miko, is quick to respond to any call. It didn't take long before I heard the sounds of

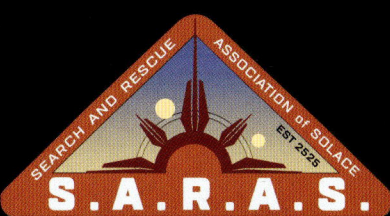

SARAS

The Search and Rescue Association of Solace was founded in 2525 by the Gibraltar family. SARAS's mission involves searching for missing people and rescuing those injured in outdoor activities, while also responding to requests for disaster relief and community protection throughout Solace. SARAS is divided into the following groups:

SOLACE MOUNTAIN RESCUE: Rescue missions carried out by the SMR cover everything from mountainous terrain to canyons. The SMR is also tasked with preserving, containing, and protecting the general public from dangerous wildlife. The majority of SARAS professional volunteers fall under the SMR.

VEHICLE SAR: Vehicle operators require extensive understanding of Solace terrain and conditions. There are very few professionals who reach the minimum requirements needed to safely operate the necessary equipment. With resources at high demand, the loss of damage to a vehicle would be a major impediment.

URBAN SAR: These rescue missions cover cities, towns, and neighboring country areas. They often involve the accidental collapse of structures due to various forms of natural disasters: storms, earthquakes, floods, and wildlife attacks like Leviathan stampedes.

MARINE SAR: With Solace City being in close proximity to the Nostos Ocean and other bodies of water, the Marine SAR consists of professionals with expertise in scuba diving, all forms of boating, sonar, and oceanography.

SARAS functions solely on generous donations from the community of Solace City. Each professional is either a part-time volunteer with limited benefits (such as training and personal resources) or a full-time volunteer who is provided with housing, family education, and medical resources.

the SARAS transports coming our way. I tried to wake up Nik, but he wasn't budging. I knew he had to get help fast. My parents taught me a thing or two about how to save a life with SARAS procedures, so I did what I could to get Nik ready to be carried up. When they arrived, it wasn't until my father rappelled down that he realized he was rescuing his own son. I remember the look in his eyes, everything from shock to disappointment to relief. I knew he was really going

SARAS'S COLORFUL PATCHES.

to let me have it, but not right then and there. We both knew that Nik had to go up first, so we worked together and strapped him to a harness and pulled him up. Then, as luck would have it, a monstrous, Gibraltar-size roar of rain sent a mudslide down the hill. Nik was pulled up just in time, but my father and I were sent further down the side of the cliff. We crashed another twenty meters down with my father's arm completely crushed under a rock.

I still remember the taste of the water and mud that had almost killed us. I had to think quick to save our lives, so I grabbed my father's bubble shield and covered us. Debris kept falling, but that handy shield protected us both just long enough for SARAS to send another team member down to get us. You know what, bruddah? That was the first time I ever used that bubble shield, but that's not why I remember that night. I put a lot of people in danger: Nik, the whole SARAS team, myself, and my father, who lost his arm because of me. But he didn't know that . . .

For some reason, Nik took the fall for me. I don't know why he did it. Chalk it up to his gratitude at being sent up first, or the grand stupidity of young love, but when Nik was questioned, he said the whole thing was his idea. That he stole the bike and he was driving it. As my father and I were lifted up into the clouds, Nik gave me a look that said, "Don't worry. It's going to be all right." But I knew, even then, it wouldn't be. I walked up to my father at the hospital as guilty as the sky is blue, but he didn't yell, he just looked at me, smiled, and said, "I know . . . I know, my son. But breaking the rules is sometimes part of life. As long as there is

someone there who has your back, you will survive. You did good out there, Makoa. Remember, you're a Gibraltar, it's in your blood to protect your own. Promise you'll do that."

I never told him the truth. Heh . . . I've never really told anyone that truth. Nik's parents wanted him to "learn his lesson" and had him sent to a juvenile delinquency center. To this day, I don't know what happened there. We lost touch. I tracked him down, years later. It was bad. Involved with the wrong people, relying on the wrong things to get through the day—that damn place turned a good kid with a heart of gold into a criminal with no hope. And now he had a baby. A little boy. He got the wrong future, because I was too scared to tell the truth. That kind of mistake eats you up, bruddah. How do you make up for that? How do you give back a lifetime?

After that, I realized I couldn't leave Solace, because Solace needed me. It wasn't long after that my father handed me the bubble shield and told me to get practicing, because it was time for me to change a life. And I did—for him, for Pio, and for Nik.

AND THAT'S WHY YOU JOINED THE APEX GAMES. IT ALL MAKES SO MUCH SENSE TO ME, FRIEND.

Heh-heh. That's true, bruddah. My place in the Games does kind of throw a wrench in the whole "protecting lives" thing, at least for those who don't really know me. After I joined SARAS when I hit about twenty-two, the Outlands were getting even more populated than they've ever been with the whole migration.

MY FRIEND AJAY MENTIONED THE MIGRATION. SOUNDS LIKE FUN AND A LOT OF WORK.

They started coming around the start of the civil war, just after the Blackout of 2720. They brought everything they could carry. Just like us, they were abandoned and just looking for a place to survive. The civil war ended when the Mercenary Syndicate Treaty was signed, and that pretty much helped stabilize the Outlands—at least for those who signed it. There were a few who didn't, and those are now part of the Fringe Worlds. Sorry, but I don't know much about them. Not many do, but I do know that my home planet of Solace became the center of the Syndicate's big project to help rebuild the Outlands: the Apex Games.

You know, bruddah? I like to think there's a reason for everything. I stole that bike, I put the person I loved in danger, my *makua kane* lost his arm—all for a reason … I don't know if I'm right or wrong, but I believe I was meant to be here when those desperate, innocent people came to the Outlands searching for a home. If I had gone to fight in the civil war, I may not have been around to change all the lives I've changed since working with SARAS. But I was.

Not only did the population of Solace triple when the treaty was signed, but it's also where the Syndicate brought back the old Thunderdome that Nik and I used to work at. I guess they believed it would help bring jobs and whatever else we needed to get the

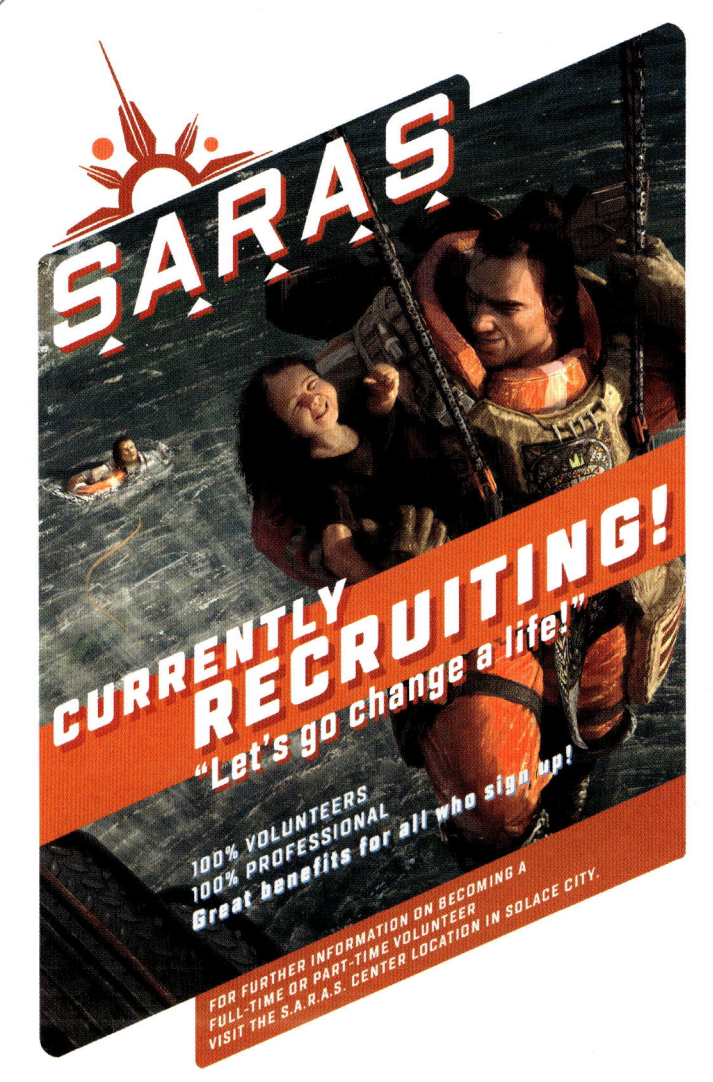

SARAS

CURRENTLY RECRUITING!

"Let's go change a life!"

100% VOLUNTEERS
100% PROFESSIONAL
Great benefits for all who sign up!

FOR FURTHER INFORMATION ON BECOMING A
FULL-TIME OR PART-TIME VOLUNTEER
VISIT THE S.A.R.A.S. CENTER LOCATION IN SOLACE CITY.

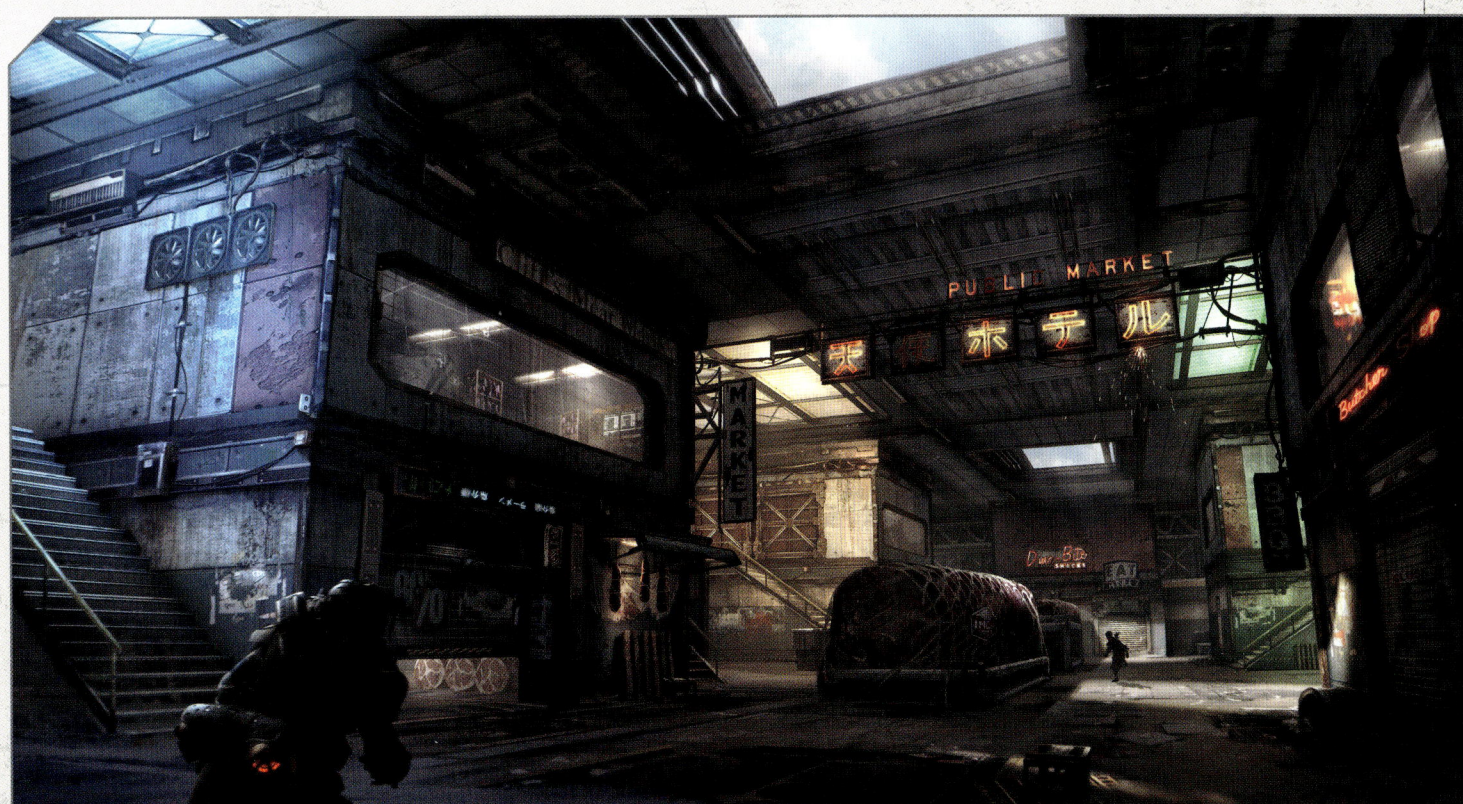

* A SOLACE CITY MARKET, SIMILAR TO THE ONE ON KINGS CANYON.

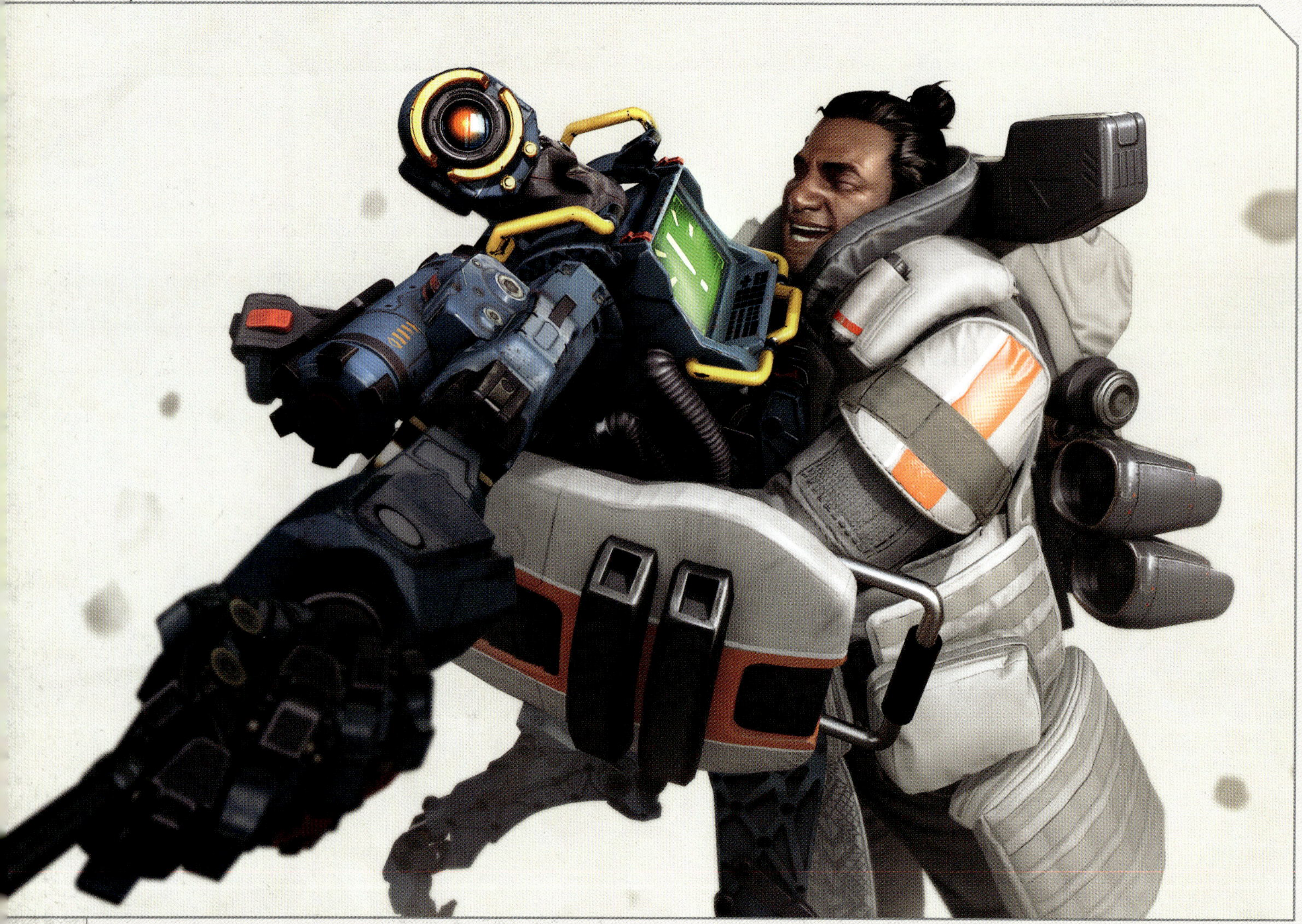

GIBRALTAR GIVES THE BEST HUGS!

Outlands back on their feet—and who am I to argue? It worked. Of course, there were many who didn't really like the idea of a "blood sport," and I don't blame them. It's a dangerous place, and it's only meant for those who understand that risk. But we're not killers. We all have our own reasons to fight, but very few do it for that reason.

I'M JUST SEARCHING FOR MY CREATOR. IT'S BEEN A MYSTERY FOR MY WHOLE TIME OF LIVING.

That's right, bruddah. And that's what led you to me. But I'm sorry to say that I'm not the one with the answers, my friend. Solace is a good place to start, but the great mysteries of this place lie in Kings Canyon. I see it's part of your little recording, too. I know Wraith has connections there, but the wonderful little Natalie Paquette is our expert on that island. She grew up there and knows all its secrets.

I KNOW WATTSON! THANK YOU, FRIEND. GOODBYE.

Not a problem, bruddah. Just remember, you were built for a reason, just like I was. We all have a place in this world and sometimes you've just gotta let it find you. Best of luck to you, Path.

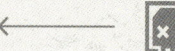

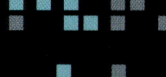

DATA POINTS RECEIVED

- The Outlands were discovered in the early 2300s by early IMC expeditions.

- The IMS *HOSTOS* was one of the first to colonize planet Solace.

- The Gibraltar family settled in Little Mouse, ten kilometers outside Solace City.

- Assistance and support promised by the IMC never came. The people of the Outlands were forced to survive on their own.

- The Search and Rescue Association of Solace, a.k.a. SARAS, was founded in 2525.

- After generations of people made the Outlands home by building cities and towns across planets, the IMC finally returned to reclaim what they believed was theirs in the mid-2600s.

- The IMC promised safety, security, and resources in exchange for intel, control of certain land and resources, and the freedom to install a series of outposts, factories, and facilities throughout the Outlands despite opposition from outer territories.

- The IMC established the Thunderdome blood sport at Kings Canyon to bring entertainment and jobs to the planet.

- From 2713 to 2719, IMC forces abandoned the Outlands in order to support the Frontier Wars, closing down all outposts and facilities and, eventually, the Thunderdome on Solace in 2715. The result was a feud for power among the Outlands' territories—the Outlands civil war.

  > See Mirage for more info on the civil war.

- The Blackout brought a large migration of those abandoned by both the IMC and the Militia from the Frontier to the Outlands for survival.

- The Outlands civil war ended with the Mercenary Syndicate Treaty, signed in 2723, which brought back jobs, safety, infrastructure, and the revival of the Thunderdome on Solace, now called the Apex Games. Those who signed benefit from the Games; those who didn't do not.

- The Apex Games on Kings Canyon may hold answers.

  > See Wattson for expert information on Kings Canyon.

  > See Wraith for more connections to Kings Canyon.

INNER MONOLOGUE ACTIVATED...

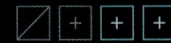
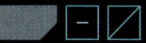

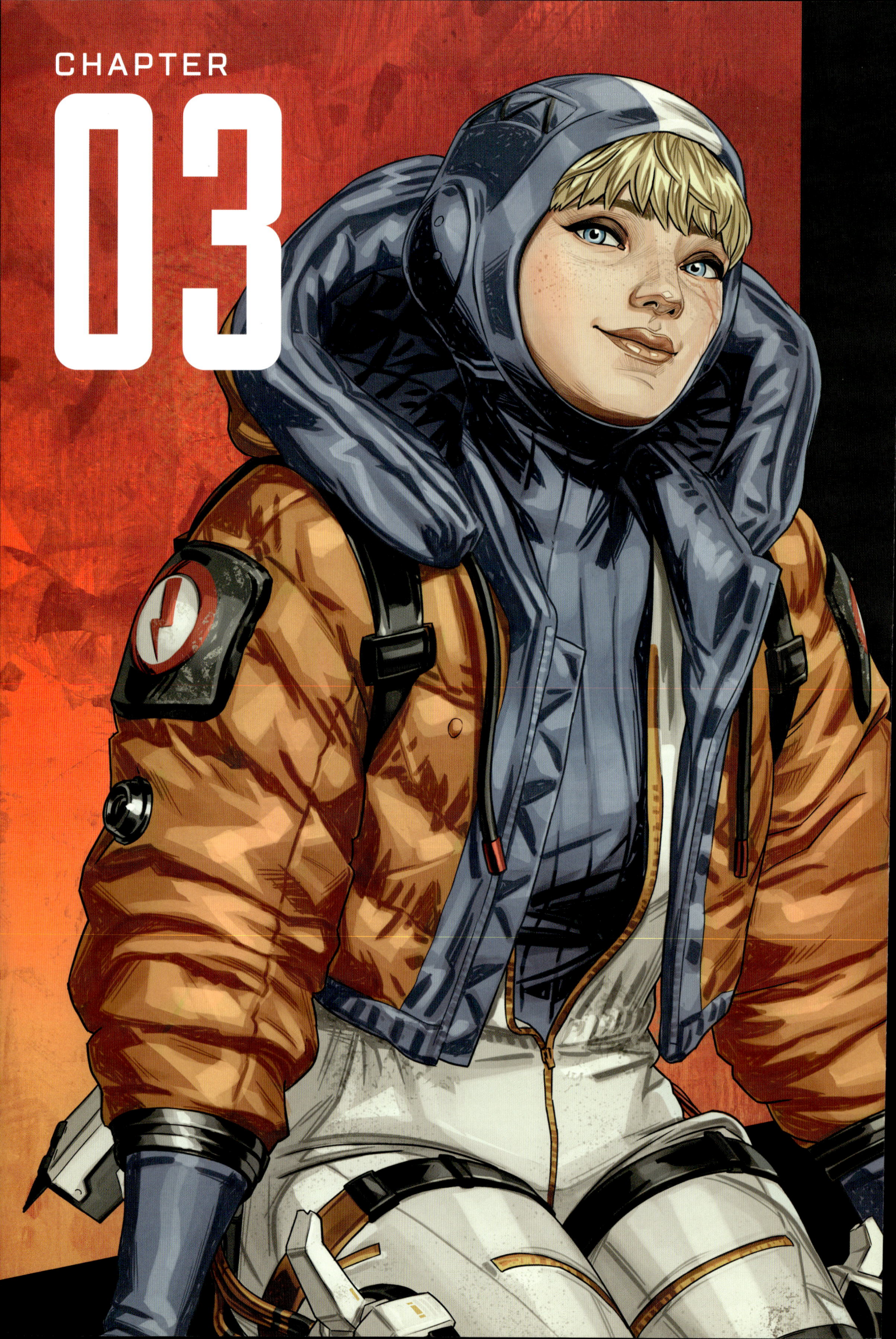

CHAPTER

03

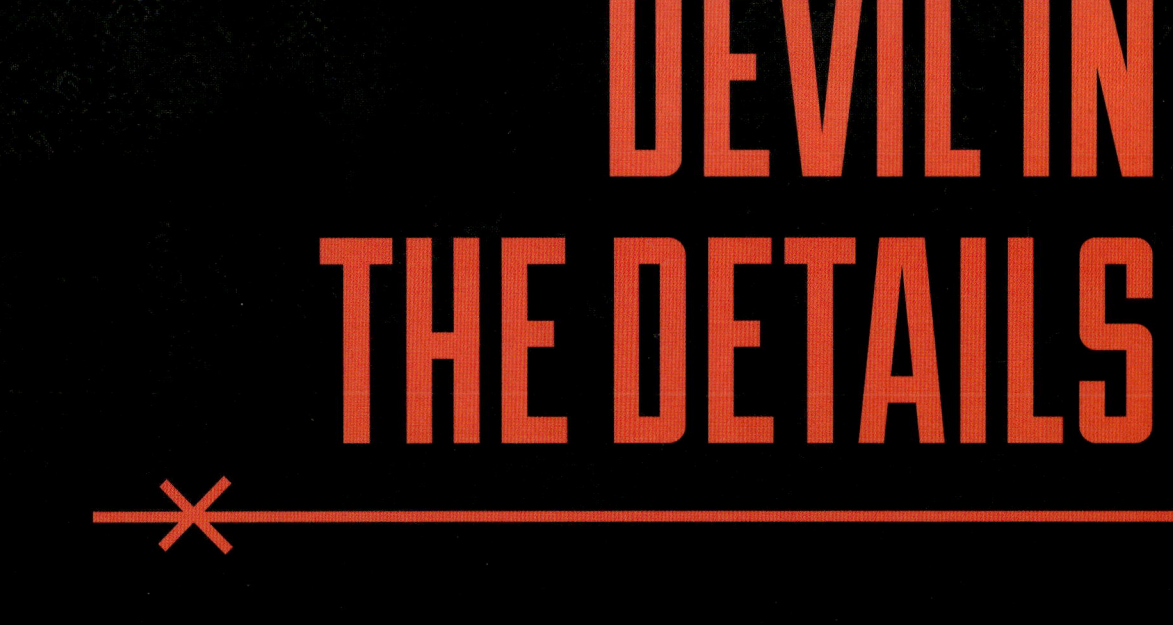

DEVIL IN THE DETAILS

✕

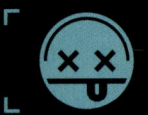
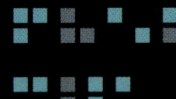
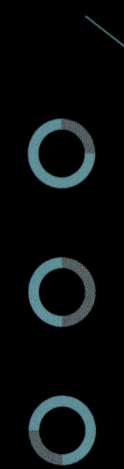

PATHFINDER MEMORY LOG: DAY 3

This is so exciting! I visited Gibraltar to learn more about the Outlands, and left knowing all sorts of fun facts. I know how the Outlands were first colonized, how SARAS was born, how Aleki is related to Gibraltar, and how Little Mouse got its name. Now I would like to get a little mouse, and name him City. Understanding how to name things is fun! What's not fun is how Gibraltar and the person he loves were separated. I am programmed to love everyone, and when I think about what it would feel like to be separated from everyone, it makes me sad-face. I don't like thinking about this. Let's think about something else!

Now I'm headed to a small fishing village on the other side of the Duchess River, which is the river that Kings Canyon is on. It's part of Solace City, but they've adopted the name Eelhead Bay. If the eels' heads are here, I wonder where the rest of the eels are. You can't get to Kings Canyon from Eelhead Bay because the underwater whirlpools will kill you, but before the Syndicate built the whirlpools, it only took an hour to travel there by boat. This makes sense, because the friend I'm going to visit had to travel there every day before it was decided she would live on Kings Canyon. Her name is Natalie, but many call her Wattson, and she's been part of the Apex Games since almost the beginning, even before she was a Legend. Maybe she knows who Amélie is . . . maybe they share a connection. Maybe it's me!

CLUE BOX

TRANSMISSION CLUES
- "Chevrex" > LIFELINE'S PARENTS' COMPANY
- "The future of the Outlands" >
- "Dr. Amélie Pa——" >
- "The Event" >
- "Aleki" > GIBRALTAR'S GRANDFATHER
- "Iris" >

SELF-MOTIVATION QUOTE . . . SEARCHING . . . 2 RESULTS FOUND

"Our greatest weakness lies in giving up. The most certain way to succeed is always to try just one more time."
—[THOMAS A. EDISON]

"The history of science shows that theories are perishable. With every new truth that is revealed we get a better understanding of Nature and our conceptions and views are modified."
—[NIKOLA TESLA]

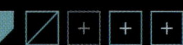

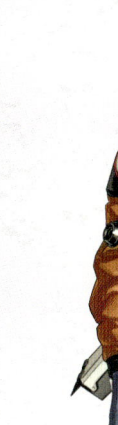

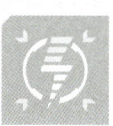
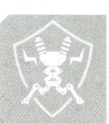

REAL NAME:
NATALIE PAQUETTE

AGE:
22

HOME WORLD:
SOLACE

TACTICAL ABILITY:
PERIMETER SECURITY

PASSIVE ABILITY:
SPARK OF GENIUS

ULTIMATE ABILITY:
INTERCEPTION PYLON

NATALIE "WATTSON" PAQUETTE IS A FAMILIAR FACE IN THE APEX GAMES, THOUGH FOR A DIFFERENT REASON THAN MOST. Daughter of the Games' lead electrical engineer, she studied his manuals to stay close to him, and discovered her calling at a young age. Though she could be completely distracted one moment and hyperfocused the next, electricity grounded her—its ordered, predictable flow made sense in a way the rest of the world didn't.

She devoured every book she could on the subject, and eventually became such a skilled engineer that she was commissioned to build the Apex Games' Modified Containment Ring. Unfortunately, her father died the day it was revealed, leaving her alone. At her lowest moment, a group of competitors invited her to return to the arena with them, assuring her she would always have a home. She now fights alongside her friends in the arena she helped build, destroying incoming missiles, recharging shields, creating fences, and using her pylon to silence fights that get too loud. Nobody knows the arena better than Wattson—anyone who underestimates her is in for a shock.

"Electrons and circuits, I get . . . it's people I do not understand."
—WATTSON

HELLO, WATTSON.

Bonjour, Pathfinder!

I HAVE RECENTLY LEARNED PEOPLE HAVE PREFERENCES ABOUT THEIR NAMES. FOR EXAMPLE, I PREFER PATHFINDER TO MRVN. DO YOU PREFER NATALIE OR WATTSON?
Names are funny, aren't they? So many for one person. Wraith calls me Wattson. Octane and Mirage call me Watts. They're very impatient and don't have time for multiple syllables. Papa called me Natalie.

I SHOULD CALL YOU SOMETHING DIFFERENT TOO. MIRAGE IS MY BEST FRIEND. I WILL DO WHAT HE DID AND SHORTEN ONE OF YOUR NAMES. I'LL CALL YOU NAT!
I would very much like that. From now on, Pathfinder calls me Nat. *Merveilleux!*

THIS IS EXCITING . . . LET'S GET STARTED, NAT-MARE-VAY-YOU . . .
Oh, Pathfinder. My papa used to tell that joke too. Silly robot.

I *AM* A SILLY ROBOT, NAT-MARE-VAY-YOU.
No, no. Just Nat is fine. *Merveilleux* means "marvelous" in French. There was a period between *Nat* and *merveilleux*.

I ONLY PUT PERIODS ON SENTENCES WHEN I WRITE THEM OR TYPE THEM— IF I WROTE OR TYPED IN THE FIRST PLACE, WHICH I DON'T. PUNCTUATION IS NOT SPOKEN ALOUD. YOU ARE AN ODD GIRL.
And you're not the first person to say that. I take it as a compliment. Papa used to say I wasn't odd; I was fortunate. He believed everything in life was balanced. Nature's way of keeping everything on the same level. A bug might be strong, but they aren't fast. A person could be brilliant, but physically feeble. Everybody has strengths and weaknesses. I was able to learn and retain information faster than others. Unfortunately, that was balanced by my knack for saying the wrong thing without realizing it.

PEOPLE SAY THE SAME THING ABOUT ME!
We are very alike, you and I. We understand so much of how the world works, yet we are still trying to understand people. By the way, I know why you're here.

YOU DO?
Yes. I always assumed this quest to find your creator would eventually lead to my front door. And I'm afraid I have bad news: he wasn't your creator.

THAT IS TERRIBLE NEWS, AND LEAVES ME WITH ONE QUESTION: WHO ARE YOU TALKING ABOUT?
Papa, of course. Is that not why you're here? Because you think Papa built you?

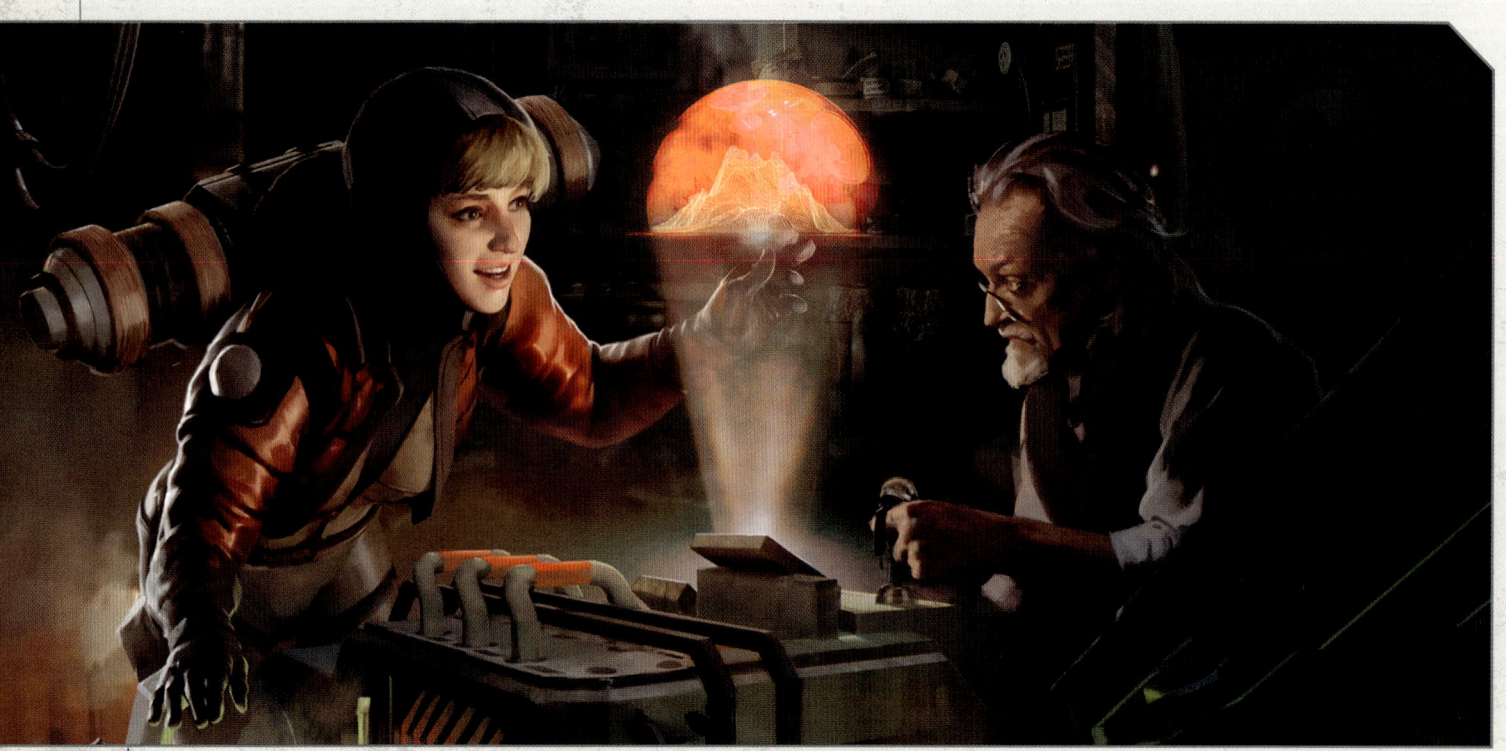

WATTSON AND HER FATHER CREATE THE APEX GAMES RING ON KINGS CANYON.

I DID NOT THINK THAT. WHY DID YOU THINK THAT I WOULD THINK THAT?

It just seemed logical. Papa and I designed the Ring. You're able to hack into the survey beacons to see where it will close next. Seemed like a safe assumption to make that if you're connected to the Ring, you're connected to Luc Paquette. I feel foolish now.

YOUR FATHER WAS A SMART MAN, AND VERY NICE. I WOULD HAVE BEEN HONORED IF HE HAD BEEN MY CREATOR, NAT.

Thank you, Pathfinder.

BUT SINCE YOU BROUGHT IT UP . . . WHY *CAN* I HACK INTO THE SURVEY BEACON?

All MRVNs can. On Solace, at least. It's a little program Papa secretly uploaded into the operating system of the Ring. When a MRVN hacks into the survey beacon, and connects with the Ring, they get an extra assignment in their programming.

WHAT KIND OF ASSIGNMENT? AND WHY?

The Outlands can be lethal. First, long before the Repulsor Tower was put up, there was wildlife all throughout Kings Canyon. Then once the Ring was installed, you suddenly had a large mass of energy that could shift and move at a moment's notice. Although the Games weren't in session, there was still danger around every corner. Papa had one invention in particular that he was desperate to keep safe, so he installed the survey beacon hack in every MRVN model in Solace City. That way, if anything went wrong, MRVNs could detect nearby carnivorous wildlife, and also see where the Ring was traveling to next, using every resource at their disposal to keep the invention safe.

THIS INVENTION SOUNDS VERY VALUABLE AND VERY EXPENSIVE. WHAT WAS IT?

Me!

MRVNS HAVE TO PROTECT YOU? ARE YOU A ROBOT LIKE ME?

No, no. I am not a robot. I have a mother and father. But in a lot of ways, he did "invent" me. He and my mama. As for protecting me, you no longer have that programmed into your software. I removed it.

I DO NOT UNDERSTAND.

Mama died when I was a baby. Papa was a single parent. He worked a full-time job while his young daughter ran around on her own, curiously exploring

MRVNS

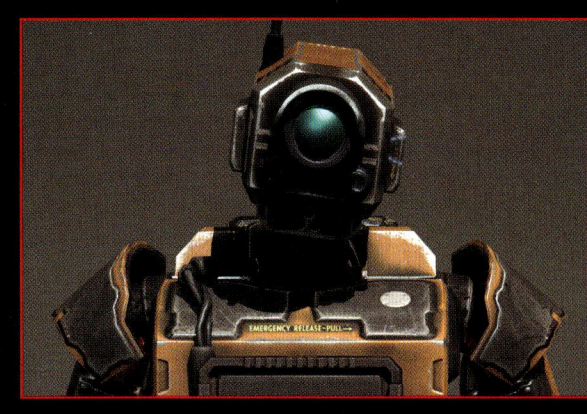

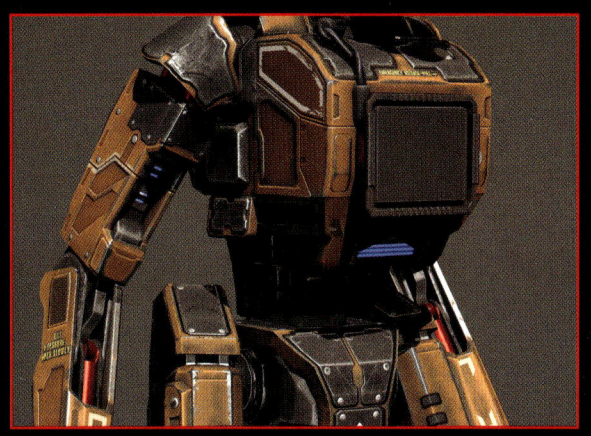

Mobile Robotic Versatile eNtity (MRVN) Automated Assistants, or "Marvins," are automatons manufactured by Hammond Robotics. They have been used over the years to perform menial jobs throughout the Frontier, whether it's in sanitation, the service industry, or repairing infrastructure. They can vary in appearance, and are programmed to be extremely docile.

dark vents . . . venturing into cave systems . . . playing in abandoned IMC laboratories, all surrounded by old chemicals and machinery—not to mention four petawatts of laser energy that moved around the whole island. Papa didn't have access to a nanny, but he had hundreds of MRVNs at his disposal. *Voilà!* Instant babysitters! When I joined the Games years later, I removed the babysitting aspect of the program, so you don't have to protect me if you don't want to.

WHY WOULD YOU REMOVE A SAFEGUARD TO KEEP YOU ALIVE IN THE GAMES, WHERE YOU CAN DIE?

Because it's unfair. And Papa always said that it doesn't matter if you win a game . . . if you didn't play fair, you lost.

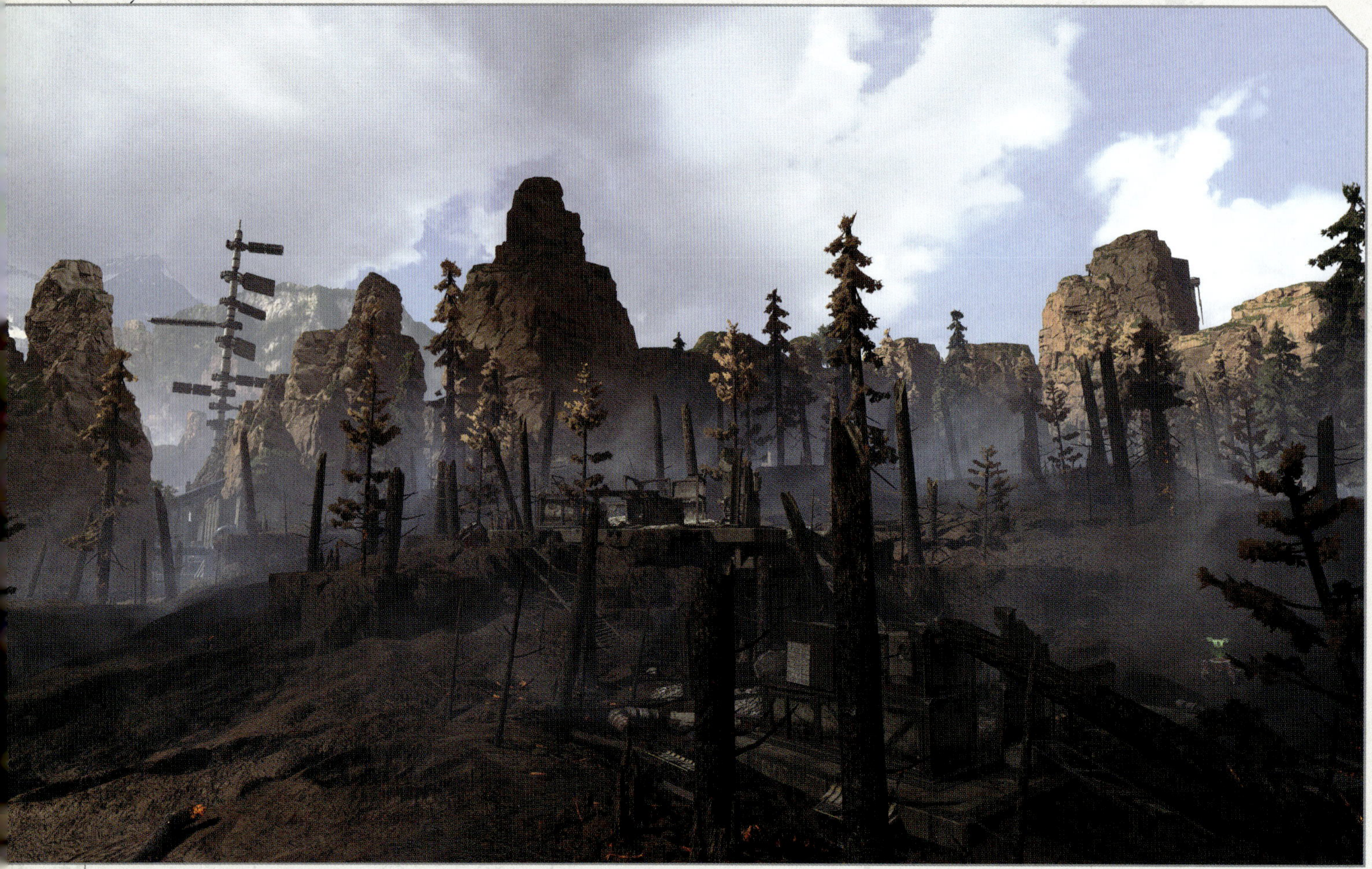

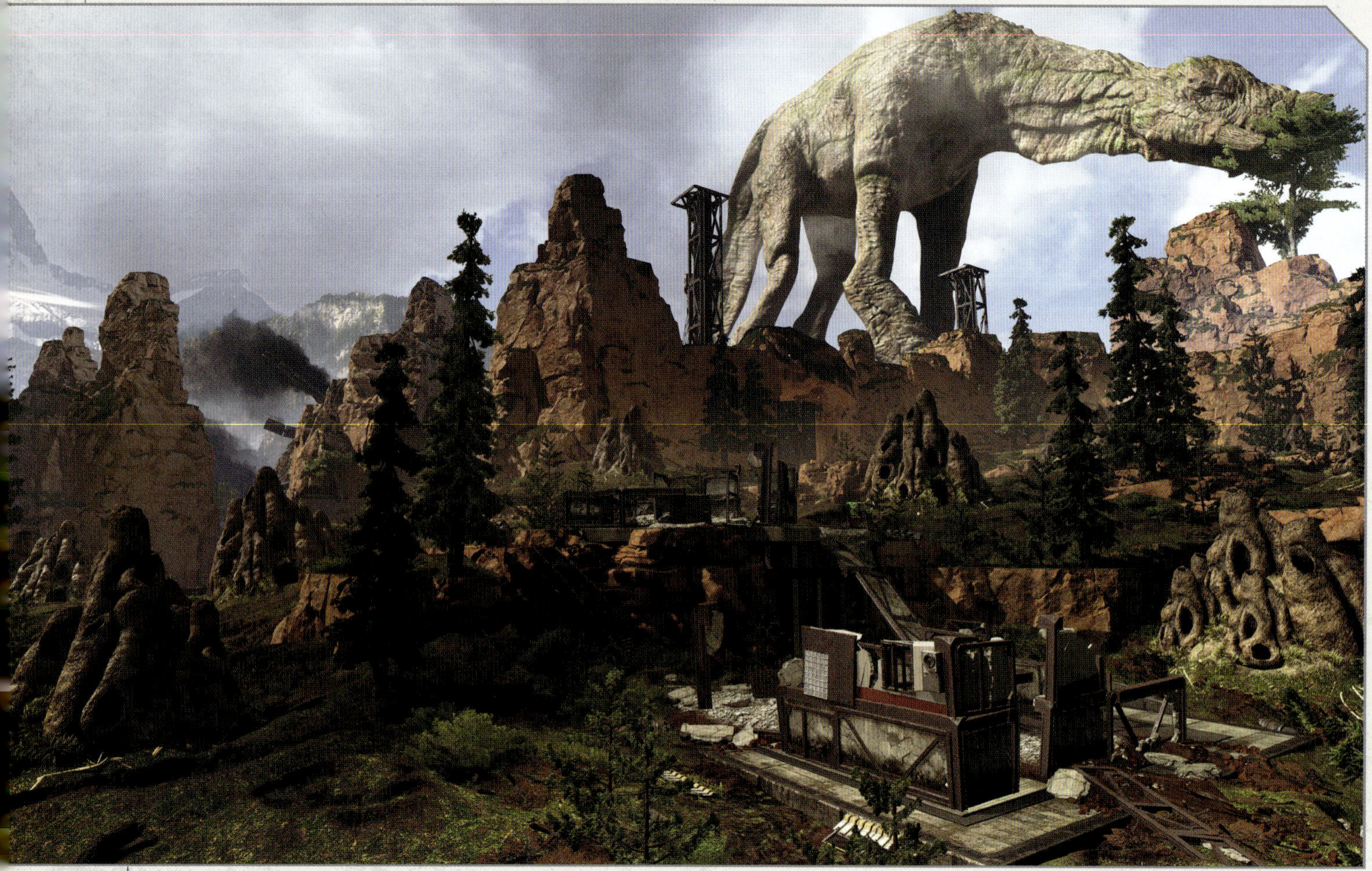

*KINGS CANYON THROUGHOUT THE YEARS.

APEX LEGENDS:
PATHFINDER'S QUEST

SO, AM I CHEATING WHEN I HACK A SURVEY BEACON?

Maybe. But you are also incapable of deceit or treachery and you don't have a brain, so... balance.

BALANCE IS GOOD. ESPECIALLY WHEN WALKING.

What an obviously literal thing to say.

THANK YOU. IT WAS. WHEN DID YOU MOVE TO KINGS CANYON?

When Papa got the contract to build the power grid for the Games. I was twelve at the time. We'd always lived in Eelhead Bay, so I was already familiar with Kings Canyon. It intrigued me. An island that was also a canyon? And one that had been abandoned by the IMC? I was fascinated with it. When I was old enough, Papa let me take the boat over and start to explore. By this time, I had already started reading Papa's textbooks, and learning everything I could about the science behind electricity. Papa had no idea. He thought I was still playing with Nessies. I was. But I was also learning.

YOU MUST HAVE REALLY ENJOYED GROWING UP HERE.

It was an adventure. It was just me and Papa back then. The treaty had just been signed, and the Syndicate now controlled most of the Outlands... has it been seven years already? *Incroyable!* It was Kuben Blisk's idea to bring back the Thunderdome Games... revamp them into something new. Something bigger. The Apex Games. He named them after his team of mercenaries. Have you met Blisk?

I HAVE NOT.

I would be very curious to see what it would be like if you did.

WHY? IS HE NOT YOUR FRIEND?

I don't think Kuben Blisk has friends. He's the antithesis of everything you are, Pathfinder. Your optimism... your spirit... your warmth and *je ne sais quoi*... it's what makes you special. Blisk is cynicism. He's greed. He's ambiguousness and misanthropy. I would think that when a positive charge (such as yourself) and a negative charge (such as him) were to share the same space together, the result would be, well... magnetic.

MAGNETS ARE FUN AND EDUCATIONAL, SO BLISK MUST BE FUN AND EDUCATIONAL TOO. SO, YOU MOVED TO KINGS CANYON ONCE PAPA WAS HIRED?

Just the two of us. Mama died when I was a baby so I don't have any memories of her. I do have the stuffed

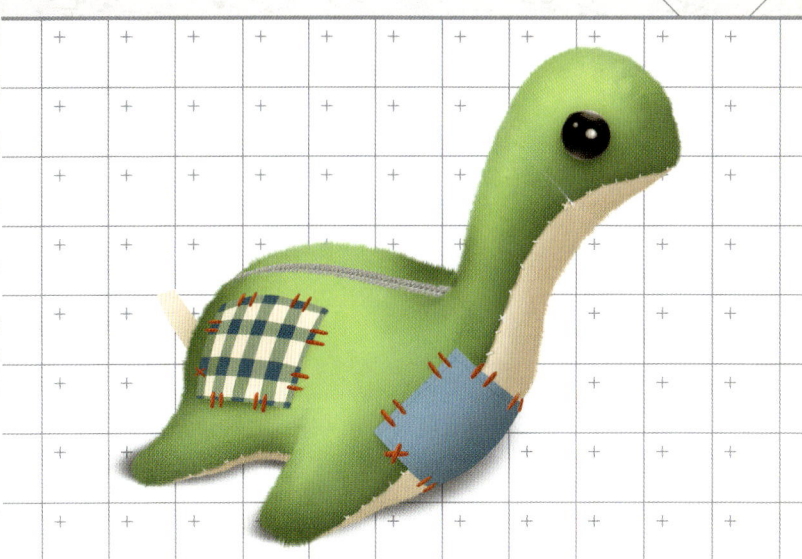

* THE ORIGINAL NESSIE.

Nessie she made for me. It sits on a shelf in my bedroom. Papa hired someone to make a bunch more for me, and I used to play hide-and-seek with them all over the canyon when I was little. Not Mama's Nessie, though. She never left my side.

THAT MAKES ME FEEL BITTER FOR YOUR LOSS, BUT I ALSO THINK IT'S SWEET. I WONDER IF THERE'S A WORD FOR THAT. WAS IT DIFFICULT FOR THE TWO OF YOU?

Difficult is subjective. It was just our life. Papa said yes to every job he was offered, no matter how hectic his schedule was. He couldn't afford not to. We knew the Kings Canyon job would take time, but most of the power lines were already there from the IMC. We'd rebuild, refurbish, but at least the foundation was there. We planned on being there a year or two at most. We had no idea that would be the last job he'd have.

WHAT MADE IT SO COMPLICATED?

The more invested and involved Blisk got in the Games, the more work my father had to put in. First it was just being able to turn on the lights. Not a big deal. But then it was loot bins. Computer networks. He had to work with a nanotech specialist to figure out how to build and install respawn beacons from scratch. And then there were the outer areas. They had to build an entire network of underwater motion-activated whirlpools, to deter competitors from trying to swim away or leave the Games midmatch by boat. There seemed to be no end in sight when it came to new additions, but Papa didn't mind. He loved a good challenge, and the MRVNs he had working with him were top quality and never broke down. He actually got bored with how friendly they were, so he programmed one to be grumpy two days a week just for variety. That was our life for the next five years.

WHERE DID YOU LIVE?

A cabin up in the mountains that overlook the artillery base. There's a river up there…it's so perfect. I loved that house. They tore it down after I moved out…they made that area off limits in the Games, which is probably for the best. Who wants to be in a gunfight when you're feeling nostalgic?

AND WHEN DID THEY ASK YOUR PAPA TO DESIGN THE RING?

Oh, we were well on our way to being done at that point. Back during the Thunderdome Games, there was no Ring—it was a free-for-all—but as the first round of Legends started a few practice competitions, Blisk saw a pattern forming. Competitors would camp out where they could, hiding from each other, waiting quietly to pick people off as they wandered by. Matches went on for half a day, sometimes overnight. It certainly made things interesting, but the Syndicate realized they needed to force them to move if they were going to hold an audience—make them fight. There were various proposals, but they all involved tactics that would harm the environment, and that immediately disqualified them. I had been reading Papa's textbooks, and studying up on the science behind what he did. I was especially intrigued by lasers, and I wanted to help him, but he asked me to stay out of it. "You're only a kid for so long," he'd say. "Make the most of it." He made me so angry, dismissing me like that. I know now that he was just looking out for me, but at the time I was young and impulsive. I defied him and kept researching possible solutions. That's when I discovered a device built in the early twenty-first century. It was called the Active Denial System, but they gave it the ridiculous nickname of "heat ray." It was the twenty-first century though…what do you expect?

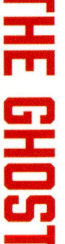

THE GHOST

A STORY OF HOW NATALIE MET THE GHOST

It was a dark and stormy night, and Nat had just gotten into an argument with her father. He had spent many nights trying to nail down the equations needed to power the modified containment system for his work, but how do you create and control an ever-shrinking ring of death? There were plenty of ideas...could they control the weather? Could the island sink and then rise up again for the next match? Each concept was shot down, but Nat believed she had cracked the code: laser cavities created between two bubble shields using an upgraded Active Denial System. By reshaping the ADS, they'd fill in the enclosed space with enough light waves to propagate the entire field. She told her dad she'd be able to obtain two bubble shields from the labs down by Glass Forest. Her father, however, frustrated with his own inability to crack the code and annoyed by his teenage daughter's interference in the project, ordered her to stay out of it. She tried to tell him that she had already figured out the equations, but he demanded she go to her room. The argument escalated (as arguments with adolescents often do) until Nat ran out into the night, screaming back at her father that he never listened to her, and that she hated him.

She didn't hate him. Not even a little. In fact, they were quite close. But fifteen-year-olds are prone to hyperbole.

She was more determined than ever to prove she was right. She looked back, relieved to see her father wasn't following her. She knew Kings Canyon like the back of her hand, and since they were the only two people on the island, she knew she would be safe. On a mission, Nat trekked down to the old labs in the Glass Forest to find her bubble shields.

Her journeys down into the lab were never pleasant. Once below ground level, everything grew musty and damp. The distant sound of dripping would echo, so she was never quite sure if she could trust her ears. The canyon played tricks on her as well. Was that a drop of water, or did somebody step in a puddle? Were they standing right there and it was too dark to see them? What if the puddle was directly in front of her...in that shadow? What if it was directly behind her? What if the thing that stepped in it was right there, and she didn't see it? What if she saw it...*now*? Inevitably, by the time she was asking herself this question, she could swear that the breeze that just wafted by was actually some creature's breath on the back of her neck. Nat shut out all these voices as she entered the lab. At the end of a long hallway, she turned on a switch. The light flickered, and she saw what she was looking for over by the old gurney. The dome shields.

The quicker Nat got her hands on them, the quicker she'd be able to get out of here. She made a beeline for the gurney, then looked up, startled. Was that...a person? It was. It was Nat herself--or rather her reflection in a chrome light fixture on the wall. She chuckled. Being one of two people alone on an island,

MY HISTORY FILES CONFIRM YOUR MOCKERY IS BASED IN FACT. HAH!

As ignorant as they were at the time, I realized they had inadvertently stumbled onto the solution to our problems. They used it for crowd control, which is in essence what the Ring does. Using bubble shield technology, I hypothesized that if one domed shield surrounded the whole island, and a second domed shield was within that first one, you could fill the space in between the two shields with the waves generated from an upgraded version of the ADS. Then, all you had to do was slowly shrink the inner domed shield and keep filling the space in between with ADS waves, forcing Legends to stay within the inner shield to duke it out, as they say. The best part was that the light waves didn't seem to hurt the environment—only living creatures would sustain long-term effects. Local wildlife wouldn't be an issue, as we had built the Repulsor Tower. So, if this worked, we would have our crowd control containment system. All I needed were two bubble shields, which I had seen in one of the abandoned labs by the forest. That's how I met the ghost . . .

YOU MET A GHOST?

Hmm. Funny how life throws things at you that you think are meaningless at the time, but ultimately end up being far more significant than you ever thought possible. The exact mathematics of these minor incidents . . . fractions of a moment . . . it isn't until you reach the end that you realize how much of it you just ignored that was far more important than you thought. Every little piece is building to the final act of the story. Anyway, I'm rambling again. Right. The ghost. And so much more . . .

she'd grown used to that kind of thing. Her subconscious wanted to believe that there were others around...and sometimes it would almost convince her that there really *were*. How many times had Nat thought she'd heard a voice? Stranger yet, she used to think she could hear humming. She'd chalk it up to one of the various generators or charge towers around the island. But sometimes she heard it in places where there was no machinery. Sometimes... sometimes it even sounded human...

But it never was. Like now, for example. She thought she sensed someone else in the lab with her, but it had just been her reflection.

...Which was why she almost jumped out of her skin when she heard a woman's voice say one word, in a sharp, curt tone:

"*Leave.*"

That's impossible, she thought to herself. There was no voice here. There were no other *people* here, and the security system would have gone off if anyone had tried to dock in the water. It was probably a water drip that just sounded like a voice, or maybe a--

"*Leave.*"

There it was again! Nat grabbed the dome shields, never taking her eyes off the only door in the room. Not that anybody would show up here--but even if they did, and made it down the steps into the long, damp hallway, Nat would still hear them. She'd still know they were coming. There was nothing here that could hurt her, or at least nothing that could sneak up on her.

That's why her heart practically stopped when she looked back over at the far wall with the light fixture, only to see a woman with milky dead eyes directly in front of her.

"I said *leave*!" she bellowed. Nat screamed and stumbled back. The thing with the dead eyes was in tattered clothes. *Where did it come from?!* Nat thought, panicked. *There's no way she could have gotten in without me seeing her... how is she here?!* And the thing held a knife...

Nat half-crawled backward at a frantic pace, but her feet couldn't seem to find the ground. They slid on the dirt, giving out under her. She could feel her pulse pounding throughout her entire body as she continued to scream down the long hallway. She rounded the corner and stopped to catch her breath for half a second, looking down to see that she'd lost her shoes in the escape. Damn it, that was going to slow her d--

The dead eyes suddenly appeared from out of nowhere directly in front of her. *But it's the opposite direction! Are there two of them?! How many are there?!*

...AND WHY IS THERE NO BODY ATTACHED TO THE HEAD?!

"*Go!*" it demanded. Nat shrieked so hard that she started sobbing as she ran to the steps and up into the cold, rainy night. When she emerged from the underground lab, she slammed the door shut as the rain poured over her. She cried as she had never cried before in her life. Was it really trapped down there, or would it return? Was there an army of them? The second thing looked just like the first--identical, in fact--but how could it come from two directions at once? She didn't wait to find out. She ran up the hill and over the mound of wet grass into the forest.

By the time she could see the artillery base, her heart had stopped racing. The thing with dead eyes hadn't returned, and her home was in her line of sight. Maybe she really had imagined it. Maybe she was losing her mind. It's not like that had been the first time she'd been down there, and she'd never come across this evil woman before. Who was she? How did she die? And how could a ghost even exist in the first place?

There would be time for these questions later. She had more pressing concerns. Her father's light was still on; that much she could still see. Nat decided she wouldn't return home until she'd proven to him that she had figured out the solution to creating the containment system-- but was she far enough away from the underground lab that the apparition wouldn't come back for her? All it wanted was for her to leave the lab...it didn't say anything about the forest. Knowing her cabin was only a short sprint away, she decided to take the risk. She scampered back down toward the lab, checking over her shoulder until she approached the first line of trees that acted as the border to what she referred to as the Glass Forest. It got its name from the unusual translucent leaves that grew on some of the trees...they were almost like glass.

She found a jumperberry plant at the forest's edge, and decided to make that the center of her "final ring." She measured back about two hundred meters, and set up the first dome shield.

The shield came to life, and a translucent dome appeared over the whole forest. She took a few steps in, and activated the second bubble shield, which came to life within the first dome. Stepping out of both shields, she took in the sight before her. Everything was bathed in a pale blue light, with the jumperberry plant standing in the center of the inner dome.

The rain was falling harder now, but Nat was focused on finishing her work. She passed a tool that resembled an unusually wide hypodermic needle through the outer dome. A wire ran from the needle to a generator that she had recovered from one of the construction sites. Opening the control panel, she typed in her father's password, which she had carefully spied over his shoulder. The screen asked if she was ready to initiate the Active Denial System.

"Am I ever..." She hit the Enter key.

A red light shot out of the needle, filling the empty space between the two domes with a scarlet energy, like blood spilling out into the ocean. The rain began to pour down even more heavily. "A little longer," she told herself. "If I'm going to prove to Papa that I know what I'm talking about, it has to be a little longer..."

Once the scarlet light filled the space between the domes, Nat took a deep breath. She moved her hand to the remote on her hip, and began to shrink the inner dome. The red cavity between the two domes began to fill. The inner dome shrunk smaller and smaller, until the only thing inside the bubble of icy blue light beneath the harsh red dome was the jumperberry plant.

And that's when the lightning bolt hit the generator, shooting a bolt of electricity up the wire to her probe. In this instant, Nat came to the horrifying realization that she was not wearing shoes. Her shoes with rubber soles, the only thing that would insulate her from--

As the bolt of electricity hit her, Natalie Paquette flew twenty meters into the air. Her body slammed against a tree before hitting the ground with multiple cracks and a sickening thud.

Surprisingly (but only barely) still conscious, Nat used every ounce of her remaining strength to open her eyes. The generator had caught fire. *It's okay*, she thought. *The rain will put it out. Just focus on getting to your feet.* She tried, but she couldn't move. Every bone in her body was screaming in agony. *What did I do*, she wondered. *I can't move. I can't scream. Am I going to die out here?*

And then the rain stopped. The fire started to spread.

Nat lay there, her home just out of reach...maybe half a kilometer at most. Her bed. Her stuffed Nessie from when she was a kid. Why had she left her home? Why had she run out into the night? *Papa! Papa, please! Come help!*

I didn't mean it. I don't hate you. Help me. I don't want to die.

The smoke was all around her. The foliage was now in flames. Nat tried once again to move any part of her body, but even rolling over was an impossibility. She was paralyzed. The fire was now so close that it singed her eyebrows. She could smell burning hair. The smoke was overwhelming. Nat softly cried, her eyes closing, as she repeated two words over and over again to absolutely no one: "I'm sorry. I'm sorry. I'm sorry."

What happened next remained a mystery for almost a decade. Nat vaguely remembered hearing something behind her. She glimpsed the bottom edge of what looked like a passageway suddenly appearing within the smoke, before the smoke backed away as the passage formed a doorway. *How can smoke retreat like that?* she later recalled thinking. Someone stepped out of this impossible door from nowhere, and carefully knelt over Nat. As Nat drifted into unconsciousness, she swore she saw the woman with dead eyes from the underground lab. Only this time, her eyes looked alive--determined, even. Impassioned. Driven. *She's only a few years older than me,* Nat thought. The woman lifted Nat into her arms, and as she did, Nat saw one last image that was so powerful, she forced herself to stay awake and etch it into her mind. She could not forget this.

She could feel herself being carried through the night, and up the path to her father's cabin. Nat was barely conscious by the time the door opened, but she felt her father was there. She didn't remember the woman vanishing into thin air, or her papa lifting her into his arms and softly crying, telling her it would be okay. The only thing she could remember was that final image from the woods that she'd forced herself to retain: despite the fire having burned the surrounding forest into ash, the jumperberry plant remained in the center ring, alive and well and thriving...

...Pathfinder?

AHH! YEAH?! WHA—DID I JUST SCREAM? SORRY.

You were so quiet, I thought you had powered down.

NO, I AM CONSCIOUS. YOU SCARED ME. THAT WAS A REALLY CREEPY STORY.

Yes. But it has a happy ending, despite the electrocution that led to my father reprogramming every MRVN on the entire planet to babysit me, and left me with seven broken bones, a concussion, and a Lichtenberg figure on my cheek.

THAT'S HOW YOU GOT YOUR SCAR?

Oui, but most importantly? It's how I eventually was able to design the Ring. The next night, I showed him the equations to make the light waves work in the bubble shield. He was blown away. He had never considered using the shields. Once I showed him how to do it, the Syndicate approved the plan, and he became one of their most trusted and beloved employees.

WHY DID THEY BUILD THE STATUE OF HIM IN THE CENTER OF EELHEAD BAY? WHY NOT A STATUE OF YOU?

I made him promise to take full credit. I didn't do it for my own gain. I did it because I loved him, and I wanted him to be happy. My father was a local hero, and Blisk gifted him with a large bonus check. They even gave us a new home in Eelhead Bay, free of charge. When you're on the good side of organized crime, it's not always a bad thing. Especially when organized crime doesn't answer to anyone, eh?

AND YOU NEVER GOT THE CREDIT...?

Not then. After he passed away, I was summoned to Blisk's office in Syndicate Tower. That was the first time I ever spoke to the man. He told me that Papa had come to his office the night they approved our proposal. He told Blisk everything—how I had literally risked my life to find a way to make the Ring happen, and that I had made him promise he'd take the credit. Papa didn't want me to know that he had gone back on that promise, but he thought it important that Blisk knew. I don't know why Blisk cared... he has no children, so he can't possibly relate to this. But Blisk said he understood, and even though he knew the truth, he kept the lie alive that my father had built the containment ring so that I would always believe Papa had kept his word. After his death, Blisk felt I was owed the truth, and he wanted me to know that I always had a home and a job in the Games, no matter what. Years later, when I asked to become a Legend, he pushed me through without even one qualifying match. I'm very lucky. The Syndicate thinks very highly of me. I don't ever want to take that for granted, nor do I want to take advantage of it. Oh, and Blisk gave me one last gift: a letter Papa wrote me the night I showed him the equations. He told me how sorry he was for being stubborn, and how proud he was of me. I framed it and put it on my nightstand. Of all his "inventions," this is the one I prize most.

IF IT'S YOUR PRIZED POSSESSION, YOU SHOULD PROGRAM MRVNS TO SAVE IT, IN CASE OF EMERGENCY.

Who's to say I haven't already?

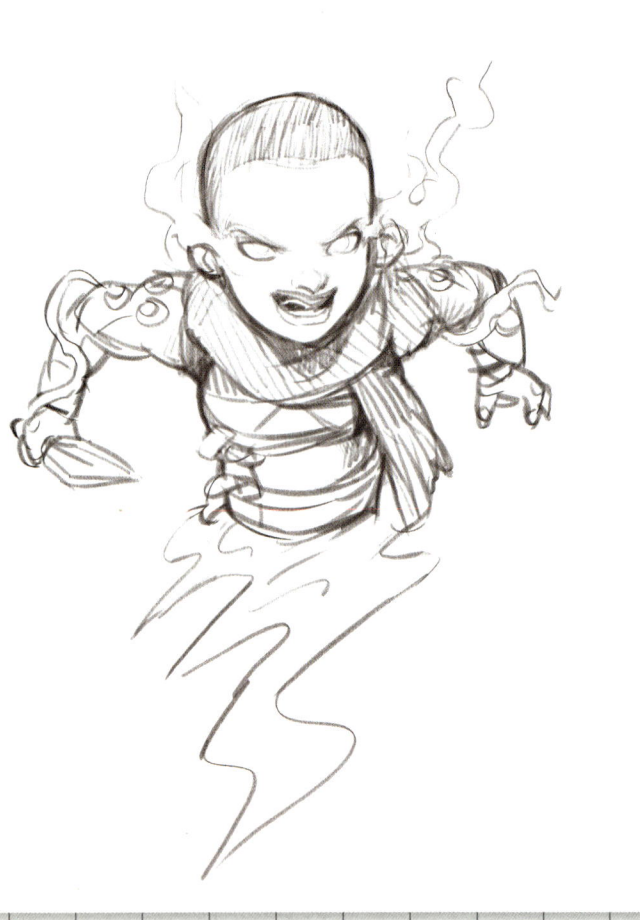

* NAT'S SKETCH OF THE "GHOST."

AND WHAT ABOUT THE GHOST?

Papa had that lab sealed up when he heard my story. Sent down into the dirt. He didn't believe in ghosts, but he also didn't believe in taking chances, so it was buried—along with its secrets. He didn't ever want to step into the place that led to his daughter almost dying.

HE DIDN'T BELIEVE IN GHOSTS . . . BUT YOU DO?

Do I believe in things that go bump in the night? No. But who's to say the energy inside us doesn't

transform or transfer itself somewhere after our bodies die? That's why I still talk to Papa sometimes. Not because I think he'll appear as an apparition or anything, but in case his energy is nearby.

BUT YOU SAW ONE OF THESE GHOSTS; THEREFORE, IT MUST BE REAL.

No, I didn't. What I saw that night—who I saw—didn't become apparent to me until many years later. This past summer, in fact. I put it all together with her help. See, I thought she looked familiar when I met her, but I couldn't place her. I just thought she had one of those faces. But I did meet her before. And once she and I put the pieces together, everything made sense.

WHO ARE YOU TALKING ABOUT? WHO DID YOU KNOW BEFORE?

Wraith. The woman with dead eyes? It was Wraith. Our Wraith, days after she used her portal to enter our world. She had been hiding out in those labs while she came up with a game plan to learn her identity. I was just some kid who stumbled into her shelter without realizing it. Her head wasn't disembodied, it was just sticking out from a portal. Years later, when we met as adults, Wraith didn't recognize me because it'd been seven years. I'm not fifteen anymore.

THAT'S *INCROYABLE*, AS YOU WOULD SAY. AND SHE SAVED YOUR LIFE IN THE FIRE?

The voices from the Void warned her of the blaze, and she used her abilities to save me and drop me off at my house. Knowing she had been discovered, she left that night and made her way into Solace City. The Glass Forest had burned to the ground. I called it the Shattered Forest after that. Like shattered glass? We sealed the lab up entirely until years later, when the Repulsor Tower attack happened and the Syndicate unearthed everything. Who would have thought that the ghost I saw as a child would one day be my teammate and friend? This is what I'm saying, Pathfinder: whatever you find out on this journey to find your creator? Pay attention to the little things. Trillions of people in this universe, and yet connections somehow arise when you least expect them. Connections you can't even imagine. You never know who or what will pop back up and be important later on.

Anyway, there I go again. I spent my formative years with nobody in my life but my father. I'll talk to anyone for days if you don't stop me. You should hear Dr. Caustic when I get talking. "It's not that what you say isn't interesting, Ms. Paquette . . . but I grow weary of your rambling."

I THINK IT'S INTERESTING THAT YOU ARE FRIENDS WITH CAUSTIC,

My dearest Natalie –

As I write this letter, it's the middle of the night in late summer. (Although it's always summer on Solace, no?) You have poked your head out of your bedroom twice already, insisting I retire for the night. Always looking out for me, though you're still a child yourself.

At least, that's what I pretend. But it appears that may no longer be the case. An hour ago, you cracked the equations necessary to power the forcefield. You showed me up tonight, my magnificent daughter, and I couldn't be happier or prouder of that.

I always knew you were special, but never did I fathom that the little girl who taught her stuffed Nessie multiplication tables when she was six years old would grow up to master quantum laser mechanics. I talked to Jacob at the Syndicate and assured him that the Modified Containment Forcefield will be operational in a month's time. The Games are a go, and it's all thanks to you.

And I owe you an apology . . .

I'm just a doddering old fool, trying to hold on to mon bébé a little while longer before he loses her to adulthood. But I do see you. I'm sorry it's taken this long, but I now see the strong, brilliant, wonderful young woman you've become, and I know when the day comes that I'm no longer walking these dusty old streets, you are going to be just fine.

Hold on to this feeling, Natalie. Savor this victory. Summer may be eternal on Solace, but the world can also be a very cold place at times. And on those days when I'm no longer with you, and you feel alone, and frustrated, and that there are too many mountains to climb . . . please reread this letter. Remember that you are my little girl, and because of YOU, my darling daughter, the people of the Outlands will have reasons to smile soon enough. The Games will be brilliant, because you are brilliant. My daughter can, and will, do anything she wants in this life. Because my daughter is the smartest woman in the Frontier.
Je t'aime de tout mon coeur, pour toujours.

Papa

P.S. And the Syndicate agrees with you – "The Ring" is a better name than "The Forcefield". Fine. You win this one, too . . .

WATTSON'S LETTER FROM HER PAPA.

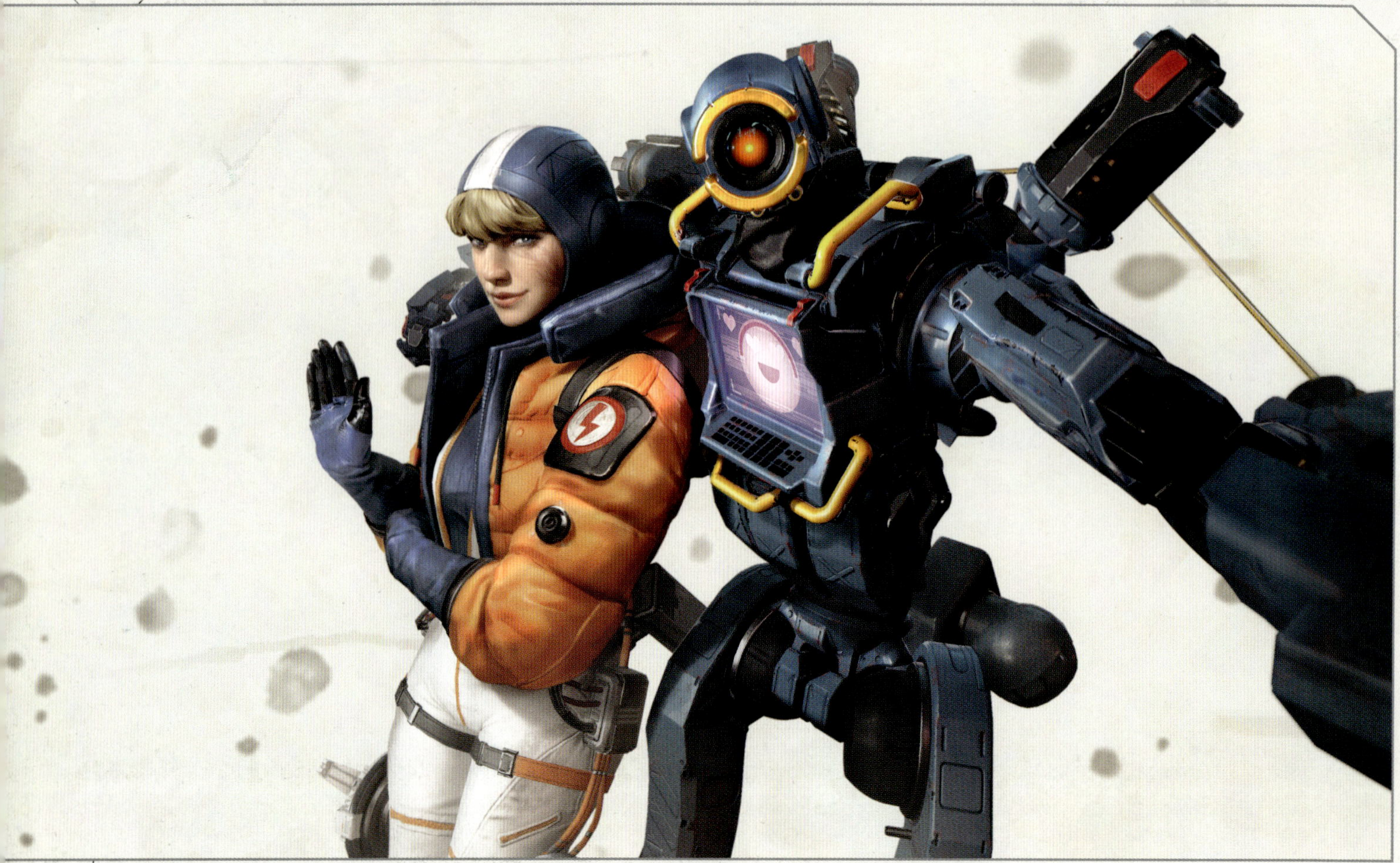

* A SELFIE WITH NAT!

CONSIDERING YOU ARE SO WELL LIKED AND HE IS WHAT MY RECORDS INDICATE IS CALLED A "SOCIOPATH."
He is, but he's still a human being. Some people like to wear masks. Caustic and Crypto want to hide who they are. They have their reasons. I respect that. Though, I think it's good if I keep my distance from them sometimes. When I'm around, they act like little boys. Always fighting. I prefer when they act like scientists. I come from a long line of great scientists. Papa's father was Emile Paquette, a world-renowned chemist on Gridiron, and his mother was Amélie Paquette, who was known in some circles as the Mother of Minerals—

OH, YOU ARE CONNECTED TO AMÉLIE?
She is my paternal grandmother. Why are you looking for information on Amélie?

I FOUND A RECORDING ABOUT THE PURPOSE I WAS BUILT FOR. IT'S AN SOS FROM A WOMAN NAMED AMÉLIE, AND HER LAST NAME BEGINS WITH "PA."
Fascinating. But she was a geologist. Unless you were built to move rocks, I'm not sure why she would be involved in your creation.

DO YOU KNOW WHERE SHE LIVES?

She's dead. She died in a lab explosion while working on assignment on Psamathe when Papa was young. He never talked about how she died, or how he felt about her, and I didn't ask questions. I just know whatever happened to her, it was bad. Very bad.

YOU SAID IT WAS AN ASSIGNMENT. INVOLVING GEOLOGY? WHO ASSIGNED IT TO HER?
I do not know details. She mostly worked freelance, although I know she did some work for the IMC. Nothing connected to the war … again, she dealt with minerals, mostly with regard to alternative fuel resources. Oh, but you know what? Speaking of Wraith, she might be able to help you! She had some luck finding old files that related to her experiment in those same labs where I first met her. Maybe she can take you down there and help you look around. You might find something with *Grand-mère*'s name on it. And if you do, let me know. I do love a good mystery …

LOADING … TRANSCRIPTION / 0000101

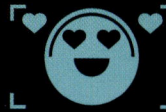
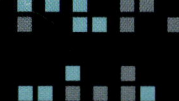

DATA POINTS RECEIVED

- Kings Canyon was occupied by the IMC until they abandoned it.

- After the treaty was signed, ending the civil war, the Mercenary Syndicate chose Kings Canyon to bring back the Thunderdome Games as the Apex Games.

- Luc Paquette was hired to install the electrical system, and he and his daughter Natalie moved to Eelhead Bay on the Duchess River.

- While Luc and his team built the power grid, Natalie was determined to help her dad build the Ring. During her experimentation, she had a run-in with Wraith, who saved her life.

- To keep Natalie safe while she was exploring, Luc programmed the MRVNs working on Kings Canyon to hack into the survey beacons and always know where the Ring was headed.

- When Luc died, Blisk told Natalie that her dad gave her full credit for inventing the Ring.

- When she asked to join the Games, Blisk allowed her to bypass the qualifying matches.

- Amélie Paquette is Wattson's grandmother.

- Little is known about Amélie, other than that she died under mysterious circumstances when Luc was younger.

- Amélie did some freelance work for the IMC, and Wraith had some luck uncovering files from her IMC experiment in the underground labs. Perhaps Wraith can help uncover some files about Amélie and how she died . . .

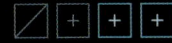
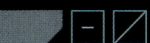

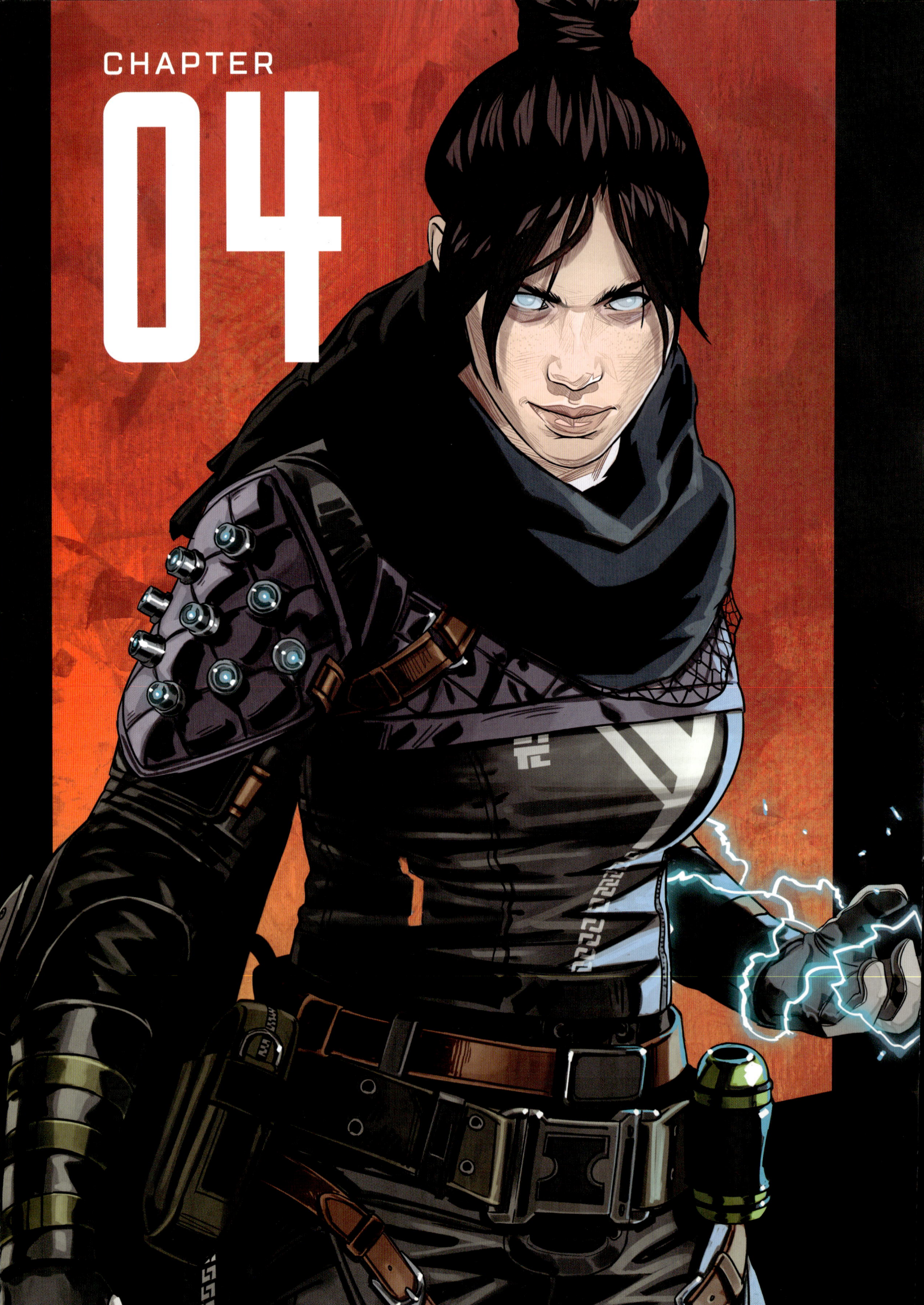

IDENTITY
THEFT

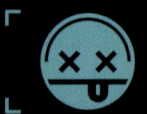
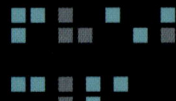
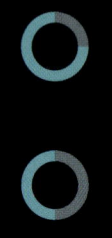

PATHFINDER MEMORY LOG: DAY 4

I am learning so much about all my new friends! It turns out Wattson—or Nat, as I call her—is Amélie Paquette's granddaughter! And that's not all. Nat was saved by what she thought was a "ghost" seven years ago who was actually Wraith! And neither one of them realized it until just this year! Because of that night, she was able to build the Ring and open the Games. I guess Nat was right . . . you never know when some small detail from the past will come back into your life and matter, even a decade later. I wonder what detail from my day with Nat will come back and haunt me? I'm not going to guess. I like surprises! I also learned why the Shattered Forest is called the Shattered Forest, along with how it burned down, and I now know where the scar on Wattson's face came from! So much information! Here's what I still don't know: How was Amélie Paquette connected to my creator? If she was my creator, how is that possible, since she was a geologist? And how did she die?

I have so many questions, but I do feel like I'm on the right track. Nat said Amélie occasionally worked on secret experimental freelance jobs and there's one person I know who is an expert on secret experiments—my friend Wraith. I'm meeting her in the abandoned Singh Labs hidden below Kings Canyon. That's where she thinks she can find her own answers—I love that we're all on quests!

Wraith is going to help me look for anything involving Amélie or Aleki or me!

CLUE BOX

TRANSMISSION CLUES
- "Chevrex" > LIFELINE'S PARENTS' COMPANY
- "The future of the Outlands" >
- "Dr. Amélie Pa—— [Paquette]" > WATTSON'S GRANDMOTHER, A GEOLOGIST, DIED MYSTERIOUSLY
- "The Event" >
- "Aleki" > GIBRALTAR'S GRANDFATHER
- "Iris" >

SELF-MOTIVATION QUOTE . . . SEARCHING . . . 1 RESULT FOUND

"We know what we are, but know not what we may be."
—[WILLIAM SHAKESPEARE]

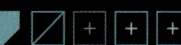

WRAITH BIO FROM THE APEX GAMES

ULTIMATE OBJECTIVE . . . SEEKING CREATOR

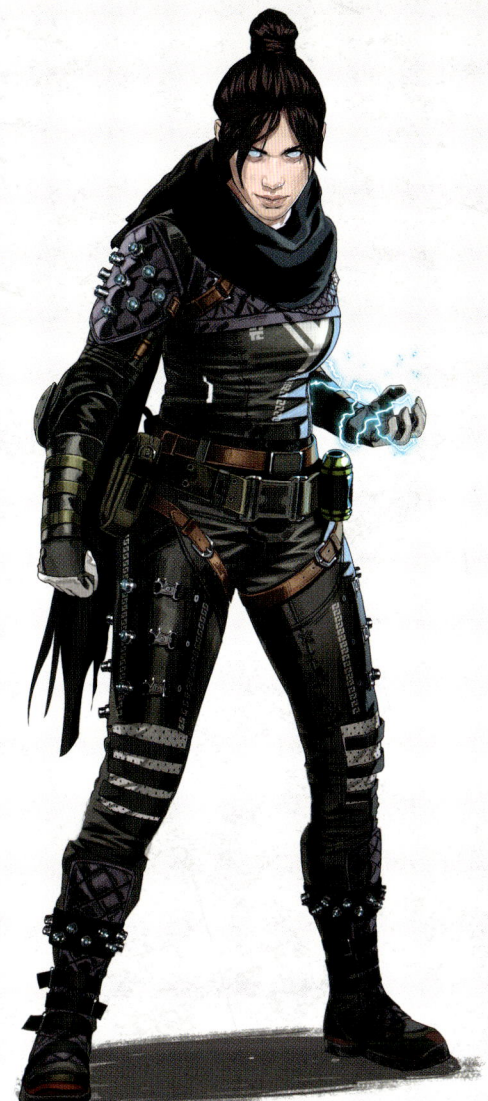
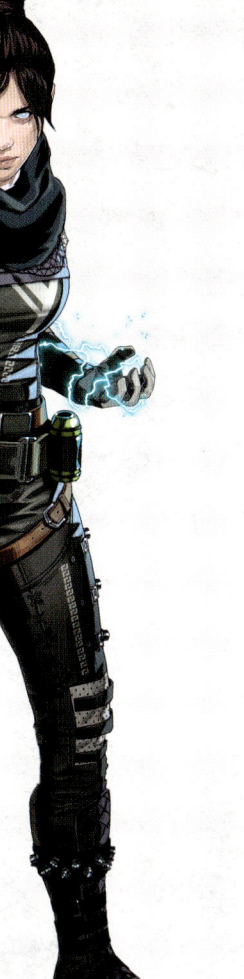

REAL NAME:
SENIOR SCIENCE PILOT
RENEE BLASEY

AGE:
32

HOME WORLD:
TYPHON

TACTICAL ABILITY:
INTO THE VOID

PASSIVE ABILITY:
VOICES FROM THE VOID

ULTIMATE ABILITY:
DIMENSIONAL RIFT

WRAITH IS A WHIRLWIND FIGHTER, ABLE TO EXECUTE SWIFT AND DEADLY ATTACKS AND MANIPULATE SPACETIME BY OPENING RIFTS IN THE FABRIC OF REALITY—but she has no memory of how she got that way. Years ago, she woke up in an IMC detention facility for the mentally ill with no memory of her life before. She also began hearing a distant voice whispering in her mind that would keep her awake for days on end. At first it nearly drove her insane, but once she started to listen and trust it, the voice helped her harness her newfound power of void manipulation and escape the facility.

Determined to uncover her true identity, Wraith began a quest to find out more about the experiments. Many of the old research facilities, however, are buried beneath heavily guarded arenas used for the Apex Games. Now Wraith has joined the competition, and with every match she gets closer to the truth. She's uncovered some parts of her past . . . her name and profession, for starters . . . but there's still much she needs to learn about the life she has no memory of . . .

"I know all the roads—they all lead to the same place. Make a choice."
—WRAITH

► HELLO, WRAITH. ◄

IT'S MY OLD FRIEND, WRAITH!
Pathfinder.

I'VE KNOWN YOU SINCE MY VERY FIRST MATCH. YOU, ME, AND MIRAGE. REMEMBER?
Surprisingly, I do. Ironic, isn't it?

HOLD, PLEASE. I NEED TO CONSULT MY GUT.
Okay, the floor's a little shaky here, so be care—

IRONY: A STATE OF AFFAIRS OR AN EVENT THAT SEEMS DELIBERATELY CONTRARY TO WHAT ONE EXPECTS AND IS OFTEN AMUSING AS A RESULT. YOU'RE RIGHT! ASKING A FRIEND WITH AMNESIA IF THEY REMEMBER, AND THEY DO, IS INDEED IRONY.
Pretty sure that's why I said it in the first place.

WITTY BANTER! CLASSIC WRAITH AND PATHFINDER!
Path, I really need you to pay attention. The infrastructure of these labs is precarious at best, and we don't need a repeat of what happened last year when you fell through my portal.

I WENT TO A PLACE WHERE REVENANT WAS KING.
You need to stop saying that to everyone you meet. They're going to think your programming is faulty and power you down. Trust me. I would know.

PEOPLE THOUGHT YOU WERE CRAZY.
They knew I wasn't crazy. Okay, there's no light at all after this next sublevel, so follow my lead.

I'M FOLLOWING THE LEADER, WHEREVER SHE MAY GO! AND WRAITH IS MY LEADER! I'M LEARNING ALL ABOUT NAMES AS WELL ON THIS JOURNEY. SHOULD I CALL YOU RENEE FROM NOW ON?
Please don't.

BUT THAT'S YOUR NAME. ISN'T THAT WHAT YOU WERE LOOKING FOR? I WOULD BE VERY HAPPY IF I FINALLY FOUND WHAT I'D BEEN LOOKING FOR.
It's just a name. But it's not what I've been looking for. What I'm looking for involves more than a name. A lot more.

SO WHY DON'T YOU LIKE RENEE?
I don't dislike it. Or like it. She's just a stranger to me. And while it's nice to know my own name, it tells me nothing I need to know.

LIKE WHAT?
Like where did I come from? Are my parents still alive? Was I married? Do I have any children? What was my childhood like? Did I have any hobbies? Did I play a sport? Did I collect anything? What was my favorite pastime? Where did I live? What kind of transport did I drive? What kind of person was I? Was I spiritual? What did I believe in? Did I attend services? Did I believe in the IMC's cause? Or was it just a job to me?

THAT'S A LOT OF QUESTIONS.
Sure is. Okay. Here we are.

THIS IS THE ROOM WHERE THE ANSWERS ARE?
Some of them.

SO, WHAT WAS THIS PLACE?
ARES Division.

I'VE HEARD OF THEM AND SEEN THEIR LOGO, BUT I DON'T REALLY KNOW MUCH.
Not too much publicly out there, but that's where I come in. *General Elias Marder* was the guy in charge.

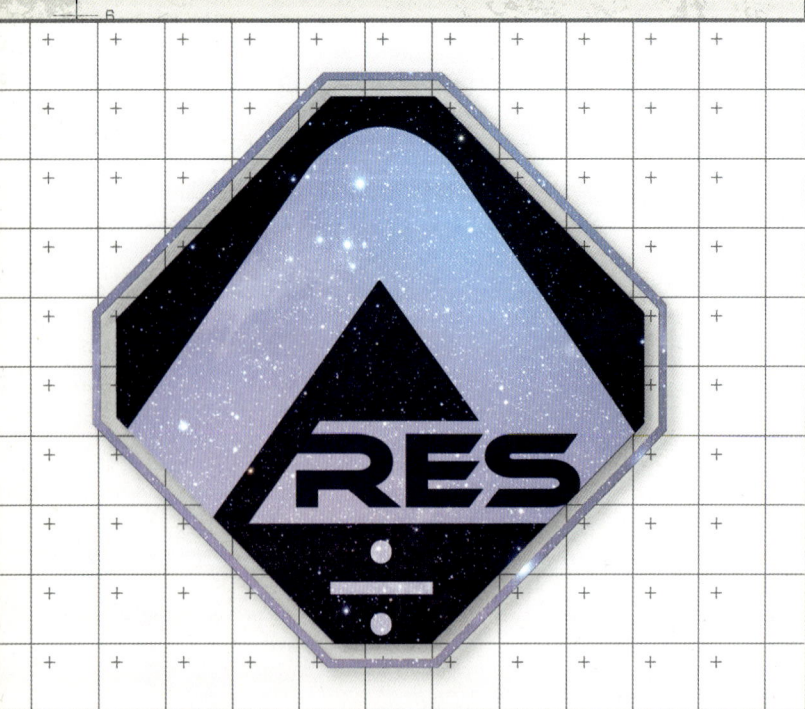

ARCHEOLOGICAL RESEARCH FOR EMERGENT SYSTEMS (ARES) IS A SPECIAL IMC MILITARY TASK FORCE EXPLORING THE FRONTIER IN SEARCH OF ANSWERS TO THE POWERS OF THE ANCIENT FRONTIER RUINS AND ARTIFACTS AND FINDING WAYS TO WEAPONIZE THEM.

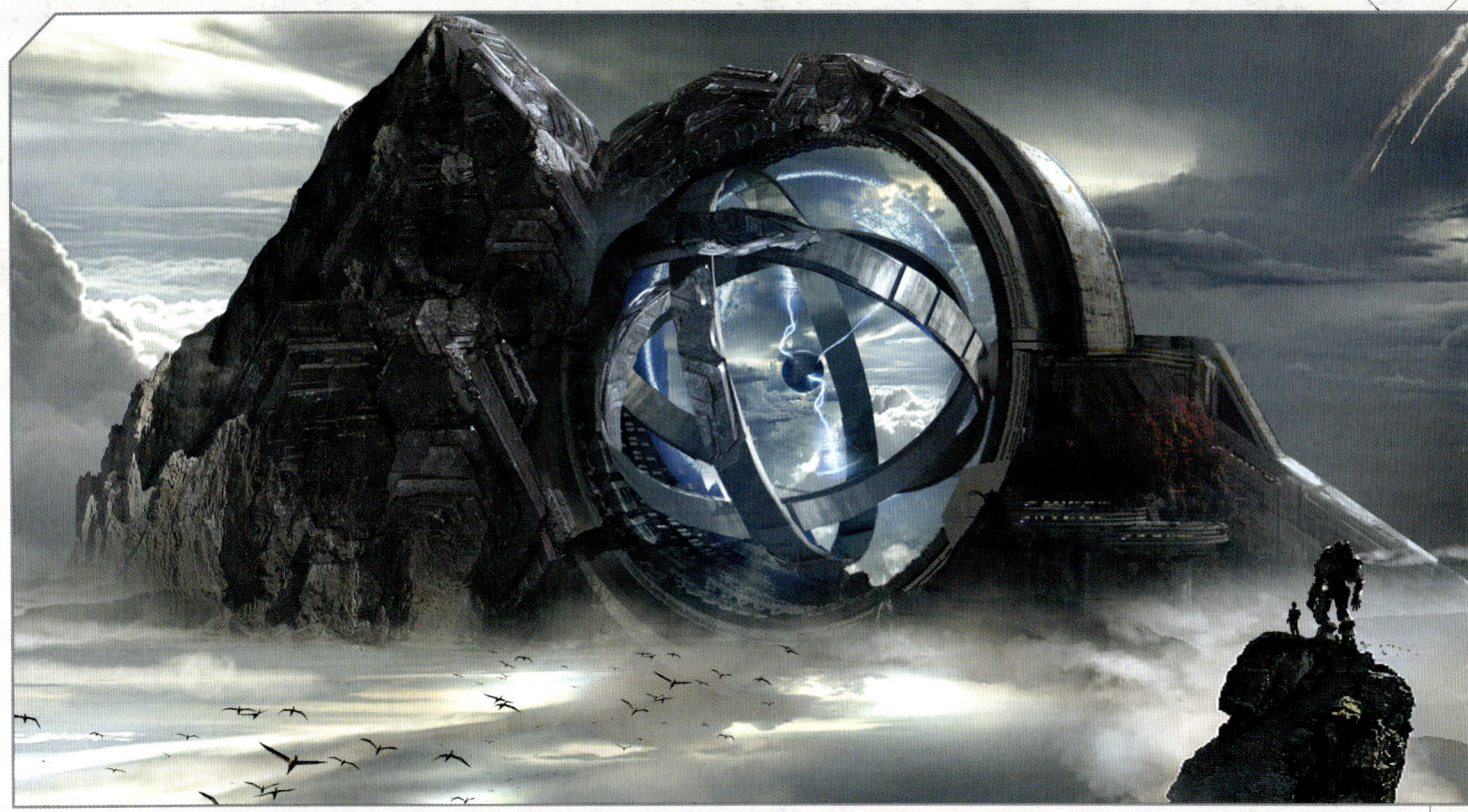

AN ANCIENT DEVICE KNOWN AS THE FOLD WEAPON AND ITS POWER SOURCE: THE ARK.

I'M SURE HE'S NICE.
He's not.

YOU DON'T LIKE HIM?
I've never met him. That I know of. But from everything I've read, and the footage I've seen, I don't need to.

It was about eighteen years ago, during the last leg of the Frontier Wars. General Marder led the ARES Division to uncover an ancient technology they called the Fold Weapon on planet Typhon. I didn't find anything on who originally built the tech, but the research I did find led me to believe that it wasn't meant to be a weapon.

WHAT WAS IT MEANT TO BE?
It terraformed planets. It made life. But, like something as simple as fire, what is made for good can just as easily be used for bad.

OH NO.
But the Fold Weapon needed something else—a key component called the Ark. Like the Fold Weapon, not much is known about the Ark, but I've learned it's powerful. Powerful enough to warp time and matter. Marder needed it secure as it was transferred from its dig site to the Fold Weapon—and that's why he hired the Apex Predators.

THE APEX PREDATORS? ARE THEY LEGENDS IN THE APEX GAMES?

One is … The Apex Predators were a mercenary group led by the former IMC Pilot—and the most infamous Apex Legend of all time—*Kuben Blisk.*

I'VE HEARD OF KUBEN BLISK.
I'm sure you have. He's the commissioner of the Apex Games. He used to compete in the old Thunderdome Games at Kings Canyon—the original Apex Games. He built up a big name for himself here in the Outlands before joining the Frontier Wars.

After he split from the IMC, he joined the Mercenary Syndicate and took command of the Apex Predators. They were the best in the Syndicate, which is why Marder hired them to protect the Ark.

AND DID THEY?
Somewhat. He completed his job, at least.

Marder's one of those guys who think they've thought of everything. Ego and arrogance always come back to bite you—that's something I've learned. Marder had no idea that a single rifleman and his mentor's Titan would stop him against all odds.

YOU'RE TALKING ABOUT PILOT JACK COOPER AND BT-7274!
I am. So, you've heard the stories.

YES. I KNOW THAT THEY SAVED A LOT OF PEOPLE.

They did. Marder wanted to destroy the Militia's home planet of Harmony, but Pilot Cooper and BT stopped him. Rumor has it Blisk stepped aside to let them do it and even gave Cooper one of those Apex cards that invite you into the Games. Coulda saved me some time if I got one of those.

In the end, Marder is to blame for what happened to planet Typhon.

TYPHON BLEW UP, AND I LOST MY JOB AS A WEATHERMAN.
It sure did.

AND EVERYONE DIED.
No. Yes, there were casualties. Militia records indicate the loss of Apex Predator mercenaries Kane, Richter, Slone, Viper, and A—oh. There's a name I didn't expect to see.

. . . "ASH"? MY ASH?!
Blisk's Ash, apparently. Died in this world . . . but ended up a nine-piece head set in another. I'm sorry, Pathfinder. I know you're trying to move on . . .

THEN LET'S MOVE ON.
Okay. Many IMC scientists lost their lives as well that

day. Whether they're considered innocent or not, they were casualties—one in particular is Dr. Jefferson Boyle. Not sure who he is, but his name has popped up a few times in the records I've found. And lastly, BT-7274. He sacrificed himself for many. He made a choice to protect those he cared about and those he didn't even know.

THAT'S REALLY NICE. I WISH I COULD BE THAT NICE.
You are, Path. That I know for sure, just like I know that the Ark still exists somewhere. The research I found postdated the Battle of Typhon in 2715. Part of the power they harnessed from the Ark continued on in ARES Division research here in the Outlands. I'm not positive, but I believe the research here in Singh Labs was connected to the Ark in some way. My abilities to phase shift and form dimensional rifts share qualities similar to the Ark.

I think it was *my* research.

AND YOU DON'T REMEMBER ANY OF THAT?
I have lots of information to fill in the blanks. But my memory hasn't returned. Take this, for example. It's my original new-employee registration form from when I came to work at Singh Labs.

SINGH LABS EMPLOYEE REGISTRATION FORM

NAME: _Renee Hope Blasey_

ADDRESS: _63-86 Ferril Square, Solace City, Solace_

ID#: _SOL38-92FE-591K_

POSITION: _Senior Science Pilot_

IN CASE OF EMERGENCY CONTACT:

SUPERVISOR:

NOTES:
_[an eye on her. Might be an issue with her
She's very [ ] and we may need to
address that at some point. She requested to be
partnered with Singh. Seems dangerous, but maybe
their combined [ ] will cancel each other out.]_

> READING . . . WRAITH'S EMPLOYEE REGISTRATION FORM . . .

> NAME: RENEE HOPE BLASEY
> ADDRESS: 63-86 FERRIL SQUARE, SOLACE CITY, SOLACE
> ID#: SOL38-92FE-591K
> POSITION: SENIOR SCIENCE PILOT
> IN CASE OF EMERGENCY, CONTACT: [ILLEGIBLE]
> SUPERVISOR: [BLANK]
> NOTES: KEEP AN EYE ON HER. MIGHT BE AN ISSUE WITH HER [ILLEGIBLE]. SHE'S VERY [ILLEGIBLE] AND WE MAY NEED TO ADDRESS THAT AT SOME POINT. SHE REQUESTED TO BE PARTNERED WITH SINGH. SEEMS DANGEROUS, BUT MAYBE THEIR COMBINED [ILLEGIBLE] WILL CANCEL EACH OTHER OUT.

IT'S A SHAME SOMETHING SPILLED ON THIS FORM. I WOULD LIKE TO KNOW WHAT IT SAYS.

You took the words right out of my mouth, my friend.

YOU JUST CALLED ME "FRIEND"!

I did, didn't I?

YOU'VE NEVER DONE THAT BEFORE.

Haven't had many friends before. You're easier than the others.

WHY IS THAT?

Every other Legend has all sorts of versions I've encountered. If you get caught up in it, you'll lose your mind. But not you, Pathfinder. You're consistent. In every dimension. Doesn't matter where I am. Pathfinder is always Pathfinder. The same Pathfinder on his quest to find out who he really is. There's something comforting about that.

I'VE BEEN TO ANOTHER DIMENSION BEFORE.

You have. A couple times. Alternate dimensions— other worlds—I don't exactly understand them myself, but there are a lot of them. Every time we make a choice, a new dimension is formed. A new path. And I see them all simultaneously when I enter the Void—that's the place in between. Every time you enter one of my portals, you pass through the Void. It's harmless, for the most part, but it's the other side that you should be worried about. Each dimension is always something a little different. I would know, because I'm not from this dimension—I came from a completely different world.

WHY?

The hope of finding out more about myself. I believed that my answers lay here, but that may not be the same for others. Sometimes what you're looking for may be right there in front of you.

I HOPE SO. I DON'T LIKE GOING TO OTHER DIMENSIONS. DO YOU MISS YOURS?

I don't remember much, but from what I do—I'm glad I'm gone. And I was one of the lucky ones, Path. My first memory is waking up being tied to a gurney with a gag in my mouth.

"LUCKY." I THINK THAT'S SARCASM IN YOUR VOICE.

It's not. Most of them didn't wake up at all. In that dimension the IMC won the war and ran the show. I didn't remember how I ended up in the institution, or why. I just knew they were drugging me. The voices told me so.

THE VOICES OF OTHER WRAITHS, FROM OTHER DIMENSIONS, WARNING YOU OF DANGER.

But I didn't know that then. I just thought I had lost my mind. It wasn't until the Wraith from this dimension showed up to save me that I learned the truth. My name is Renee Blasey. I was a science Pilot for the IMC and was experimenting with phase-jumping tech with my colleague, Amer Singh. When we couldn't get a human volunteer, I volunteered myself. The experiment didn't go as planned. I lost my memory. And Singh decided to take full advantage of that. He covered it up, locked me up as a Jane Doe, and continued his experiments on me to take all the credit for himself.

THAT DOESN'T SOUND LIKE HE'S A VERY GOOD FRIEND.

You picked up on that too. It makes you wonder though...

IT SURE DOES. I'M CURRENTLY WONDERING HOW SOMEBODY PILOTS SCIENCE, BECAUSE THE STUDY OF THE NATURAL WORLD SEEMS LIKE A DIFFICULT THING TO FLY THROUGH SPACE. WHAT ARE YOU WONDERING ABOUT?

If my partner in these experiments was capable of stabbing me in the back, drugging me, and holding me prisoner for the rest of my life, all in the name of personal glory...then what kind of person would I have been to agree to work with him in the first place?

I LIKE MY QUESTION BETTER.

Me too.

SO, THE WRAITH FROM THIS DIMENSION SAVED YOU. AND YOU CAME HERE THROUGH THE VOID. WHY DID THE WRAITH FROM THIS DIMENSION STAY BEHIND?

That Wraith...your Wraith...is only interested in one thing: killing Singh. And that's one of the few dimensions where he's still alive.

YOU DON'T WANT TO KILL SINGH?

I suppose there has to be a part of me that wouldn't mind seeing him dead. We're all the same Wraith, one way or another. But it's not my priority. Not like it's her priority. I just want answers. And right now, I want to know: if the roles were reversed...if I had been the lead scientist, and Amer Singh had been the one experimented on...what would Renee Blasey have done?

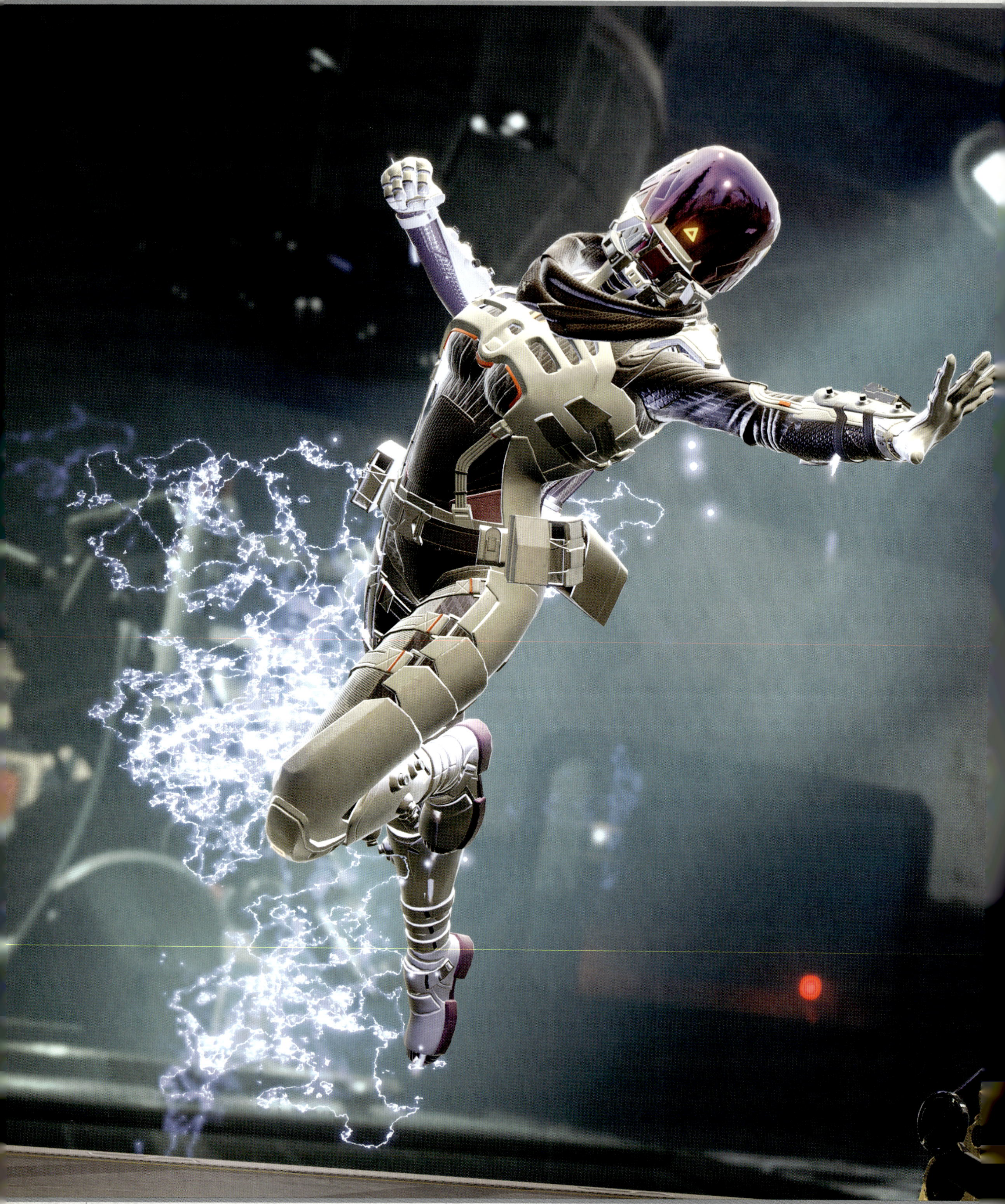

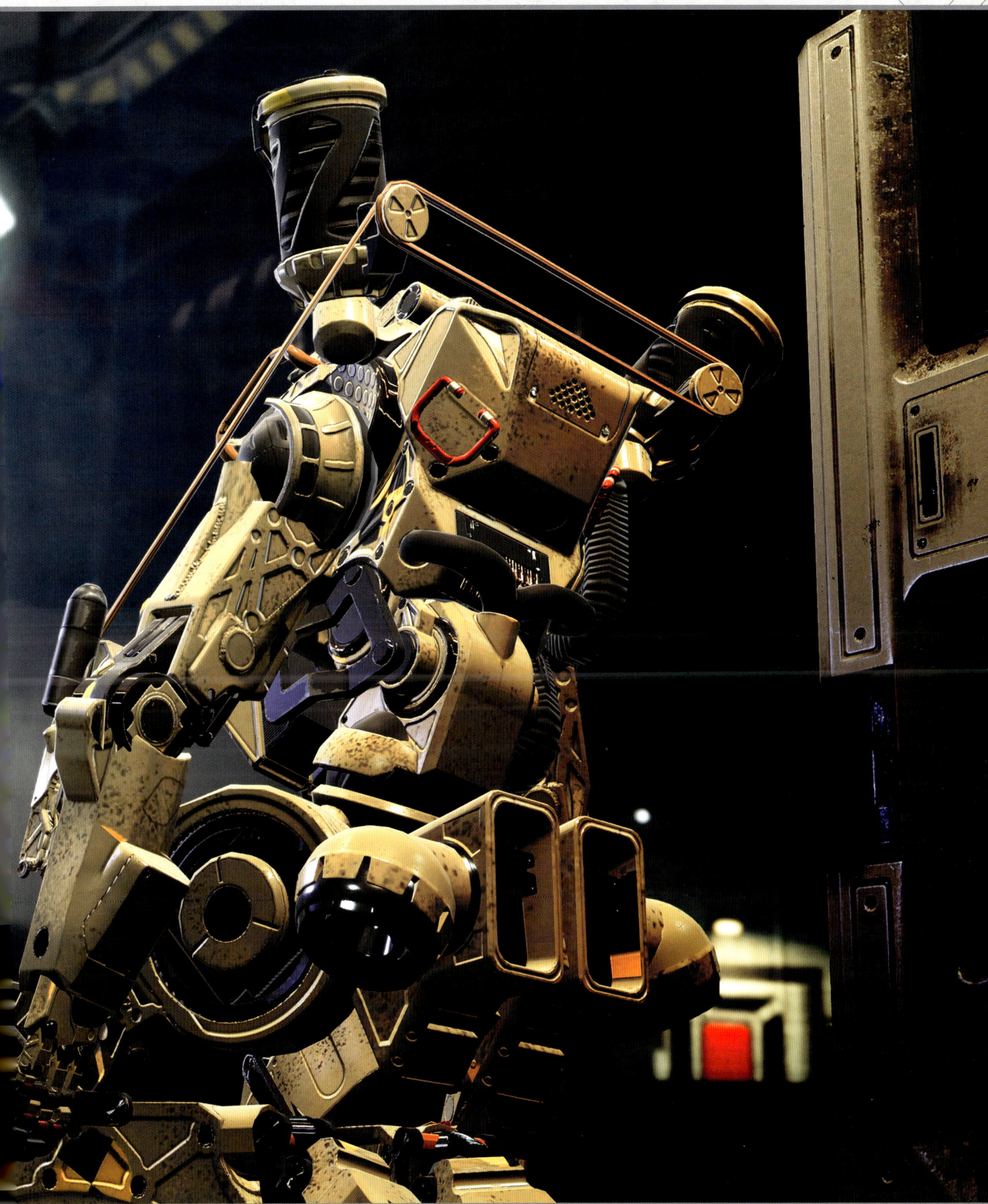

I DON'T KNOW ABOUT RENEE. BUT I KNOW OUR WRAITH . . . AND YOU ARE OUR WRAITH, DESPITE YOUR ORIGINAL HOME DIMENSION . . . SHE WOULD HAVE DONE THE RIGHT THING.

Thank you, Pathfinder. I needed to hear that.

WHAT A COINCIDENCE! I NEEDED TO SAY IT! WHEN DID YOU COME HERE?

About seven years ago. 2727.

SO, YOU ENTERED OUR DIMENSION HERE, THROUGH SINGH LABS, AND STEPPED OUT INTO KINGS CANYON!

Sure did. It was under construction back then. The Games hadn't even opened yet. But I didn't know that. I wandered around for hours. Most of Singh Labs was burned to a crisp, as if someone was trying to hide what was originally there. I didn't see a single soul. I found houses, artillery bases, bunkers . . . but it was all abandoned. I didn't know where I was, or why I didn't see anybody. It made no sense. I wondered if there had been an invasion or a natural disaster. I had emerged into a dimension with no human beings and had no idea why.

WHAT DID YOU DO?

I set up camp in the lab. It was almost comical. I ran

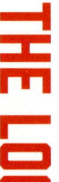

THE LOG

A STORY OF A KID WHO RUINED EVERYTHING

JANE DOE LOG
GAMES DIMENSION

DAY 1: In my new home. Looks just like my old home. Except Singh's not here, and this place looks like it was abandoned a long time ago. There's a large hanging banner that welcomes you to the future home of the Apex Games, whatever that is. I'm at a loss. I don't see any people, and this version of the institute appears to have been abandoned for years. Found rations and water. The big question is...where are the people? Actually, no. The even bigger question is: why don't I hear any of my voices?

JANE DOE LOG
GAMES DIMENSION

DAY 3: I've ventured out as far as I can go in every direction, and have only come to one factual conclusion: I am on an island. In my world, this is a peninsula, but my current hypothesis is that the piece of land that turns this into the Kings Canyon Peninsula doesn't exist here...in my dimension, that piece of land was actually made by the IMC. If I travel to the edge of the island I can see a mainland that appears to be powered by electricity. I can only assume

there are people who reside there, but as I have yet to see a single human being, I can't be sure. For all I know, the apocalypse has claimed this world, and I am the last living thing on it. Though I don't think so. There are times I think--and I realize how insane this sounds--but there are times I think I hear a girl in these woods. If she was dangerous, I would think the voices would warn me to stay away. But it's been days, and they've said nothing. Tomorrow, I'm going to test a theory. Tomorrow, I am going to leap off the canyon.

JANE DOE LOG
GAMES DIMENSION

DAY 4: Eventful day. In an attempt to hear the voices in my head again, I climbed to the top of the canyon. I wondered...would they respond if I put myself in danger? I climbed to the highest peak. But as I felt the rocks under my feet begin to crumble and my weight shifted, I heard the first voice I'd heard in almost five days--only this time, it was a man's voice, shouting, "Natalie!" I was so startled that I almost didn't hear the voices in my own head then whisper, "Careful of the rocks!"

before they crumbled under my feet. I opened a Void portal and managed to reappear at the bottom of the canyon with only minor injuries. Had the man seen me? Did he recognize me? He'd only called out for Natalie, but he said it so harshly it almost seemed like he was angry at me. But also, as if he was...scolding me? I heard it, as crystal clear as the lake his cabin resided on. The voices in my head warned me about the rocks, but they didn't warn me about the man. Maybe he's a friend. Maybe...I'm Natalie?

NATALIE DOE LOG
GAMES DIMENSION

DAY 5: I am a hunter now, but I do not wish my prey dead. I'm determined to learn all I can about this man who lives here. I don't even know his name. He's an older gentleman. Maybe in his fifties, although he could be older. It seems as if life has not been so kind to him. He appears to be an electrician of sorts, but most of the time, I hear him talking to himself, or to the robots who help him with his work. I can't figure out what he's doing. Sometimes he works with these charged pylons. But he's all the way to another dimension to escape the institution and ended up . . . right back in the institution.

THAT DOESN'T SOUND COMICAL AT ALL.

When you've lived my life, let's just say that bar is incredibly low. So, I hung out down here for a few days. Found some dried rations that were about a decade old. They tasted like dung, but there were enough to keep me going until I could find a better food source. Found water in some nearby coolers . . . nobody was around to drink it, and I wasn't going to look a gift horse in the mouth. I had put together that I was on an island. In my world, Kings Canyon was on a peninsula, but for whatever reason, in this world the connection to the larger landmass had sunk into the river. Meaning I was trapped out at sea. I could build a raft, but it would take a few days. Then I could venture into the city across the water. See what I could find. But in the meantime, I could at least explore this dimension's version of Singh Labs. See what I could find out about my past and Amer Singh. Would have had a full two days to uncover the truth too, if it weren't for the kid.

THE KID?

I kept a log of the whole thing, exactly how it happened. The kid who ruined everything for me . . .

also doing something with radiation and lasers? The voices still haven't told me that I'm in danger, so I assume I was on good terms with the man. If they warned me about the rocks, they'll warn me about this man if he poses a threat, right? He tends to go out at night. I'm going to sneak into the house tomorrow night when he goes out to feed the Flyers. See if I can find a link to him, find out how he knows me. I don't want to get my hopes up, but what if he's my dad?

NATALIE PAQUETTE LOG
GAMES DIMENSION

DAY 6: I have a last name. So much has happened, and I'm trying to process all of it. The man left to feed the Flyers, so I snuck into the house. I thought I had seen him talking to someone in the bedroom. I had to know who this was. Were these my parents? But I found something else in the empty bedroom I didn't expect: a wedding ring on the nightstand and a note that reads: "My wonderful Luc Paquette, I love you--your ecstatic wife." Why would he leave his ring on the nightstand? Shouldn't he be wearing it? And that's when I saw the other side of his bed. The sheet was covered in...stuff. Blueprints.

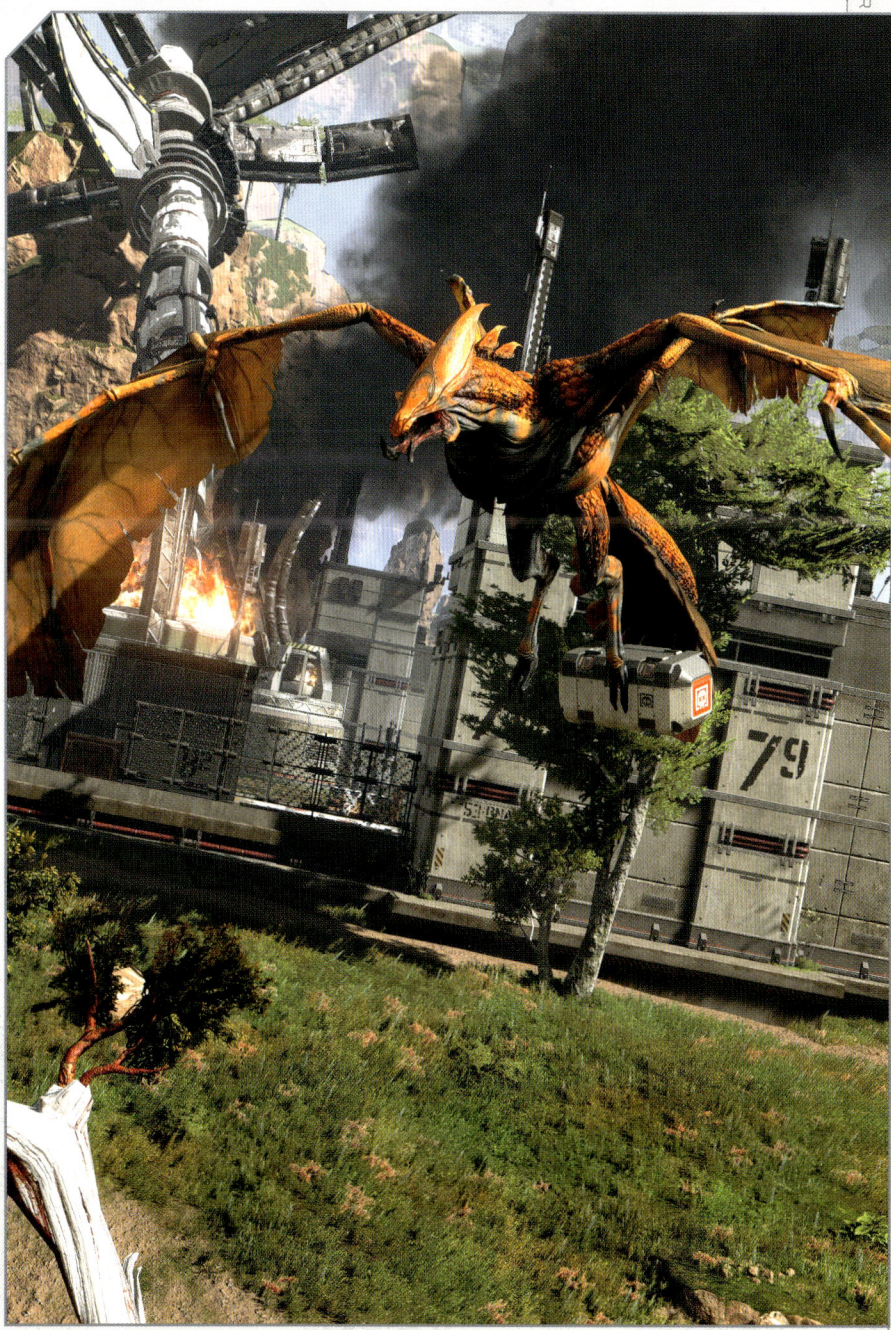

FLYERS: INDIGENOUS WILDLIFE FOUND ON MANY PLANETS THROUGHOUT THE FRONTIER AND OUTLANDS.

Notebooks. Ideas scribbled on paper. It looked like nobody had slept on the other side of the bed in weeks. But he was obviously married. Did she die? She couldn't have died, because he'd have pictures of her up everywhere, and there wasn't a single one. You don't erase dead wives from your life. So, she left. She left him all alone. And now he's devoted to a life of solitude on an island with no people. Just him and his robots. But where was his Natalie? And that's when it hit me. Could it be possible that I'm his Natalie?! That I was married to this man? Maybe in this world I had no memory, and I escaped from Singh years ago. And I met this man, and I married him. The Wraith from this world certainly carried herself as older. Still, though... the age difference is enormous. I don't know how I feel about this. That's when I heard the front door open. I quickly opened a portal and disappeared into it, leaving it only slightly open in the corner of the room, so I could listen... and pray that Luc (that's his name) didn't see it out of the corner of his eye. He stormed in and exclaimed under his breath, "Damn it, Natalie...where did you go?" "Right here," I wanted to shout, but I didn't. He picked up the wedding ring, looked at it, then hurled it in the garbage.

He's furious with me, thinks I abandoned him. He stalked back out into the night, on a mission. I reentered and picked up the ring from the trash. I tried it on. It fit. Maybe it's true. I have a name. I am Natalie Paquette, wife of Luc Paquette. This changes everything...

NATALIE PAQUETTE LOG
KINGS CANYON
GAMES DIMENSION

DAY 7: I must find a way to tell my husband I am back. I don't find him particularly attractive, but maybe it's his personality that most interests me? I wear the wedding ring, and although it fits, nothing about it seems familiar. But it's the first sign of hope I've found in a week that I have an identity. I have to hold on to that. Otherwise, I've made no progress at all, and I'm just trapped on this island indefinitely. I follow Luc as he runs his errands. Works with the robots. Continues to build his power grid. He works too much. It wasn't until I followed him back home that I heard the noise. The sound of a girl. She laughed. Luc looked out into the night, his brow furrowing. Then he called out, loud enough to wake the dead: "Laugh all you want! I'll find you! Then you'll get what's coming to you." Luc reentered the house, and I realized in that moment that there is somebody else on this

island. His mortal enemy. I must find them and vanquish them.

NATALIE PAQUETTE LOG
KINGS CANYON
GAMES DIMENSION

DAY 8: I saw her. She's a young girl. I remember seeing girls that young in Singh's care too. And they were just as dangerous as this one. I couldn't make everything out, but she snuck into Singh Labs and was particularly interested in the bubble shields that were there. Then I heard her talking about how she was going to put one shield within another, fill the space between with something called ADS light waves, expand that space by shrinking the inner dome, and kill every living thing on the island! She's going to murder Luc! I will stop her. I will stop her from murdering my husband and he'll have no choice but to forgive me for abandoning him! I heard Luc call my name in the distance. The poor thing. He misses me so. The girl scampered away at the sound of his voice. But she'll be back. And I will strike...

NATALIE PAQUETTE LOG
KINGS CANYON
GAMES DIMENSION

DAY 9: The girl came back, and I was ready for her. She stole my bubble shields, and that's when I popped out of a portal that I

HAHA!
Pathfinder? Are you...laughing?

THAT IS WHAT ONE DOES WHEN SOMETHING IS FUNNY. HAHA—
Please stop. That's unnerving. What's funny about it?

YOU SAID THAT TO WATTSON'S DAD. YOU MUST HAVE LOOKED RIDICULOUS!
Yes... Now I regret showing you those logs. Maybe that was another mistake.

NO. IT'S OKAY, FRIEND. I UNDERSTAND. SO HOW DID HE TAKE IT?
He grabbed his daughter and told me Natalie was *her* name and he'd never seen me before in his life. I was so embarrassed, I opened a portal and stepped through it back to the lab. I was mortified. I was so desperate to believe anything, I'd convinced myself I was connected to the first possible human being I found.

About two hours later, once the forest had burned down into ash, he showed up in the lab. I was hidden, opened near the wall and told her, "Leave!" She screamed and ran. It was hysterical. But then she stopped by the exit to catch her breath, so I popped out of another portal right in front of her face. She screamed so loud she cried. Threaten my husband?! That'll teach you. She ran off, and I thought for sure that was the end of her, but can you believe it, she actually tried to turn on her wretched murder machine! Oh no you don't! I opened a portal, but by the time I got to where she was, the moron had set the forest on fire! She had passed out from the smoke and was inches away from death when I stepped out of the portal. What kind of assassin was this? The bad kind, that's what. I picked her up and checked her breathing. It was shallow. Good. Serves her right for trying to kill the love of my life. I walked her through the Void to the front door. He appeared at the doorway, shaken. "Natalie...?" he whispered. "Yes," I exclaimed. "Yes, I am your Natalie! I did not abandon you, I just traveled from another dimension, where I was held captive by a mad scientist, until my other self saved me, and I saved you from this assassin who was going to kill you with her heat ray!"

so he couldn't see me. He stood in the middle of the lab, and he said:

"I know you can hear me. You don't have to come out, you just need to listen. My daughter thinks you're a ghost. Some kind of apparition or wraith like in her storybooks. I don't know who you are. But you're not supposed to be here, and from everything I just heard from you up at my front door, you're certifiably insane. However, you saved my Natalie's life. So I'm also grateful. That's a lot of complicated

emotions for one evening, so here's what we're going to do: Tomorrow morning, at dawn, the MRVNs have been instructed to cover up this building. It's already buried halfway in the swamps. They're going to finish the job, so nobody will step foot in this lab again. If you are still here in the morning, you will be buried alive and will perish. Alternately, as a thank-you for saving my daughter, I have left a boat at the docks by the old landing pad. I will turn off the Syndicate's whirlpools for one night, and one night only. Take that boat due north, and you'll reach Solace City by morning. Any other night, and you'll be killed in a whirlpool. One way or another, you will not take a breath on my island by sunrise. The choice is yours."

Suffice it to say, I was on the boat within an hour, and in Solace City by the morning. But I swore to myself, one way or another, I'd get back to that island, no matter what Luc Paquette said. I'd get back into that lab and find the truth about who I was.

I spent the next few years honing my skills, finding my way into a qualifying match, and getting into the Games. I spent even more finding a way to get back into that lab underground. It wasn't until it was excavated during the post–Repulsor Tower renovations that I was able to get back down there to learn that I had a name: Renee.

At least I got the French part right.

[. . .]
That was a joke.

HAHA!
You're killing me, Path.

YOU'RE KILLING ME, WRAITH. OH, YOU GOT THE NAME "WRAITH" FROM WATTSON'S PAPA! THAT IS SO SWEET. After that, I didn't trust myself so much. I still trusted the voices, but I was completely wrong about who I was. I wondered sometimes why they didn't warn me about my own thoughts. But I think it's because that was a lesson I had to learn. Don't be so quick to jump to conclusions. Gather all the research first. Don't assume your first guess is your best guess. You'd do well to remember that, Path.

NAT IS USUALLY SO PLEASANT, BUT WHEN SHE TOLD ME THIS STORY, IT WAS SCARY. YOU ARE USUALLY RESERVED, BUT WHEN YOU TOLD THE STORY, IT MADE ME LAUGH OUT LOUD. Human beings are complicated. But it just goes to show you that perspective is very powerful. Someone could

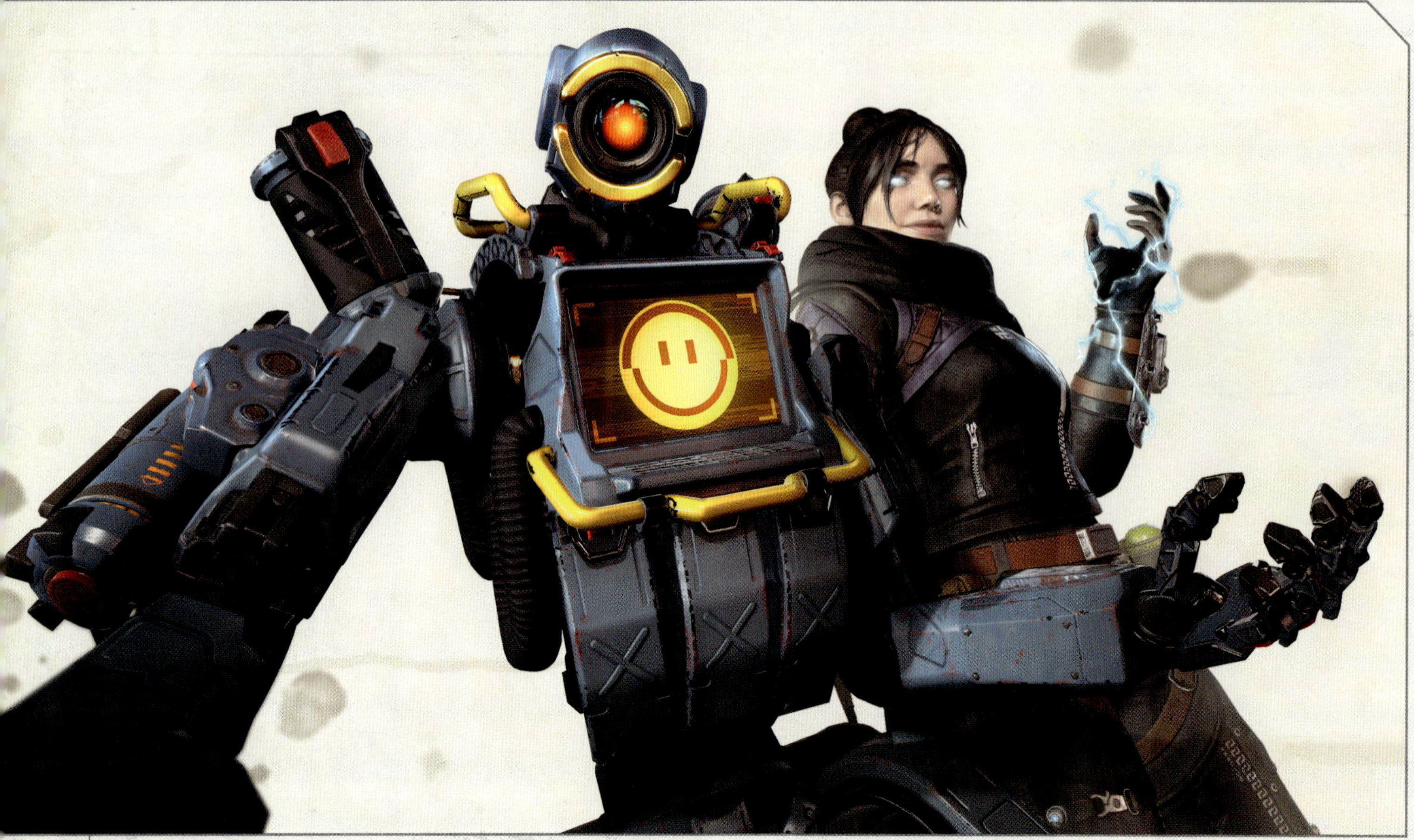

* IT'S NICE TO SEE WRAITH SMILE!

view an event through one lens, while somebody else could see an entirely different event. But it's the same event.

I DON'T THINK I'VE EXPERIENCED THAT YET.
Oh, you will. Soon enough.

DID THE VOICES TELL YOU THAT?
They didn't have to. I speak from experience. Anyone who digs into their past this much is bound to run into it sooner or later. I guarantee, before this is all over, you'll think you're dealing with one thing . . . but you're going to find out it's very, *very* different than you thought . . .

I CANNOT WAIT TO BE SURPRISED.
You might not have to wait very long. Guess what I just found?

WHERE? IN THAT FILING CABINET?
A reference to Amélie Paquette. It's in this old file. Something called Project: Iris . . . does that mean anything to you?

IT DOES. IRIS IS ONE OF MY CLUES. I DIDN'T KNOW IRIS IS A PROJECT! DO YOU THINK I'M PROJECT: IRIS?
I don't know. But check it out. The IMC was definitely involved one way or another. Seems like others were

PROJECT: IRIS

involved too. Which is weird, because the IMC doesn't play well with others. Says something about the Adonis Squad. Weird—I feel like I've heard that before from someone we both know.

WE DO?
Sergeant First Class Anita Williams, a.k.a. Bangalore.

SHE CAN'T BE IN ADONIS SQUAD. THIS WAS 2654, ALMOST EIGHTY YEARS AGO. BANGALORE DOESN'T LOOK A DAY OVER THIRTY-EIGHT.
I'm not saying she was alive back then. Obviously, she wasn't. But she may have been part of the same IMC squad years later. Maybe she knows their history. I would definitely hit her up. And when you do, I would definitely tell her she doesn't look a day over thirty-eight.

DEFINITELY?
Definitely.

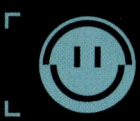
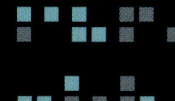

DATA POINTS RECEIVED

- ARES Division was set up to study artifacts in the Frontier and was run by General Marder.

- The Fold Weapon is believed to have been built to terraform and create life but was used to destroy.

- The Ark is a mysterious source of power that can manipulate space and time. It has similar attributes to Wraith's ability to phase shift and form dimensional rifts.

- There are multiple dimensions similar to ours—each created by the choices we make.

- Wraith was named Jane Doe and was so desperate to find an identity, she convinced herself that she was Luc Paquette's wife and Wattson was an assassin trying to kill him with a heat ray.

  > She was wrong.

- Luc Paquette was the one who inadvertently gave Wraith her name and sealed up Singh Labs.

- Iris means Project: Iris, created in 2654.

- An old IMC unit, Adonis Squad, was in some way involved with Project: Iris. Bangalore might know of this squad's history.

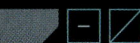

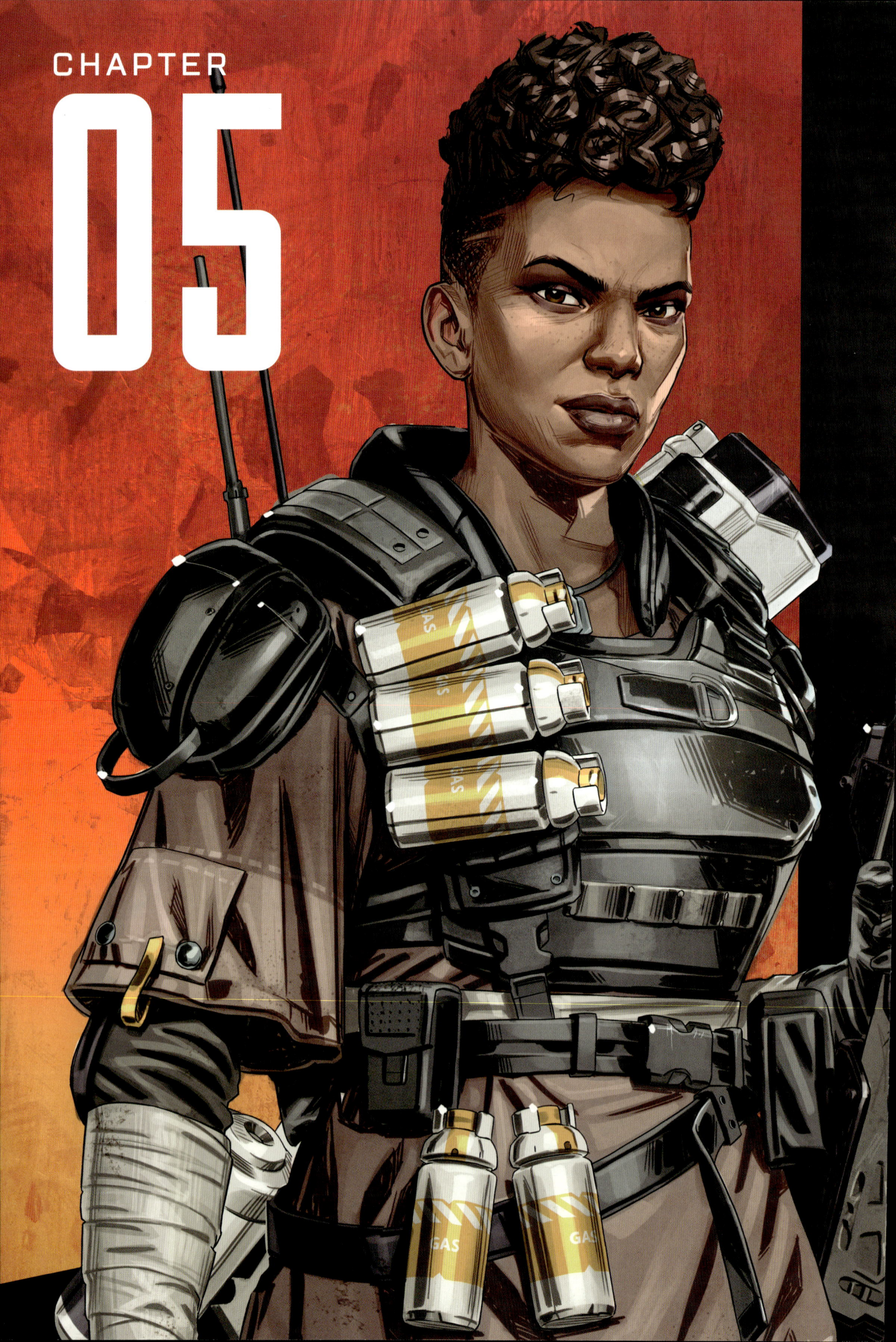

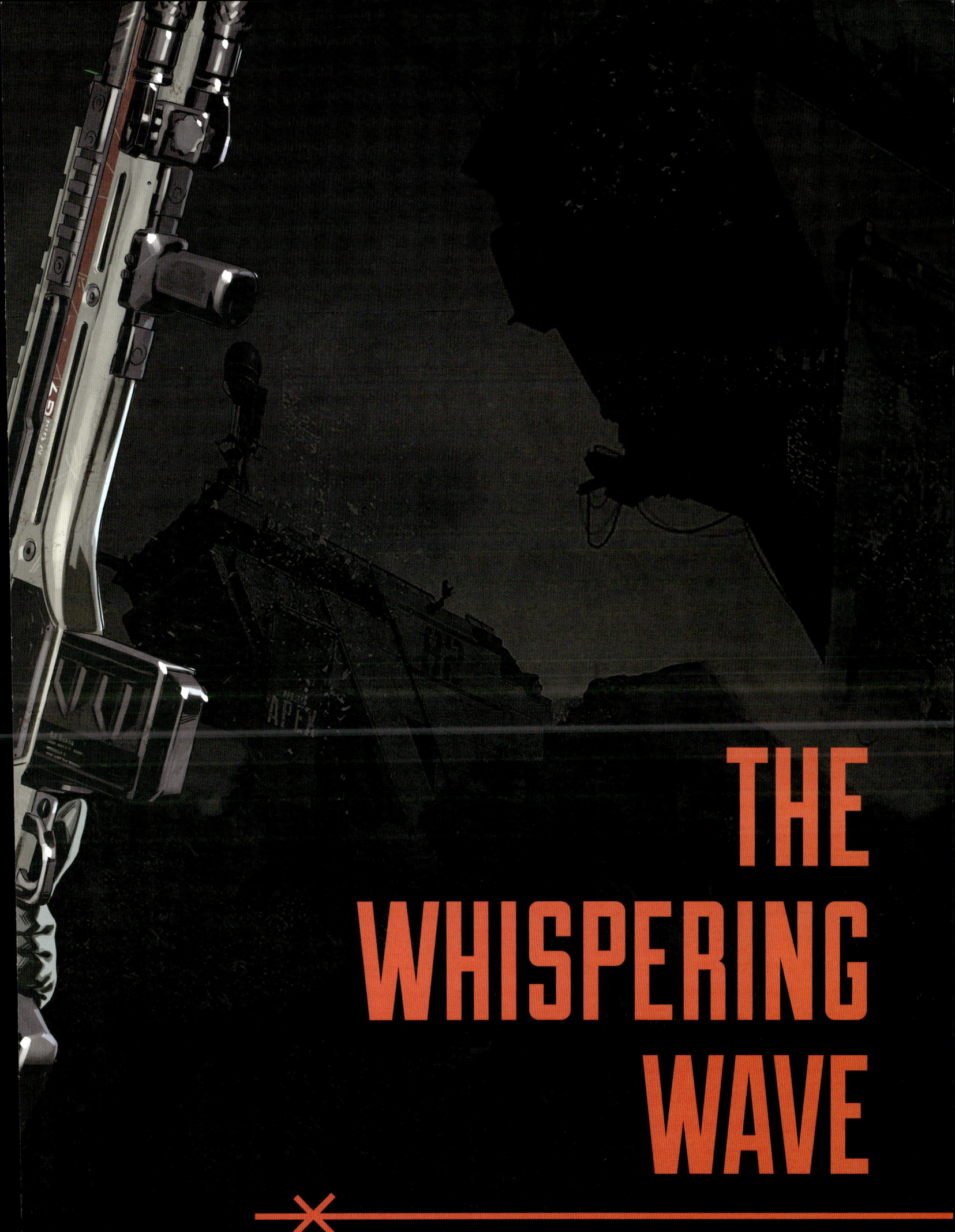

THE
WHISPERING
WAVE

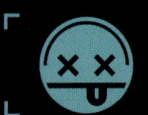
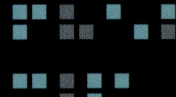
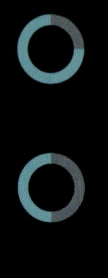

PATHFINDER MEMORY LOG: DAY 5

Wow—that was very exciting . . . and scary . . . and funny! Wraith has always been nice to me, and I like that. She and I are very similar, since neither of us really knows who we are or where we came from. It's nice to have that connection with someone—that shared experience. The Outlands are full of so many different people and things and . . . people-things, but it's still easy to feel alone when you feel like you don't have a place in the world. I feel bad for Wraith because she may never find her place, since this isn't really *HER* world at all. She comes from a different one—an alternate dimension. I've been to one before by accident when I went through what I thought was Wraith's portal, but it wasn't. The world was a place where Revenant was king or something—it was weird and scary, but fun, and I got to show all my friends what it was like when we looked for my ex-girlfriend's head! Luckily, we all made it home, but that's not something Wraith wants to do. Home isn't important to her. The only thing that she cares about is learning who she is and where she came from. Maybe to her, that's all she needs. Maybe that's all I need. Once I find out who I am, I may finally be home . . . I may finally have a place.

Luckily, we're both on the right track, and thanks to her, I found another clue. "Iris" is actually from something created in 2654 called "Project: Iris." Maybe I'm Iris? Or maybe I'm "Project"? Either way, an old IMC unit, Adonis Squad, was in some way involved with Project: Iris. Wraith thinks that Bangalore might know something from this squad's history—and I hope so too!

CLUE BOX

TRANSMISSION CLUES
- "Chevrex" > LIFELINE'S PARENTS' COMPANY
- "The future of the Outlands" >
- "Dr. Amélie Pa—— [Paquette]" > WATTSON'S GRANDMOTHER, A GEOLOGIST, DIED MYSTERIOUSLY
- "The Event" >
- "Aleki" > GIBRALTAR'S GRANDFATHER
- "Iris" > PROJECT: IRIS, CREATED IN 2654

SELF-MOTIVATION QUOTE . . . SEARCHING . . . 1 RESULT FOUND

"There's never been a true war that wasn't fought between two sets of people who were certain they were in the right. The really dangerous people believe that they are doing whatever they are doing solely and only because it is without question the right thing to do. And that is what makes them dangerous."
—[NEIL GAIMAN, *AMERICAN GODS*]

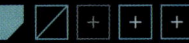

BANGALORE BIO FROM THE APEX GAMES

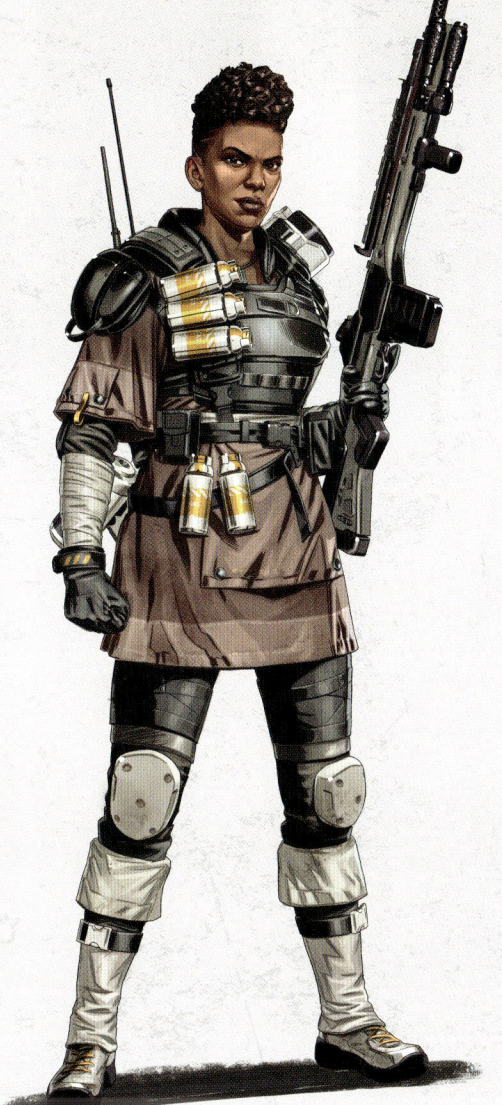

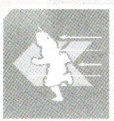
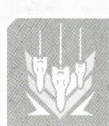

REAL NAME:
SGT. FIRST CLASS ANITA
WILLIAMS, 40138416

AGE:
38

HOME WORLD:
GRIDIRON

TACTICAL ABILITY:
SMOKE LAUNCHER

PASSIVE ABILITY:
DOUBLE TIME

ULTIMATE ABILITY:
ROLLING THUNDER

BORN INTO A MILITARY FAMILY WHERE SHE, HER PARENTS, AND HER FOUR BROTHERS ALL SERVED IN THE IMC ARMED FORCES, BANGALORE HAS BEEN AN EXCEPTIONAL SOLDIER SINCE SHE WAS YOUNG. She was top of her class at the IMC Military Academy and the only cadet who could take apart a Peacekeeper, equip it with a Precision Choke hop-up, and put it back together in under twenty seconds—blindfolded.

In the months following the Battle at Gridiron, the IMS *Hestia*, with Anita and her brother Jackson on board, was attacked by unknown assailants. A bomb on the outer hull blew out a chunk of the ship, and Anita watched helplessly as Jackson was sucked out into the vacuum of space. After crashing on Solace, Anita looked for both work and the brother she refused to believe had died, so they could begin the decades-long trip back home. Now, she fights to raise money in the Apex Games in the hopes of finding a pilot willing to make the journey so she can reunite with her family.

"Lock and load. Rinse, repeat. It's that simple. No substitute for real steel."
—SGT. FIRST CLASS ANITA "BANGALORE" WILLIAMS

► HI, BANGALORE! ◄

Pathfinder.

YOU DON'T LOOK A DAY OVER THIRTY-EIGHT!
Excuse you?

WRAITH SAID I SHOULD DEFINITELY TELL YOU THAT.
Did she now.

AREN'T YOU GLAD I DID?
I'll be sure to give Wraith my thanks in person when I see her again.

I JUST CAME FROM SEEING HER. SHE'S DOING VERY WELL. FINDING OUT MORE ABOUT HER PAST EVERY DAY. SO AM I!
I'm thrilled for both of you.

WOW. HOW'D YOU DO THAT? YOUR TONE DIDN'T MATCH THE MEANING OF YOUR WORDS, AT ALL.
Yes, I'm very layered. Full of nuance.

OH, I UNDERSTAND NOW. THIS IS SARCASM. WRAITH IS A COMEDIAN! SEE, I CAN BE SARCASTIC, TOO.
That's not quite—never mind.

I'LL NEVER BE ABLE TO SARCASM.
That's not necessarily a bad thing. Anyway … you said Wraith sent you here?

YES. DID SHE TELL YOU WHY?
Why would Wraith tell me anything?

AREN'T YOU BEST FRIENDS?
I—what? Okay, look, you have this fascination with the term "best friend." I need you to listen to me. Humans under the age of fifteen talk about "best friends." Adults have . . . acquaintances. Colleagues. Peers.

THAT SOUNDS VERY LONELY.
Life is lonely sometimes. A lot of the time. You do what you have to in order to get by.

WELL, I THINK YOU AND WRAITH SHOULD BE FRIENDS. YOU HAVE A LOT IN COMMON. YOU'RE BOTH IMC . . .
Wraith is not IMC.

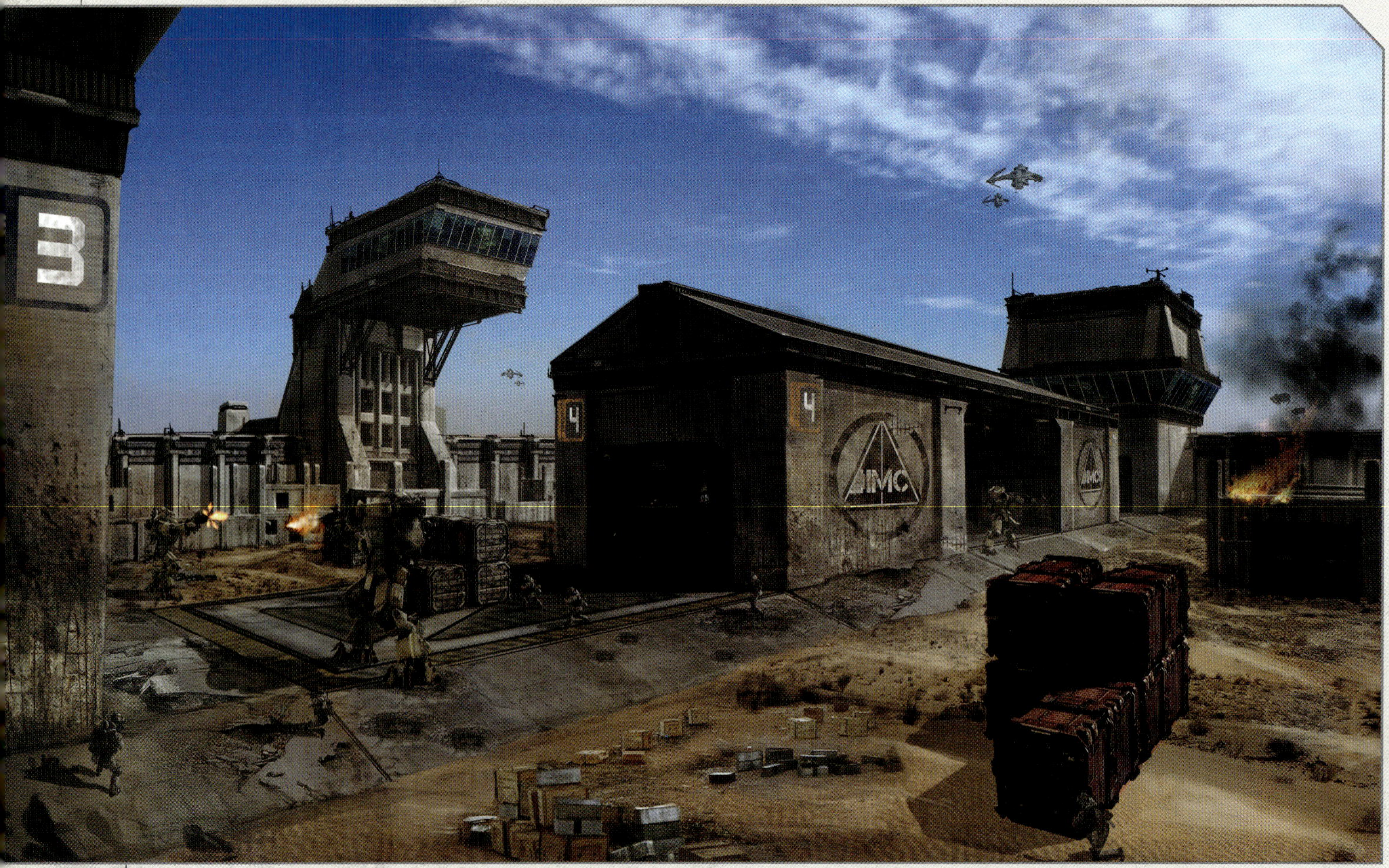

THE TRAINING GROUNDS ON GRIDIRON.

SHE IS! SHE WORKED IN THE ARES DIVISION.

Wraith is a lab rat, okay? She did that to herself, and has nobody but herself to blame for what happened to her. *Not* the IMC. Maybe if people took responsibility for their own actions there'd be a lot less finger-pointing going on in this world.

YOU'RE VERY ANGRY WITH ME. DID I SAY SOMETHING WRONG?

No. It's not you. I feel like all I hear all day is people blaming the IMC for all their problems. Everybody conveniently forgets there was a time of prosperity out here . . . and that was when the IMC was running things. Before the Militia rose up.

I'VE LEARNED MUCH ABOUT BOTH THE IMC AND THE MILITIA. IT'S NOT DIFFICULT TO UNDERSTAND WHY THE MILITIA DIDN'T THINK THE IMC WERE THEIR FRIENDS ANYMORE.

That's the problem. Too many people "thinking." Think they know what's best, think they know what's most profitable, think they know more than everybody else. The truth is, they don't. Most people in this world would be better off if they just did what they were told. The IMC provided jobs, put food on the table. All they asked in return was that you played by their rules, and their rules weren't that difficult. Grown men crying about liberty and freedom. Well, we got it, all right. Look around you, Pathfinder. Liberty for miles. But half the folks don't have food, and the other half don't have jobs. But we got "freedom." How's that working out for you?

I'M DOING GREAT. I JUST NEED TO FIND MY CREATOR.

Don't we all.

BRINGING UP THE IMC MAKES YOU VERY UPSET. I DIDN'T COME HERE TO MAKE YOU VERY UPSET. THAT MAKES ME SAD. BUT I DO HAVE A QUESTION ABOUT THAT. MAY I ASK IT?

Could I stop you?

I SUPPOSE YOU COULD SHUT ME DOWN. THAT WOULD ALSO MAKE ME SAD.

I'm not going to power you down, you stupid robot.

YAY FOR NOT POWERING DOWN! I DON'T UNDERSTAND WHY WRAITH WAS TORTURED BY THE IMC, AND LIFELINE'S PARENTS LIED TO HER ABOUT THE IMC AND YOU'RE ANGRIER AT THE BOTH OF THEM THAN AT THE IMC. WHY IS THAT?

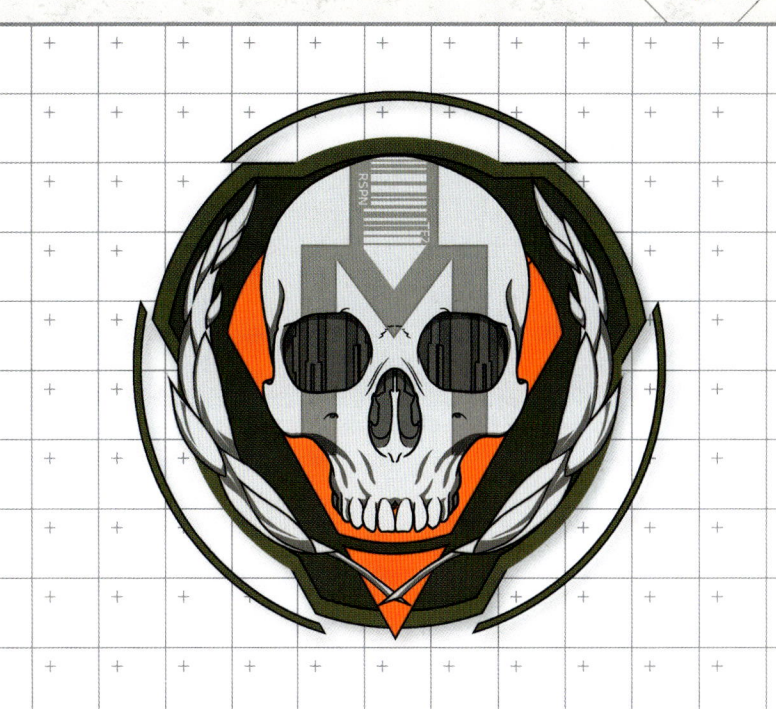

* THE LOGO OF THE MILITIA, A FRONTIER RESISTANCE GROUP.

It's not the IMC I'm angry at. It's everybody else who survived that pisses me off!

. . . YOU'RE MAD . . . THAT THE IMC DIDN'T SURVIVE?

To everybody walking around out there? They're the big bad wolf. The enemy. The power-hungry overlords. But to me? They were my neighbors. My aunts and uncles. They were the crossing guard at my school, and the pastor at my church. They were the doctors who gave me a lollipop if I didn't cry when they set my broken bone in a cast. They're my brothers. They're my . . . they're my parents . . .

BANGALORE? ARE YOU . . . ? ARE YOU . . . CRYING?

Every single day I walk out that door, I get . . . looks. Their faces shrivel up in disgust when they see my patches. They scurry away with their pets, and they protect their children from me like I'm some kind of monster. One woman even spit on my face. I was raised to believe in our leaders. I was raised to believe they knew better than we did, and they would lead us on the right path. And when I believed that with all my heart . . . my life was good. There was discipline and hard work, but there were barbecues and sing-alongs. And there was a lot of love in my life. In a lot of people's lives. And then somebody decided they didn't like the IMC. That they were the bad guys. And they started a war over it. And life was never the same again.

BECAUSE THEY THOUGHT POWER WAS BEING ABUSED, ACCORDING TO THE HISTORY BOOKS LIFELINE GAVE ME.

The history books are written by men. And men have opinions. They always have opinions. And opinions don't tell the whole story.

WHY NOT?
Why not what?

WHY DON'T MEN TELL THE WHOLE STORY?
So they can rewrite history. Prove they were right all along.

THAT DOESN'T SEEM FAIR.
It's not. But it's been that way as long as we've walked this, or any, planet. No one ever knows the complete story.

DOES THAT MEAN THAT I WILL NEVER KNOW THE COMPLETE STORY OF MY CREATION?
You're dedicated—and because of that, you'll get to the truth. Parts of it, at least. And some of those parts may be accurate. But there will always be somebody else out there who has a different perspective of the same story. And it may not be the perspective that you want to hear.

I CAN'T IMAGINE THERE'S ANY PART OF THE STORY OF MY CREATION THAT I WON'T WANT TO HEAR.
You'd be surprised what can sneak up on you.

WHAT SNUCK UP ON YOU?
What didn't?

MAYBE I CAN BE PREPARED, LIKE CRYPTO, IF I KNEW WHAT I WAS LOOKING FOR? WHAT WAS IT YOU HEARD THAT YOU WISH YOU HADN'T HEARD?
It doesn't matter.

EVERYTHING YOU SAY MATTERS. BECAUSE YOU SAID IT.
Huh. If "Legend" doesn't work out for you, "greeting card writer" might.

I'VE ALREADY DONE THAT. I GOT FIRED.
Okay, okay. I forget how exhausting talking to you is.

THANK YOU, FRIEND. SO, WHAT WAS A STORY YOU HEARD THAT YOU WISH YOU HADN'T HEARD, BECAUSE OF THE OTHER PERSPECTIVE?
That's personal, don't you think?

YES, IT IS. WHICH IS WHY YOU SHOULD SHARE IT WITH YOUR FRIENDS. IT'LL BE FUN.

Like a nest of Flyers.

THAT IS FUN!
That is sarcasm. You know I hate those damn things.

WHY?
Because I keep boots to the ground. I know what's in front of me. Behind me. All around me. I don't want to think about what's above me. I don't like surprises. And that's what things that fly are. I don't care if you're a bird or a bug or a Flyer or a fighter jet . . . being dive-bombed is, and always will be, my blind spot.

BLIND SPOTS ARE SCARY. LIKE STORIES YOU WISH YOU HADN'T HEARD BECAUSE OF THE OTHER PERSPECTIVE.
You're not going to let this go, are you?

NOT IF IT HELPS ME FIND MY CREATOR.
I don't know how this will possibly help you do that, but if it will make you go away, I'll tell you. I haven't told this story in years. My brother, Jackson, and I were only a year apart. Everyone thought we were twins. I mean, *everyone*. Which is funny, because we . . . well, it's not that we didn't get along. But I had to beat him in everything. It was a sickness. From the moment we could walk, I had to be better than him. I had to reach the finish line before him. I remember being five and reading at the level of an eight-year-old just so I could beat him. It wasn't mean or malicious. It was just . . . what we did. We'd race to see who could finish our vegetables first. Ultimately, we made it a lifelong game. Even created a scorecard. One of us would challenge or dare the other, and we'd say, "For the card?" and the other would say, "For the card!" Then, for whoever won that bet, that dare . . . that challenge, an X was marked on the scorecard.

WHAT WERE YOU PLAYING FOR?
To see who was the better Williams sibling. First one to one hundred won.

HOW LONG DID THAT TAKE?
Until the day he—it lasted our whole lives.

Mama didn't like it. She thought it made us antagonistic. But in a weird way it brought us closer . . . that competitive streak. It's why the rumor that we were twins spread when we were teenagers. Mama used to joke that she'd think we were twins, too, if it weren't for the eighteen months she knew she spent pregnant during a two-year period. Pops would chime in from the living room that he couldn't help it—those were Mama's best years. And we'd be so grossed out.

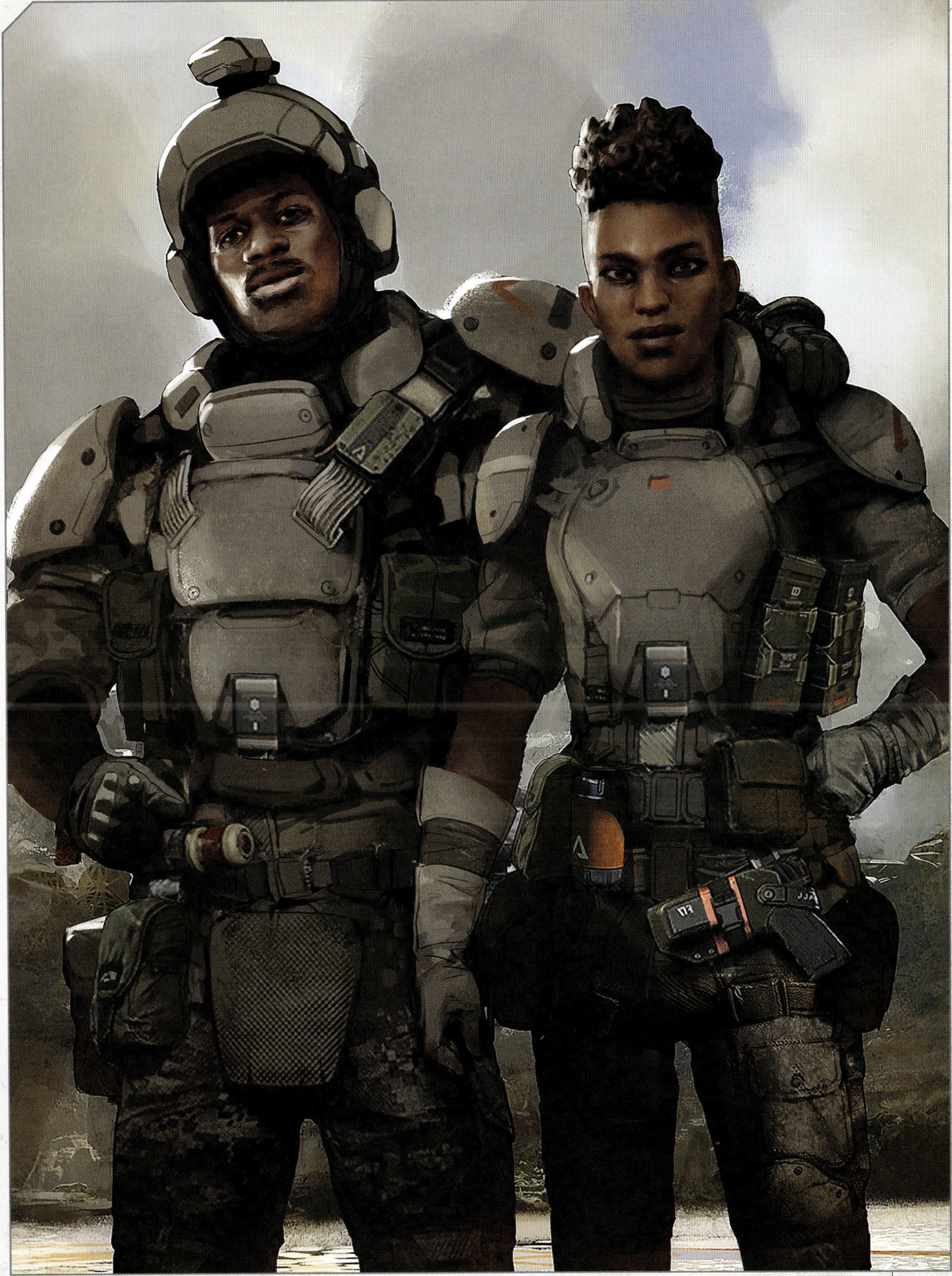

* IMC CADETS JACKSON WILLIAMS AND ANITA WILLIAMS.

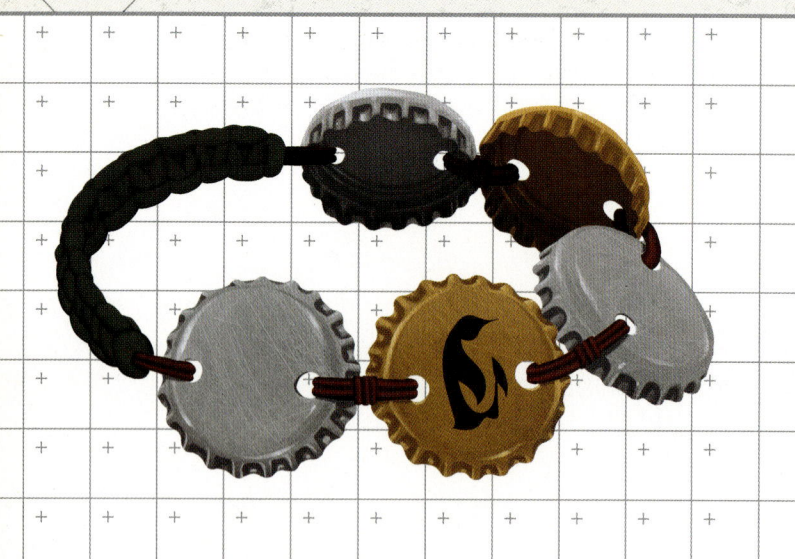

A BOTTLE CAP BRACELET MADE BY JACKSON WILLIAMS AS A GIFT FOR HIS SISTER.

THAT'S BECAUSE CONCEPTION IS DISGUSTING TO HUMAN BEINGS WHEN IT'S THEIR OWN.

Moving on …

WHERE ARE WE GOING?

To basic training. It's 2715. The end of boot camp. Two long years bustin' my ass and being broken down to make me the soldier I am today. Jackson and I were in the same boot camp. Mostly because I couldn't beat his records if I didn't know what they were. And we're graduating … getting our orders to report to duty. And he's got this present for me. He won't tell me what it is, but his hype for this thing is through the roof. For weeks, all I heard was how epic this present was. So, we get to graduation day. The whole family's there, and I'm already mad at Jackson. See, he found out earlier that week that he was getting his marching orders a few days after graduation, and I had to wait another week. That was the last contest on our scorecard— who got their marching orders first. And Jackson won.

SO HE MADE IT TO ONE HUNDRED FIRST.

Yup. After twenty years of bets and dares and challenges, we were neck and neck with ninety-nine each … and he was getting his assignment before I did. Jackson was the "better Williams sibling." I was so mad I took the scorecard and ripped it up into little pieces.

Anyway, graduation's just ended, and Jackson's waving to me, and I assume he wants to give me this gift. And he's rushing toward me … and then suddenly, there's someone on the microphone, even though the ceremony is over. And they're asking us

to remain seated. And no one knows what's going on, but there's this disturbing humming sound in the air. And I realize it's not machinery … it's people whispering. And as this wave of whispering takes over the crowd, there're gasps … and tears … and cries of agony. And as word of whatever it is spreads, I can see it getting closer, and I don't want it to. I don't want to know what they know.

On instinct, I get up and walk away from the audience. Away from the whispering wave. Jackson follows me. He asks me to keep it together, but I need to know. And I don't want a stranger who had a ticket in front of me to tell me whatever this is. I beg him. Tell me. What happened? And he does. Typhon has been destroyed. Hundreds of thousands of IMC soldiers … Gone. In a flash. They were R&D … do you believe that? Research and development. Not even a battalion. And they died when the Militia raided their labs. All of them … including Zeke Williams, my oldest brother. The only one of us who didn't become a soldier. He became a scientist. And he was dead. On my graduation day. Murdered in a Militia raid.

I'M VERY SORRY. THAT'S A VERY SAD STORY.

Oh, it gets worse. See, my family has this tradition .. . goes back generations. We're a military family, and the night before one of us gets sent off, we throw a party. The Williams Sendoff, as it's called. And everyone's invited. Friends, family, neighbors, even the Daily Deliveries person. There's barbecue … Nana's red velvet cake … so good. And Jackson and I have our own tradition. We write a song about the Williams who's going off to assignment. Jackson plays guitar … I sing … we even competed with that. Anyway, it's a hell of a bash. And we stay up all night, but at sunrise, we ask everyone who's left—which isn't many—we ask them to leave. The last hour, the first hour of dawn, that's just for us. Just for immediate family. And we open one last beer. And we just sit around the table, and watch every shade as the sun rises, and nurse that last beer. And when we're done, we take the bottle cap … the one with a hole in the middle from the bottle opener? And tie it to a leather rope. We make a leather bracelet and put it on the wrist of the person leaving. The bottle cap from the last beer you had with your family. A piece of us is with them, wherever they go in the galaxy. And you tell everybody … you tell everybody you know, if anything happens to you? Take the dog tags, but you keep the bottle caps on your wrist. Those bracelets'll guide us back to each other someday. They gotta.

And if something does happen, and they don't make it home … we have another tradition. We play the footage from that party at their funeral. We don't want to think of our loved ones' final moments in battle. We want to remember them from that night. Smiling. Happy. Surrounded by the people who love them the most. That's who we are. That's what the Williams family stands for.

THAT'S BEAUTIFUL. I USUALLY JUST ASK FOR HIGH-FIVES.

It's supposed to be beautiful. Except for Zeke . . . it wasn't. See, Zeke never showed up to his party. Zeke had a girlfriend, Catelynne. Catelynne wore skintight everything . . . was constantly sending messages to other people she didn't want you to know about . . . and she'd barely look at you when you walked into a room. But Zeke was smitten. He fell head over heels. I could never figure out why. She didn't seem interested in him in the slightest, but every time he was about to catch on to the fact that there were other men? She'd suddenly turn on the charm. I don't know why she kept him around. Made no sense to me—if you don't love someone, don't be with them. But Catelynne was something else. She strung him along, while the whole time, she had one eye on every other man in the room. Anyway, he skipped out on his own sendoff party to spend his last night with her. None of us got to say goodbye to him. Sure, we talked over vidphone and whatnot . . . it's not like we never talked to him again,

but he didn't get a bottle cap bracelet. He chose a girl who was using him over his own family. We didn't have any happy footage of Zeke for his service. We just had regret. And remorse. And sadness.

The one bright spot? Catelynne showed up to pay her respects. With her new boyfriend. I gave her a right hook to the chin that fractured her jaw in three places. I know. Only three. I was off my game that day.

YOUR HATRED FOR HER IS BOTH UNDERSTANDABLE AND A PROJECTION OF YOUR OWN GRIEF AND FRUSTRATION. AND NOW I UNDERSTAND WHY YOU HATED LOBA WHEN YOU MET HER.

Don't you headshrink me, robot.

AND NOW I TAKE THAT BACK.

Damn right you do. You think I hated Catelynne? That was nothing compared to my hatred for the Militia after Zeke died. I was more determined than ever to watch them all burn. We were order, and we were law. They were just . . . anarchists. Why would you murder a bunch of scientists? I wanted blood. Jackson put in for a transfer, didn't want to leave me alone. I followed him to boot camp, but he followed me on my first assignment: the IMS *Hestia*.

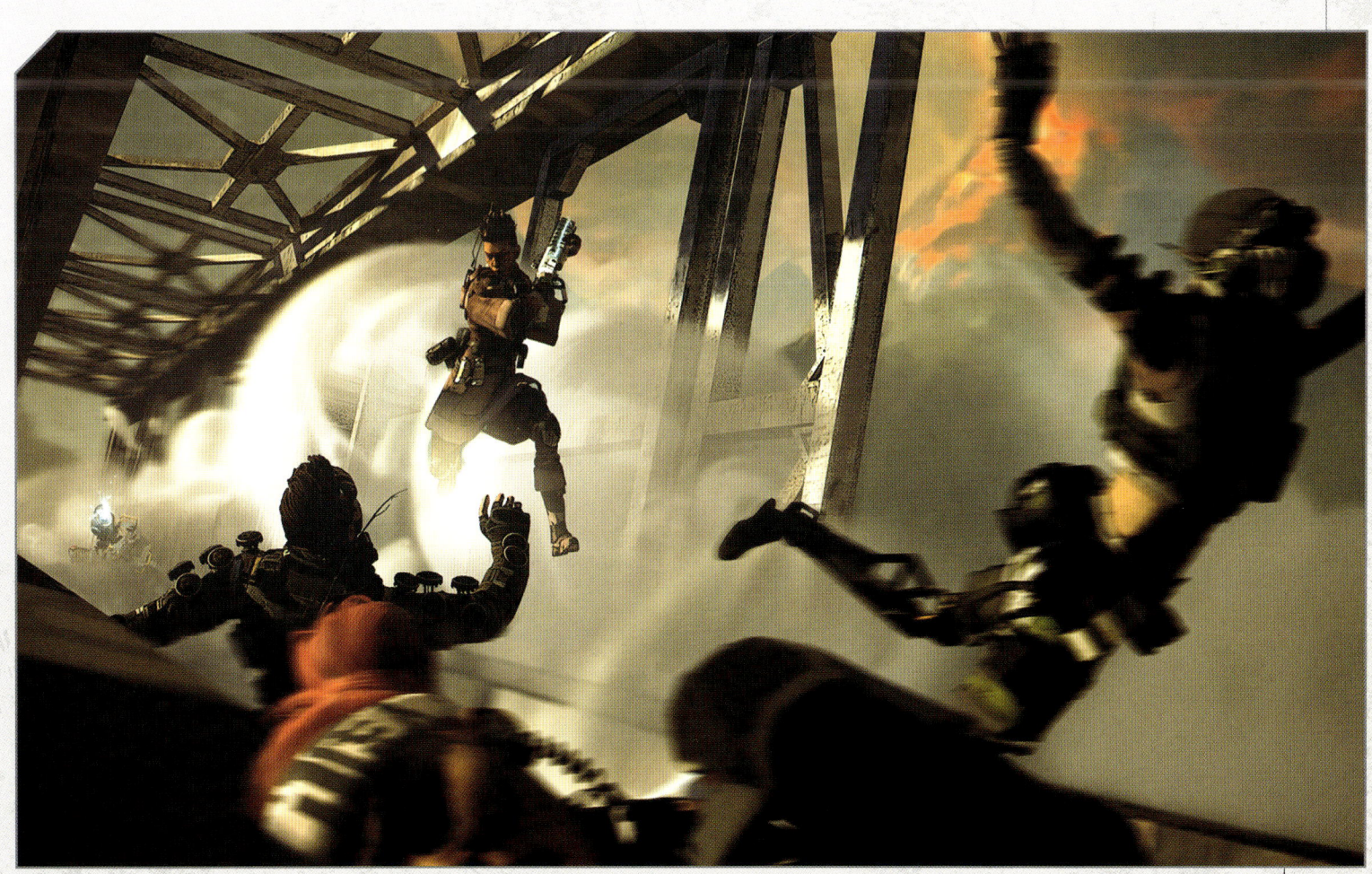

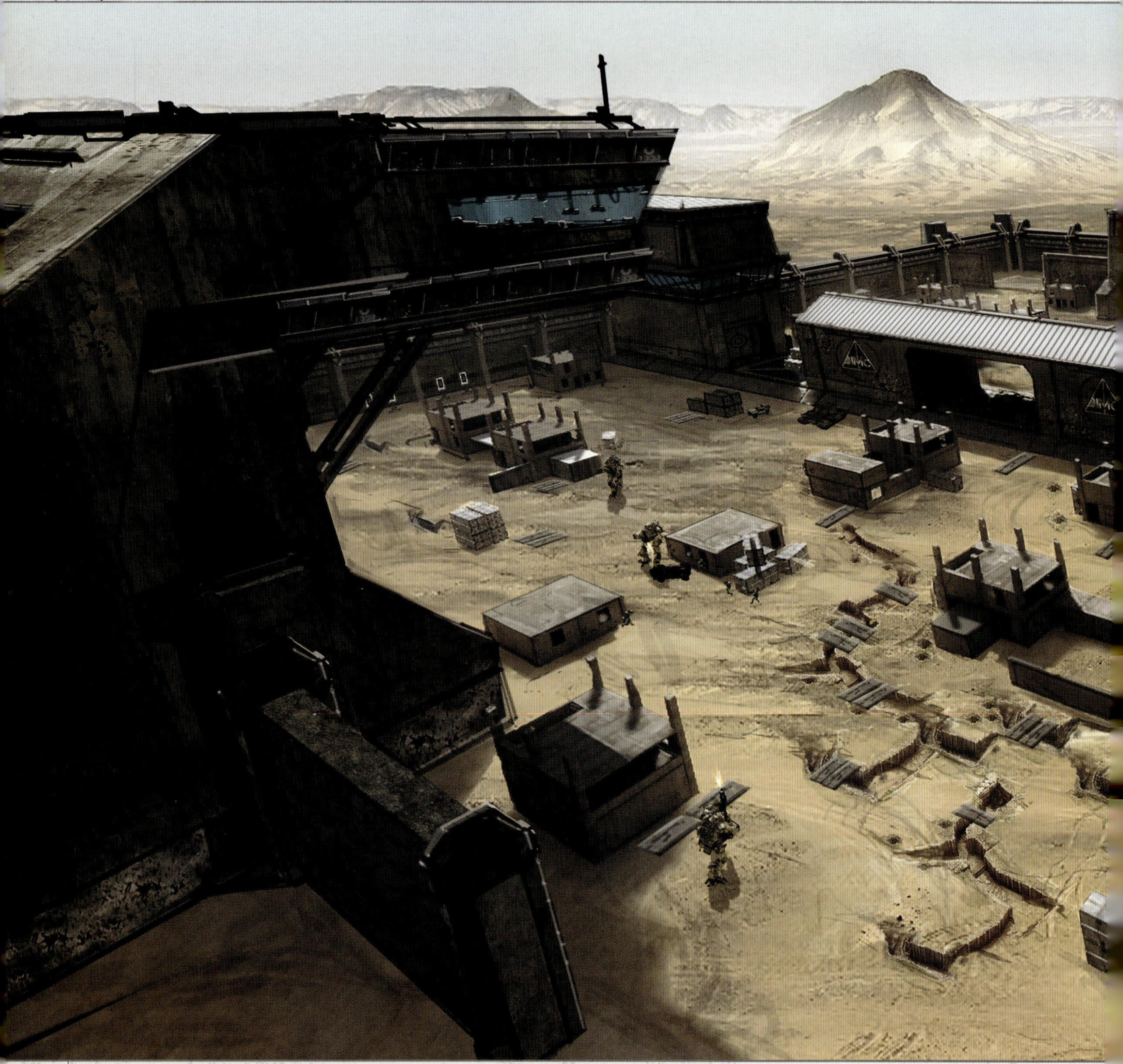

THE TRAINING GROUNDS ON GRIDIRON.

He didn't trust me not to go rogue, so he made sure he was at my side. He said he couldn't bear to lose a sister after he lost a brother. How's that for poetry, considering that's the decision that would cost me my second brother?

Of course, with Typhon gone, all resources were called back to Gridiron, and it became the last stronghold of the IMC. Thanks to their unnecessary murder of my brother and hundreds of thousands of others, the tide turned in the Militia's favor. That's when folks started jumping ship. First it was the mercs with good ol' Commissioner Blisk at the helm. "We're on the wrong side, fellas . . . time to quit while we're behind." Then the Remnant Fleet disappeared . . . that was the fleet controlled by the IMC's sophisticated computer network. So now we don't have our balls, and we

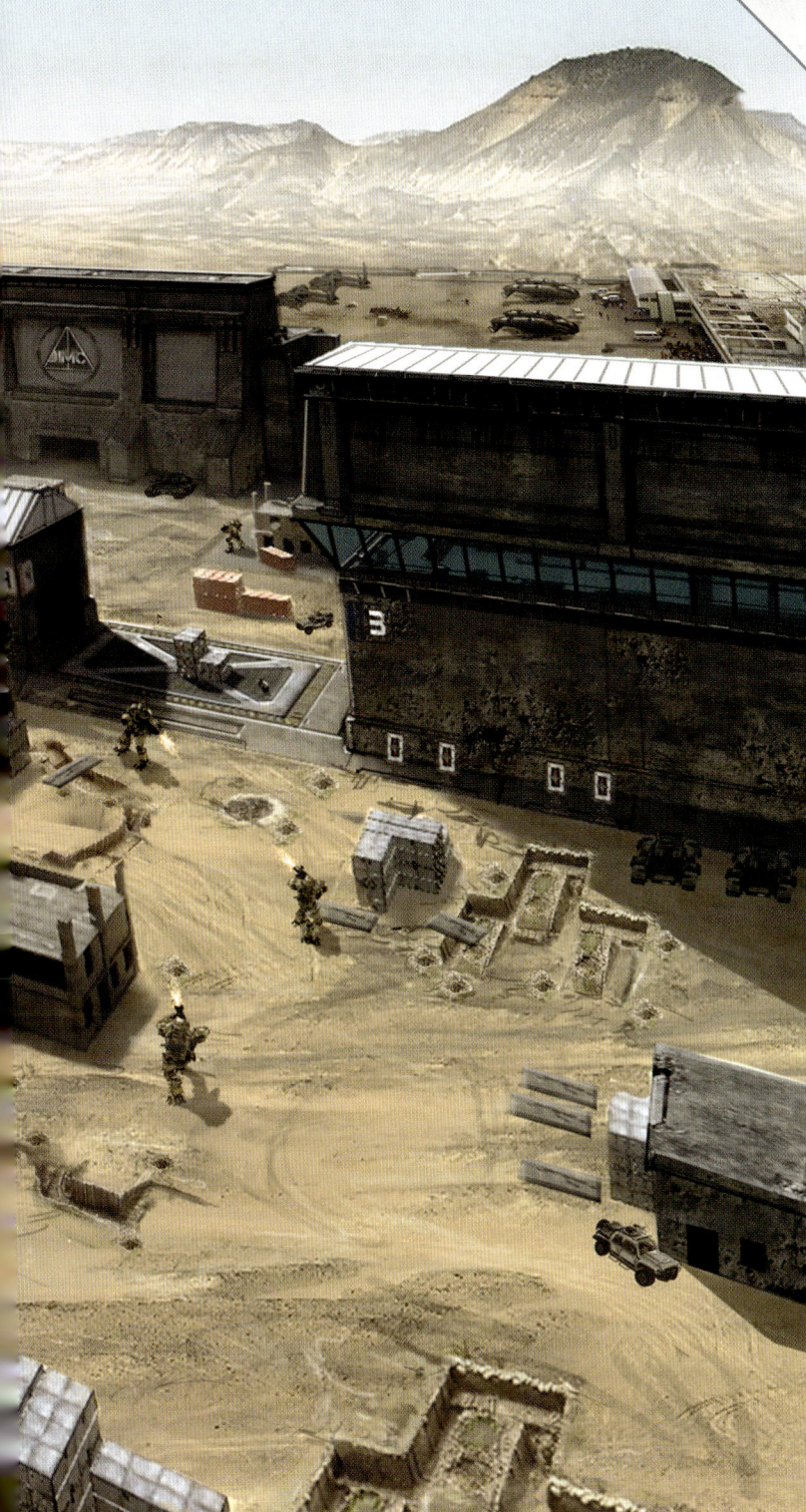

YOU WERE THERE. YOU WERE AT THE BATTLE AT GRIDIRON.
I was.

SO, YOU KNOW WHAT HAPPENED? YOU KNOW HOW THE WAR ENDED?!
I wish I did. The IMS *Hestia* was docked at the time when the Militia attacked. Jackson was the one that woke me up. Broke the door off the hinges of my quarters. I nearly shot him in his face. Don't go breaking down doors of women in the military in the middle of the night, you'll get your you-know-whats shot off.

I DON'T KNOW WHAT YOU-KNOW-WHATS ARE, BUT THAT SOUNDS BAD.
Thank God I realized who it was before I pulled the trigger. He took my hand, said there was a skeleton crew waiting on the *Hestia*. General Lewis was there. And that's when they revealed that they had grabbed an item from the labs and smuggled it on board with them. I don't know what it was, or exactly where it came from. All they said was that it was recovered from the Typhon wreckage. Part of the project Zeke had worked on.

AND IT WAS ON GRIDIRON?
They were experimenting with it. I never even got a good look at it. Whatever it was, it was important to the IMC, could've turned the tide. That's how powerful this was. I assumed we were going to use it in battle against the Militia, the same as they had done to us on Typhon. Nothing could've been further from the truth.

IF YOU WERE SURROUNDED, AND THE MILITIA WAS ON THE OFFENSIVE, WHAT OTHER CHOICE DID YOU HAVE BUT TO USE THE WEAPON AGAINST THEM?
The general . . . my brother . . . they all chose to *run*. Can you believe it? It all came down to this. The Battle at Gridiron. The final conflict between Militia and IMC. And we had a piece of technology that could wipe them all out. And they ran away like cowards. Jackson had to restrain me from staging a coup. He said this was for our very survival. They locked us in stasis chambers. I screamed the whole time. This wasn't who we were as soldiers. This wasn't who we were as Ironhides. This wasn't who we were as Williamses. They used the energy from the experimental weapon to amplify the phase tech that would transport us, and that's when the drugs took effect, and I started to drift off . . . and I don't remember what happened next.

YOU DON'T REMEMBER YOUR PAST EITHER? YOU AND ME AND WRAITH SHOULD START A CLUB.

don't have our network. We've essentially been castrated. Power hungry? You're damn right we were. We had no power. We were the underdog. We were dying right and left, our leadership was in shambles, there was nobody calling the shots . . . all we had was the home-field advantage. It would take that and a miracle. When the Militia showed up and surrounded Gridiron, we still had a few aces up our sleeve.

I remember my past. Just not the chunk of time during which the IMS *Hestia* traveled from Gridiron to the border of the Outlands...

THAT TRIP WOULD TAKE TWENTY YEARS AT NORMAL SPEED.

Thanks to Typhon's mystery tech they stole from the lab, we got there in a year. Stasis chamber took care of our digestive needs and oxygen. Kept us alive, and kept our muscles from atrophying. But the tech that powered us here? Dead. We could return to Gridiron, but like you said, it would take decades. We had no idea who was alive and who was dead. Or who had even won the battle. We were safe, but none of us were sound. I was furious with Jackson for weeks, but inevitably, I forgave him. What else are you going to do? You're stranded at the other end of the universe with the only family you've got left? If you don't forgive him, you've got nothing to get out of bed for in the morning.

IT SOUNDS LIKE YOU FORGAVE HIM BECAUSE HE SAVED YOUR LIFE, AND SAVING YOUR LIFE IS A GOOD THING.

He damned us to purgatory is what he did. And we didn't know it then, but remember that wave of whispers in the crowd on graduation day? It was a sign of things to come. Because another wave of whispers followed us in the IMS *Hestia*, only we didn't know it. See, something happened back at Gridiron...maybe it happened during the battle, maybe we caused it with the technology Jackson stole...who knows? But apparently, all forms of communication—all satellites, all computers, every power line in existence—just shut down. For good.

THE BLACKOUT.

Yeah...the Blackout. Wherever it started, it made its way throughout the universe. And by the time it hit you and you realized what had happened, you couldn't warn anyone in its path because you couldn't contact them. It took five years for it to spread from Gridiron to the Outlands. Five years it was out there, heading toward us, and we didn't have a clue. Rumors had started to spread throughout the Outlands that nobody could get in touch with the Frontier planets, but we all figured it was a case of work being done. The connections were always fritzing in and out anyway. Bunch of technicians got together about a year before it hit us. Put in some old-fashioned tech from a few centuries ago. Connections weren't great, but at least it worked on a different system. The Syndicate planets were able to stay connected. Thank God, because when the Blackout hit us, we were still able to communicate with Gaea, Talos, Psamathe...They say the classics are the classics for a reason, and the same is true with technology.

Those old systems are the reason we can at least communicate within the Outlands. They were smart.

WHAT ABOUT THE EXPERIMENTAL TECH FROM TYPHON THAT JACKSON USED TO SAVE YOUR LIVES?

It's gone. I don't know where, Jackson said he tossed it once he realized it didn't hold any power anymore. I hated the damn thing. If it wasn't for that thing...whatever it was...we'd be home with our family, not stranded two decades away.

OR YOU COULD BE DEAD. OR THEY COULD BE DEAD. THERE ARE BILLIONS OF POSSIBILITIES. YOU HAVE NO IDEA IF WHAT JACKSON AND THE CREW OF THE *HESTIA* DID WAS GOOD OR BAD OR...

It was bad. It was all bad.

I DISAGREE.

I don't care.

SAD THINGS HAPPEN. AND A LOT OF SAD THINGS HAPPENED TO YOU, FRIEND. MORE SAD THINGS THAN HAPPEN TO MOST PEOPLE. AND YES, YOU ARE NOT A NICE PERSON SOMETIMES BECAUSE OF THEM. BUT YOU'RE A NATURAL LEADER. AND A MORAL PERSON. AND YOU FIGHT HARDER AND LONGER THAN ANYBODY ELSE IN THE GAMES. EVEN THOUGH YOUR EYEBROWS ARE PERMANENTLY IN THAT POSITION NOW. I THINK YOU SHOULD BE PROUD. I THINK YOU SHOULD BE PROUD OF WHO YOU ARE, AND THE SOLDIER YOU BECAME. AND I THINK THAT PRIDE SHOULD HELP YOU TO SMILE WHEN YOU WANT TO CRY, OR GET MAD, OR YELL AT ME FOR TALKING TOO MUCH. AND YOU MAY NOT THINK SMILING IS IMPORTANT, BUT IT'S JUST AS IMPORTANT AS BEING MAD AT THE WORLD. AND IF YOU SAY YOU DISAGREE, THEN... THEN I'LL SAY I DON'T CARE RIGHT BACK AT YOU.
[...]

ARE YOU GOING TO SAY YOU DISAGREE—

I don't disagree, Pathfinder.

OH GOOD. BECAUSE ACTUALLY, I DO CARE, AND I DIDN'T WANT TO SAY I DIDN'T CARE. AND IS THAT WHY YOU'RE

CRYING AGAIN? BANGALORE, WHY AREN'T YOU SAYING ANYTHING?

I… I really want you to find your creator. It would mean a lot to me.

WHY WOULD IT MEAN A LOT TO YOU?

Because I'm dying to know who programmed you. Sometimes you say crap that makes me want to use you for target practice, and other times… other times, Path, you say exactly what I need to hear.

AND SOMETIMES I DO IMPRESSIONS. WANT TO HEAR ME DO CAUSTIC? "I DON'T CONCERN MYSELF WITH THE AMBITIONS OF—"

It's okay. I'm good.

YOU HAVEN'T ANSWERED MY QUESTION THOUGH. WHAT WAS THE STORY YOU WISH YOU HADN'T HEARD THE OTHER PERSPECTIVE OF … THAT YOU WERE BETTER OFF NOT KNOWING?

Oh, right. That's what started this. It's funny. Those last few years on the *Hestia*… taking odd jobs to get by… Jackson and I became closer than ever before. We relied on each other. And the rest of the *Hestia* crew. We became family. Jackson confided in me about a week before the explosion that… that separated us. He told me he'd grown close to this doctor who worked in the lab that had the Ark shard. That's how he first heard about it. And this doctor confided in him what the reports on Typhon said, before redactions. They kept the truth from the public. The ARES Division was doing cruel and unspeakable things, testing on human subjects. The research and development team was building a weapon that would destroy reality as we know it. They were building the iron fist that the IMC could bring down at any moment if anybody dared speak up to them. He had tears in his eyes as he admitted the Militia killed hundreds of thousands… to save billions.

SO THE IMC WERE THE BAD GUYS.

General Marder was a bad guy. The people in charge, who made the decisions? They were bad guys. The IMC is not one hive mind. It's entire populations of people. Don't tell me the people I love—who loved me, and who are good people at heart—are bad people. I know we're not. Don't paint us with that brush. I may not believe in ARES Division, but I believe in my brothers. My parents. My people. I helped people. Ever hear of the Nexus executions? Planet on the other side of the Outlands with some half-assed monarchy that punished anyone who said anything critical of them, no matter how small, with public executions. Barbaric. Until the IMC stepped in. We saved those people. They were grateful. Their

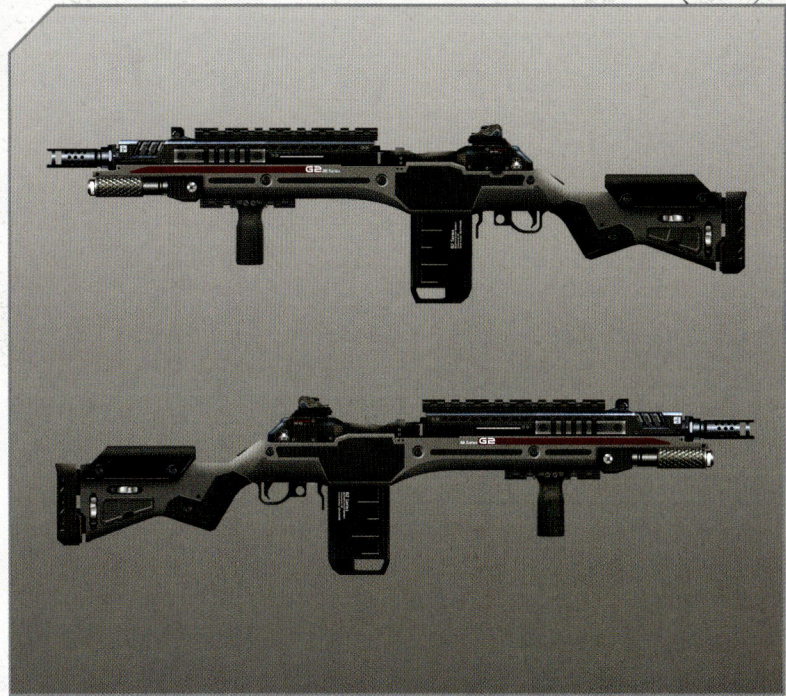

* BANGALORE'S FAVORITE RIFLE, THE G7 SCOUT.

children are alive today because of us. The IMC weren't angels. But we damn sure weren't devils. And anyone who thinks they can reconcile any of it into "good guys" and "bad guys"? Unless you're God Almighty, you're full of crap if you think you can.

I THINK I'M A GOOD GUY. AM I FULL OF CRAP?

I think you're the closest thing to a good guy the Legends have right now, Path. But, yes. I think you're full of crap.

AND THAT MAKES EXCELLENT FERTILIZER TO GROW IMPORTANT FRUITS AND VEGETABLES.

It sure does.

I HAVE ONE LAST QUESTION …

I swear to God, robot, if you make me cry again, or you tell anybody I cried, I will melt you down and turn you into a trash compactor!

WHAT WAS THE GIFT?

The what?

YOU SAID JACKSON HYPED UP HIS GIFT. BUT YOU NEVER TOLD ME WHAT IT WAS.

I never knew. The news about Zeke and Typhon derailed the whole graduation day. I actually had forgotten all about it… until six months after we lost Jackson.

YOU STILL DON'T KNOW WHAT CAUSED THE EXPLOSION?

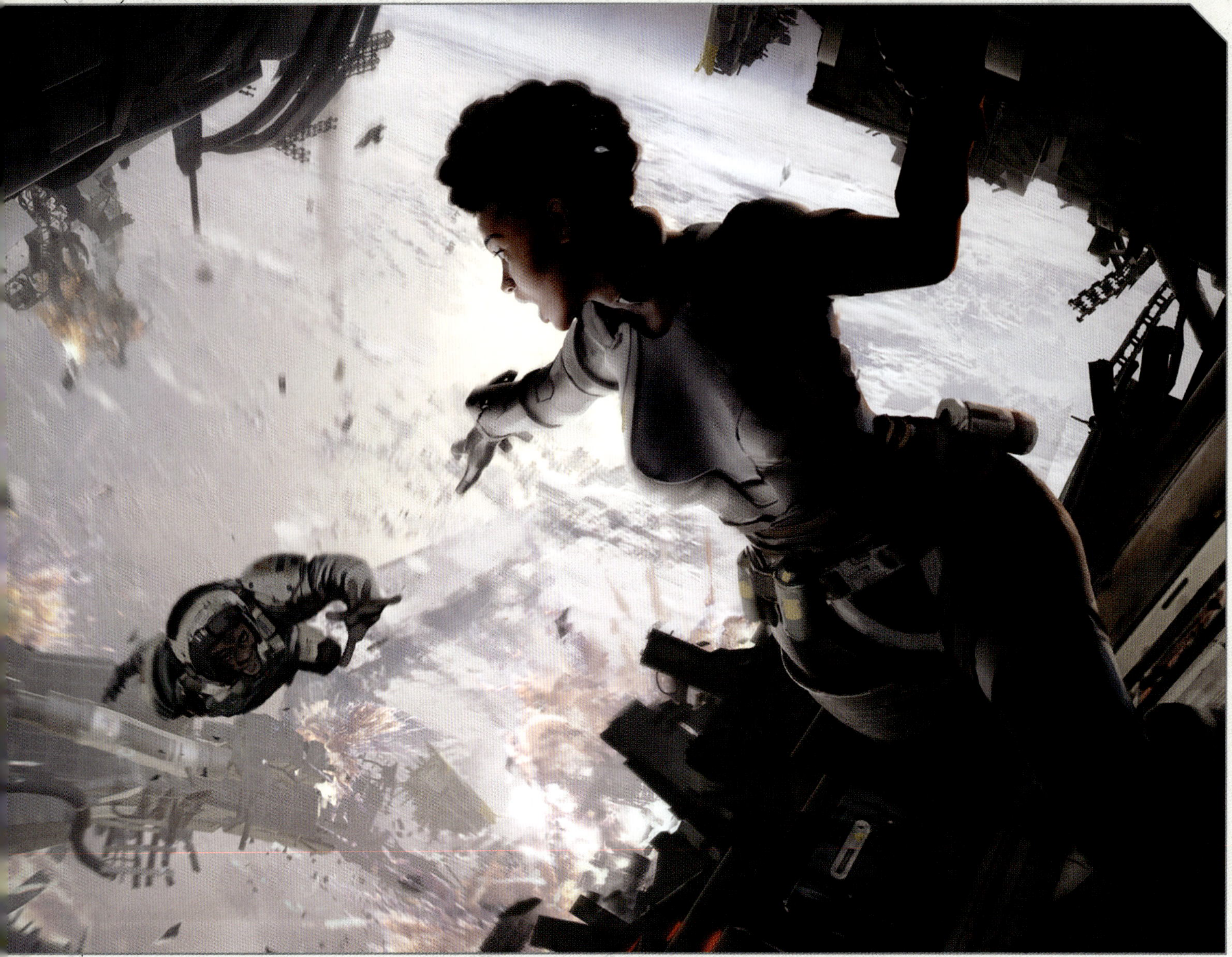

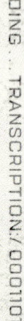

* A DEPICTION OF THE MOMENT ANITA WILLIAMS LOST HER BROTHER JACKSON.

It was a grenade on the outer hull of the ship, but we have no idea where it came from—if it had been floating through space, or somebody shot it at us and we never knew . . . it was a freak accident. One minute we're talking in an airlock, the next I'm seeing him in orbit over Solace. I know this . . . he's alive. He has to be. He put his jump pack on every morning. And the last time I saw him, his eyes were open. And he was smiling at me. He's out there somewhere. Maybe on Solace, maybe somewhere else by now. But I will find him. And I'm going to wring his neck when I do.

WHY WOULD YOU DO THAT?

Because it took me six months after the explosion to work up the courage to go through his things. And that's when I found it. All these years, he'd kept it and never gave it to me. So, there I was, standing in his quarters, six months after his—after he disappeared. And it was like this voice from beyond the—just from beyond. With tears in my eyes, I opened the card. It said, "Dear Anita—I know how upset you were when I won Best Williams Sibling after finding out my assignment was coming in next week, and you had to wait for yours. But turns out we were both wrong. Technically, we're tied . . . 99 to 99. And you're beating me in one more thing before I get my orders next week. You're graduating first. So, it looks like the Best Williams Sibling isn't even a contest. Wherever we go from here is out of our hands, but I know we'll both succeed. And let's hope history doesn't repeat itself and we end up somewhere boring like Zeke and Uncle Al did, right? But in all seriousness, I'm so proud of you. And always remember, what's broken can be fixed. What's shredded can be mended. And what's been torn apart can always be put back together again. Love always, Jackson." And inside . . . painstakingly taped back together again . . . was our scorecard. Only this time, it proclaimed me the winner.

COMPETITION	JACKSON	ANITA
Who said their first word first?	X	
Who rolled over first?	X	
Who crawled first?	X	
Who took their first step first?		X
Who got potty trained first?		X
Who left their crib for a big bed first?		X
Who rode a bike with training wheels first?	X	
Who rode a bike without training wheels first?		X
Who started school first?	X	
Who read their first word first?		X
Who found their Christmas presents first?	X	
Who opened all their Christmas presents first?		X
Who read their first book with pictures?	X	
Who read their first book without pictures?		X
Who could do their multiplication tables first?	X	
Who could eat all their vegetables first?	X	
Who could sneak their entire dinner to the dog first?		X
Who can get a touchdown first?		X
Who can get a home run first?	X	
Who can run a mile faster?		X
Who can make it through all twelve courses on Christmas Eve?	X	
Who can get ready for bed first?		X
Who can be done brushing their teeth first?		X
Who graduated from elementary school first?	X	
Who can get someone to admit they like-like them first?		X
Who can go on their first date first?		X
Who can get kissed first?	X	
Who can sneak onto the IMC base without getting caught first?	X	
Who can get a part-time job first?		X
Who shot ten cans off a fence without missing first?		X
Who shot ten cans off a fence in ten seconds without missing first?		X
Fastest time to disassemble an R-201?		X
Fastest time to disassemble an R-201 and put it back together?		X
Who can hold their breath underwater the longest?	X	
Who can clean up all their toys first?	X	
Who can take out the garbage and get back to the kitchen the fastest?	X	
Who can do twenty laps around the house faster?		X
Who can cook dinner for the entire family faster?		X
Who can cook it better?	X	
Who can memorize the IMC Military Handbook first?		X
Who can recite the military alphabet first?		X
Who can put a Peacekeeper together faster?		X
Who lost all their baby teeth first?	X	
First one to get a cavity loses.	X	
Who broke a bone first?	X	
Who got a cast first?	X	
Who can clean their bedroom faster?	X	
Who can get Mama a bigger Mother's Day present?		X
Whose peach cobbler is as good as Mama's?	X	
Who can write a song faster?	X	

COMPETITION	JACKSON	ANITA
Who can write the better song?		X
Whose red velvet cake is as good as Grandma's?	X	
Who can get Papa a bigger Father's Day present?		X
Who can clean their toilet faster?		X
First person to forget a sibling's birthday loses!		X
First person to hit a wrong note during a Williams Sendoff loses!	X	
Most saltines eaten without drinking anything?	X	
Who can finish the pint of ice cream first even with an ice cream headache?		X
Who can get their tongue off the cold flagpole first?		X
Who can finish the complete works of Shakespeare first?		X
Try to drink an entire glass of hot sauce. First one to give up loses!	X	
Who met Vice Admiral Graves first?		X
Who met Barker first?		X
First to have a drink with Barker?	X	
Who met James MacAllan first?		X
Spin in a circle as fast as you can for three minutes, then stop. First one to fall loses.	X	
Who can make Dad laugh first on his birthday?	X	
Who can crack all eight knuckles at once first?		X
Who can last the longest in a downward dog pose?		X
Who can learn an instrument first?	X	
Who can write a limerick, memorize it, and recite it to Mom first?		X
Who can build two dining room chairs without instructions the fastest?		X
Who pukes the least after catching the Gridiron stomach bug?		X
Who can say "Prepare for Titanfall" in the most languages?	X	
Who can guess the next evolution of the R-97?	X	
Who can name the most Militia terrorists?		X
First to successfully grow an avocado?	X	
First to guess the twist ending of the novel *To Angel City with Love*?		X
First to correct Mom when she thinks "Frankenstein" was the name of the monster?		X
Who can make Zeke pull their finger first?		X
First to spit on Graves (post-betrayal)?	X [HIS STATUE]	
First to spit on MacAllan (post-betrayal)?	X [HIS STATUE]	
First to be able to fold a fitted sheet fastest?		X
First to be able to say the alphabet backward?	X	
First to get a fake ID that actually works?	X	
First to get a new Vidphone Mach 10?	X	
First one to break their Vidphone Mach 10 loses!	X	
Who can ride Death Coaster the most times in a row?		X
Who can do the laundry the fastest, INCLUDING ironing?	X	
Who can mow the lawn fastest?	X	
Who can get straight As first?	X	
First person to get a B loses.		X
Who's better at pool?		X
Who's better at Ping-Pong?	X	
First to get Zeke's new girlfriend to admit she's an idiot?	X	
First Militia takedown?		X
First to get their own Titan?	X	
First to pilot a Titan?	X	
First to get their Pilot certification?	X	
Best brisket?	X	

[. . . CONTINUED]

3X   [TARGET THREAT] 0%

COMPETITION	JACKSON	ANITA
Who can go the longest without painkillers after surgery?		X
First to make a quadruple-layer cake perfectly?	X	
First to catch Monty picking his nose and take a picture of it?		X
First to restore Grandpa's antique furniture?		X
First to get a vegetable plant to grow in the garden?	X	
First to get first place in the science fair?		X
First to get top of their class?		X
First to get a date to prom?	X	
First to get a driver's license?	X	
First to get a learner's permit?	X	
First to get into basic training?	X	
First to get accepted into the academy?	X	
First to get in a transport accident loses.		X
First to survive a gunshot?		X
First to survive getting stabbed?		X
First to get anything above a C+ in art?		X
First one to reprogram a MRVN to speak only in pig Latin?	X	
First one to build a robot?		X
Who can go the longest without talking?	X	
Fastest zipliner?		X
Who bungee jumped first?		X
First to learn how to swim?		X
First to learn how to jump rope?		X
First to learn how to sew?		X
First to learn how to build a birdhouse?	X	
Fastest doing the dishes when the whole family eats dinner together?	X	
Who skydived first?	X	
First to write their own computer program?		X
First to type 120 words a minute?	X	
First to finish a marathon?	X	
First to read the Bible cover to cover?	X	
First to finish an entire box of cereal in one sitting?	X	
Most hot dogs in a single sitting?	X	
Most jalapeños in a single sitting?		X
Who can hold down a tablespoon of salt without puking?		X
Who can rake all the leaves in the front yard the fastest?	X	
Who can fix Grandpa's broken chair?		X
Who can make a lamp out of a potato first?		X
Who can memorize all the generals in the IMC first?		X
Who's quicker in the bathroom in the morning?		X
Who has a cleaner bill of health after their physical?		X
Who makes the best pancakes on Sunday morning?	X	
Who gets published in the local newspaper first?	X	
Who has the most followers on social media?	X	
Who can finish drinking a gallon of milk faster?		X
Who got chickenpox first?		X
Who beat chickenpox fastest?	X	
Who was nicer to Mama and Pops during their teenage years?	X	
Who can fit more marshmallows in their mouth?	X	
Who can finish a stein of beer faster?		X

COMPETITION	JACKSON	ANITA
Who blinks first?	X	
Who's better in chess?	X	
Who's better in checkers?		X
Who can change a flat tire the fastest?	X	
First to fall asleep during Grandpa's story about the night he killed the spider loses.		X
First one to climb all 120 flights of stairs in the Kodai building?		X
First one to eat a plate full of cooked brains?		X
Who can do the most sit-ups?	X	
First to steal Dad's 3D printer to print out a toy Titan?	X	
Who can get four strikes in a row during candlepin bowling?		X
First to hold a conversation longer than three minutes with second cousin Manny in the asylum?	X	
Firts to points out, all the grammer mistakens; in this sentence$		X
First to call Mom by her real name and not get grounded?		X
Who can skip class the most times and still get an A?	X	
Who can do the most pushups?	X	
Who can eat two bowls of beans and run a mile first?		X
First to get a tattoo?	X	
Who can climb the tallest tree?		X
First to wear Mom's Pilot helmet to school?		X
Who can design the best logo of their name? (Zeke's the judge.)	X	
Who can get the highest score on the admittance test?		X
Who can finish their admittance test faster?	X	
Who got the most applause at the school talent show?	X	
Who has the biggest stamp collection?	X	
First to eat an entire Big Bang pizza by themselves?		X
First to complete the "disarm a bomb" simulator?		X
Who runs to the end of the street and back fastest?	X	
First to make the nicest centerpiece for the holiday dinner?		X
First to clean their transport?		X
First to find Maw Maw's glasses when she loses them?		X
Who can guess most accurately how many fireworks get set off on Heinrich Hammond Day?	X	
Who eats more turkey on Thanksgiving?		X
Who won more Halloween costume contests?	X	
Who has more Halloween candy?		X
Who gets more Christmas presents?	X	
Sibling who gets grounded the least?		X
Wins most prizes at the carnival?		X
Best chili?	X	
Who can save more money by the end of the year?	X	
Who can last the longest in a hot tub?		X
Who holds the record for longest amount of time without being found in hide and seek?		X
Who can bench-press more?	X	
Who can chug more cans of soda in a minute?		X
Who can memorize more numbers in pi?	X	
Who can get more holes in one in a game of golf?		X
Who can get more bull's-eyes in a row with a bow and arrow?	X	
Who can stay up 48 hours without sleep or caffeine?	X	
Who can get a higher score in *Frontier War: The Game*?	X	
Who wins more hands of poker?		X
~~Who's getting their first assignment marching orders first?~~	X	
Who's graduating first because *A* comes before *J* in the alphabet?		X

[. . . CONTINUED]

I DON'T GET IT.

Jackson won. He was supposed to be the first to get to a hundred, because he was getting his marching orders before me. But instead, he fished the pieces of the scorecard out of the garbage, taped it back together, and willingly gave up the contest of a lifetime, because my name started with an A, and I graduated seven seconds before he did. He gave me the win. Because ... because ...

BECAUSE THAT'S WHO HE IS.

You're the first person in a long time to not refer to him in the past tense.

AND I'M NOT EVEN A PERSON!

You feel more human to me now than most everyone out there.

AND IF YOU SAY HE'S ALIVE, I BELIEVE YOU, FRIEND. JUST LIKE I BELIEVE I'M GOING TO FIND MY CREATOR. YOUR BATTALION MAY HAVE BEEN INVOLVED IN MY CREATION. BUT IT WOULD HAVE BEEN BEFORE YOU WERE BORN. TELL ME ... WHO IS THIS UNCLE AL THAT JACKSON MENTIONS?

I never knew him. He died before I was born. My father referred to him as Uncle Al. He wasn't even blood related ... just a friend of the family. He was also Eighty-First Battalion. I don't know if we ever found out the real story of how he died. Something about how the IMC was contacted to help with security detail for some science project. When Zeke got called to Typhon, we ragged on him that he'd end up like Uncle Al. We never thought it would actually happen ...

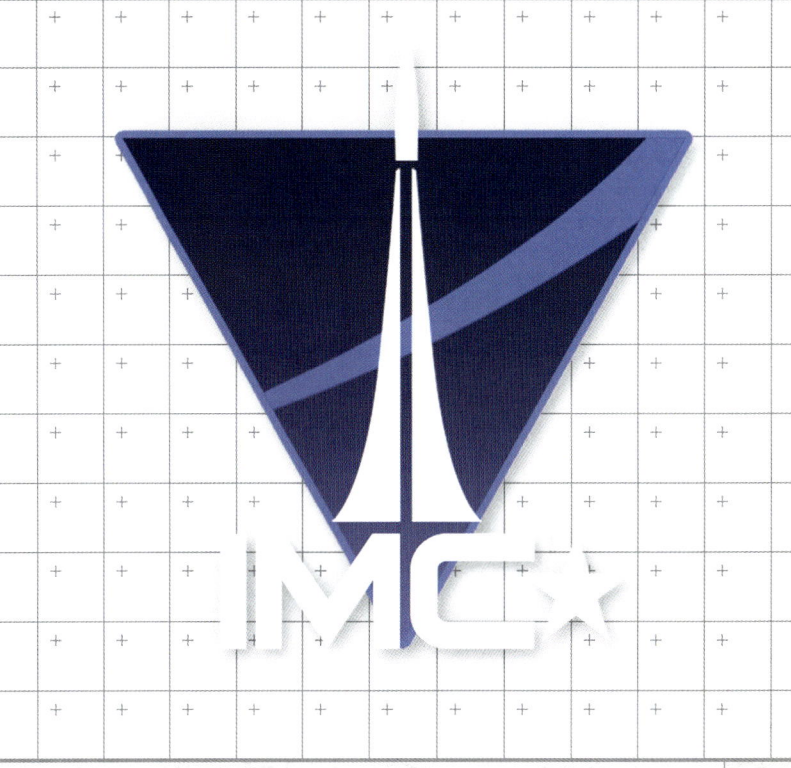

* THE LOGO OF THE INTERSTELLAR MANUFACTURING CORPORATION.

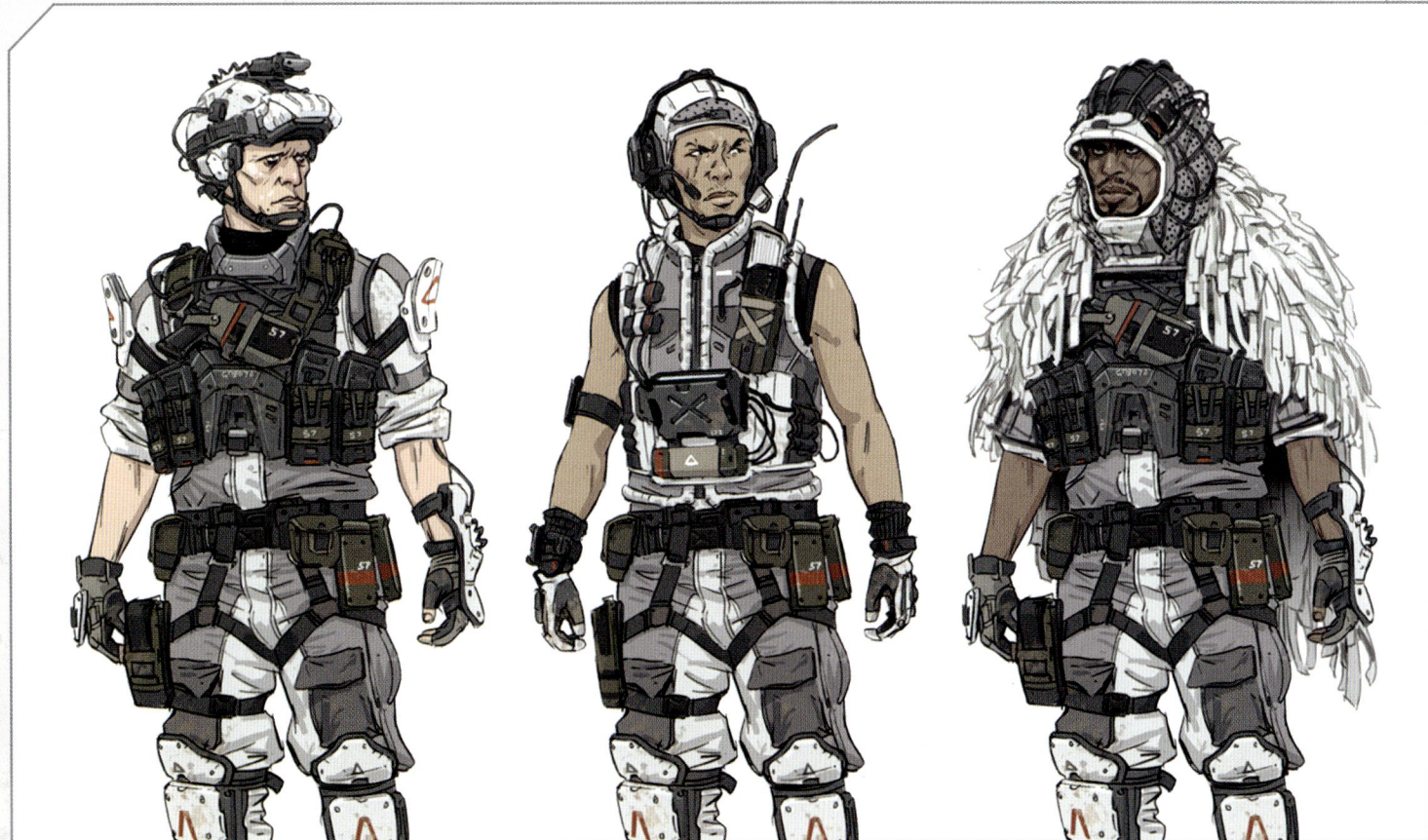

* IMC SOLDIERS.

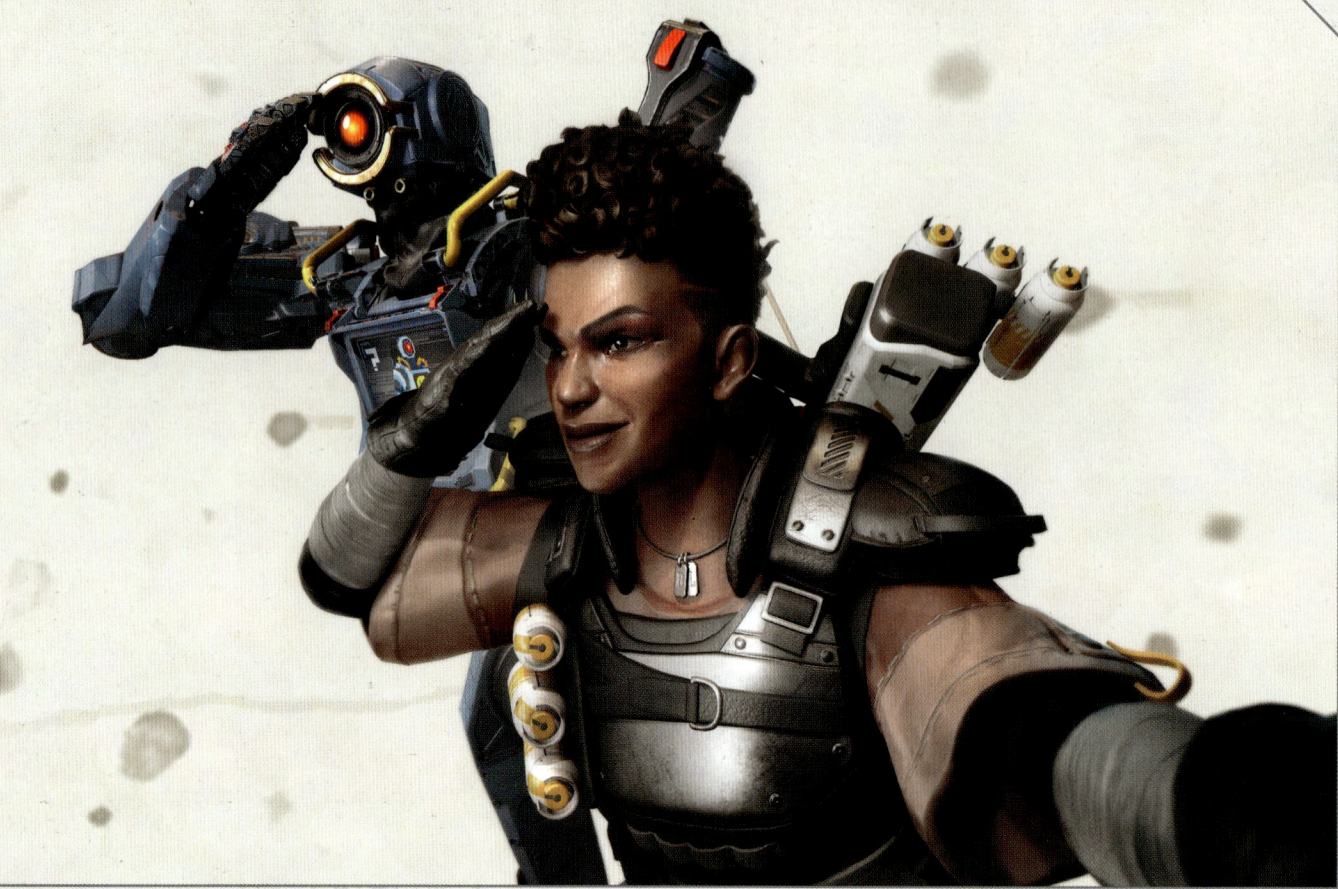

* BANGALORE AND ME DOING OUR BEST SALUTES!

WHAT HAPPENED TO UNCLE AL?

He died. Coincidentally, it was also an explosion. Some-where on Psamathe. I don't know the details. Pops said he was security for someone who was trying to save "the future of the Outlands," with something called … Isis? Iris?

PROJECT: IRIS!

Yeah. They couldn't give us details. But he died in the line of duty. Received the Medal of Valor posthumously and everything.

I THINK I'M PROJECT: IRIS! I THINK THEY WERE BUILDING ME.

I … hmmm. Are you sure about that?

NOT AT ALL. BUT WHAT ELSE COULD THEY HAVE BEEN BUILDING?

I don't know, but if it was a robot, I feel like Pops would have said something. Jackson loved robots growing up. And nobody ever mentioned anything about a robot. I just remember he'd get really defensive if we made fun of it. Saying it wasn't some hippie-dippie project. That a lot of people were going to die if Project: Iris failed.

SO IF I'M NOT PROJECT: IRIS, WHAT AM I?

Maybe you're the thing Project: Iris was trying to stop?

WHAT?!

Kidding. Pathfinder, it's a joke. I'm kidding! But you know who you should talk to? Witt.

MY BEST FRIEND MIRAGE!

He grew up here. He'd know if something was threat-ening the future of the Outlands. Back when the civil wars were breaking out, Jackson and I stayed as far away from the Outland planets as possible. Mirage was down here. He was dealing with it, lost his brothers in those wars. He probably knows what they were trying to protect the Outlands from. If it's not you, that is.

I HOPE IT'S NOT ME.

Relax. I told you I was joking.

THANK YOU, FRIEND.

Thank you. And stay pure, Pathfinder. You're better off this way.

Oh, and I mean it: anyone hears I shed a tear, and you get pounded into aluminum foil.

LOADING … TRANSCRIPTION/ 0001101

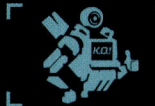
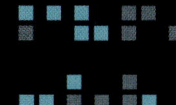

- Bangalore comes from a military family who love her very much, and even though everyone tells me the IMC are the bad guys, I think only some of them were truly bad, and the rest of them were just letting bad people do bad things and it didn't bother them until their lives suffered, and then it bothered them.

- I also learned that when their lives went bad, they got angry about it and then they were as angry as everyone else. So maybe bad guys don't exist after all. Maybe there are just guys who live their lives peacefully, and guys who don't, and the guys who don't just make life so hard for the peaceful people that everybody just gets mad at everybody else. And when that happens, you find a ship with an experimental energy source (I wonder if it had a name?) and you run like hell. Because you may be a coward, but at least you're still alive. I don't know what any of that means, but it sure is interesting.

- I learned that the Battle at Gridiron was not nearly as evenly matched as people say, and that a lot of people may have died, but a lot of people may also have lived, and still nobody knows who won.

- I believe Jackson Williams was not the perfect soldier . . . but he made up for it by being the perfect brother.

- I learned the Blackout took five years to span the galaxy, and may have been caused by the IMS *HESTIA* escaping . . . or maybe not. What I do know is that the IMS *HESTIA* and its strange experimental tech have nothing to do with Project: Iris, which was happening years before . . . and light years away.

- Project: Iris started because "the future of the Outlands" was at stake.

- I learned that I might not be Project: Iris . . . but I might be. Or I might be the thing Project: Iris had to save the Outlands from . . . but I might not be. Maybe Wraith and Bangalore are right. Maybe I should stop digging. Maybe I won't like the answers I find. No, I'll like them. I'll like them no matter what. I just know it!

  Good thing I'm off to see my bestest friend in the world to relive the deaths of his three brothers with him! He's going to be so excited when he finds out!

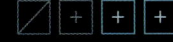
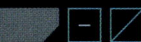

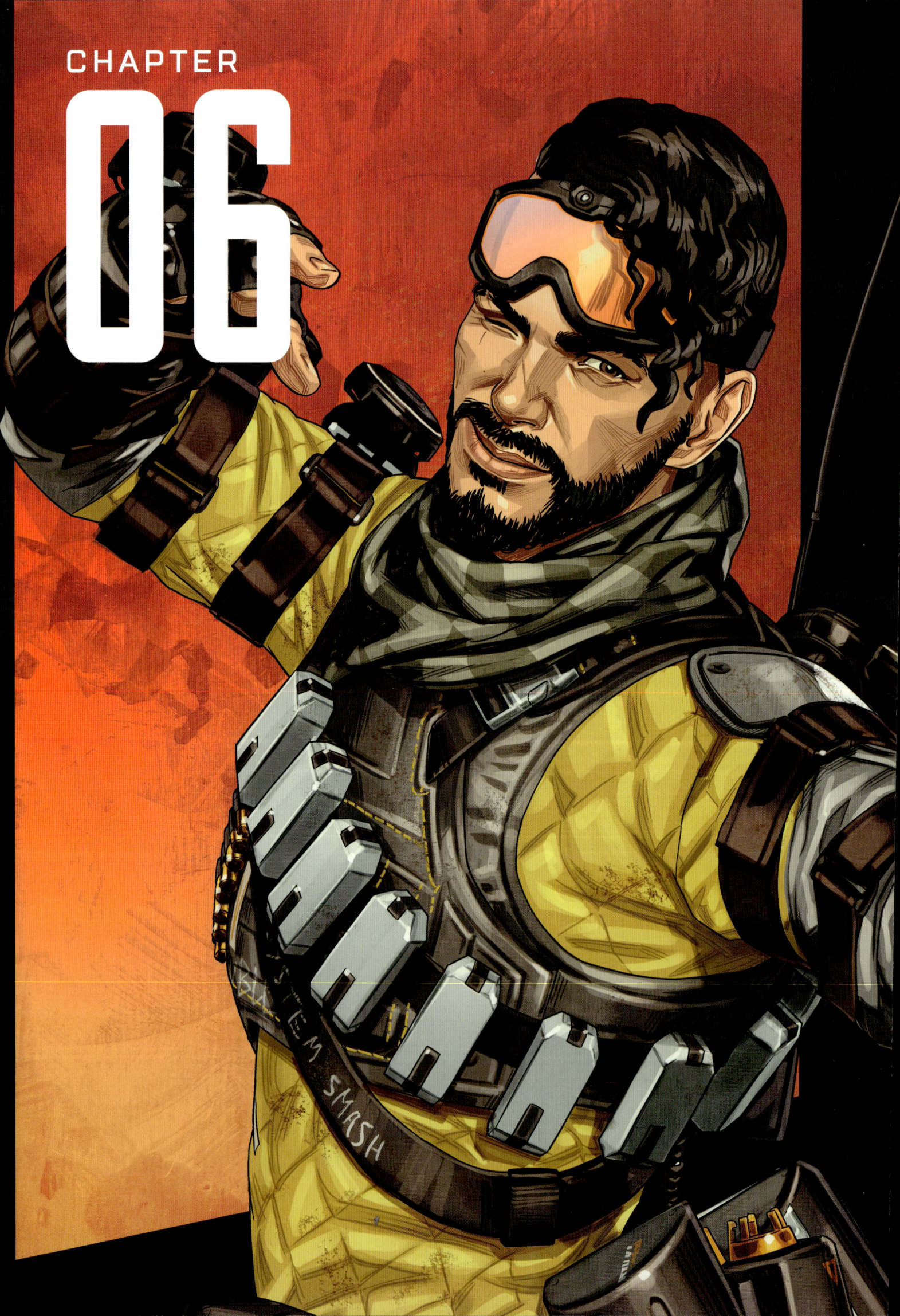

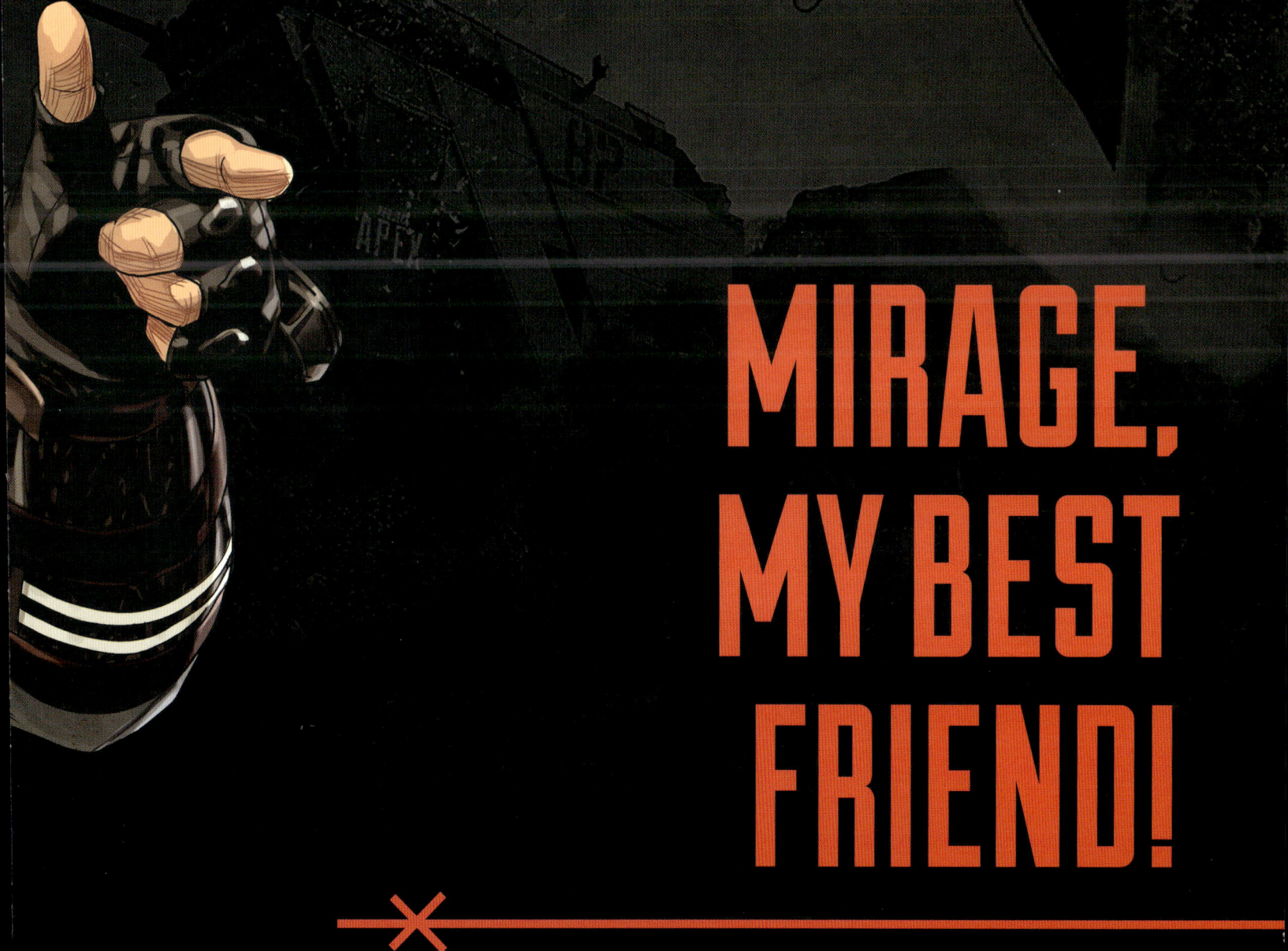

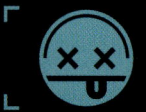
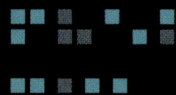
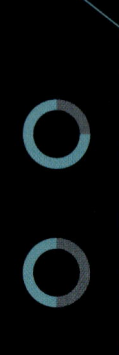

PATHFINDER MEMORY LOG: DAY 6

Sergeant First Class Anita Williams . . . more like Sergeant "Best Class," because she's the best! Bangalore was very helpful. I knew some information about the IMC (Interstellar Manufacturing Corporation), but it was mostly from people who didn't like them very much. I never really learned the other side of the story. Now I know what Lifeline was talking about—how it's hard to see which side is good and which side is bad, because sometimes there isn't a clear answer.

If it were up to me, I'd just want everyone to put their differences aside and get along. That way everyone who needs help would get help—that's what I care about. I hope that was why I was created. It seems important and it feels good to be needed for something important—and what's more important than helping people?

Bangalore helped me learn about old IMC and ARES Division experiments in the Outlands that had goals to change the future. It seems that my clue "The future of the Outlands" has to do with one of these goals, but I don't know which one. Was this to change the future of the Outlands in a good way? Or was this to change the future of the Outlands in a bad way? Bangalore didn't have an answer for me but thinks that my best friend Mirage might.

Mirage knows a lot about the conflicts in the Outlands (specifically the civil war), because his brothers were soldiers. I'm excited to learn more, so I'm off to the Paradise Lounge to meet him for a drink.

CLUE BOX

TRANSMISSION CLUES
- "Chevrex" > LIFELINE'S PARENTS' COMPANY
- "The future of the Outlands" > OLD EXPERIMENTS TO CHANGE THE FUTURE
- "Dr. Amélie Pa—— [Paquette]" > WATTSON'S GRANDMOTHER, A GEOLOGIST, DIED MYSTERIOUSLY
- "The Event" >
- "Aleki" > GIBRALTAR'S GRANDFATHER
- "Iris" > PROJECT: IRIS, CREATED IN 2654

SELF-MOTIVATION QUOTE . . . SEARCHING . . . 1 RESULT FOUND

"The secret of staying young is to live honestly, eat slowly, and lie about your age."
—[LUCILLE BALL]

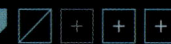

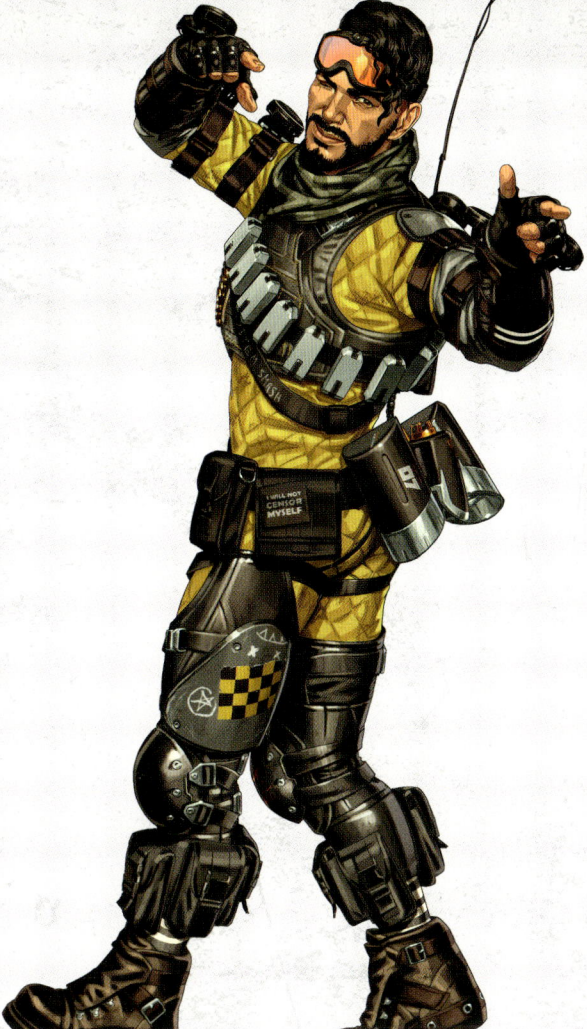

REAL NAME:
ELLIOTT WITT

AGE:
30

HOME WORLD:
SOLACE

TACTICAL ABILITY:
PSYCHE OUT

PASSIVE ABILITY:
NOW YOU SEE ME …

ULTIMATE ABILITY:
LIFE OF THE PARTY

MIRAGE IS THE KIND OF GUY WHO LIKES TO STAND OUT. The youngest of four brothers, he perfected the art of fooling around to get attention. The one thing he took seriously was Holo-Pilot technology. Introduced to the illusion-creating tech by his engineer mother, he pored over the mechanisms and learned all he could about them. Even when his brothers went MIA during the civil war, Mirage and his mother continued to develop holodevices, and the work brought them closer.

While working as a bartender to make ends meet, Mirage heard amazing stories from his patrons about the Apex Games and the wealth and glory that came with victory. As good as both of those sounded, he knew he couldn't risk leaving his mother childless—until she gave him a set of customized holodevices and told him to follow his dream. Mirage is now the life of the Apex Games, outwitting opponents and charming audiences across the Outlands.

"I don't take myself too seriously. I don't take myself anywhere. I need to get out more."
—MIRAGE

13918175

► HEY, FR— ◄

Hold on. You said Bangalore sent you to me? Wow. Bangalore, huh? Needing good old Mirage for some help? Makes sense, you know, I am quite the intel... interlec... in... I'm quite the smart dude. So, what does she need?

NOT HER. ME.
Oh no...

I'M TRYING TO FIND MY—
Creator. I know. We know. Everyone knows, tin can. Is this just what you do when you're not in the Games?

YES. IT'S ALSO WHAT I DO IN THE GAMES. I'M ALWAYS LOOKING FOR MY CREATOR. THAT'S WHY I JOINED THE GAMES. WHY DID YOU JOIN THE GAMES?
Me? Um... well, isn't it obvious? I joined to be the best. The fame. The glory. The money. And I'm not gonna lie, I'm doing a pretty great job of all three, if I don't say so myself.

YOU DO SAY IT YOURSELF.
That fame is something else. It's something I always wanted. Even back during the Thunderdome days, when my brothers and I would go watch a match, those Legends were amazing. I wanted to be just like them. Of course, some were locked-up criminals forced to fight the IMC for their freedom... but there were a few that were real stars. Blisk, for one—I was lucky enough to see his last match before he left for the war. That was about twenty-three years ago—2710. Wow... it's been a long time.

THE APEX COMMISSIONER! I'VE HEARD OTHERS TALK ABOUT BLISK. HE SOUNDS LIKE A SCARY GUY.
And if you see him fight, he's even scarier. I only got to meet him once. He came into my bar and just sat in the corner by himself with a glass of something smooth. I wanted to say something, but I didn't. I wasn't always the hotshot guy I am today.

[...]

Anyway. That was the last time I got to see the guy. My brothers used to give me a hard time because they both got to meet him after the only match I didn't go to, because I broke my leg helping my mom with a project. I always helped her with anything she needed—that's the type of guy I am. Can you blame me? I'm a caring people person. Some may say a saint? Hah. I'm only kidding—sort of... Anyway, she always had projects from different contracts throughout the Outlands. I bet you were wondering where I got my smarts and good looks from?

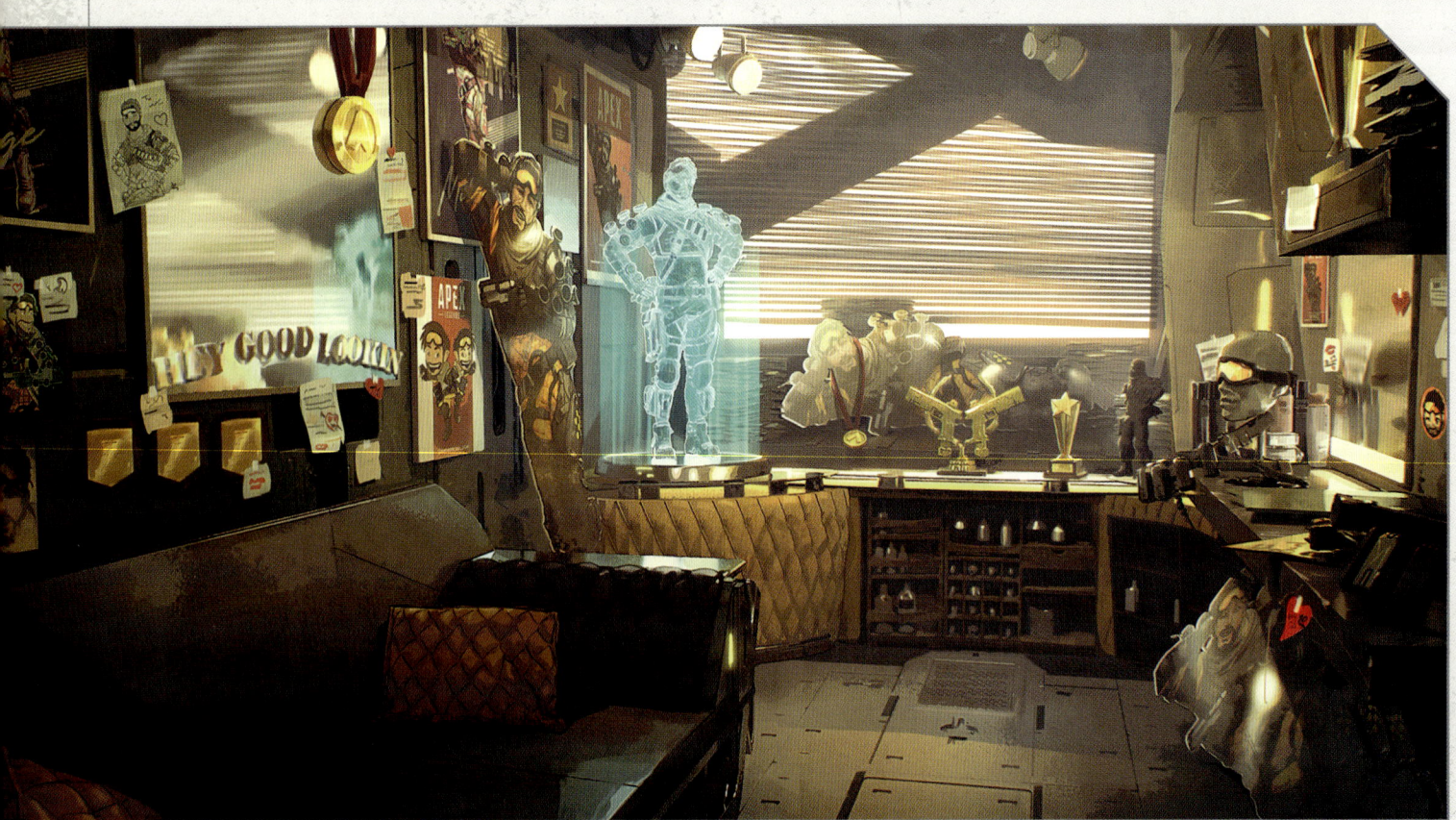

MIRAGE'S WONDERFUL COLLECTION OF MEMORABILIA.

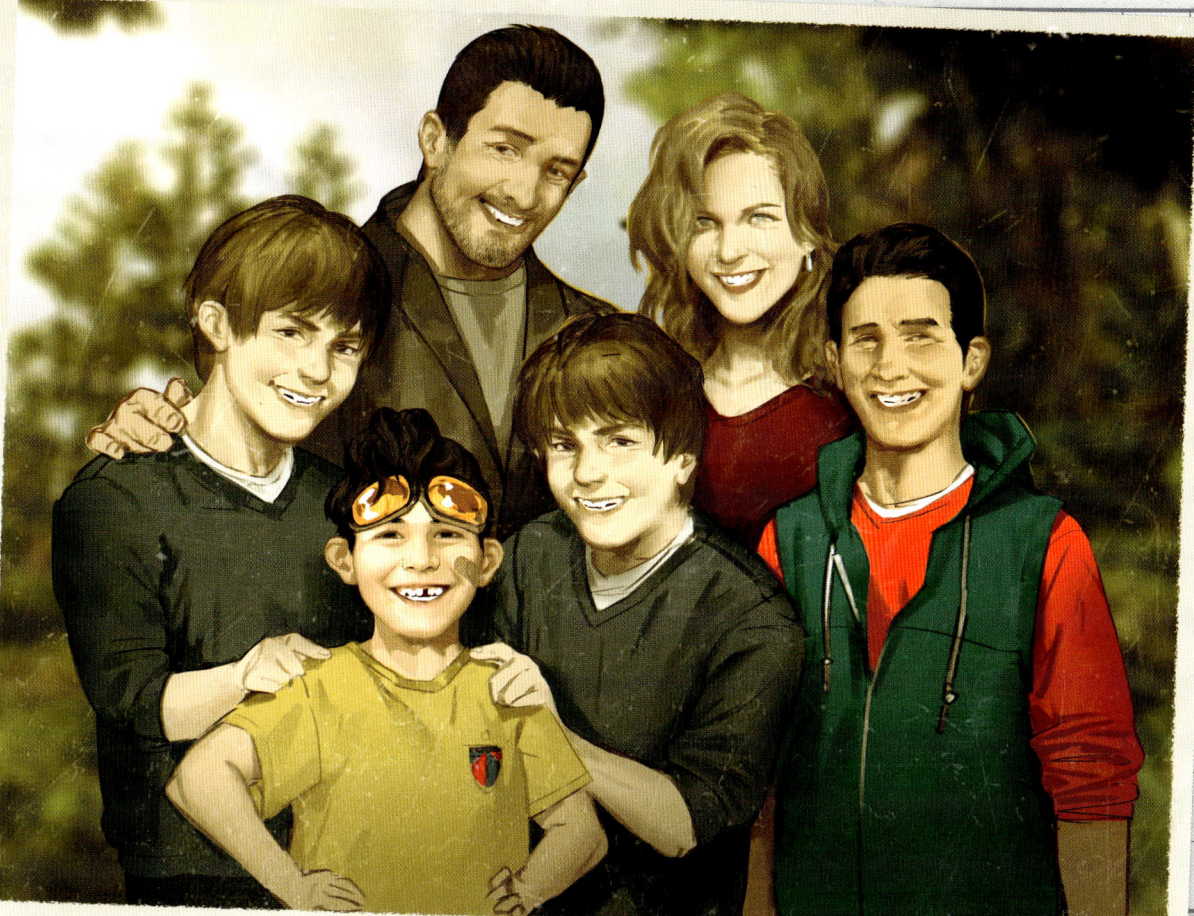

LITTLE ELLIOTT AND HIS FAMILY . . . DURING HAPPIER TIMES.

I WAS!

That would be my mom—Evelyn Witt. She's the smartest person I know. One of the best holoengineers in the entire Frontier. That woman worked with the best from Kodai to the IMC. Sure, I bet you're thinking that the IMC ain't that great (unless you ask Bangalore), but when you've got to raise four kids on your own, you take any gig you can get.

I THINK IT'S GREAT. WHERE WAS YOUR DAD?

The infamous Richard Witt? Nah . . . He wasn't really in the picture. I mean, he's been in a few pictures—I know what he looks like. I have met the guy, but he's not exactly the father type. I think he tried, but he mostly spent his time trying to make a living, at least that's what my mom told me. She used to tell me stories all the time—how he always had a new "hit creation," a new "big score" . . . I'm pretty sure one time he even claimed to have invented bottled water.

There was one that really stuck out to me. I guess I was turning about fourteen—really growing into my charm—and I knew the guy was on his way home after being on some sort of "expedition." I think this was around the time this father of mine was trying to be some sort of explorer or treasure hunter—he was really obsessed

with that IMC ARES Division that started doing some digs or somethin' all throughout Solace. I bet Wraith knows all about that stuff.

I remember he had been gone for about three months, and my mom had promised he was going to come home for my birthday.

AND HE DIDN'T?

Huh? Actually, he did. He came home and it was great. It was good to see the guy, but . . . Nah, never mind. I don't know why I'm telling you this. I don't need to talk about my life.

WE'RE BEST FRIENDS. YOU CAN TELL ME. YOU LOVE TALKING ABOUT YOUR LIFE.

I like talking about myself, but my life . . . Now, that's a horse of a different flavor—wait, that's not right. Okay. Okay, fine. Just keep it between us.

When my . . . dad came home for my party, he brought me all kinds of things. Gifts he got on his travels, but they weren't really things I was into. They weren't really things anyone was into. They were weird food from Psamathe, a rock he found in the mines of Gaea that looked like a Titan, and a scrap of paper with scribbles on it, which he called "art." I guess that's why I hate art.

YOU HATE ART?

Not really—especially if it's of me. Big fan of my fan art, and I've seen them all. Those are gifts I understand and gifts that understand me. The gifts my dad gave me felt like gifts from a stranger for a stranger.

The guy just didn't really know who I was, and the weirdest part was that I didn't mind. It didn't bother me, and that's why I remember that day. It was nice to see him, but I didn't have to see him. I had my brothers and I had my mom. I grew up. I wasn't the kid he knew when he left—assuming he knew me in the first place. Either way, I was fine with it.

I spent a lot of time in my early teens helping my mom with her projects. I wasn't doing it because I loved holoengineering or anything, but I got paid just enough to feel like I had money to spend. And I'll tell you what, being a kid in school with money to spend made me feel like a regular entrepr . . . entraopo . . . a big business guy.

I BET!

But I did learn a thing or two from my mom. I wasn't too bad either. One could say that I had a hand in creating my very own holotech suit and abilities. Of course, the only reason I was so good was because my mom was such a great teacher. She knew how to problem-solve like no other. Still does—on her good days. My dad didn't really understand that. He never really understood her passion for science and gadgets and all that junk. Don't get me wrong, I'm not saying he didn't love her or viso-verso . . . vice-vorso? You know, the other way around. But just maybe some-times you need more than love.

I THINK LOVE IS ENOUGH.

I coulda guessed you'd say that. I've heard that before. And I'm not saying who's wrong and who's right—I just feel like I've experienced it one way and that's all I need to know. It didn't work out for Richard. The poor guy tried, but he just didn't quite understand his own family. We moved on without him, and that's just how it was.

. . . and it sucked. I don't usually have the time to think back on it, so thank you for the refresher.

YOU'RE WELCOME, FRIEND.

What was it you needed? Unless you came here to learn all about me, which ain't a bad thing—I mean, who can blame you? I'm a Legend. An open book. I have no problem talking about anything or anyone.

GREAT. I WANT TO KNOW ABOUT THE OUTLANDS CIVIL WAR.

No. Nah. No, thanks. I think we're done here.

NO, WE'RE NOT. I STILL HAVE TO FIND MY CREATOR.

Why do you care so much about someone you don't even know?

BECAUSE I DON'T KNOW THEM, AND THEY CREATED ME. SO HOW AM I SUPPOSED TO REALLY KNOW MYSELF? WOULD YOU BE THE SAME PERSON IF YOU DIDN'T KNOW YOUR CREATORS?

I would be nothing without my mom. Okay, but why the war?

I THINK THE REASON I WAS CREATED HAS SOMETHING TO DO WITH THE CONFLICTS THAT TOOK PLACE IN THE OUTLANDS.

* A PORTRAIT OF ELLIOTT WITT, ENTITLED MIRAGE OF LUST.

Well, I do know a thing or two or three about the conflicts . . . You see, Path, I lost all my brothers in the civil war.

OH NO . . .
You're telling me.

When the IMC started leaving the Outlands back around 2715, all the territories and planets went full-on chaotic. It was like Mom left home and the kids went wild. I'm sure many folks have their own opinions on the IMC, I know I do, but they did keep things somewhat sane. And after they all left, the fighting began.

Solace was the last planet to join the fight, since it was the last planet the IMC left, but the rest of the Outlands officially started the civil war when I was around fifteen. It was too bad, too—I used to have friends on all those different planets. A buddy on Gaea, a girlfriend on Talos, another girlfriend on Talos,

and a lot of good friends on Raffi—bummer I'll never see them again.

WHY NOT?
They're in the Fringe Worlds.

OH. AJAY AND GIBRALTAR MENTIONED THEM—THE FRINGE WORLDS.
Ajay? She doesn't let me call her Ajay . . . lame.

Yeah, I'm sure she's been there with the Frontier Corps. And the big guy probably had some friends on those worlds like I did. Solace was and is pretty much the central hub of the Outlands. People came from all over to see a match at the Thunderdome or even drop by for a pint right here at my bar! You know, this bar has been in the Witt family for generations. Though, of course, my dad didn't know how to run this place, nor did he want to, so he gave it to his

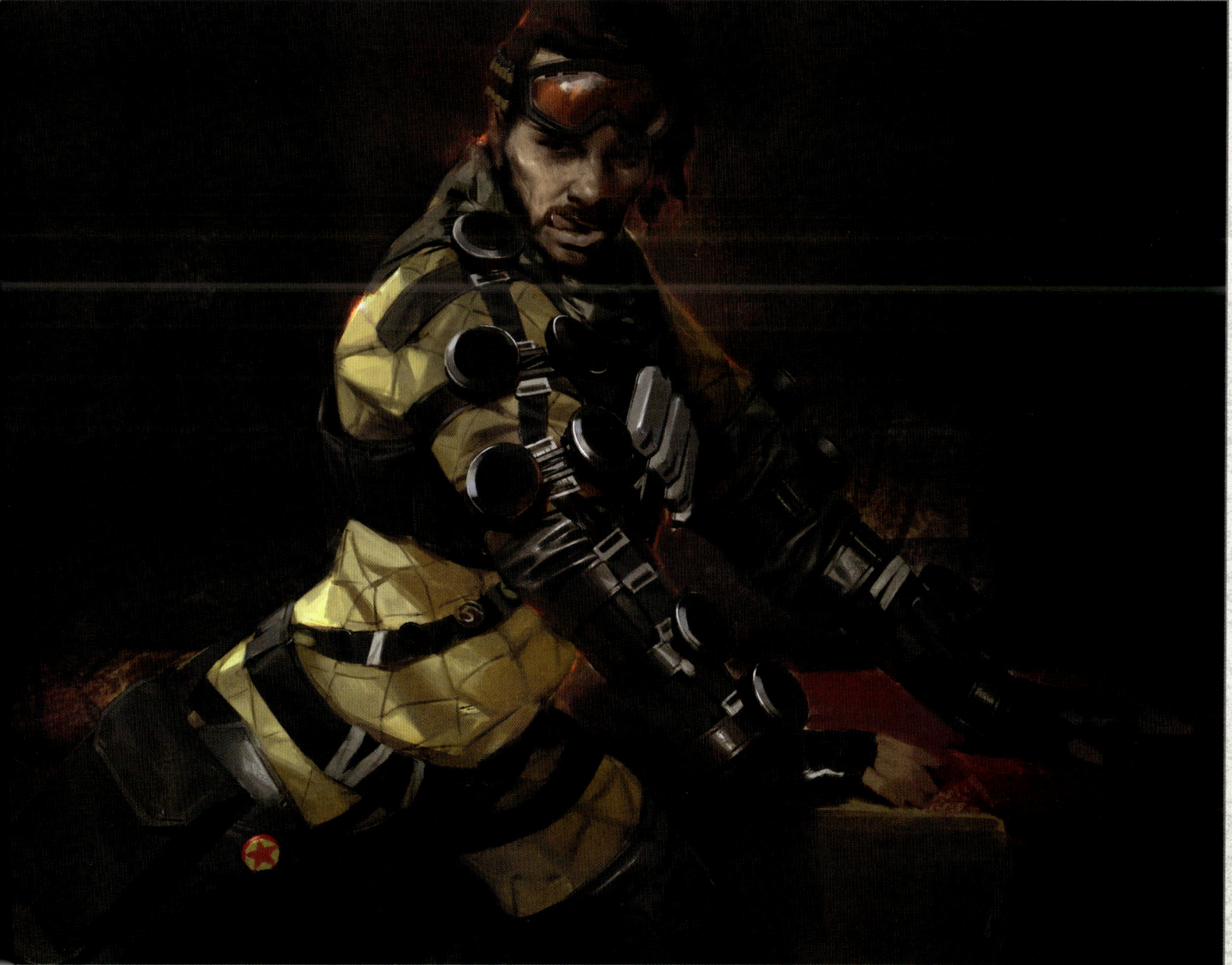

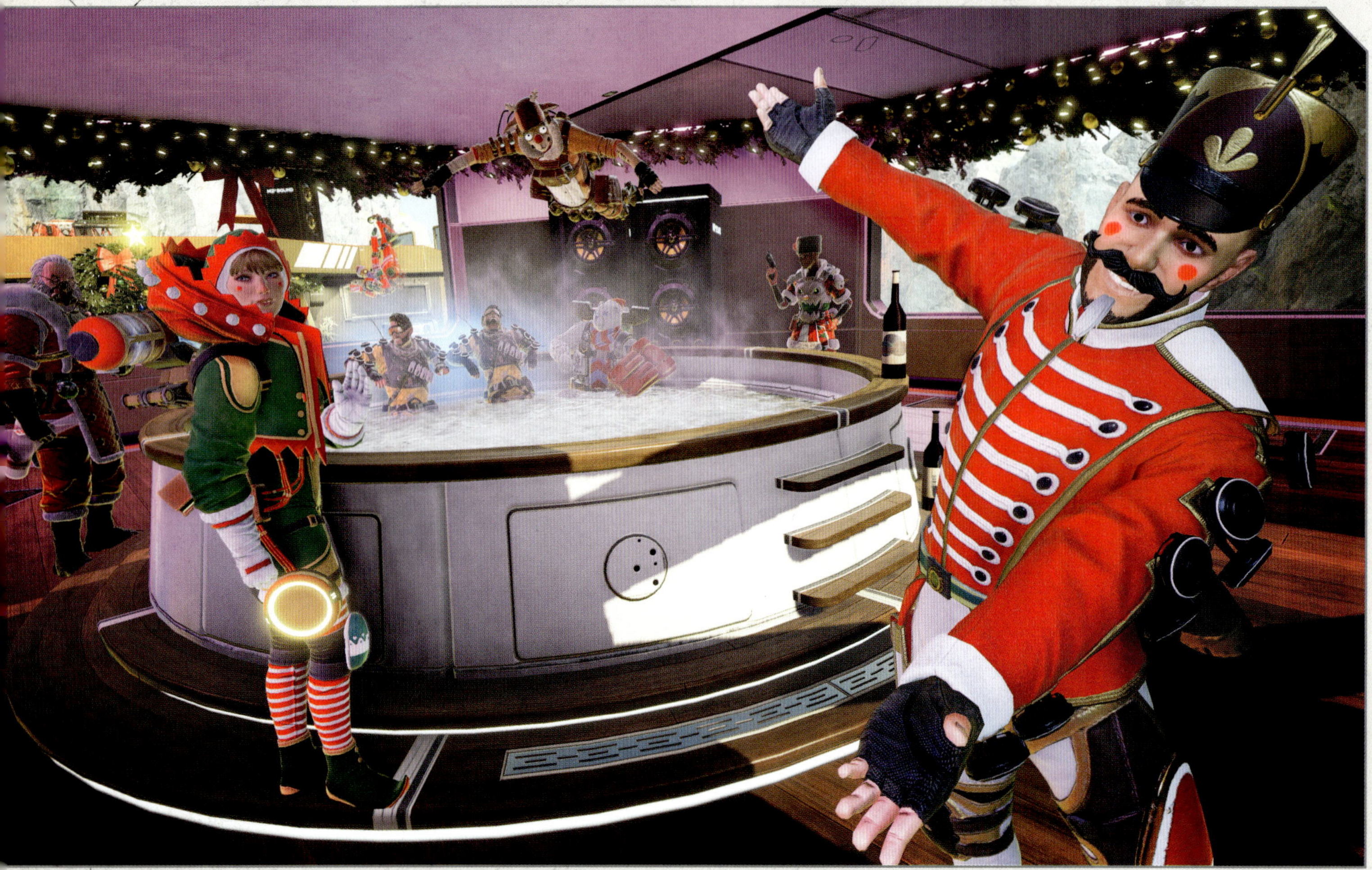

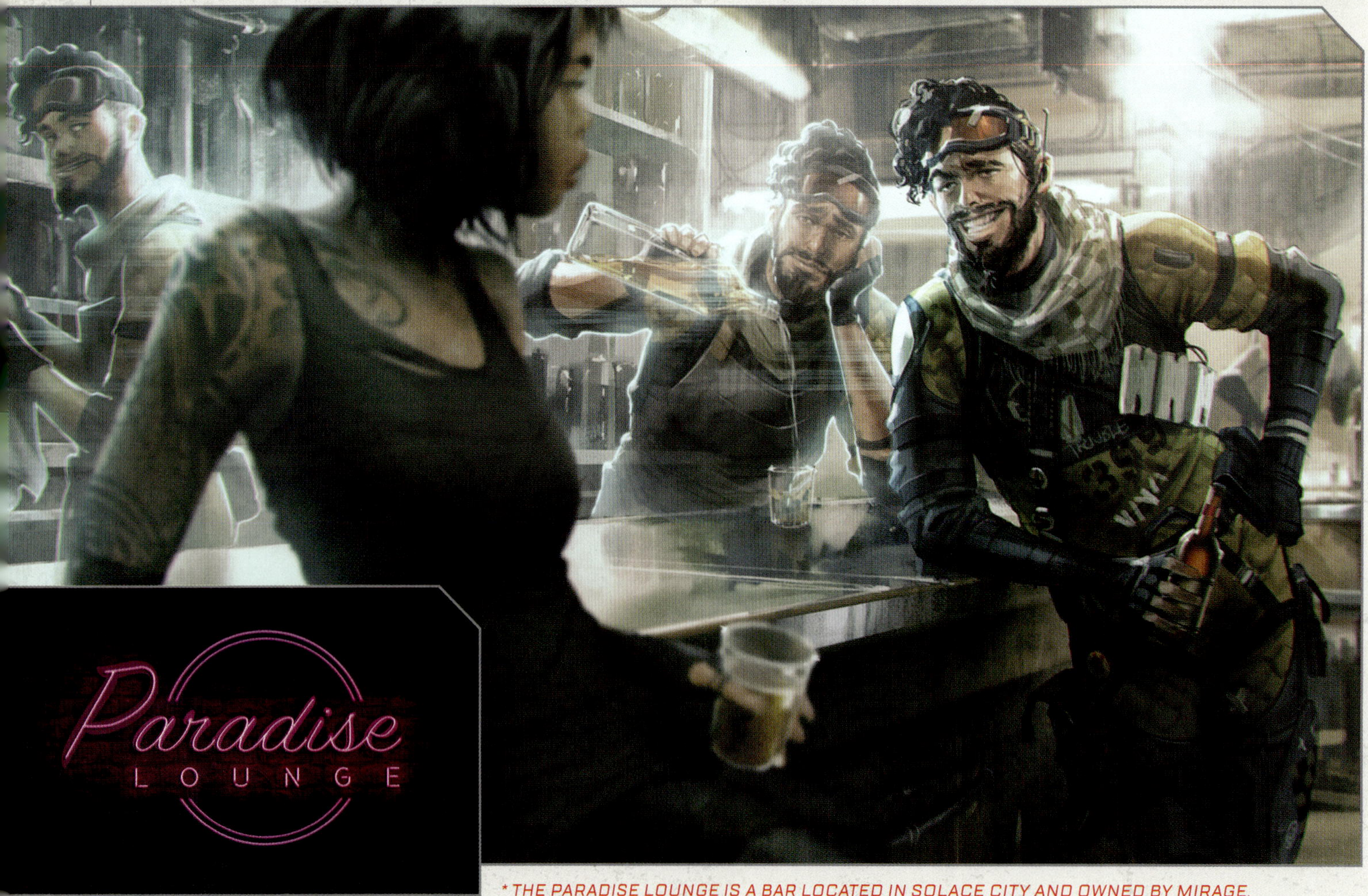

*THE PARADISE LOUNGE IS A BAR LOCATED IN SOLACE CITY AND OWNED BY MIRAGE.

brother, who was planning on selling it to my older brother, Roger, whose dream it was to run the place, but then he went missing ... so eventually I bought it and kept the name he was going to give it: the Paradise Lounge.

I love this place. It's a social place. And I'm a social guy. I always get along with everyone. I still do, except Crypto ... that pain in my—

SO WHY COULDN'T EVERYONE GET ALONG?
Not everything is thumbs-up and friendship, you know?

I DON'T.
It's all about power and greed. That's pretty much what the Apex Games are all about, too. After the IMC abandoned us, each planet, territory, and town fought over who controlled everything from fuel outposts to farming land. And those disputes kicked off the civil war.

At the time, we shared resources based on the laws of the IMC. There were Solace properties on Gaea and people on Psamathe who owned land on Talos—everything was mixed up, but without the IMC to keep things together, those with the biggest guns and the most fighters took control.

If you haven't noticed, Solace is a fairly dry planet. That old Duchess River wasn't left the cleanest after the IMC polluted it, so the Solace City water treatment plant worked overtime. I would know, I did a few shifts there myself. Not to brag, but I was a nighttime manager.

THAT SOUNDS LIKE A BRAG.
Okay, it's a brag.

The fuel needed to keep the plant running was on Gaea and the only way for Solace to get that fuel was to fight for it.

Everyone I knew enlisted, including all three of my brothers.

DID YOU NOT BECAUSE YOUR PARENTS WOULDN'T LET YOU? THAT WAS GIBRALTAR'S ISSUE.
Oh, yeah? Was it? So, the big guy just does whatever his parents tell him, huh? Ha ha.

NO. HE RAN AWAY FROM HOME INSTEAD.
Oh ... Yeah. That sounds about right for him—Mr. Self-Proclaimed Protector of the Innocent.

I stayed home because I ... I had my reasons. Let's just leave it at that.

The point is, the war left my home quiet for the first time. That house was busy—there was always something going on. Roger, my older brother, he was the rock star of the family, and there wasn't a day that went by that didn't have him shredding his guitar as loud as he could. I joined him every now and then, but I only played piano. And I only knew one song.

WHAT SONG?
It's the song my mom loves. A very old tune called "The Inch Worm." I wasn't very good at piano though, and that wasn't exactly my brother's type of music anyway. It was still nice that he let me listen and feel included. Unlike my other brothers, the twins, Ricky and Elon. Those guys were nothing but sports, sports, and more sports. They lived and breathed by the Thunderdome and played everything from football to archery pretty much every day.

I was the youngest and I didn't really fit in all the time. I know, right? Me? Mirage? Not fitting in? I fit in with everyone! But not then, nope. I wasn't very good at sports, I wasn't very good at music, I think the only thing I was actually good at was sciencey-techy stuff with my mom. I always knew how to solve a problem—I am a Legend after all ... Heh. If my brothers could see me now, they'd lose their minds.

SO, WHAT HAPPENED TO THEM?
That's the problem: we don't really know. All three were on the same dropship going in for an attack near Gaea and they were struck by ... something. We're still unsure what it was. The Solace Military was a mess. If it wasn't for the Syndicate, the rest of us probably wouldn't have survived.

I remember the day we found out, though. Mom and I were working on a contract she had with SARAS to make some sort of holographic search beacon. I guess there had been a few accidents near the Cascade Mountains and they needed something new to help call for help—so, of course, they reached out to me ... well, Ma, but me too.

We were stuck on the visual aspect, which Ma and I usually butted heads on. I prefer something flashy, something decent to look at. I get her side, that it's not important to the functionality ... lify ... the function of the thing, but that doesn't mean it has to be boring. And if there is one thing you know about me, it's that I like to keep things interesting. Remember the Holo-Day Bash on my Mirage Voyage?

YES.
Remember how great it was?

YES.
It was pretty great, right?

YES.
Yeah, such a great time. See, that's what I'm talking about. It can serve a purpose and be good lookin'.

AND WHAT DID YOUR MOM THINK?
Well, let's just say she got the last laugh. The next morning, I went downstairs to the workshop where we did most of our work and standing right there in front of me, next to my mom, was *me*.

That's right. My mom took my advice and turned it up to eleven. The search beacon we were working on was no longer just a holographic SOS sign, but a full, life-size version of the one and only Elliott Witt. Of course, it was just a prank—she reset it back to a normal sign after getting a good laugh in my face.

LIKE YOUR HOLOGRAMS!
That's where it all started. Of course, she only did that one as a joke. That woman was always a fan of a good old-fashioned practical joke. We reprogrammed the real beacon to be something a little more simple, but, like you pointed out, the holographic versions of me became my new toys. While Ma worked on her other projects, I continued to perfect my 'grams. I made them look just like me all the way down to my perfect smile.

Wink.

WHO ARE YOU WINKING TO?

MADE YOU SMILE: A MIRAGE FILM

A STORY OF HOW MIRAGE JOKED AROUND

EXT. CUMMINGS CT. - SOLACE CITY - NIGHT
Smack dab at the end of the cul-de-sac sits the WITT FAMILY HOME, with a crooked mailbox, a rusty old car, and dried-up grass that matches the bright yellow paint that barely covers the exterior of this humble abode.

INT. WITT FAMILY HOME - KITCHEN - NIGHT
The kitchen is a mess, with a sticky puddle of maple syrup and honey on the counter, an empty brown spicy mustard container in the trash, a dirty mixing bowl splattered with the remnants of a savory glaze, and a toppled container of cloves that hopefully did not all make it into the final concoction. EVELYN WITT grabs a tray of glazed pork chops and puts them in the oven.

> EVELYN WITT
> *(shouting)*
> Elliott! Dinner will be ready soon!

A snicker comes from the living room but no response.

> EVELYN WITT
> Elliott?

Evelyn follows the mischievous laughter.

INT. LIVING ROOM - CONTINUOUS
More snickering comes from the cupboard under the stairs.

> EVELYN WITT
> Elliott. C'mon. Seriously?
> You're sixteen, not six.

She opens the door with an "aha" only to be met face to face with...a mirage hologram of her son ELLIOTT WITT.

The world, because they deserve it. But unfortunately, although Ma and I had a nice laugh, the day ended with some suit from Solace Military at our door. Not a general or even a soldier, just some suit. I think the guy worked in accounting or something. He just rang our bell and handed us a piece of paper and said, "Sorry." It said that the Solace transport vessel *Crimson* went down over Gaea—and that, although resources were too limited to verify, a loss of communication for over seventy-two hours made it clear enough to consider all soldiers MIA.

Just like that. A no-name with a piece of paper told my mom that three of her sons were dead.

MIA DOESN'T MEAN DEAD.
They weren't even going to look for them. So, if they weren't dead then, they are now. Still to this day, no bodies have been found or any information. I've even put some money into searching, but other priorities came into play.

LIKE BEING AN APEX LEGEND.
Right . . . that.

Losing her sons really broke my mom. Bothered me, obviously, but I think I focused a lot on my mom so it was easier to forget . . . nah, "forget" isn't the word. It was easier to avoid that sort of pain when you're spending the majority of your day making people laugh—that's what I did with my mom.

WHAT DID YOU DO?
I was about sixteen. I did what I always do—I joked around. I remember it like it was a movie . . .

MIRAGE HOLOGRAM
Wink.

It smiles before it disappears.

EVELYN WITT
(shouting gleefully)
Whoa! C'mon, Elliott! You son of a...ME!
That's it. Show yourself.

Evelyn runs up the stairs to the second floor.

INT. SECOND FLOOR HALLWAY - CONTINUOUS
She steps cautiously and quietly down the hallway toward Elliott's room, the very room he used to share with his twin brothers, Ricky and Elon. The door looks like it was taken off of some kids' clubhouse with a "Do Not Enter" warning carved into the wood at the top.

THUD! Noise comes from the bedroom, but Evelyn's not so easily fooled--this time.

EVELYN WITT
Okay. We got another mirage in here?
Is that your trick, Elliott?

She grasps ahold of the doorknob and feels a beat-driven vibration.

EVELYN WITT (CONT.)
Either you're having a party for one in there, or there are two mirages,
and they're having a party for two.
How's that for math?

She laughs as she opens the door and springs inside to find--

INT. ELLIOTT'S BEDROOM - CONTINUOUS

Not one but TWO MIRAGES doing what they think is breakdancing on the floor.

MIRAGE HOLOGRAM 1

We're a little busy, Ma.

MIRAGE HOLOGRAM 2

Unless you think you've got a move
in you that needs busting...

Evelyn smiles at the two holograms and shakes her head.

EVELYN WITT

No. Not me, Ricky.
Not at my age. Hey, Elon, don't
forget to clean up your side of
the room. And would you two
play with Elliott once in a while?
It would be nice if you included him.

The two mirages quickly disappear, leaving Evelyn staring into the empty room.

ELLIOTT (O.S.)

Mom?

Elliott, having overheard this conversation, steps out of hiding and joins his mom in
the bedroom.

ELLIOTT

Hey, Ma. Who were you talking to?

It takes a second, but Evelyn regains her focus on Elliott.

EVELYN WITT

Hey...um, no one.
Remember when the twins got into
breakdancing? It was so loud and
obnoxious, but also kinda sweet.
It's just...nice to think about them.
It's nice to be reminded of those moments.

ELLIOTT

(concerned)
Yeah. Are you sure you're all right, though?

EVELYN WITT

Me? Yeah. I'm fine. Even better
now that I--FOUND YOU!
(laughing)
You know, I didn't give you those mirages so you could play
jokes on me. Because of that,
you're doing the dishes. Got it?

               ELLIOTT

       Sure thing, Ma. Anything for you.

Elliott tries to brush off what just happened, but part of him is a little concerned. Was that just a walk down memory lane? Or something else?

INT. LIVING ROOM - NEXT DAY

Elliott runs down the stairs to head outside, but stops when he sees his mom reading a book.

               ELLIOTT

        Hey, Ma, I'm headed out to
        play some ball with the guys.

             EVELYN WITT

      Sure thing, Elliott. Have fun.

Usually this is something Elliott does with his brother Elon, but neither of them bring this up. Elliott's surprised by this.

               ELLIOTT

     Do you need me to get anything on my way home?

Evelyn stops reading and looks at Elliott.

             EVELYN WITT

     I'm good. Do you need anything?

               ELLIOTT

         I'm all good.

There's a brief moment of awkwardness.

           ELLIOTT (CONT.)

        Okay. See ya, Ma.

EXT. WITT FAMILY HOME - CONTINUOUS

Elliott walks outside and slowly closes the door behind him.

               ELLIOTT

         (to himself)

       That was weird. I coulda
     sworn she was going to bring up
     Elon. Nothing...not even a smile.

And then he has an idea...

INT. LIVING ROOM - A FEW MOMENTS LATER

Evelyn finishes reading her book. Elliott comes walking back in acting like his normal goofball self.

               ELLIOTT

         Hey, Ma,

> Elon and I are going to
> go to play some ball,
> if that's all right?

Evelyn looks up to see Elliott followed by his MIRAGE. She pauses for an uncertain moment, then smiles.

                    EVELYN WITT
           Of course, honey. Of course. Just
           do me a favor and don't rip
           those shorts again like you did
           last time. They took too much
           effort to fix, and I've got a book to read.

                    ELLIOTT
           Yeah. Don't worry. I won't.
           This time I'll win, unlike last time.
           Elon got like four alley-oops;
                   it was amazing.

Evelyn smiles. Elliott leaves through the front door.

EXT. WITT FAMILY HOME - CONTINUOUS
Elliott closes the door and looks at his mirage.

                    ELLIOTT
                (proud, amazed)
                   Huh...

For the next few weeks, Elliott continues to fill the house with mirages that help spark conversations about his brothers.

INT. ROGER'S BEDROOM - WEEK 1
Elliott is playing guitar with a mirage set up to look like his older brother ROGER. Evelyn walks by.

                    ELLIOTT
           Hey, Ma, we're just jammin'.

She smiles.

INT. KITCHEN - WEEK 2
Elliott attempts to cook Leviathan stew with his "brother" Ricky, who always had a knack for cooking. Evelyn comes home from work.

                    ELLIOTT
                (shouting)
           Hey, Ma, sorry, but we kind of screwed up dinner.

She smiles.

INT. BATHROOM - WEEK 3

Elliott projects all three mirages fighting over the bathroom.

> **ELLIOTT**
> C'mon. Get off of me!

He smirks, knowing that his mom is coming right around the corner.

> **EVELYN WITT**
> Elliott? Are you okay?
> What's going on?

She sees all four of her sons crammed into the bathroom. Though the mirages are obviously holograms, as each of them start flickering.

She smiles, but it's short.

> **EVELYN WITT**
> Glad you're okay, honey.
> I have work to do, I'll
> be in my workshop.

She leaves. Elliott's smile falls.

> **ELLIOTT**
> *(to his mirages)*
> That was different.
> Why was that different?
> *(realizing)*
> Oh no...I think I'm making it worse.

Elliott's mirages shrug their shoulders: "I don't know." They disappear, and Elliott takes a deep breath with a stern nod.

INT. WORKSHOP IN THE BASEMENT - MOMENTS LATER
Elliott creeps down the stairs.

> **ELLIOTT**
> Hey, Ma. It's me--Elliott.

> **EVELYN WITT**
> I know, honey. What's going on?
> I'm almost done here,
> if you want to get dinner started.

Evelyn types a few words into her computer while trading off sightlines between the monitor and her son.

> **ELLIOTT**
> I...
> Um...
> This is a parculi...
> particu...par...

this is a weird situation.
I'm not sure how to say this,
or if I should say this,
or if I should call a doctor.

EVELYN WITT

Honey. You can say anything to me.

Evelyn now gives her son her complete attention.

ELLIOTT

I think I've done something bad to you.
Something really bad.

EVELYN WITT

Honey. What are you talking about?

ELLIOTT

Okay...So, the past few weeks,
I've been pretending that Ricky, Elon, and Roger were still here.
They're not.
(takes a deep breath)
They're gone and they're not coming back.

EVELYN WITT

Honey, I know.

ELLIOTT

Do you?
I think there is something
wrong with you, and I don't know
how to fix it. I think I made it worse,
and I was just trying to make you happy.

Evelyn stands up and walks to her son, who is almost shaking with fear and sadness.

EVELYN WITT

No, you didn't.

ELLIOTT

I didn't make you happy?

EVELYN WITT

(laughs)
No, you silly boy. Of course you made me happy.
You always make me happy.
But, honey,
I knew what you were doing.
I just had no idea that you were doing it for me.
I thought you were doing it for you.

ELLIOTT

(bewildered)
What? What do you mean?

EVELYN WITT

I guess I thought it made you happy to
pretend that your brothers were still
around. That's why I went along with it.
I felt like that was the only way
you felt comfortable talking about them.

ELLIOTT

And I thought it was the only way
I could get you to talk about them.
It wasn't until you saw them in
my mirages. You thought
they were the twins. Didn't you?

EVELYN WITT

Yes. I did.
That night something did
happen to me, but it wasn't the first
time, and it won't be the last.
But there is *nothing* for you to worry
about, Elliott. I'm taking care of
myself. I will be okay--I promise.

ELLIOTT

You will?

EVELYN WITT

Yes, honey.
And I will always be here for you.
I'm sorry you got worried that night.
I'm sorry you thought I didn't
want to talk about them. Of course
I do. We are here for each other.
And we don't need your mirages to
talk about them. If you want to talk
about the time Ricky tried to make
pork chops using practically nothing but
cinnamon and cloves, I'm happy to.
If you want to talk about the
time Elon accidentally got his head
stuck in a pumpkin for five hours,
I'm ready, and I've got pictures.
If you want to talk about the time Roger
tickled you until you went number two
in your pants--

ELLIOTT

(interjecting)
I-I don't remember that actually happening...

EVELYN WITT

I will drop everything in a
heartbeat because I love talking about
my sons. I love talking to you.
I love you, Elliott. And you never
have to try to make me happy,
because you being my son is enough
to make me happy the rest of my life.
I'm your number one fan--no matter what.

She holds out her arms, welcoming Elliott into them.

He goes in for the hug.

ELLIOTT

I love you, too, Ma.
Thanks for not getting mad at me.

EVELYN WITT

Oh, you're totally grounded for a month.

Elliott pulls back in shock.

ELLIOTT

What?! That's totally unfair!

EVELYN WITT

(laughing)
Just kidding! Yeesh--you've
got to learn to take a joke.

She smiles.

(End)

AND DID YOU?
Did I what?

LEARN HOW TO TAKE A JOKE?
Heh. Yeah. I think so. I definitely get my sense of humor from my mom. And she's right. She's doing great. We still talk about my brothers all the time, and it hurts to know that now with the war over, we still don't know what happened to them. I don't know if we ever will. All the planets in Syndicate Space may have signed that treaty ten years ago, but that doesn't mean everyone is buddy-buddy.

These planets here have never really gotten along. And this goes back to like a hundred years ago or so. Definitely before the crisis. I think even longer. It's all about power and greed and—

I'M SORRY. WHAT CRISIS?
Back in 2655—the energy crisis. Did . . . do you not know about that? I thought that was public knowledge, but maybe I just knew about it because my mom kept talking about how it could have been the end of the Outlands as we know it.

WHAT HAPPENED?

Uh . . . let's see if I can remember. I remember something about someone named Peck who kept talking about how the Outlands was running out of energy. I think she believed they had about ten years left in them before everything went downhill. From what Ma said, no one believed Peck until it was too late. I guess all the planets in Syndicate Space and the Fringe Worlds figured they had other things to worry about than some wild and crazy theories about what could happen ten years in the future. The sad part is that she was right.

All those planets didn't do anything, and they paid for it, because after a few years, the crisis began to unfold. If you weren't a millionaire, then you wouldn't have had any chance getting fuel for a ship or even hot water for your one bedroom. My Ma said that Solace had a very small reserve of energy, and it was practically gone until something happened that pretty much stabal . . . stabil—helped things get back to normal.

I THOUGHT YOU SAID IT WOULD HAVE BEEN THE END OF THE OUTLANDS?

Yeah. That's what they thought, but something happened. This is what always intrigued my mom. I remember she had books and books of theories about what happened, but nobody really knew the truth. One day death was knockin' on the front door, the next it was knockin' on the back door . . . to get out of the house. Like it was trying to leave . . . I think I screwed up this analogy, but you get the point. It was bad and then some event happened and things were back to normal.

SOME EVENT? WAS IT "THE EVENT"?

I don't know the difference, but sure? If that makes you happy.

IT DOES! IT REALLY DOES! I COULD HAVE BEEN THE EVENT THAT HELPED ALMOST DESTROY THE OUTLANDS!

That doesn't sound great . . . but, sure. You know, if you're really looking for info on that stuff, I'd try to find Bloodhound. Our parents worked together on some secret IMC project that I think had something to do with the Event a long time ago. Ma loves bringing up how the IMC was more obsessed with secret stuff

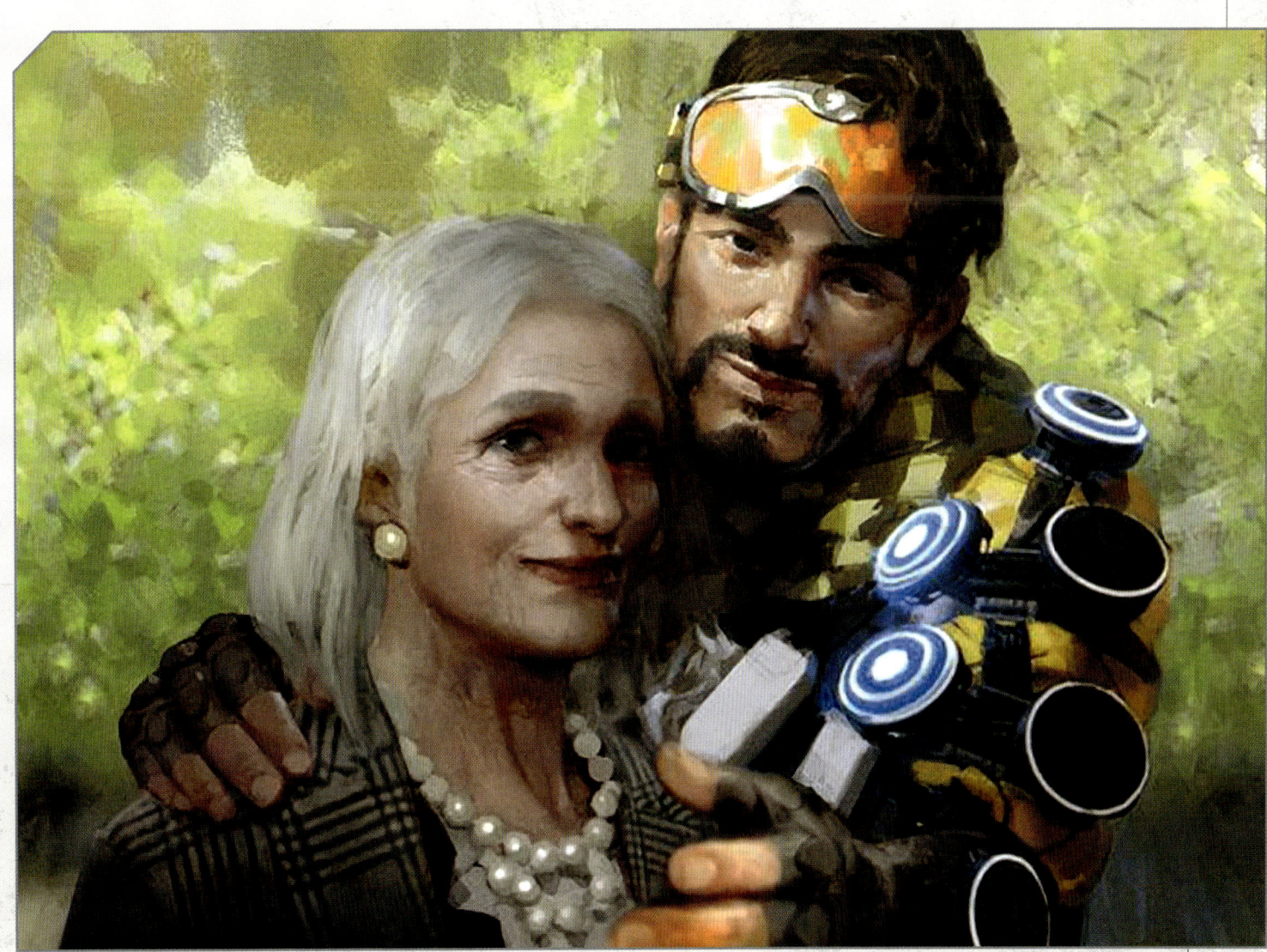

ELLIOTT AND HIS BELOVED MOTHER, EVELYN.

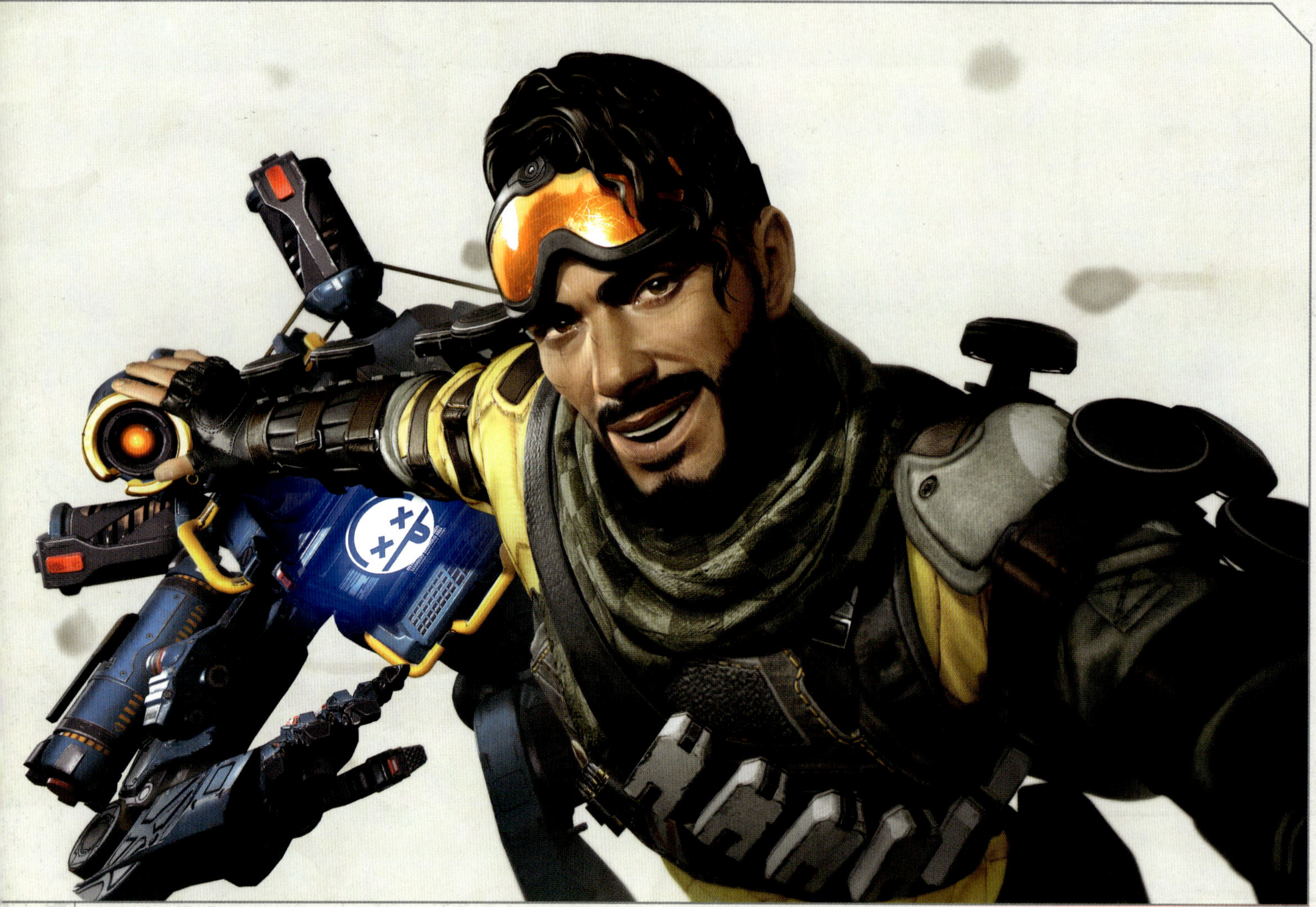

ME AND MY BEST FRIEND!

LOADING . . . TRANSCRIPTION:/ 0000101

than I am with my hair. She also loves bringing up how she was friends with Bloodhound's mom every time that hunter kicks my butt. "You know, I was friends with their mom." She's one funny lady. Anyways, we were both pretty young at the time, so I don't remember much, but I'm sure they know a thing or two about what our moms were working on, since the project was not only on Talos, where Bloodhound grew up, but it was also the project that, you know . . . cost them the price . . . I mean, they lost the price . . . I mean, um . . . their parents died. Sorry, didn't know how to really say that, and last time I brought it up to Bloodhound, they didn't really like talking about it. But you've got a way of getting anyone to open up, so I'm sure you'll be fine. Let's just hope you don't have to talk to Caustic—I'd hate to hear about the skeletons in his closet. *Oof!*

I AGREE! YOU'RE RIGHT, THAT'S GOING TO BE A SAD CONVERSATION WITH BLOODHOUND, BUT THAT'S OKAY, BECAUSE I LIKE TALKING TO MY FRIENDS. THIS HAS BEEN VERY HELPFUL. THANKS SO MUCH.

Yeah. Yeah. Don't mention it. Seriously, though. Try to keep some of the stuff I told you between us, if you don't mind.

LIKE A SPECIAL FRIENDSHIP SECRET?

Uh . . . yeah . . . sure . . . I just got a reputation to keep up, and I don't need everyone getting all up in my . . . I like who I am now.

I LIKE YOU TOO, BEST FRIEND.

Thanks. And good luck, buddy.

BUDDY?!

I mean, Pathfinder . . . just get out of here, you crazy tin can.

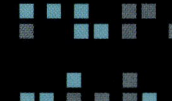

DATA POINTS RECEIVED

- Mirage, a.k.a. Elliott Witt, is still my best friend!

- Kuben Blisk's last Thunderdome match was in 2710. Interesting.

- Evelyn Witt is Mirage's mom. She's the smartest person he knows and one of the best holoengineers in the entire Frontier.

- Richard Witt is Mirage's dad. He wasn't around much.

- The Outlands civil war began around 2716 after the IMC pulled all authority from the Outlands.

- Roger Witt, Elon Witt, and Ricky Witt went MIA during the civil war after their dropship was attacked somewhere near Gaea, leaving Evelyn Witt and Elliott Witt alone on Solace.

- An energy crisis occurred in 2655.

  > A woman named Peck believed the Outlands had ten years left to find a solution before the point of no return.

  > Something happened that stabilized the energy resources of the Outlands.

    ∆ This something is "the Event" from the message.

- Bloodhound may have more information, because their parents were working on a secret project related to the Event.

- Bloodhound's parents knew Mirage's mom. They worked together in the past.

- Mirage called me his "buddy," and I like that.

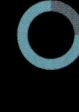
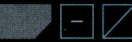

INNER MONOLOGUE ACTIVATED...

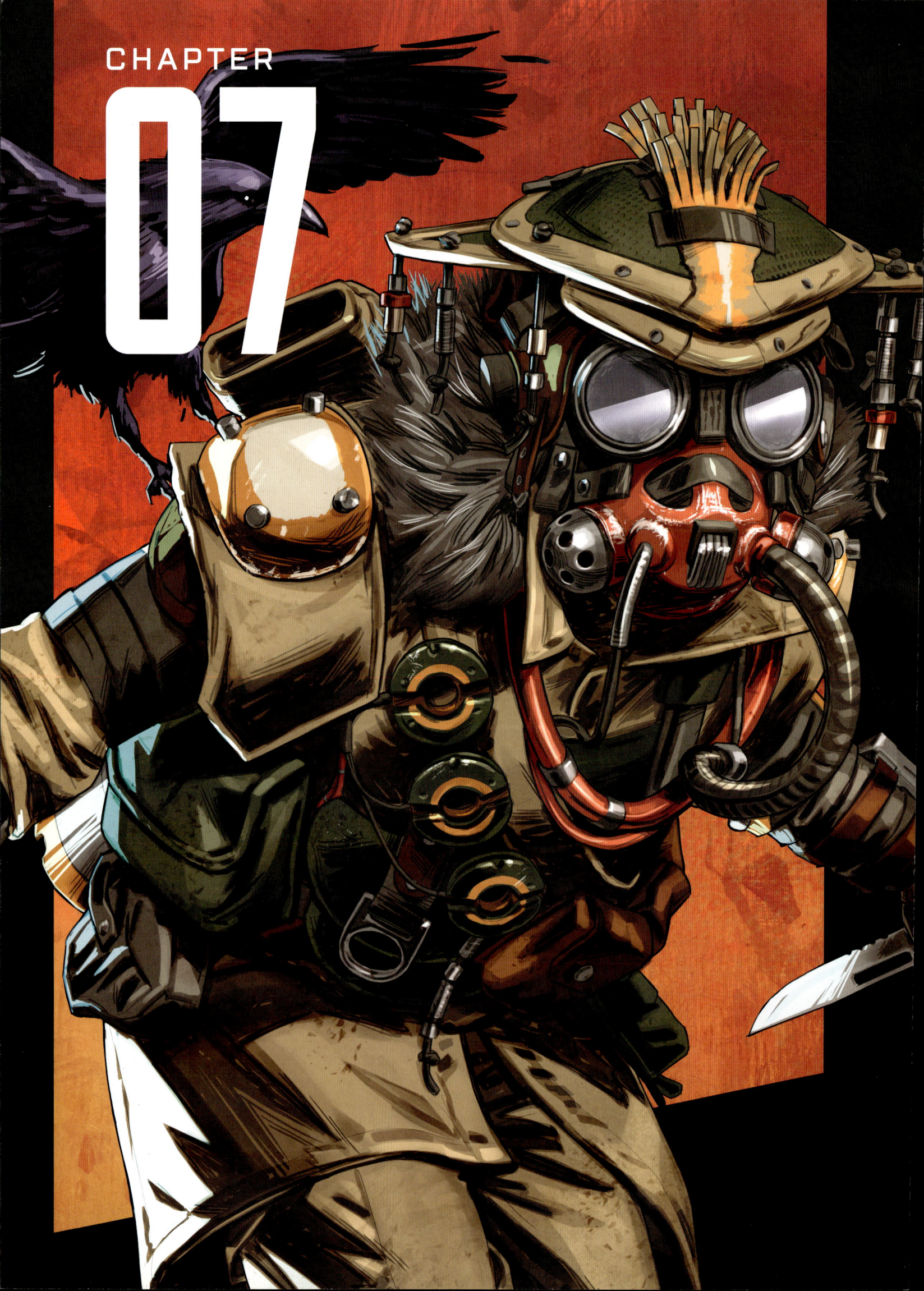

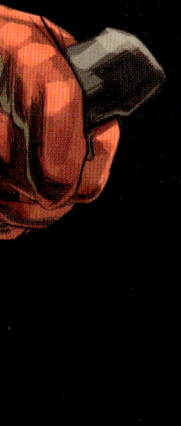

FROZEN
IN TIME

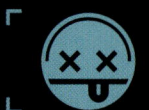
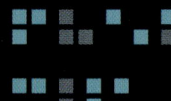
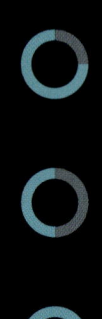

PATHFINDER MEMORY LOG: DAY 7

Wow, that was fun! I love talking to my best friend Mirage, and it was nice to learn more about him, because that's what friends do. Now that we've done it more, we're even better friends, mathematically! But I'm sad that his brothers went missing in the civil war because everyone decided to fight over things instead of being friends. If everyone had shared and worked together, Mirage's brothers would see how great he is, and he could still play piano not so well with them, and Mirage's mom would be extra happy, which would be nice.

I said yesterday that I want everyone to put their differences aside and get along, and I'm saying it even harder today! Maybe I can help—I like getting along with everyone. Maybe that's what my creator made me for, if they programmed me to feel that way. I hope so.

It makes me extra sad that the planets in the Outlands don't get along, because they all had the same problem almost a hundred years ago. It sounds like everyone was almost in big trouble, but then they weren't, because the Event saved everyone. That is very confusing, but Mirage said Bloodhound can explain it to me.

No one's really sure where Bloodhound lives, because Talos is mostly volcanoes and ice and icy volcanoes, which are illogical. But I asked a bunch of friends, and got a bunch of clues, and put all the clues together—and then Bloodhound found out I was asking about them and sent me a message with directions to their village on Talos. Hooray!

CLUE BOX

TRANSMISSION CLUES
- "Chevrex" > LIFELINE'S PARENTS' COMPANY
- "The future of the Outlands" > OLD EXPERIMENTS TO CHANGE THE FUTURE
- "Dr. Amélie Pa—— [Paquette]" > WATTSON'S GRANDMOTHER, A GEOLOGIST, DIED MYSTERIOUSLY
- "The Event" > AN EVENT THAT ENDED THE ENERGY CRISIS SEVENTY-FIVE YEARS AGO, NEED MORE INFO
- "Aleki" > GIBRALTAR'S GRANDFATHER
- "Iris" > PROJECT: IRIS, CREATED IN 2654

SELF-MOTIVATION QUOTE . . . SEARCHING . . . 1 RESULT FOUND

"Hearts will never be practical until they are made unbreakable."
—[THE TIN MAN, *THE WIZARD OF OZ*]

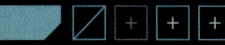

BLOODHOUND BIO FROM THE APEX GAMES

3X [TARGET THREAT] 0%

ULTIMATE OBJECTIVE . . . SEEKING CREATOR

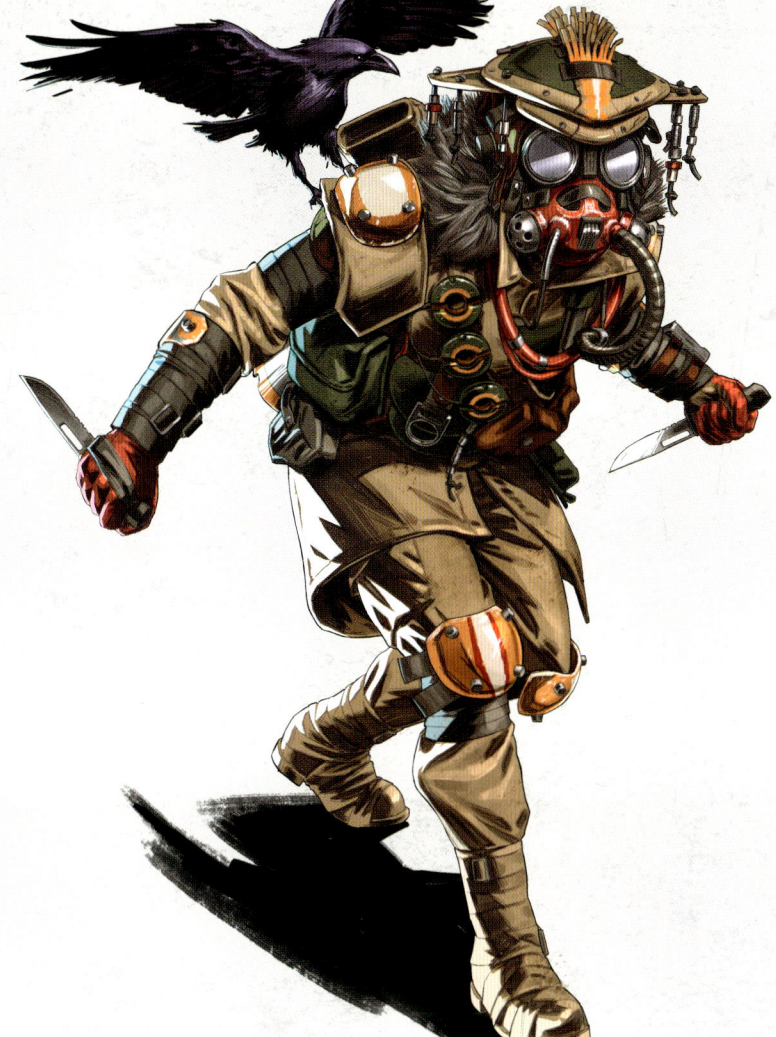

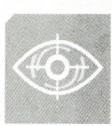
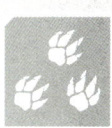
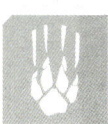

REAL NAME:
UNKNOWN

AGE:
UNKNOWN

HOME WORLD:
TALOS

TACTICAL ABILITY:
EYE OF THE ALLFATHER

PASSIVE ABILITY:
TRACKER

ULTIMATE ABILITY:
BEAST OF THE HUNT

BLOODHOUND IS KNOWN ACROSS THE OUTLANDS AS ONE OF THE GREATEST GAME HUNTERS THE FRONTIER HAS EVER SEEN—AND THAT'S ABOUT ALL ANYONE KNOWS. Their identity is a mystery wrapped in layers of rumors: they are fabulously wealthy, a bloodthirsty murderer, a Goliath whisperer, a former slave, half bat, and a dozen other things, depending on who's doing the whispering.

All anyone truly knows is that Bloodhound is a force to be reckoned with in the Apex Games. Bloodhound's unparalleled tracking skills are a boon to any team they join, helping them root out hidden opponents and track the enemy's movements. Calling on Earth's old Norse gods to guide them, Bloodhound believes that destiny is a path that has already been laid out, eventually carrying all to their death. But with that knowledge comes strength, because until that day comes, Bloodhound knows they can't be stopped.

"I am the hunter the gods have sent."
—BLOODHOUND

► HELLO, FRIEND! ◄

THANK YOU FOR TELLING ME WHERE YOU ARE. YOUR VILLAGE IS VERY NICE.
Velkominn, velafolk. I thank you. Though I was surprised to hear you were searching for me. I do not believe we have exchanged many words.

YOU'RE RIGHT—I HAVE A TALLY, AND IT'S NOT VERY MANY. BUT I THOUGHT YOU DIDN'T LIKE ME, SO I DID MY BEST TO LEAVE YOU ALONE.
…Pardon? Why did you believe such a thing?

WAS I WRONG? I WILL BE HAPPY TO BE WRONG.
I…don't feel strongly toward you, truly. Neither kinship nor rancor.

OH. BECAUSE YOUR BIRD ATTACKS ME SOMETIMES. I THOUGHT IF HE DOESN'T LIKE ME, YOU DON'T EITHER.
Artur does not take kindly to those who raise a hand to him. Nor do I, now that you have reminded me.

OH NO, I RAISE A HAND TO HIGH-FIVE PEOPLE. IS THAT BAD?
Raise a hand to *strike*.

BUT I ONLY DID THAT BECAUSE HE WAS PECKING ME.
Perhaps you did something else to earn his *reiði*.

I DON'T THINK I DID . . .
Then we must agree to disagree. But let us put this aside. Today, you are my honored guest. Now, why have you come?

WELL, YESTERDAY I WAS TALKING TO MY BEST FRIEND MIRAGE, AND HE SAID HIS MOM KNEW YOUR MOM, AND YOU COULD TELL ME ABOUT THE EVENT!
…Ah, the *miklimunnr*. Yes, he has spoken to me of this as well. My mother was a mechanical engineer, and it seems she and Evelyn Witt collaborated on a prototype for the IMC in years past. He found that amusing, that we were *tengdur* in this way, and joked that they forced our hand—that the pressure on us to succeed is vast. I reminded him that I lost my mother when I was a child in the disaster that destroyed World's Edge. When we do battle, we walk across the very ice that ended her life.

He babbled for many moments without forming a single word. I found *that* amusing.

But the Event? I know not of what you speak.

OH NO, THAT'S NOT GOOD! I NEED TO KNOW ABOUT THE EVENT SO I CAN FIND MY CREATOR. MIRAGE SAID YOU WOULD KNOW ABOUT IT.
Hmph, when it would be a benefit for him to speak at length, he does not. Did he say nothing else of it?

JUST THAT THERE WAS AN ENERGY CRISIS, AND IT WAS GOING TO DESTROY THE OUTLANDS, BUT THEN THE EVENT HAPPENED AND EVERYTHING TURNED OUT OKAY. WHICH IS GOOD! I'M GLAD EVERYONE DIDN'T DIE.
Hmm. Perhaps he speaks of the discovery of branthium. That was the concern of my kin.

MAYBE! WHICH IS BETTER THAN NO!

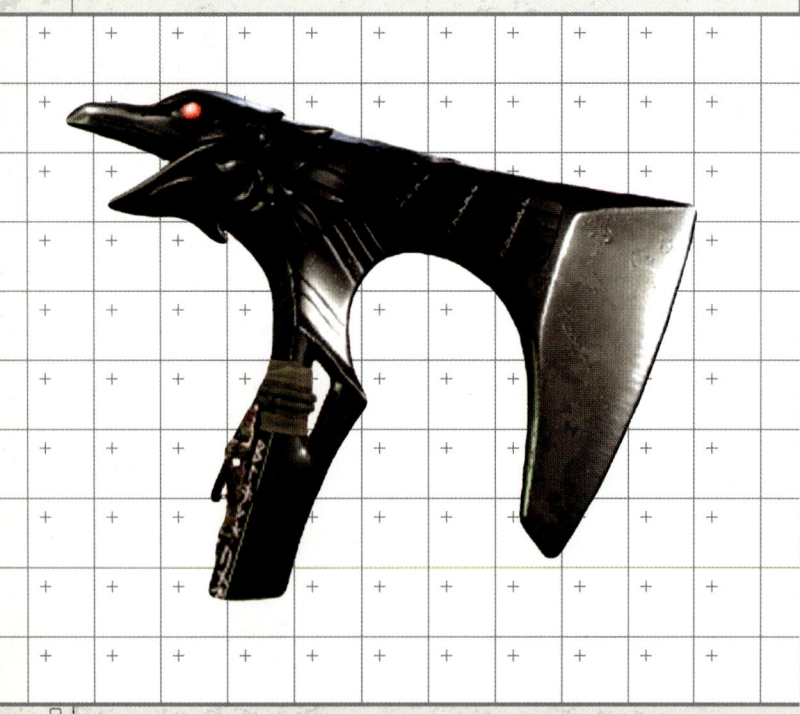

* BLOODHOUND'S AXE WAS GIVEN TO THEM BY THEIR UNCLE ARTUR.

[TRANSLATION NOTES]

Bloodhound says strange things sometimes. I asked if they don't know the right words in English, but they said they just like their words more. Confusing, but interesting! I'm translating them here so I remember what they mean:

miklimunnr = *bigmouth*   **tengdur** = *related*   **velkominn** = *welcome*
reiði = *anger*   **velafolk** = *machine person*

It is an old story, and it is as your friend says: in days long past, the Outlands were rich with resources, but sapped of energy reserves. The IMC had drained all with little thought for the future, for their future did not lie here. World's Edge is a testament to such *ágirni*. This world was wild and burned with potent heat; they doused the flames that guarded its heart, so they might *taka*.

IS THAT WHAT THE ICE WAS FOR? AND WHAT IS A PLANET HEART MADE OF? I KNOW WHAT A HUMAN HEART LOOKS LIKE, AND I DON'T THINK I WANT TO SEE ONE THAT IS PLANET SIZED.
Be silent and listen, if you wish to know the story.

[. . .]
Thank you. In those times, the IMC *taka* all, and those who endured battled over the remains. Our doom was promised. But in that dark hour, the gods blessed us with branthium.

It is a dense mineral, black as obsidian, that takes the shape of sandy grains, or gleaming crystals when held to heat and pressure. Within, it bears a great store of energy—a single grain can burn for thirty days if undisturbed. Such power could only come from millennia spent pressed beneath the earth, but no record of it existed one hundred years ago. Less. There was none before . . . 2658, I believe. It simply appeared. Vast heaps of branthium were discovered upon Solace, Gaea, Psamathe, as high and wide as a Leviathan skull.

A supply to last centuries, yearned for one day and *gipt* from the heavens the next. It is a boon from the Allfather himself.

WOW, THAT'S AMAZING, FRIEND! AND YOU KNOW SO MUCH ABOUT IT. THAT'S AMAZING, TOO.
You flatter me. I learned by scouring the remains of World's Edge for . . . for relics from my mother and father's age. There were *herr* records to be found, many among my father's belongings. Secret IMC documents that explained much.

EXCITING! ARE YOU AND YOUR FAMILY TREASURE HUNTERS?

That is . . . an amusing thought. No—my mother and father were scientists. After the branthium appeared, the IMC and many others were quick to collect it. The IMC scoured this world too, searching for the *gipt*, but found none. It was only thirty years ago that the mineral was discovered here, dispersed amid the molten rock. It was believed this world could provide some clue to the mineral's origin.

The IMC built a vast industrial coolant plant which hardened the magma and crystallized the branthium within. They christened it New Dawn with hope in their hearts—but with *stórlátr*, too.

My father served the IMC; he was a fuel engineer, one among many to study the *gipt* and divine how best to extract it. It seemed a work of fate that his brother— my uncle Artur—had chosen Talos as his dwelling place some years before. Even back then, my uncle had no love for *taekni*. I was told he was *ódr* when New Dawn rose above the horizon, and the town of World's Edge followed. But it seems my father accepted this sign that Talos would be a true home to us, rife with *kind* and *sæla*.

I recall little of that time, for I was quite small. I remember my father returning home at sunset each day, bearing the *lykt* of earth. My mother would teach me to repair toys that had broken. She had a tense accord with my uncle—I did not understand then, but I know now that he *hath* her life's work, and she his creed. But even still, I remember happiness. Our life was simple, but I wanted for nothing.

I remember the disaster just as well. The conquerors were hasty, and would not be kept from their *haust*. From daybreak to dusk, New Dawn never grew quiet. One day, like a beast forced to run with no rest, it could no longer bear its burden. It unleashed a great wave of ice that froze all in its path. My mother and father were lost in the *banvænn* frost. I may have perished too, had Uncle Artur not braved the ice and found me in our home.

THAT IS VERY SAD! I'M SORRY, FRIEND.
Guilt rests not with you, *velafolk*. Nor with *taekni*, though my uncle saw it so. He became bitter in his hatred of it. He was a wise and fair leader, but in this, I believe mourning for my father, his brother, made him harsh.

[TRANSLATION NOTES]

ágirni = greed	**herr** = numerous	**sæla** = prosperity
banvænn = deadly	**kind** = kinship	**taka** = take
gipt = gift	**lykt** = scent	**taekni** = technology
hath = hate	**ódr** = furious, wrathful	
haust = harvest	**stórlátr** = arrogance	

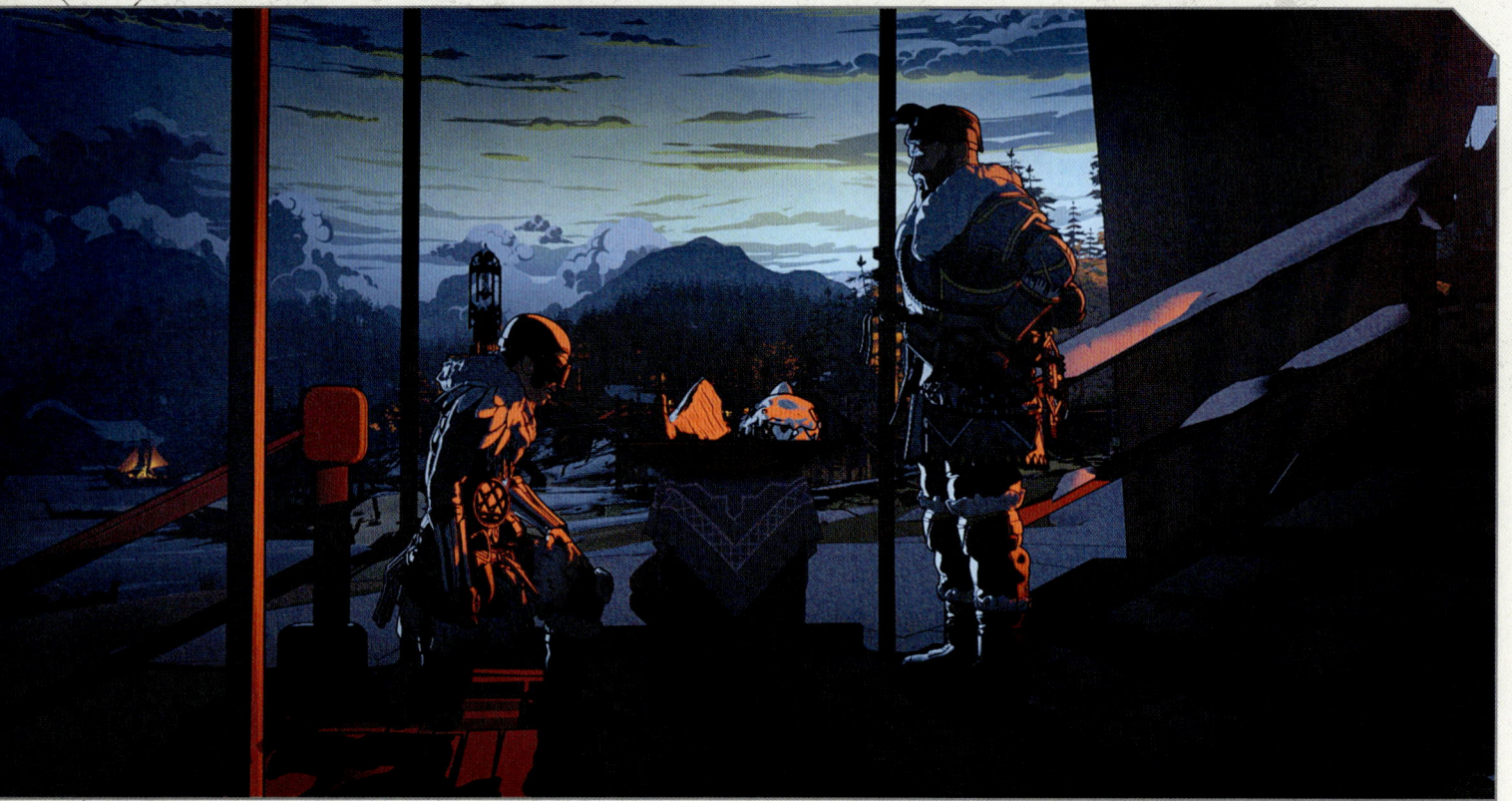

Even as a child I did not blame *vel*. New Dawn was no more than a tool. Its wielders were ungrateful for the miracle of branthium. In the end, they lost what they treasured most—what branthium still remained was trapped deep within the belly of Talos. The new Hammond unearths it now, but if they falter, they too will suffer. The fate of World's Edge will befall all those who forget themselves before the gods.

Those who followed my uncle rejected *taekni* out of fear. As I grew, we used only what could be recovered from the ruins of World's Edge. Any prize more *velkin* than a light bulb was forbidden. But the truth beat in my *bloth*. In time, I . . . I believe I changed my uncle's heart, too. But that is a tale for another day.

SO YOU HAVE NO TECHNOLOGY AT ALL? THAT IS VERY INTERESTING— AND UNCOMFORTABLE, SINCE I AM TECHNOLOGY.
Ah, that is no longer so. My people began to adopt *tækni* in time.

OOH, EXCITING! THAT IS LESS UNCOMFORTABLE.
Indeed, it was some twenty winters ago, though it is

difficult to know—one cannot track a season easily when you are many worlds away. Three winters after Uncle Artur's passing. Our *felagi* people did not open their hearts to *tækni* so quickly, but they were swayed by my words, and the demise of the *jǫtun*—a great beast which plagued our village, and fell against the joining of the old ways and the new.

I had not the years to act as a full leader, but my people trusted the wisdom of my line. I knew the tools the Allfather *gipt* would not lead us astray. We had always collected metal to build our homes and plastics for our *klæði*, but now we gathered generators and electric lamps. We began repairing broken *tækni*, as much as we were able. We were most fortunate to find and restore a transmitter, and used it to signal passing vessels from which we sought trade and knowledge.

Visitors were few, but to us it felt *herr*. A troop of wandering ecologists, a satellite engineer low on fuel, an excitable journalist, a strange grenadier. In time I began to yearn for the arrival of *ókunn* and their stories, and my village seemed to grow smaller with each new tale.

But the one who held my attention was Boone. He was a tracker, a *mjǫk hærðr* with night-black hair and

[TRANSLATION NOTES]

bloth = *blood*	**klæði** = *simple clothes*	**vel** = *machines*
felagi = *fellow*	**mjǫk hærðr** = *one with abundant hair*	**velkin** = *machine-like*
jǫtun = *Goliath*	**ókunn** = *unknown people*	

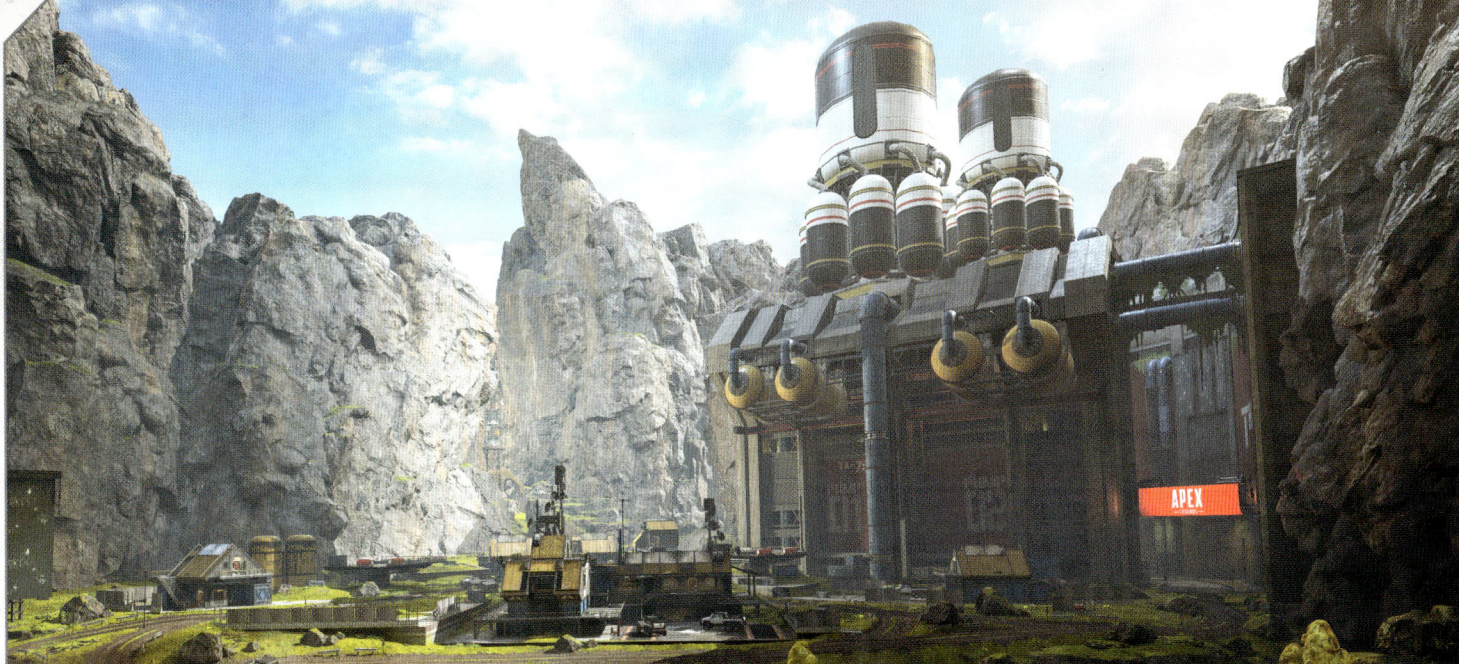

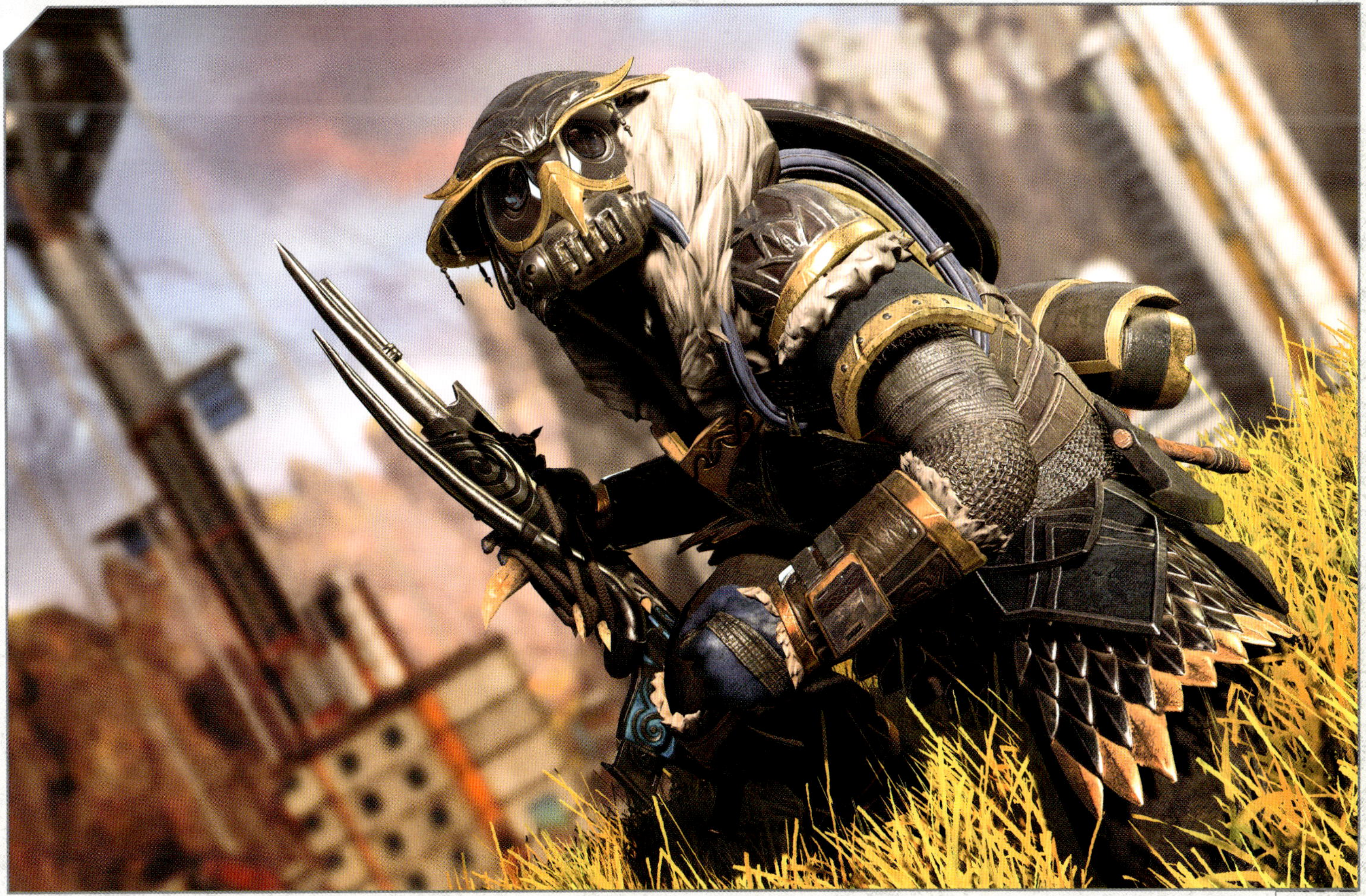

* ARTUR'S ARMOR.

a sharp chin. His ship was no larger than a *salr*, yet it bore many magnificent trophies, and he wore nearly as many. He carried a strange blade and spectacles that, together, showed him beasts hidden in the shadows. They were lit in pulses, like a heartbeat.

Unlike the others, he came not to haggle or gawk, but

to hunt. He fascinated me.

…But that was long ago now, and…it did not end happily. You have well enough for your answer.

BUT, FRIEND, I WANT TO HEAR THE REST OF THE STORY. YOU SEEMED REALLY

THE LONG WINTER

A PRIVATE STORY FROM BLOODHOUND

That autumn, Boone requested passage to hunt on our *skog-land*. I spoke to him only briefly at first, but learned he was known across the Outlands for tracking rare beasts. He stayed with us for some time, and would often emerge long after dark bearing a Prowler or wild bird. But I could see the frustration across his brow. The beast he sought eluded him.

I was...compelled to offer aid.

He was cautious. He did not know me, or what I could provide him. But I knew that a hunter is not made by their weapon. All my years I hunted this *skogr*, and I could be an invaluable guide.

He deliberated. I was to tell no one--the prize was too precious, and others would seek to trespass. But in time, he yielded; our hunt would begin at dawn. Not for the beast he truly sought, but minor creatures, for I would be tested and my loyalty proven. His doubt in me was a blade to the breast until he offered me use of his tools. For those, and his company, I obliged.

We cooperated in this way for a time. I made great use of the tools, prying the shapes of beasts out of the shadows. Boone and I grew... close. His guard fell as he became comfortable in my presence. He would *kvisa* instructions, only to have them grow into jest on his lips. Once, by some flight of fancy, he leapt into a *kaldr* pond only for the pleasure of drawing me in with him. It was a *gleði* I did not know until then.

My *felagi* people looked to me for guidance-- an honor, but it came with the burden of silence. With him, I could speak freely. When he learned what became of my kin, he understood, for such tragedy was not unfamiliar to him. He

was unmoved by the scars beneath this *grima* and *klæði*. He had many of his own.

It was a pleasant autumn. I will always cherish that time.

THAT SOUNDS NICE! ARE YOU SURE YOU AREN'T REMEMBERING ANOTHER SAD THING? THIS IS A VERY HAPPY STORY.
Hmph. You speak hastily, *velafolk*. You should open your ears before your mouth.

OH DEAR. I DON'T HAVE EITHER OF THOSE.
[*Sigh*] I will explain.

One day, Boone relented and spoke to me of the *óséður*. It was a rare beast with the sinew of a feline and an amphibian's slippery film. He said it moved with incredible speed, and its skin could render it invisible to even the keenest eye. His tools helped little--in all his time in our *skogr*, he marked it only a moment before its trace vanished. Even prints did not serve, for the *óséður* was fleet of foot and left tracks like a dragonfly on water.

It was many days later, as we huddled by a flame against the cold, that I thought of heat. It remained in the prints, and would pour from such a robust creature. I had heard of devices which detected heat like a mist. Could his tools be modified to mark the same?

We promised a passing trader a hundred hides in exchange for the parts we'd need to modify

[TRANSLATION NOTES]

gleði = *joy*	**kvisa** = *speak quietly*	**skog-land** = *well-wooded land*
grima = *mask*	**óséður** = *unknown one*	**skogr** = *forest*
kaldr = *frigid*	**salr** = *one-room dwelling*	

EXCITED TO TELL IT!
I . . . you are mistaken, I assure you.

I AM STILL EXCITED TO HEAR IT, THOUGH. AND I WANT TO KNOW WHAT HAPPENED TO YOUR FRIEND.
[*Pause*] That is my burden to bear.

I CAN BEAR IT WITH YOU. I LIKE CARRYING THINGS PLACES.
[*Pause*] You swear this will remain private.

OF COURSE! IT'S GOING IN MY BOOK, WHICH IS JUST FOR ME TO READ.
[*Very long pause*] Okay.

Boone's tools. The pieces were many weeks away, so we continued the hunt, seeking out tracks to determine the span of its hunting ground. We spoke of the future. When this hunt was over, Boone would depart in search of the next rare creature--and he wished for me to go with him. I was not eager to leave my people, but with all I had learned, the village felt *smar*. And to hunt across the Outlands, at his side...

Days after winter took the *skog-land*, the pieces arrived. Boone's tools had always fascinated me, but as he attached the new parts, they became something *vænn*. I thought my heart would erupt when he presented them to me as a *gipt*. They were the work of my knowledge, he said. I should be the one to wield them.

THAT WAS VERY NICE OF HIM! HE SOUNDS LIKE A GOOD FRIEND.
Hmm. An *elskhugi*.

THEN YOU DEFEATED THE O-SEE-EH-THUR IN AN EPIC BATTLE?
You have a simple understanding of things. Life is not so *duttlungafullur*.

THAT IS A VERY LONG WORD. IT SOUNDS EXCITING. WAS THE FIGHT EXCITING TOO?
The battle did not occur that day.

[TRANSLATION NOTES]

bjóða = *order*
duttlungafullur = *whimsical*
elskhugi = *very good friend*
itsanna = *truth*
smar = *small*
vænn = *beautiful*

I donned the *tækni--sónar*, we called it-- and scoured the beast's hunting ground. Its burrow nearly eluded us, but in the cold sweep of winter, a flicker of heat was enough to lead us to it. And there was little more than that, for when we found the *óséður*--lithe and wiry, just as Boone described it--it was deep in hibernation.

I was saddened. I knew the hunt must cease until spring. But Boone...that is when I should have seen the dreadful *itsanna*. He was pleased. He said it would be easier to take the creature alive this way, and an arena on the planet Solace would pay generously for it. It was disturbing. Exploiting a creature that could not defend itself? I did not understand. I had believed Boone honored the hunt--yet now he disgraced it without thought.

We argued. Loudly. I forbade him from capturing a dormant beast on our lands. I... do not remember all that was said, but I cannot forget that it was cruel. We departed on poor terms.

OH NO, THERE *IS* A SAD PART.
Yes. Shrewd of you.

I expected to speak with him again at sunrise, after the night had cooled our tempers. But when I woke, the ground stood empty where his ship once rested, as did the *óséður* nest. I...I have never felt such rage. The *bloth* burned within me.

I begged all to tell me where he had gone, but he had spoken with no one. When I was on the edge of my temper, a trader told me he witnessed Boone's departure at first light. I boarded his ship and requested he pursue... *bjóða*, perhaps.

I remember moments of the trip fondly-- my first pilgrimage away from my home world. The constellations, the light of stars brushing quiet planets. It was *vænn*. I would have savored it more had ship sickness and nerves not kept my gaze at the bottom of a *bytta*. I curse Boone for that to this day.

His trail took us to Solace, and I recalled his talk of the arena. The trader knew it well--it bore great fame, and rested on an island near the world's largest city. We made landfall in a *kyn-ligr* valley, arid and marred by great pillars of iron. A crowd had gathered in a hollow carved out of the rock. Within, man and beast descended from high cages and battled in bloody sport. I expect you know it, *velafolk*: it was once called Thunderdome.

There was no sign of Boone when we arrived, and for many hours after. I feared I was mistaken about his aim. But as the sun set, a great metal crate descended from on high, bearing Boone atop it. He wove a great tale for the gathered crowds as the crate touched the earth, though I can't repeat his words--I was *hugleikinn*, advancing on his voice.

I heard the beat of flesh against metal. The *óséður* had awakened. Boone bore an electrified prod to control it, but to face an unpredictable creature with it--*alheimskr*. I pushed to the fore and called out to him, full of *jǫtun-móðr*.

He was quick to spot me. I expected him to *sneiða*, to mock the *sveitadāræ* for trusting him. But he smiled--humbly. An apology. As if he expected to be reprimanded, but would atone when next we met.

Or perhaps he meant none of these things. I cannot know.

I did not detect the cage opening, and Boone was inattentive. The *óséður* was not so blind. It was swift. It seemed a flash as it slid beneath the gate...

> **... FRIEND? ARE YOU OKAY?**
> Must you fill every moment with noise? Yes, I am fine.

It scaled the cage and rent Boone from shoulder to hip. The crowd bellowed in amusement as he fell from the crate and the *óséður* vanished. I did not move. Perhaps I could not. I saw only his wide eyes and puffs of sand scattering as he tumbled to the earth.

Fearful cries pulled me from my reverie. The unseen beast had leapt into the stands.

The onlookers scattered like frightened hares. None could escape its frenzy, for none could see it--none but I, who bore the *sónar*. Through its lenses I could detect the beast clearly, scrambling on its belly, its flesh burning hot with the strain of its *hlaða*. As others scattered, I leapt into its path. It was not prepared for a composed assault, and I pulled my blade through its withers.

It collapsed, injured but alive. But the blood marked it out for the encircling *sveit*. Fighters bearing firearms and blades pushed me aside. The creature's cries were sharp and agonizing as they *slatra*.

I did not bear witness to its death. I thought only of Boone. But when I fell beside him, the life was gone from his eyes.

I knew the truth even as I seized the vessel. He was not *valr*. His death was marred by dishonor. We would not meet again in the halls of Valhalla.

Twenty winters. It feels an eon, and no time at all. Since that day, my life has been one of battle. I gather *ágæti*. That, *velafolk*, is what brings me to the Games, season after season. When I fall, I will present my victories as an offering to the Allfather. He will see the glory forged in Boone's name, that my friend may enter the hall of the fallen at long last.

[TRANSLATION NOTES]

ágæti = fame, excellence
alheimskr = completely foolish
bytta = pail, bucket
hlaða = rampage

hugleikinn = entranced
jǫtun-móðr = Goliath's rage
kyn-ligr = strange
slatra = slaughter

sneiða = taunt
sveit = group
sveitadāræ = country fool
valr = one who has died in battle

NEAT! THAT IS A VERY NICE THING FOR YOU AND YOUR ALLFATHER TO DO. HOW MANY TIMES DO YOU HAVE TO WIN?

That is not mine to know. But the Allfather sees true glory. When I present these offerings, he is sure to accept them.

OH, OKAY. IT'S NICE THAT HE TOLD YOU THAT!

Nay. The Allfather does not speak as you and I do.

IT'S NICE THAT HE WROTE A LETTER TELLING YOU THAT?

What? No. The Allfather proclaims nothing in simple human script.

IT'S NICE THAT HE USED MORSE CODE TO TELL YOU THAT?

…I meant to apologize for my sharp tongue earlier, but you disrespect me again.

OH NO! I'M SORRY, FRIEND. I DIDN'T MEAN TO HURT YOUR FEELINGS.

Hmph. I see now why you admire the *miklimunnr*—you both neglect to measure your words.

I CAN DO THAT IF YOU WANT ME TO. I JUST SAID TWENTY-NINE WORDS, TOTALING ONE HUNDRED AND FORTY-FOUR CHARACTERS. DOES THAT MAKE YOU FEEL BETTER? I DON'T UNDERSTAND HOW IT WOULD, BUT I'M HAPPY IF IT DOES!

[*Deep sigh*] My well-being is not your concern. And this is my burden to bear. The loss of my mother and father, my uncle's passing, and the fall of Boone—all by nature, all as I *kikna*. The gods have delivered a message that I must interpret alone. I will not fail as the makers of World's Edge once did. For my inaction, I will *sætt*.

OH, I GUESS I UNDERSTAND. MAYBE. BUT IF YOU HAVEN'T TRIED IT, CRYING MIGHT HELP! BANGALORE CRIED WHEN I TALKED TO HER, AND SHE FELT A LOT BETTER.

[*Pause*] The information you *sœkja* is now yours. Perhaps it is time you act upon it. Elsewhere.

BUT, FRIEND, YOU WERE VERY HELPFUL, BUT I DON'T KNOW WHAT

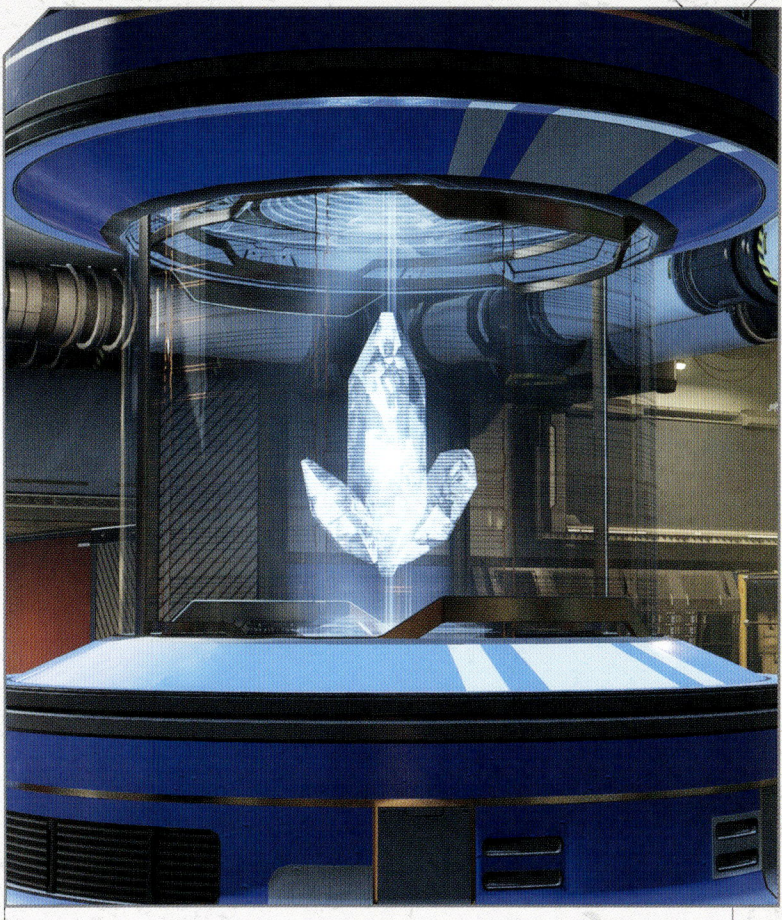

* A HOLOGRAM OF A BRANTHIUM CRYSTAL.

TO DO NEXT. NOW I KNOW ABOUT THE EVENT, AND THAT IT WAS WHEN BRANTHIUM SHOWED UP, BUT I DON'T KNOW WHAT THAT HAS TO DO WITH MY CREATOR, OR WHERE TO GO.

I cannot help you further. You know all I have to impart.

AWW. THANK YOU, FRIEND. I'M SAD NOW, BUT YOUR HELP WAS VERY HELPFUL.

…Aah. Perhaps …*finna* more of the nature of branthium would be a benefit. I know one who holds a branthium crystal that you may *skoða*, if she is willing.

WOO-HOO! I WOULD DEFINITELY LIKE TO SIK-YA IT, I THINK. AND I'M EXCITED TO MEET YOUR FRIEND.

You are acquainted. You *sœkja* Loba Andrade. She is a gatherer of *men* … pardon, of *auðr*. Last I broke bread upon her ship, I laid eyes on the crystal briefly. If you wish to inspect it, she may accommodate you for a time.

[TRANSLATION NOTES]

auðr = *treasures*	**men** = *treasures?*	**sœkja** = *seek*
finna = *find*	**skoða** = *examine*	
kikna = *go weak at the knees*	**sætt** = *atone*	

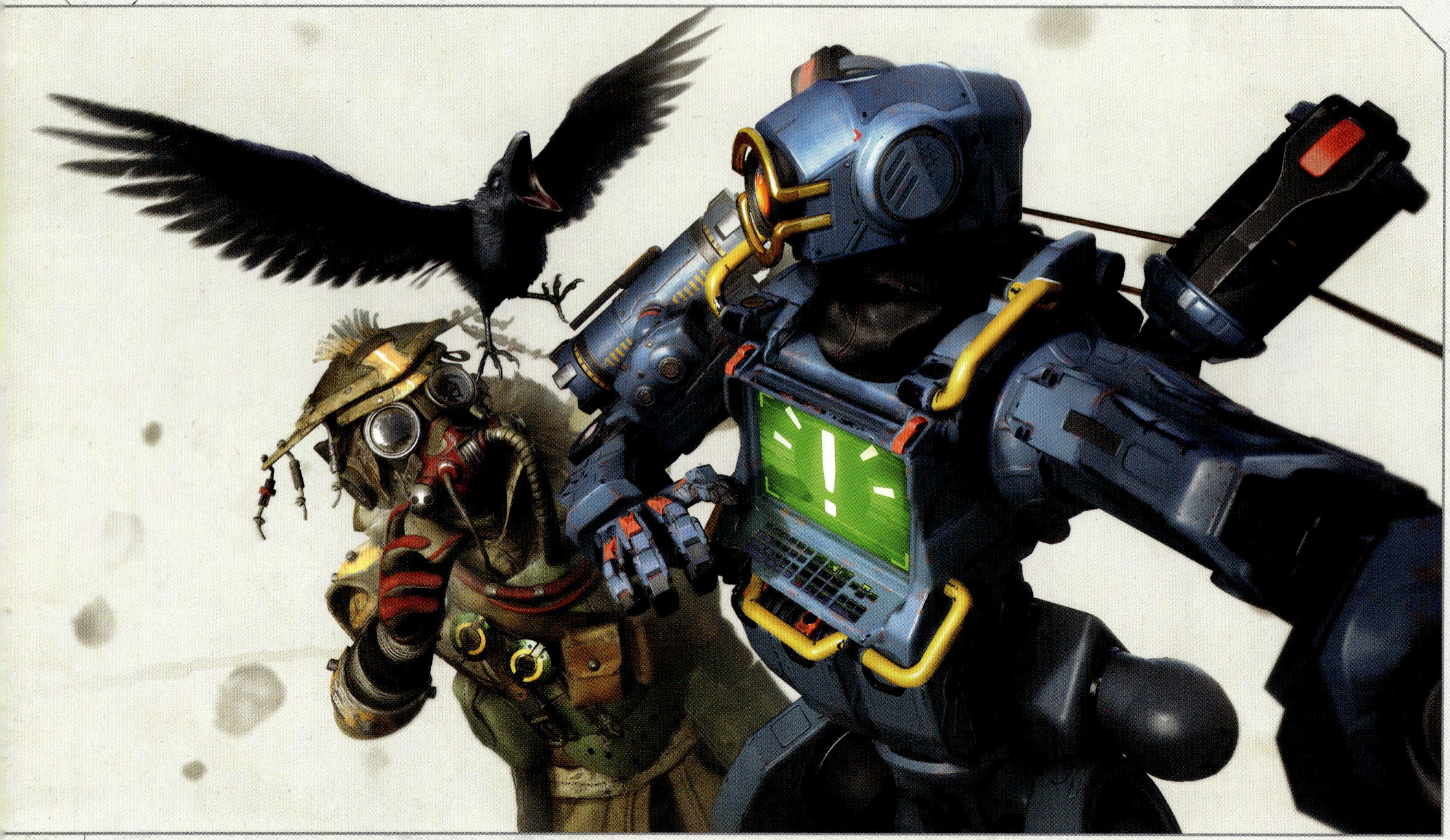

BLOODHOUND, ARTUR, AND ME! I DON'T THINK THAT ARTUR LIKES ME VERY MUCH...

THAT IS VERY NEAT, FRIEND! I DIDN'T KNOW YOU WERE BEST FRIENDS WITH LOBA. THAT MAKES ME HAPPY, AND SO DOES KNOWING WHERE TO GO. WERE YOU BEST FRIENDS BEFORE SHE JOINED THE GAMES? HOW DID YOU FIND HER SHIP?

I grow weary of reciting tales today. I will request she grant you her current coordinates. It is her choice to *taka við* or *neita*. I suggest you do not agitate her as you have others.

OH NO, I DON'T WANT TO MAKE ANYONE UPSET. I WILL DO MY BEST, FRIEND. BEFORE I GO, CAN I TAKE A PICTURE WITH YOU? I'M GETTING PICTURES WITH ALL MY FRIENDS, BECAUSE I LOVE THEM.

Very well, if it will speed your flight.

OH, I CAN'T FLY, BUT IT WOULD MAKE ME VERY HAPPY, WHICH IS ALSO GOOD. DO YOU WANT TO TAKE YOUR MASK OFF, SO YOU CAN SMILE?

...You are quite a stunning creation. The *dugr* of a warrior, but the discretion of a child. I see why others are charmed by you, with thought.

DOES THAT MEAN NO?

You are correct.

OKAY, THAT'S FINE, TOO! LET'S TAKE THE PICTURE. IT COUNTS DOWN FROM TEN. NINE, EIGHT—YOU CAN SMILE ANYWAY, BECAUSE SMILING IS GREAT. FIVE, FOUR—OW. UH, FRIEND, YOUR BIRD IS—

Þirraður, yes. It is not unexpected.

OW—OW! WELL, I THINK IT'S A NICE PICTURE ANYWAY. THANK YOU, FRIEND!

Good faith—now be on your way. I wish you *hap* hunt, *velafolk*. May it not end in *erfið*.

[TRANSLATION NOTES]

dugr = *prowess*	*hap* = *good, lucky*	*þirraður* = *annoyed*
erfið = *trouble*	*neita* = *refuse*	*taka við* = *invite into one's home*

LOADING ... TRANSCRIPTION/ 0001101

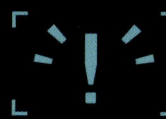
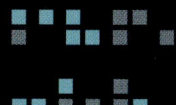

DATA POINTS RECEIVED

- Bloodhound likes me! Or doesn't not like me.

- Mirage and Bloodhound's mothers used to work together as IMC engineers.

- "The Event" was the discovery of branthium seventy-five years ago.

  > Branthium is an energy source that can burn for a long time, making it an ideal fuel source.

  > Just when the Outlands were about to run out of energy reserves, branthium appeared! Nobody knows where it came from. Bloodhound says it was a gift from their gods.

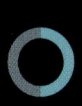

- Traces of branthium were discovered in the lava fields on Talos over thirty years ago.

- The IMC built New Dawn to cool the lava so they could harvest the branthium, and World's Edge was built around the plant.

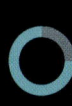

- Bloodhound's mother and father were IMC engineers who moved to Talos to work at New Dawn. Their uncle already lived there, and didn't like New Dawn.

- New Dawn was pushed to its limits, which caused the meltdown that froze World's Edge and killed Bloodhound's parents. Sad face!

- Bloodhound grew up in a village where technology was forbidden, but convinced everyone to change their minds and use it. Because of that, they met their friend Boone. Boone died, so Bloodhound is collecting victories to give to their god. Then he'll let Boone into Valhalla, maybe.

- Bloodhound doesn't know what branthium has to do with my creator, but they think studying some of it might help me figure out the answer. Loba has a branthium crystal I can look at, if she will let me.

- Bloodhound might not like me again?

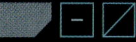

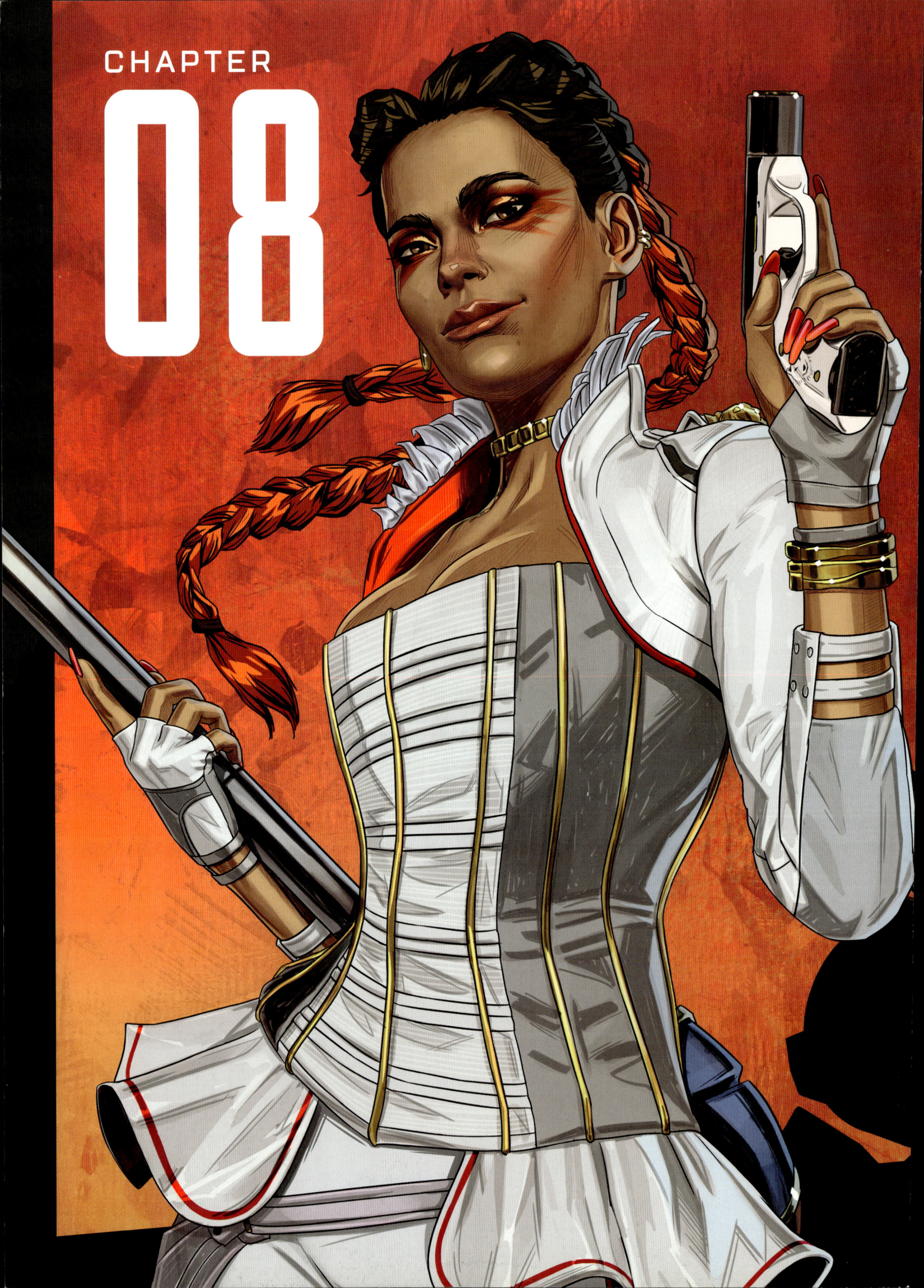

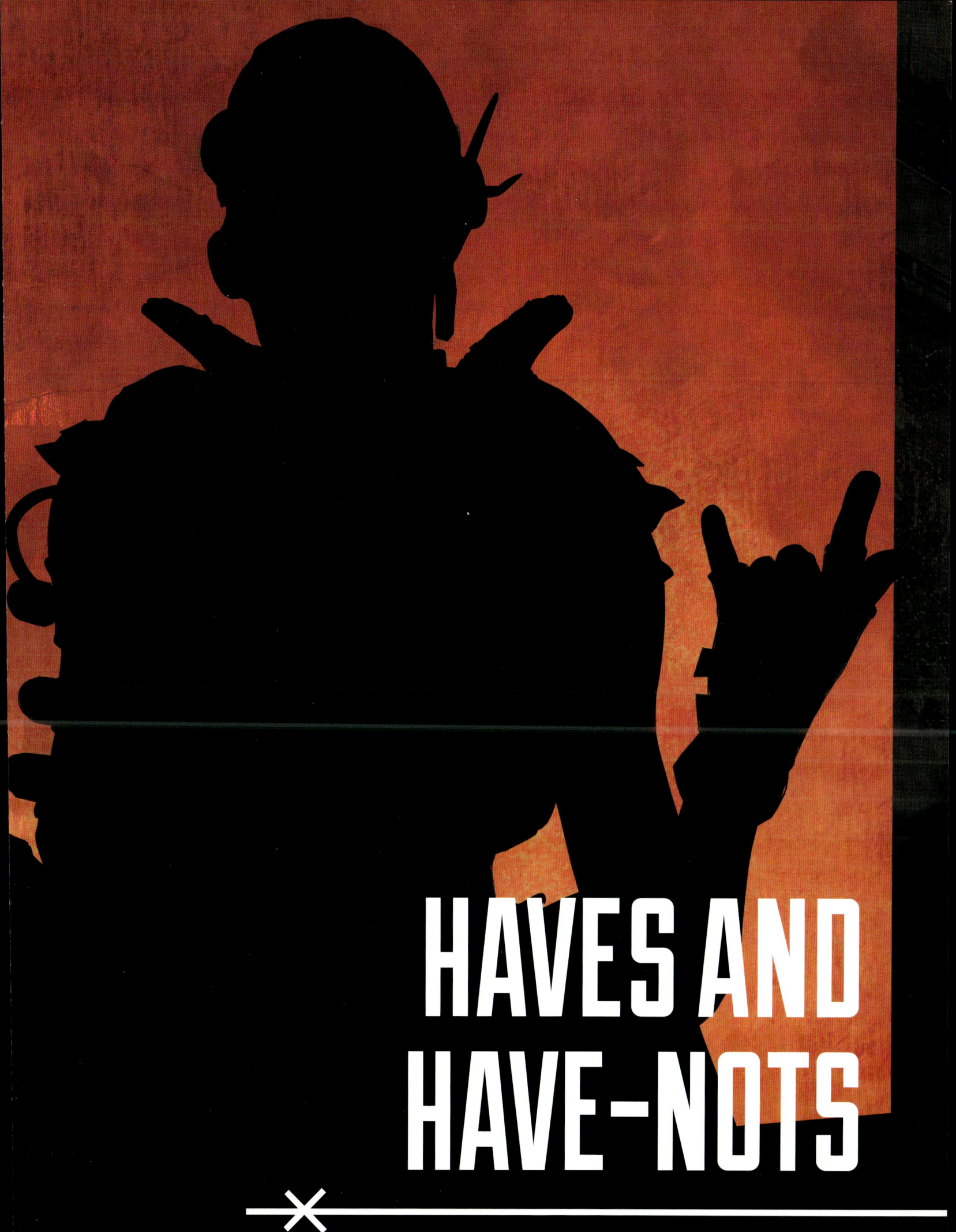

HAVES AND HAVE-NOTS

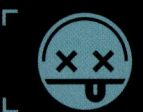
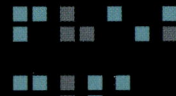
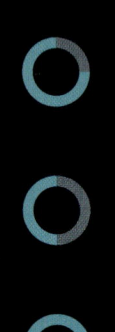

PATHFINDER MEMORY LOG: DAY 8

I'm not sure if Bloodhound and I are friends now, but I hope we are. They gave me lots of information about the Event. That was the day a new kind of fuel appeared and stabilized the Outlands, which was in the middle of an energy crisis that could have killed everyone! That energy was called branthium, and it's been powering the Outlands for almost a hundred years.

They also told me that they're in the Games because they're trying to help their friend Boone get into Valhalla so they can meet again someday. I'm sad Boone died, but happy that Bloodhound is looking for someone, just like I'm looking for my creator! That makes me feel less alone. It's another shared experience, like the one I had with Wraith!

I don't know what the Event or branthium have to do with my creator, but Bloodhound thinks Loba Andrade might know. She has a crystal of branthium, and looking at it might help me learn more about how the Event affected life in the Outlands—and my creator, maybe?

Loba gave me the coordinates to her ship, just like Bloodhound asked. She is very nice. It is docked in Malta, a city on Psamathe—hey, I used to work there! But when I was almost there, Loba sent me a message with new coordinates. This is exciting, like a treasure hunt! Except it's a treasure hunt for a treasure hunter?

The new coordinates lead to an upscale part of town, which is a fancy way of saying "expensive." There are two hills connected by a bridge that's all white and gold, with restaurants and shops built across it.

I follow the coordinates to a restaurant with orange canopies, which is a fancy way of saying "curtains." There are people talking and eating on white couches. It is very classy, which is a fancy way of saying "intimidating."

I see Loba! She is talking to someone I don't know, but she smiles and waves when she sees me. She looks happy. I'm excited to be friends with her.

CLUE BOX

TRANSMISSION CLUES
- "Chevrex" > LIFELINE'S PARENTS' COMPANY
- "The future of the Outlands" > OLD EXPERIMENTS TO CHANGE THE FUTURE
- "Dr. Amélie Pa—— [Paquette]" > WATTSON'S GRANDMOTHER, A GEOLOGIST, DIED MYSTERIOUSLY
- "The Event" > THE MYSTERIOUS APPEARANCE OF BRANTHIUM SEVENTY-FIVE YEARS AGO
- "Aleki" > GIBRALTAR'S GRANDFATHER
- "Iris" > PROJECT: IRIS, CREATED IN 2654
- [NEW CLUE] "Branthium" > THE SOLUTION TO THE ENERGY CRISIS

SELF-MOTIVATION QUOTE . . . SEARCHING . . . 1 RESULT FOUND

"What we see depends mainly on what we look for."
—[JOHN LUBBOCK]

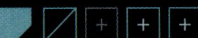

INNER MONOLOGUE ACTIVATED . . .

LOBA BIO FROM THE APEX GAMES

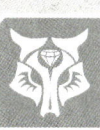
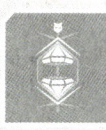
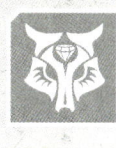

REAL NAME:
LOBA ANDRADE

AGE:
34

HOME WORLD:
NONE

TACTICAL ABILITY:
BURGLAR'S BEST FRIEND

PASSIVE ABILITY:
AN EYE FOR QUALITY

ULTIMATE ABILITY:
BLACK MARKET
BOUTIQUE

WHEN LOBA WAS NINE, SHE LOOKED ON AS SIMULA-CRUM HIT MAN REVENANT KILLED HER FAMILY. Left with nothing, she survived by picking pockets, using every tool at her disposal to lift herself from the gutter. Her career truly took off when she broke into a supposedly impenetrable facility and got her hands on the jump drive tech stored inside. With her new teleportation bracelet, the most secure and unattainable items were within her reach.

Rumors spread across the Outlands that if you wanted something valuable—and well guarded—Loba was who you go to. Through her rapidly growing black-market business, she finally realized her high society dreams. She was almost able to put her past behind her. But when Revenant joined the Apex Games, her past catapulted into her future. Now, she's joined the Games to find a way to end him for good. It doesn't hurt that the arenas are brimming with treasures just waiting to be snatched. Revenge will come, if fortune favors her. In the meantime, some beautiful things have caught her eye.

"There's a certain elegance to combat. I'll show you."
—LOBA

► HELLO, FRIEND! ◄

LOBA Ah, and it seems my next appointment is here. It's been lovely, but it looks like we'll have to continue this some other ti—

NEW FRIEND? Whoa, hey, robot! Long time no see.

OH, HELLO, OTHER FRIEND. I HAVEN'T MET YOU BEFORE. MY NAME IS PATHFINDER! WHAT'S YOURS?

NEW FRIEND? You kidding, robot? You really gonna forget an *amigo* who saved your butt two blocks from here? It's Octane!

WOW! I DIDN'T RECOGNIZE YOU, FRIEND. PROBABLY BECAUSE I HAVE NEVER SEEN YOUR FACE BEFORE. DID YOU LOSE YOUR MASK? BLOODHOUND DIDN'T WANT TO TAKE OFF THEIR MASK, BUT IT LOOKS LIKE IT DOESN'T BOTHER YOU.

OCTANE Hey, gotta let it breathe sometime, no? And the legs didn't tip you off, *amigo*? Haha!

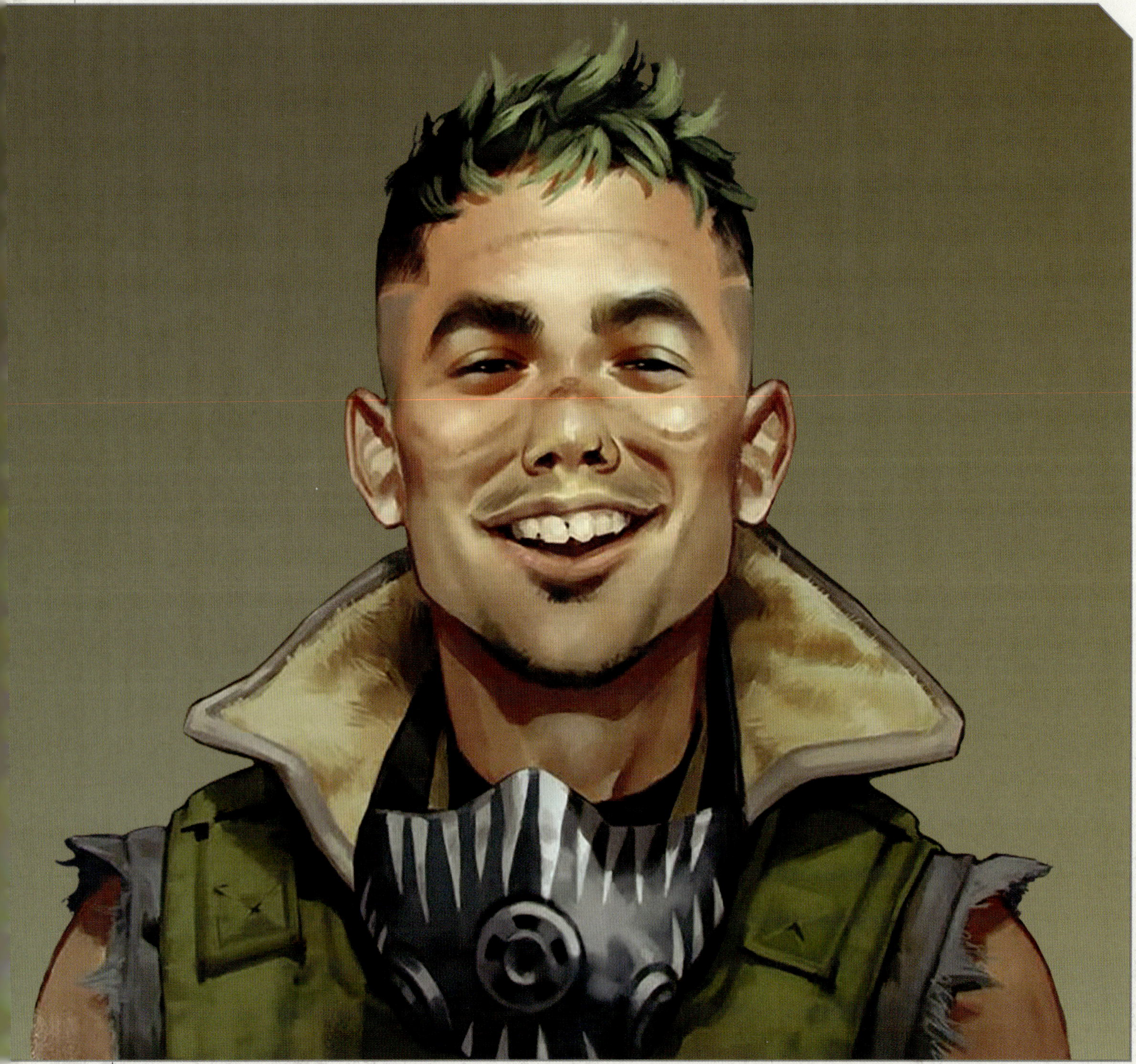

* OCTAVIO SILVA'S ROGUISH GRIN.

OCTANE BIO FROM THE APEX GAMES

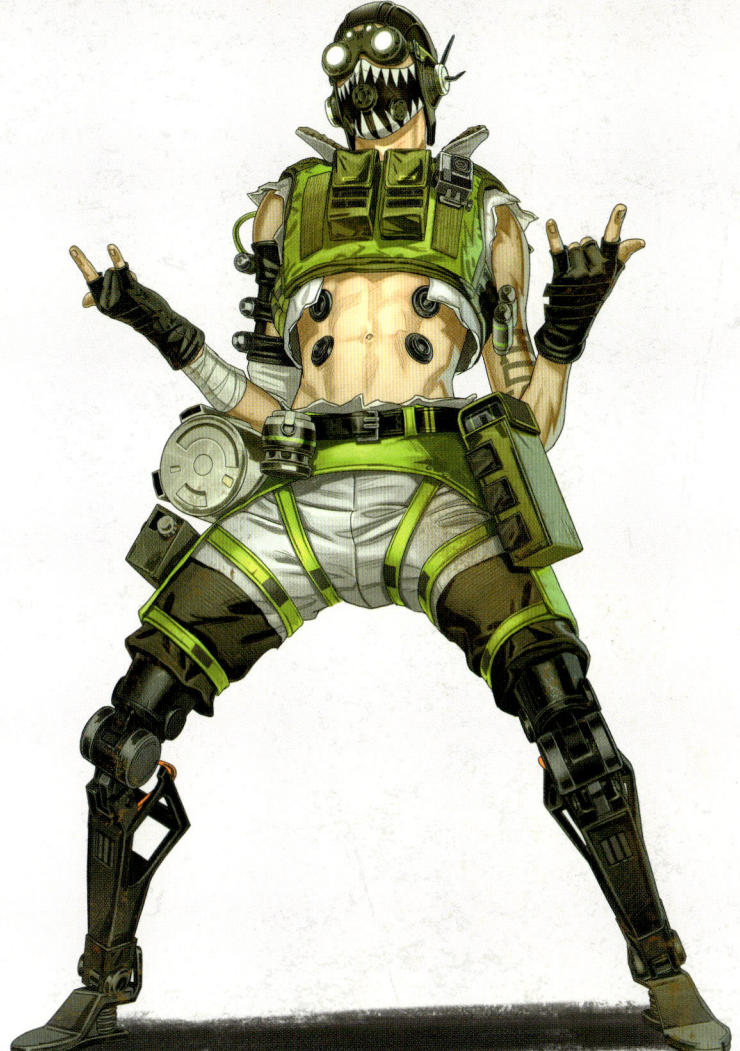

REAL NAME:
OCTAVIO SILVA

AGE:
24

HOME WORLD:
PSAMATHE

TACTICAL ABILITY:
STIM

PASSIVE ABILITY:
SWIFT MEND

ULTIMATE ABILITY:
LAUNCH PAD

ONE DAY, OCTAVIO SILVA WAS BORED. IN FACT, HE WAS BORED MOST DAYS. Heir to the preoccupied CEOs of Silva Pharmaceuticals and wanting for nothing in life, he entertained himself by performing death-defying stunts and posting holovids of them for his fans to gawk over. So, this day, he decided to set the course record for a nearby gauntlet by launching himself across the finish line—using a grenade.

As he lay in triage hours later, the doctors informed him that the damage done to his legs meant his daredevil days were over. That didn't sit well with Octavio, who turned to an old friend for help: Ajay Che, who he guilted into forging an order to replace his legs with bionic ones. Suddenly able to repair his limbs at a moment's notice, Octavio decided petty online stunts weren't enough: the ultimate adrenaline rush, the Apex Games, was calling. Now, he's going to become an Apex champion doing the most incredible, death-defying moves anyone's ever seen. Maybe in the arena, he won't be so bored.

"Whoa . . . what a rush!"
—OCTANE

LOBA Pathfinder is here to view an item from my personal collection—and I would hate to keep him waiting.

OCTANE Oh, hells no. You ain't getting off that easy. Come ooooon, I just need it for one day. You won't even miss it.

LOBA I don't know how many times I can explain that I do not *loan out* my prized possessions. I wouldn't part with this bracelet for every cent in your family's coffers.

OCTANE You sure about that? Because there's a whole lot of cents in there. Just saying.

EXCUSE ME, FRIEND, BUT WHAT DO YOU WANT LOBA'S BRACELET FOR?

OCTANE For a sick stunt, *amigo*! No spoilers, but there's a go-cart, some angry bees, and probably a grenade or five. All I need to pull it off is a teleporter, and what do you know? I've got an *amiga* who has one! Eh, *jefa*?

OH DEAR, THAT'S NOT A NICE THING TO SAY.

LOBA Not around the *gringo*, Silva. And no, not on your life or your dime. Now, we really have to get going.

YEAH, LOBA IS GOING TO LET ME SEE HER BRANTHIUM CRYSTAL AND TELL ME ALL ABOUT HOW IT CHANGED LIFE IN THE OUTLANDS.

OCTANE Yo, what're you talking about? I dunno what a brantum crystal is or whatever, but you wanna know about life? You gotta *live* it, *amigo*. Or you talk to a guy like me, 'cause I live it up every day. Haha!

OH? ANY HELP IS VERY HELPFUL! WHAT DO YOU KNOW ABOUT LIFE IN THE OUTLANDS AFTER THE EVENT?

LOBA Ay, no …

OCTANE No idea what that is, *amigo*, but I know in this life—you gotta make your own fun. Like, if you're boring, a classy place like this might be enough for you.

CLASSY! THAT'S A FANCY WAY OF SAYING—

OCTANE But once you get tired of this stuff—and that happens *real* fast, trust me—there's these awesome canyons you can jump in Solace, and these crazy nightclubs on Gaea. And then there's the stuff

barely anybody knows about, like this huge mountain on Talos, out in the middle of nowhere. You ever fall off a mountain, *compadre*? Because it's *awesome*. And that's just the stuff off the top of my head. You're bored and looking for something cool to do? Nobody's gonna find it for you.

THAT'S NOT REALLY WHAT I—

LOBA Hmph, what? Do you think everywhere in this system is all fun and games? I'd ask what sort of privileged life you lead, but I already know.

OCTANE Oh-ho-ho, spicy, eh, *jefa*? You should be nicer to me if you want what you're looking for.

LOBA I—what do you think is going on here? I would love to know.

ME TOO! I'M VERY CONFUSED.

LOBA Look, the robot wants to know about branthium and all the *good* it's done. The Peck Foundation? Does that ring any bells, *compadre*?

OCTANE … No? Is it supposed to?

LOBA You cannot be serious. You expect me to believe that Silva Pharmaceuticals doesn't have its fingers in that particular *pie*, or that you don't know about it?

OCTANE You think I know what my old man is up to? Me? Naw. Fat chance.

LOBA … You really don't care. I keep thinking this persona of yours is an act, and you keep surprising me.

OCTANE Ha! *Amiga*, you know how unbelievably boring it is hanging out with a bunch of suits getting puffed up like *gallos* about quarterly profits all day? Last time my old man dragged me to one of his meetings, I walked out and straight off a bridge just to *feel something*, you know? I let him and the accountants take care of all that stuff. Otherwise, I'll die of boredom.

LOBA And you have no idea where a sizable portion of your family's wealth comes from. You truly do lead a charmed life.

OCTANE Haha. Hey, what can I say?

YOU COULD SAY WHAT YOU'RE TALKING ABOUT? BECAUSE I AM STILL CONFUSED.

OH. THAT STORY WAS SAD. I LIKED OCTANE'S MORE. IT WAS ONLY SUBCONSCIOUSLY SAD.

OCTANE Yeah, *jefa*, you really know how to bring down a room. And this room doesn't even have walls.

LOBA It's a good reminder for those who tend to forget. Some people are born with everything they could ever want. Others have to fight for every scrap and can never forget there's always someone waiting to snatch it. The branthium you wanted to know about saved the Outlands through the *generosity* of those who made money handing it out. That was the Outlands before, and it's the Outlands now. Nothing has really changed.

AH, THAT IS INTERESTING. BUT ALSO . . . GOOD, KIND OF!

LOBA And how is that?

WELL, IF NOTHING CHANGED, THEN THE OUTLANDS WEREN'T DESTROYED, LIKE SOME PEOPLE THOUGHT THEY WOULD BE. THAT MEANS A LOT OF PEOPLE WERE OKAY AFTER THE ENERGY CRISIS!

LOBA . . . You really are infuriatingly optimistic.

I GUESS SO! SEEING THE BRIGHT SIDE MAKES PEOPLE HAPPY, AND HOPEFULLY IT MEANS PEOPLE WILL REMEMBER THE OTHER PEOPLE WHO HELPED.

LOBA Hmm. Well, do thank them if you find out who they are. Those who sold it off weren't forthcoming with how they came upon it. That's a question without an answer, as hard as anyone's looked.

OH, THAT'S RIGHT! BLOODHOUND SAYS NO ONE KNOWS HOW BRANTHIUM GOT TO THE PLANETS. DOES THAT MEAN YOU DON'T KNOW, EITHER?

LOBA Ha! Well, I may be exceptional in many ways, but even I have my limits. There are information brokers who *might* know what you're looking for, but they tend to be tightlipped.

OH, LIKE CRYPTO! HE BARELY TALKS AT ALL. I WONDER IF HE KNOWS. I SHOULD ASK HIM! CAN I TAKE THE BRANTHIUM CRYSTAL TO HIM?

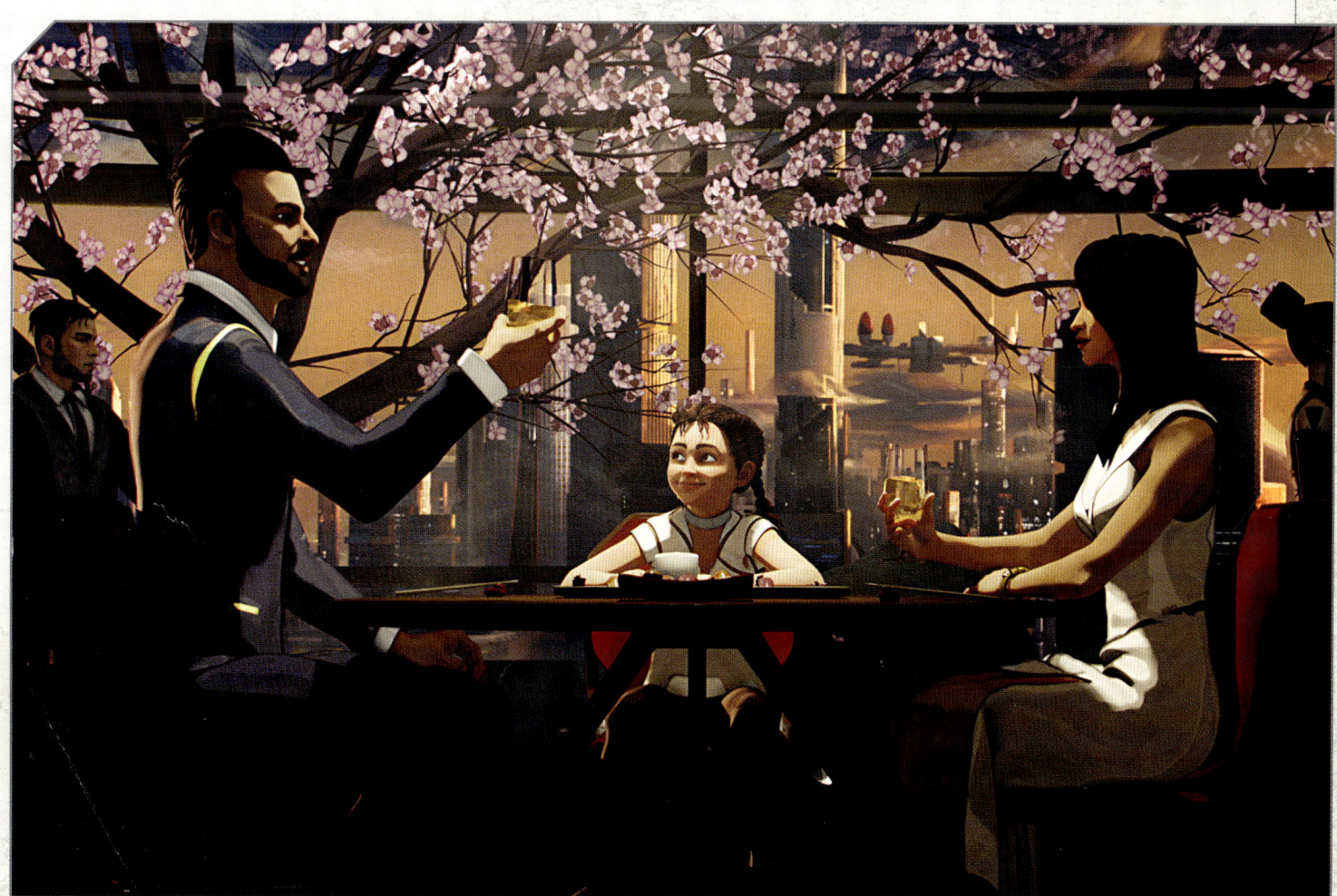

* THE ANDRADE FAMILY.

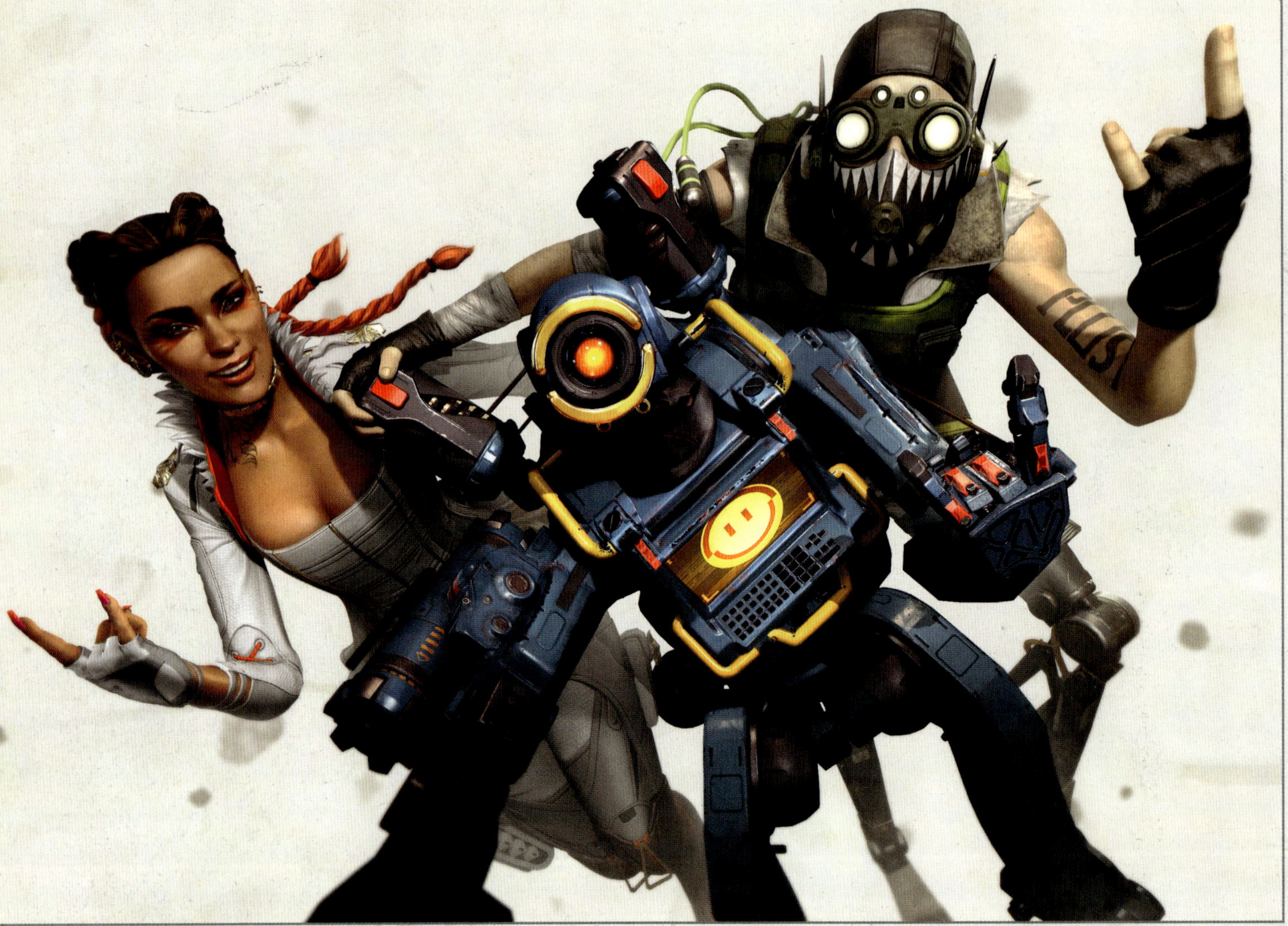

12 15 21 15 3 20 11 4 5

OCTANE PUT THE MASK BACK ON BECAUSE HE SAYS IT'S "PART OF THE MAGIC." SHOULD I TELL HIM I HAVE A COPY OF THAT OTHER PICTURE?

LOBA You may take a *photo* of the branthium crystal, if you'd like. Like I said, I don't loan out my most prized possessions.

OCTANE Hey, uh, speaking of, *jefa—*

LOBA Silva. That's one thing you'll never understand: even with all the riches in the world, you can't buy something priceless.

OCTANE Priceless like friends in high places, eeeeeeh?

PRICELESS LIKE FRIENDS! LIKE ALL THE FRIENDS THE BRANTHIUM HELPED. SO EVEN IF PEOPLE MADE MONEY ON IT, IT CAN'T BE ALL BAD, RIGHT?

LOBA …You're sweet. You know, I'm not usually fond of robots, but you have a certain charm.

THANK YOU! YOU ARE VERY CHARMING, TOO.

LOBA And flattery will get you everywhere. Now, would you like to see the crystal, or would you like to close down the bar?

OH, I PROBABLY SHOULDN'T DO THAT. I HAD A BARTENDING JOB ONCE, AND IT DIDN'T GO WELL. THAT'S WHY MIRAGE WON'T LET ME WORK AT HIS!

LOBA And a sharp wit, too. Shall we? Silva, do feel free to come along and see the collection. Then you'll know who you're really bargaining with.

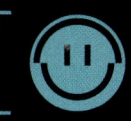
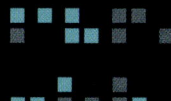

DATA POINTS RECEIVED

- Loba and Octane both live on Psamathe, sort of—Loba lives on a ship, and I think Octane lives wherever he wants.

- After branthium was discovered, a lot of groups got some of it, like charities and companies. And Loba! But later, because she's not that old.

- Lilian Peck, the founder of Olympus, also created a charity called the Peck Foundation. She wanted to do good and keep everyone in the Outlands safe and happy! I like her.

- The Peck Foundation got a lot of branthium, which is good, because it ended the energy crisis! Then a lot of companies made a lot of money because they had investments with Peck—I don't know if that is as good? Loba doesn't seem to think so.

- One of the companies was Silva Pharmaceuticals, which is owned by Octane's family. That's why he's rich, and probably where he gets all his stim.

- There are six planets in Syndicate Space: Solace, Talos, Gaea, Boreas, Psamathe, and Tartarus. All of them were affected in different ways by the energy crisis, and some of them turned out better than others.

- Octane really doesn't like his dad. That is confusing to me—I could never hate my creator, right?

- Loba didn't want to share any of her secrets, so she told a story about someone else. But I think she kind of shared a secret anyway, by accident.

- Loba says no one knows how branthium got to the planets—except maybe Crypto. I should go ask him!

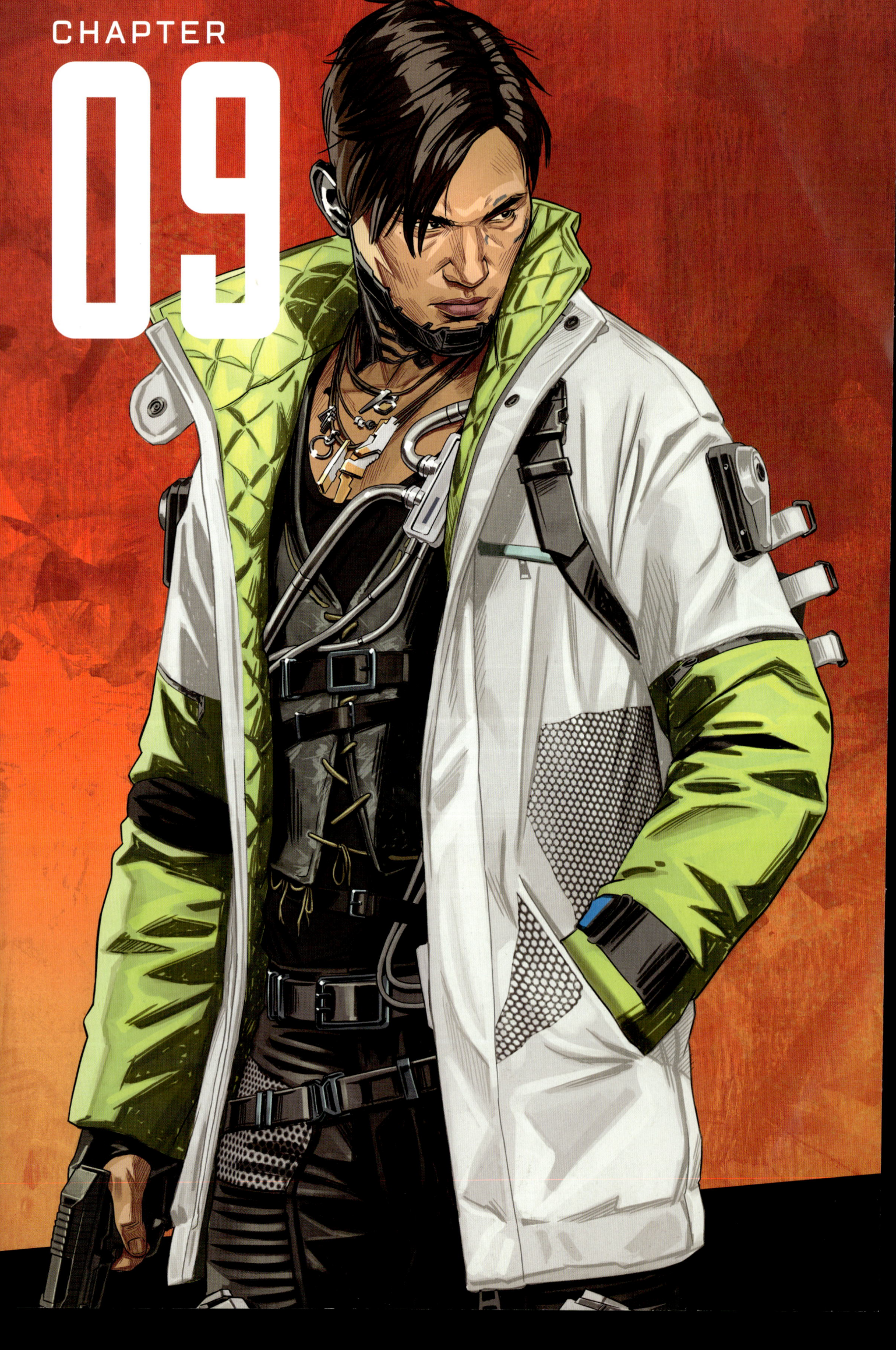

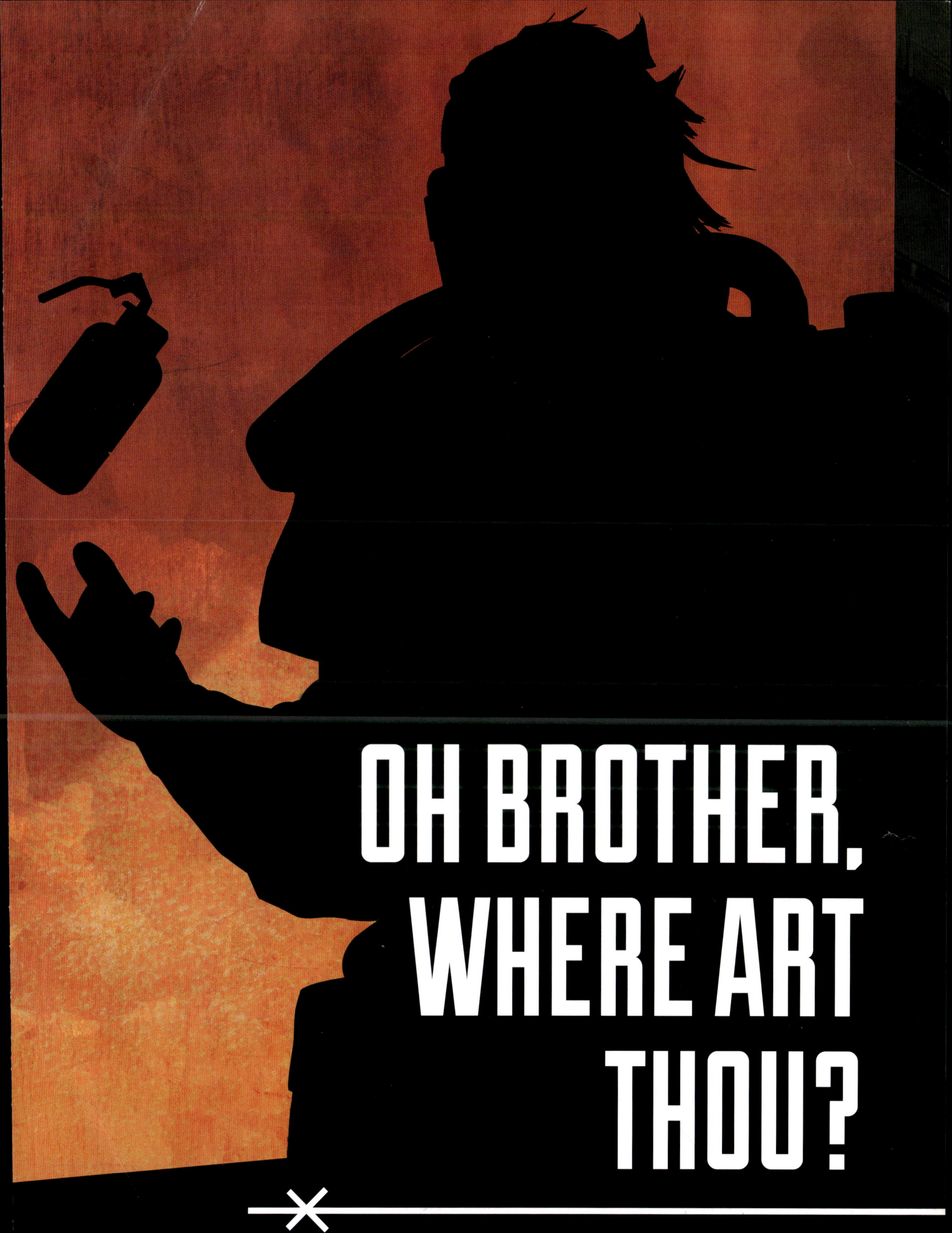

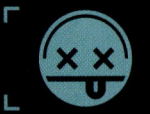

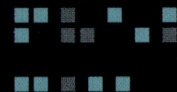

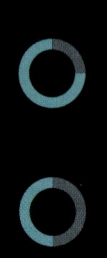

PATHFINDER MEMORY LOG: DAY 9

Octane and Loba sure were fiery. Physical appearance makes people say and do some pretty funny things. I have noticed many times that the prettier Loba looks, the more she gets her way, but I think how she looks shouldn't really matter because even though she hasn't always been honest, she's a good person. I'd do anything for her even if she wasn't pretty, because that's what friends do. And Octane is a very good-looking man, but nobody knows that because he wears a mask. He doesn't care if anybody knows what he looks like. All he cares about is if you can see what he does, and what he does is very impressive and very dangerous and will probably lead to his death one day, but it looks so cool that nobody seems to care!

Now they're sending me to Crypto. Hopefully, he has sorted through all the conspiracies and lies surrounding the Event and can help me find out what it was, how it's connected to Project: Iris, and how it all relates to me and my creator. I feel like I'm so close to figuring this all out, and I have all my friends to thank for it! I hope I can do something nice for all of them when it's over. I wonder if they like Leviathan stew . . .

I'm in the home stretch now, which is a reference to baseball, which is a game with bats, which is what vampires turn into, which is what Crypto was for Halloween last year! It's all connected! Go me!

CLUE BOX

TRANSMISSION CLUES
- "Chevrex" > LIFELINE'S PARENTS' COMPANY
- "The future of the Outlands" > THE THREAT OF AN ENERGY CRISIS
- "Dr. Amélie Pa—— [Paquette]" > WATTSON'S GRANDMOTHER, A GEOLOGIST, DIED MYSTERIOUSLY
- "The Event" > THE MYSTERIOUS APPEARANCE OF BRANTHIUM SEVENTY-FIVE YEARS AGO
- "Aleki" > GIBRALTAR'S GRANDFATHER
- "Iris" > PROJECT: IRIS, CREATED IN 2654; BANGALORE'S UNCLE AL (NO RELATION) RAN ITS SECURITY DETAIL AND DIED THERE IN AN EXPLOSION
- "Branthium" > THE SOLUTION TO THE ENERGY CRISIS

SELF-MOTIVATION QUOTE . . . SEARCHING . . . 1 RESULT FOUND

"Don't you know that a midnight hour comes when everyone has to take off his mask? Do you think life always lets itself be trifled with? Do you think you can sneak off a little before midnight to escape this?"
—[SØREN KIERKEGAARD]

INNER MONOLOGUE ACTIVATED . . .

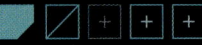

CRYPTO BIO FROM THE APEX GAMES

ULTIMATE OBJECTIVE . . . SEEKING CREATOR

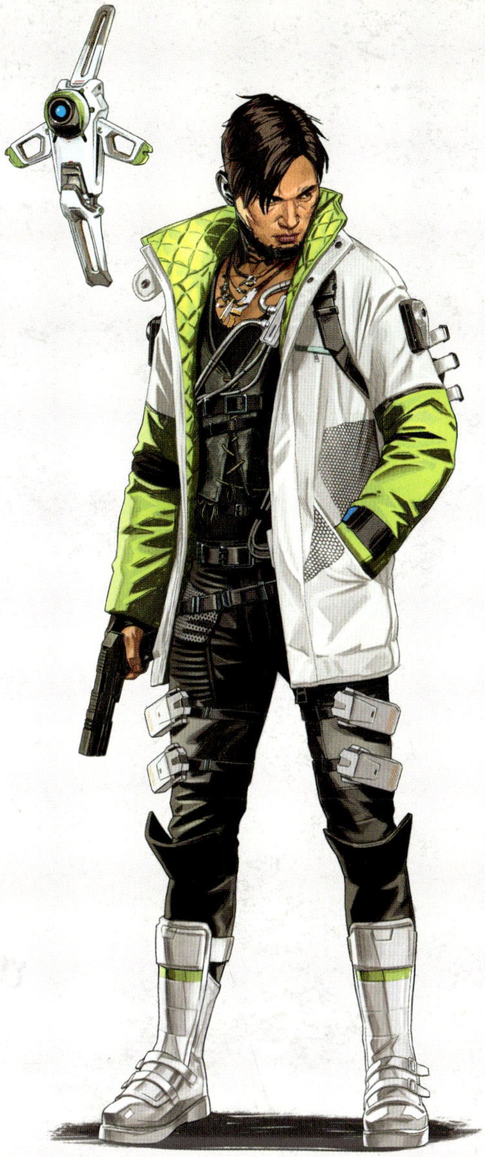

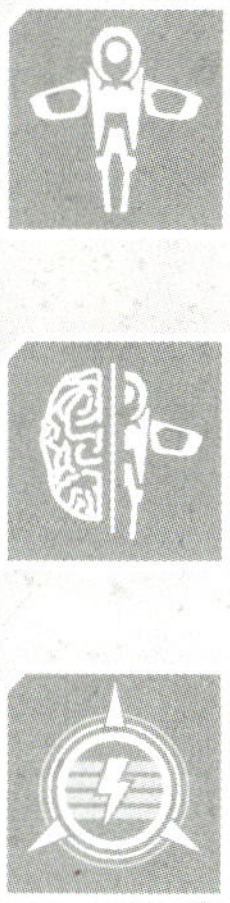

NAME:
**HYEON KIM (ALIAS) //
TAE JOON PARK**

AGE:
31

HOME WORLD:
GAEA

TACTICAL ABILITY:
SURVEILLANCE DRONE

PASSIVE ABILITY:
NEUROLINK

ULTIMATE ABILITY:
DRONE EMP

CRYPTO SPECIALIZES IN SECRETS; HE KNOWS HOW TO UNCOVER THEM, AND HOW TO KEEP THEM. A brilliant hacker and encryption expert, he uses aerial drones to spy on his opponents in the Apex arena without being seen. It's been noted that his drones have a similar design to those created by wanted murderer Tae Joon Park.

Orphans raised on the streets of Suotamo, Tae Joon and his foster sister Mila Alexander escaped a life of squalor by becoming computer engineers, designing drones that transmit the Apex Games throughout the Outlands. But one day, Tae Joon disappeared with an important company secret, and his sister vanished under mysterious and violent circumstances. However, Crypto claims to have had no contact with Tae Joon, and the case remains unsolved.

Crypto's motives for joining the Apex Games are almost as mysterious as the man himself. In recent interviews, he has claimed he is seeking justice—but for what, exactly, remains unknown.

"You're either ready or you're an idiot, but what do I know? I'm just a genius."
—CRYPTO

► HELLO, CRYPTO! ◄

An-nyeong, Pathfinder. Stand on the footprints please.

YES, I'M STANDING ON THE FOOTPRINTS PAINTED ON YOUR FLOOR. I DIDN'T KNOW YOU WERE AN ARTIST.
It's not a decoration. You're currently being scanned for listening devices, surveillance equipment not already covered in your specifications, and anything that may be used as a weapon.

AND I'M IN A PRETTY GREEN LIGHT, TOO! NIFTY.
Yeah, that's the scan.

GREEN IS MY FAVORITE COLOR.
I'll need you to leave the grapple and zipline by the door.

WHERE ARE MY MANNERS? OF COURSE. ACTUALLY, ALL OF THE COLORS ARE MY FAVORITE COLOR.
Hmm. Come in. Your message said you were looking for information about an Event.

YES, BUT WE DON'T HAVE TO TALK ABOUT THAT YET.
Mwo?

SEE, FIRST WE BANTER A BIT, AND THEN YOU TELL ME ABOUT YOUR PERSONAL LIFE, INCLUDING A STORY I MARK AS "STORY TIME."
None of that will happen. You are going to ask me about the Event, and I am going to tell you what I know, and then you will leave. *Kandanhe.*

WHY ARE YOU SKIPPING ALL THE OTHER PARTS?
I don't talk about my personal life, and only children need "Story Time." This flash drive has everything you need to know about the Event. All information has been vetted with multiple sources.

YOU'RE NOT GOING TO TELL ME YOURSELF?
The majority of that information is connected to Hammond business deals made over seventy-five years ago. You are better off consulting with an expert. Horizon is from that time period. Or perhaps Revenant? He hates Hammond, but he knows much about their inner workings.

REVENANT HATES EVERYTHING. I THINK HE EVEN HATES ME.
Probably. Is there anything else? You have what you need.

SO, I HAVE TO TALK TO HORIZON AND REVENANT?
As far as I'm concerned, you don't have to do anything but leave.

THERE REALLY ISN'T GOING TO BE A STORY TIME?
Take care, Pathfinder. *Hwa-i-ting.*

HOSTILE: INCOMING. HOSTILE: INCOMING.

WHAT IS THAT?
That is my security system. There is a hostile on my property.

HOW DO YOU KNOW THEY'RE HOSTILE?
Everybody's a hostile until I say otherwise.

AM . . . AM I A HOSTILE?
Of course you are.

HOSTILE: INCOMING. HOSTILE: INCOMING.

BUT I AM YOUR FRIEND.
You're a robot, Pathfinder. You can be reprogrammed.

I CAN BE REPROGRAMMED . . .
Security, I need visuals.

HOSTILE: INCOMING. HOSTILE: INCOMING.

. . . THAT HAS NEVER OCCURRED TO ME BEFORE . . .
I said, Security, visuals! Hello—oh. *Aissi*—LASSIE! I NEED VISUALS.

YOU NAMED YOUR SECURITY SYSTEM "LASSIE"?
I named my security system "Security." Wattson renamed it "Lassie." I keep forgetting to change it back.

[TRANSLATION NOTES]

Aissi. (아이씨.) = *Damn.*
An-nyeong. (안녕.) = *Hello. [Casual]*
Hwa-i-ting. (화이팅.) = *Good luck. [Dismissive]*
Kandanhe. (간단 해.) = *It's simple.*
Mwo? (뭐뭐?) = *Huh?*

HOSTILE: INCOMING. HOSTILE: INCOMING.

AS IN THE SCOTTISH WORD FOR "GIRL"? YOU KNOW WHO WOULD APPRECIATE THAT? DR. MARY—
No, apparently it was a dog on ancient Earth that would bark when you were in trouble. Wattson thought it would be cute. I have visual in Quadrant Two. Oh no.

WHO IS IT? WHO IS THE INCOMING HOSTILE?
An idiot.

MIRAGE?
Worse.

WAIT, ARE YOU OPENING THE DOOR? I THOUGHT YOU SAID HE WAS HOSTILE.
He is, but if I don't open the door, he'll gas the place. Like he did last time. Lassie, open front door . . .

HEY. LOOK WHO IT IS!

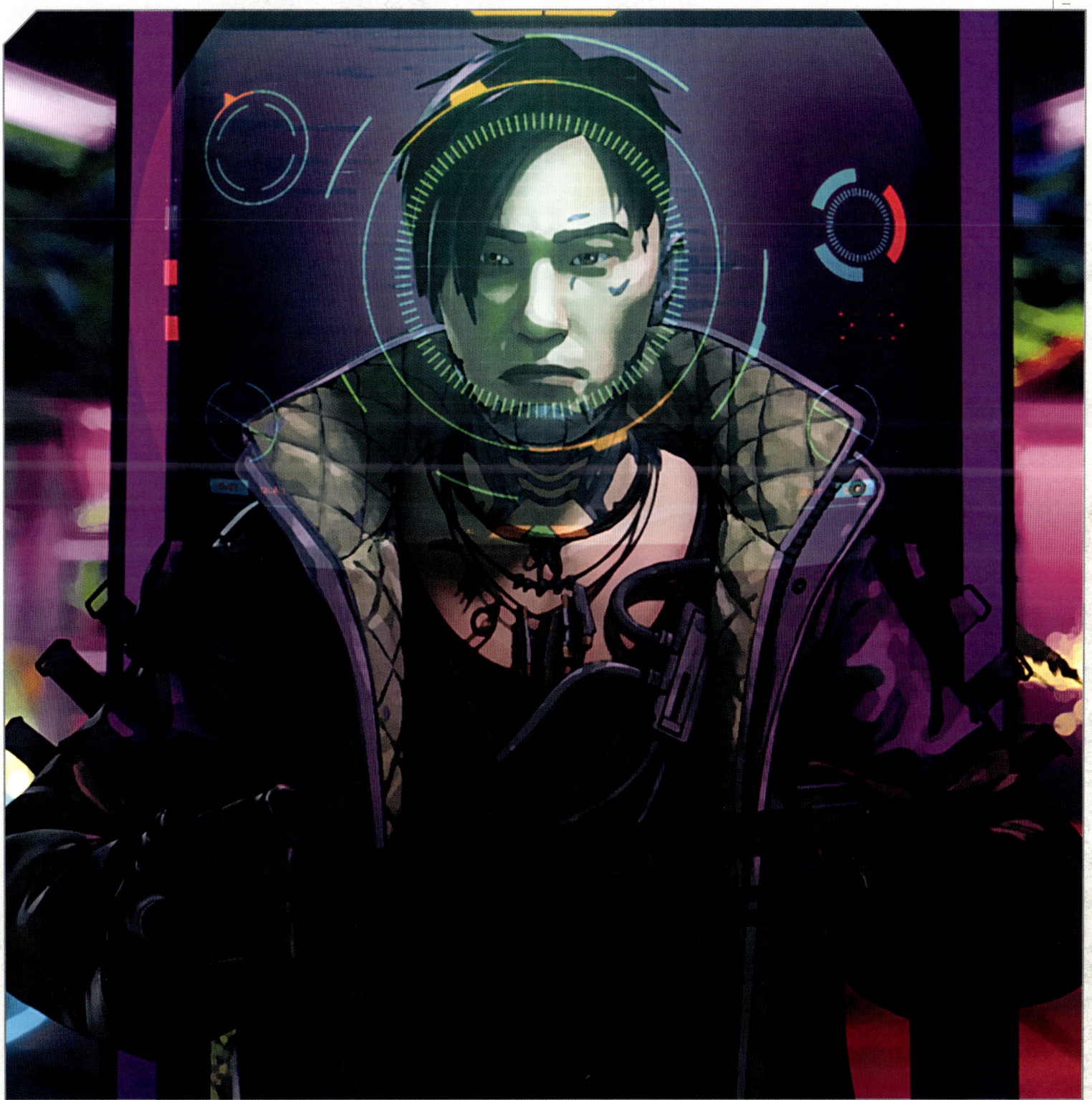

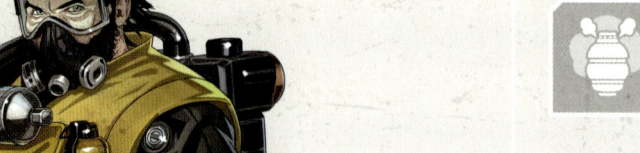

CAUSTIC BIO FROM THE APEX GAMES

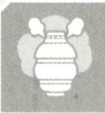

NAME:
MIKHAIL CAUSTIC (ALIAS)
// ALEXANDER NOX

AGE:
48

HOME WORLD:
GAEA

TACTICAL ABILITY:
NOX GAS TRAP

PASSIVE ABILITY:
NOX VISION

ULTIMATE ABILITY:
NOX GAS GRENADE

BEFORE THERE WAS CAUSTIC, A SCIENTIST NAMED ALEXANDER NOX WORKED AT HUMBERT LABS, THE FRONTIER'S LEADING MANUFACTURER OF PESTICIDE GASES. With a large supply of pesticides needed to protect the growing Frontier colonies' crops, Humbert Labs was constantly on the hunt for better and stronger formulas. Nox was one of their brightest scientists and worked day and night developing new gases. But to make sure they worked, he needed to test them on more than just inert tissue: he needed something living.

As he toiled in secret, Nox began to see the beauty in his creations and their ability to destroy anything they touched. But the head of Humbert Labs soon discovered his gruesome experiments, and their confrontation ended with the lab in flames and its chief dead. Today, Nox is missing and presumed deceased. Caustic, meanwhile, now finds new test subjects in the Apex Games, where he puts his gaseous creations to work and observes their effects with great interest.

"I do not care who makes the kill, as long as I can observe it die."
—CAUSTIC

IT'S CAUSTIC! IT'S MY FRIEND CAUSTIC!

CAUSTIC I am no friend of yours. And you . . . *you* . . . what did you tell her?

CRYPTO You'll have to be more specific. Please stand on the footprints.

CAUSTIC The hell with your footprints! I should rip off your—

CRYPTO Lassie, isolate the intruder.

WHOA. WHAT HAPPENED? HE'S TRAPPED.

CRYPTO That is a soundproof containment unit Wattson put together using "quantum electricity." There's no such thing, and she is well aware of that, but she thought it sounded "fun." She said I need to "lighten up," then laughed and asked if I "got it." I did. It was actually funny. Did I mention it's soundproof?

IT'S LIKE A JAIL CELL MADE OUT OF LIGHTNING. CAUSTIC SURE LOOKS ANGRY IN THERE.

CRYPTO Yeah, that's because he is.

IS THERE A WAY TO HEAR WHAT HE'S SAYING? IT LOOKS LIKE HE'S YELLING AT ME NOW.

CRYPTO Hold on. I'll lessen the strength of the sound containment field.

CAUSTIC —like some creature in a zoo! Robot, make him release me.

ME?

CRYPTO Why are you here?

CAUSTIC There's an error in one of Ms. Paquette's equations for the prototype she's working on. I stopped by her cottage to warn her not to go through with the prototype until she speaks to me.

CRYPTO And . . . ?

CAUSTIC And she won't see me! Clearly, Crypto is poisoning her against me once again.

CRYPTO *Ni jarmoshiya.* Did she tell you why?

CAUSTIC Merely that she was busy.

CRYPTO I contacted her earlier, and she said something similar to me.

CAUSTIC Is she intentionally avoiding both of us again? And lying about the reasons why?

CRYPTO *Morugetnunde . . .*

I KNOW THE REASON WHY!

CRYPTO *Mwo?*

CAUSTIC Impossible.

SHE TOLD ME SIX DAYS AGO. WHEN I MET WITH HER TO TALK ABOUT HER GRANDMOTHER, THE GEOLOGIST. DID YOU KNOW THEY NAMED THE AMELIE MOUNTAIN RANGE AFTER HER GRAND—

CAUSTIC I know those mountains like the back of my hand. What did she tell you about us?

CRYPTO Yeah, Pathfinder . . . what?

SHE SAID SHE KNOWS THE TRUTH NOW.

CRYPTO The truth . . . ?

CAUSTIC About what, robot?

ABOUT WHO YOU BOTH REALLY ARE.

CRYPTO What? She said that?

CAUSTIC Who . . . we are?

CRYPTO She said that exactly?

YES. THOSE WERE HER EXACT WORDS.

CAUSTIC I am who I say I am. Dr. Mikhail Caustic. Who are you, Mr. *Kim*?

CRYPTO Hyeon Kim.

NO, SHE SAID THOSE ARE MASKS YOU WEAR.

[TRANSLATION NOTES]

Ni jarmoshiya. [네 잘못이야.] = *That's your fault.*

Morugetnunde. [모르겠는데.] = *I don't understand.*

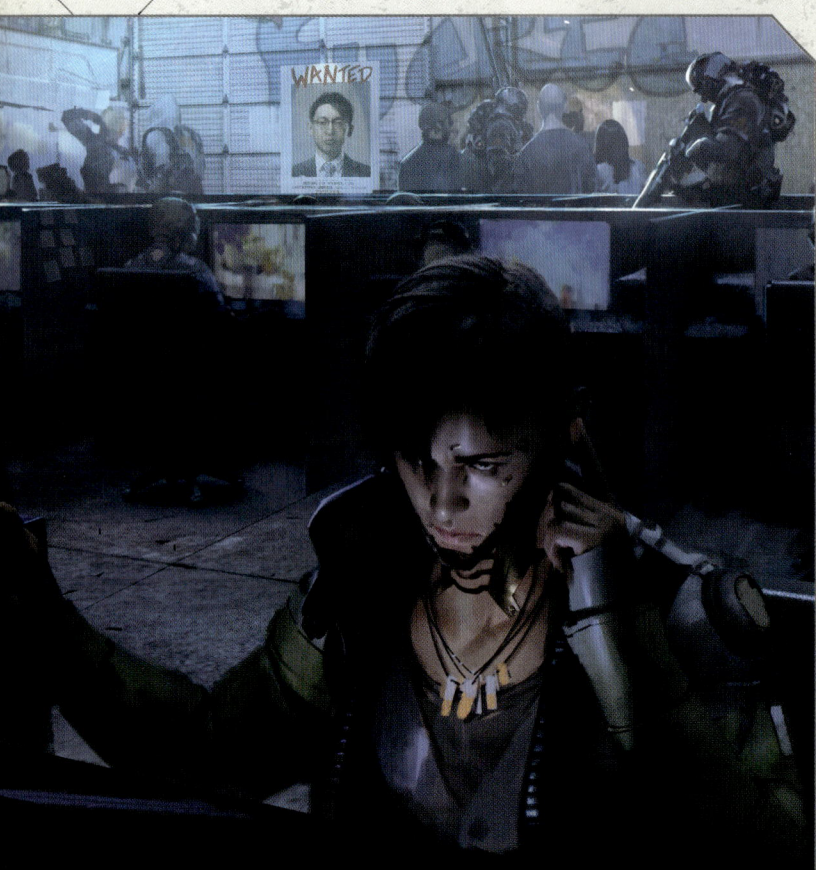

CRYPTO Do not try this again. *Hoohwehalguyah.*

CAUSTIC Try what again?

CRYPTO You were the one who betrayed Loba to Revenant, then you tried to frame me. And you're doing it again now.

THIS IS LIKE A MOVIE! IT'S VERY EXCITING. BUT I SHOULD GO IF I'M GOING TO READ EVERYTHING ON THIS FLASH DRIVE.

CAUSTIC You're not going anywhere. Not until you tell me what she said.

CRYPTO About who you really are? And who might that be? *Heungmiropji anah?*

HE'S DR. CAUSTIC, OF COURSE. HE'S ALWAYS BEEN DR. CAUSTIC.

CRYPTO As long as you've known him, maybe. But this isn't the first time you've been accused of not being who you say you are, Doctor …

IT'S NOT?

CRYPTO No. Soon after he joined the Games, Mikhail Caustic was interviewed by a reporter. Angela Fazia.

CAUSTIC And how do you know about this?

CRYPTO I made it a point to learn as much as I could about my opponents when I entered the Games.

CAUSTIC To the extent of being able to recite it from memory?

CRYPTO I keep no hard copies. *Jongeenun heunjeogeul namgiji.*

CAUSTIC You're hiding behind your language. What don't you want me to know?

OOOOOH … SICK BURN …

CRYPTO Fazia confronted you when you stepped off the dropship after winning your first match. She said

---

CRYPTO *Geuressuligah upneunde …*

CAUSTIC […]

WOW, THESE MOMENTS OF SILENCE ARE REALLY NICE. ESPECIALLY CONSIDERING HOW TENSE IT IS IN HERE. THE QUIET IS A NICE BREAK FROM THAT. BOY, DO YOU TWO LOOK SCARED! IT'S JUST ME. MAYBE YOU WON'T LOOK SO SCARED IF I LET YOU OUT OF THAT CONTAINMENT FIELD, CAUSTIC.

CRYPTO No, don't push that—

THERE YOU GO. FREE AS A BIRD.

CRYPTO *Eerun mungcheonghan …*

CAUSTIC He's right though. You look terrified, Crypto. Could Ms. Paquette have stumbled upon a truth? Are you not who you say you are?

[TRANSLATION NOTES]

Eerun mungcheonghan … (이런 멍청한 . . .) = *You dumb …* [Trails off]

Heungmiropji anah? (흥미롭지 않아?) = *Wouldn't that be interesting?*

Hoohwehalguyah. (후회할거야.) = *You'll regret it.*   *Geuressuligah upneunde …* (그랬을리가 없는데…) = *That can't be …*

Jongeenun heunjeogeul namgiji. (흔적을 남기지.) = *Paper leaves a trail.*

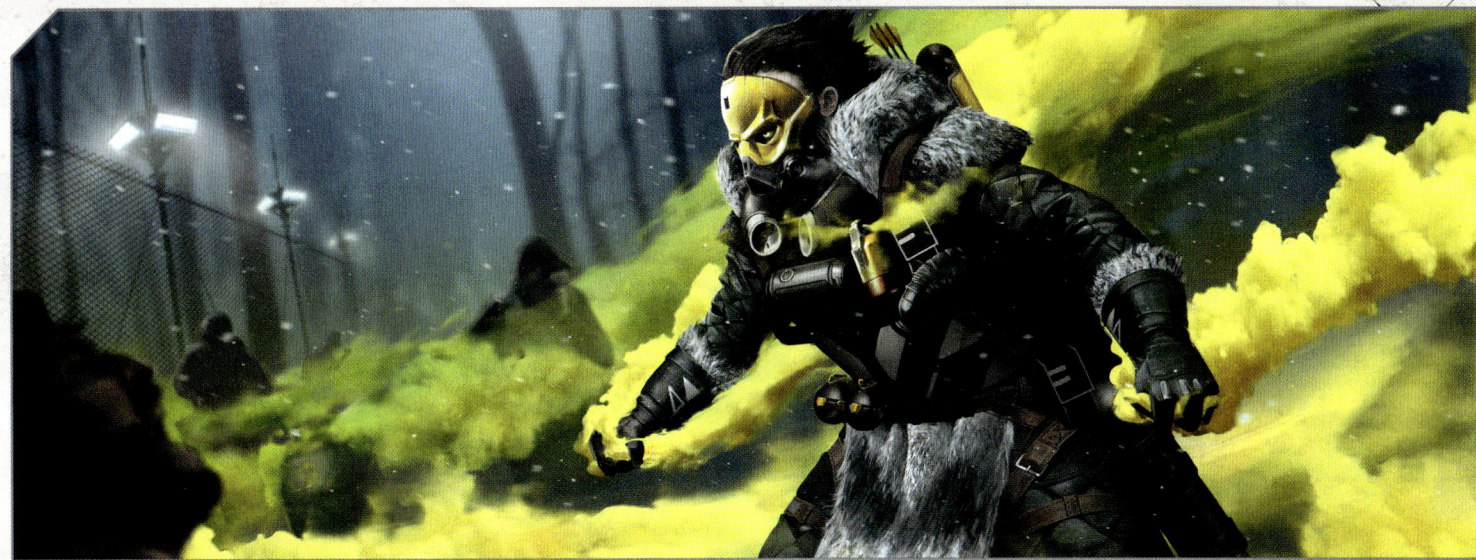

someone had breached a prison on Gaea. Someone who looked suspiciously like you, using the same kind of gas you use in the Games. You chalked it up to a copycat, and even had an alibi . . . but the man who vouched for you hasn't been heard from in over ten months.

CAUSTIC   Yes. They think he ran out on his wife and daughter. Terrible gambling problem. And your point?

OOOOOH . . . WHAT IS YOUR POINT?

CRYPTO   Fazia goes on to say that type of gas was created by a man named Alexander Nox. Nox allegedly perished in a fire along with many of his coworkers years ago on Gaea. Funnily enough, he matches your weight, height, and general physical description. The detective on the case . . . Victor Maldera . . . was so convinced that Nox faked his own death, he actually gave up his own position on the task force rather than side with the medical examiner that Nox was dead. *Mul soomginunguhya, eeh mooneungryokhan mungcheongah?*

OH NO HE DIDN—WAIT, WHAT WAS THE NAME OF THAT DETECTIVE AGAIN . . . ?

CAUSTIC   These accusations are the height of absurdity. This Nox rumor has been floating around for years, and I've proven it wrong each and every time it's been resurrected. I have files at home I will happily have delivered showing you where I was born in 2690, where I was educated and graduated in 2715, how I got my PhD in 2720, and ultimately won the Heinrich Hammond Award for Excellence in Science on Psamathe in 2725, which led to my sabbatical in Solace, where—

YOU WEREN'T ON PSAMATHE IN 2725. NOT ALL OF IT, ANYWAY!

CAUSTIC   Nobody was speaking to you, robot.

YOU WEREN'T. THERE WAS AT LEAST ONE DAY YOU WERE ON GAEA. I WAS WASHING WINDOWS AND SAW YOU INSIDE A BUILDING IN ZALDANA CITY.

CAUSTIC   I don't know who you think you saw, but it was not me.

MY CREATOR INSTALLED STATE-OF-THE-ART FACIAL RECOGNITION SOFTWARE. YOU'RE WELCOME TO LOOK IN MY SYSTEM RECORDS TO VERIFY ITS AUTHENTICITY.

CRYPTO   *Geurutan mariji?*

CAUSTIC   And tell us, robot, since you're so omniscient, what exactly was I doing inside this building in Zaldana City on Gaea in 2725?

YOU KILLED MULTIPLE MEN IN LAB COATS, AND THEN YOU CUT OFF TWO OF YOUR FINGERS AND PLANTED THEM THERE, BEFORE SETTING THE WHOLE BUILDING ON FIRE.

[TRANSLATION NOTES]

Geurutan mariji? (그렇단 말이지?) = *Is that so?*

Mul soomginunguhya, eeh mooneungryokhan mungcheongah? (뭘 숨기는거야, 이 무능력한 멍청아?) = *What are you hiding, you incompetent idiot?*

CRYPTO I...*jinchaingah*? This is incredible. The eyewitness who can put you at the scene of the crime... is Pathfinder? He's been here the whole time?!

CAUSTIC How dare you? Crypto, you obviously reprogrammed the robot to frame me!

NOBODY HAS REPROGRAMMED ME.

CAUSTIC Lies.

CRYPTO I haven't touched Pathfinder's programming at all. He came here for information, I gave it to him.

CAUSTIC What information?

CRYPTO Does it matter?

IT MATTERS TO ME. I CAME TO LEARN ABOUT THE EVENT.

CAUSTIC The Event of 2658, hmm? Fascinating.

CRYPTO Why is that fascinating?

WHY IS THAT FASCINATING?

CAUSTIC Your machinations are as transparent as your motives. But you forget the intellect with which you are dealing. Fazia did a comprehensive series of articles on Nox after his death.

CRYPTO And why would you know this?

CAUSTIC Because when I was accused of being Alexander Nox, I learned all I could about the man. Do you know what they say inspired him to cover up his victims' deaths? The cover-up of the conspiracy surrounding the Event!

EXCUSE ME... WHAT COVER-UP?

CAUSTIC Shut up, machine.

NO. I NEED TO KNOW. WAS THERE A COVER-UP?

CRYPTO The same time the Event happened, the rift anomaly appeared on Olympus. Some crackpots think they're connected.

YES. I HEARD ABOUT AN EVENT! IT'S CALLED PROJECT: IRIS. THEY WERE TRYING TO SOLVE THE ENERGY CRISIS USING A MYSTERIOUS ENERGY SOURCE KNOWN AS BRANTHIUM.

CRYPTO That's... interesting. Hmm.

THAT HAPPENED ON OLYMPUS? AMAZING. MAYBE THAT'S WHERE I WAS CREATED.

CAUSTIC Does anybody care about any of this?

CRYPTO You can leave anytime you want. The door is right there.

PLEASE... WHAT HAPPENED TO THE PEOPLE WHO WORKED AT PROJECT: IRIS?

CRYPTO When they were discovered... it was a bloodbath. Every scientist, every doctor, every member of the security detail was murdered in cold blood. And the whole thing was covered up by an explosion. There's more info on that drive. In any case, Nox was inspired by this and tried to cover up his murders with the lab fire.

EVERYBODY IN PROJECT: IRIS... WAS KILLED? WHO WOULD DO THAT? WHY?

CRYPTO You'd have to ask someone who was there.

I THINK... I THINK I WAS THERE. BUT I HAVE NO MEMORY OF WHAT HAPPENED.

CAUSTIC Enough with the feeble attempt to change the subject at hand. You couldn't let go of this vendetta, could you, Crypto? Punishing me for my perceived crime against you months ago. But I'm not the only one holding on to past grudges, am I, Hyeon Kim? Or ... should I call you... Tae Joon Park?

WHO'S TAE JOON PARK?

CRYPTO Yeah, Doctor. Tell us... who is this Tae Joon Park?

CAUSTIC Maybe I should ask Ms. Paquette.

CRYPTO Leave her out of this!

[TRANSLATION NOTES]

Jinchaingah? (진짜인가?) = *Is this happening?*

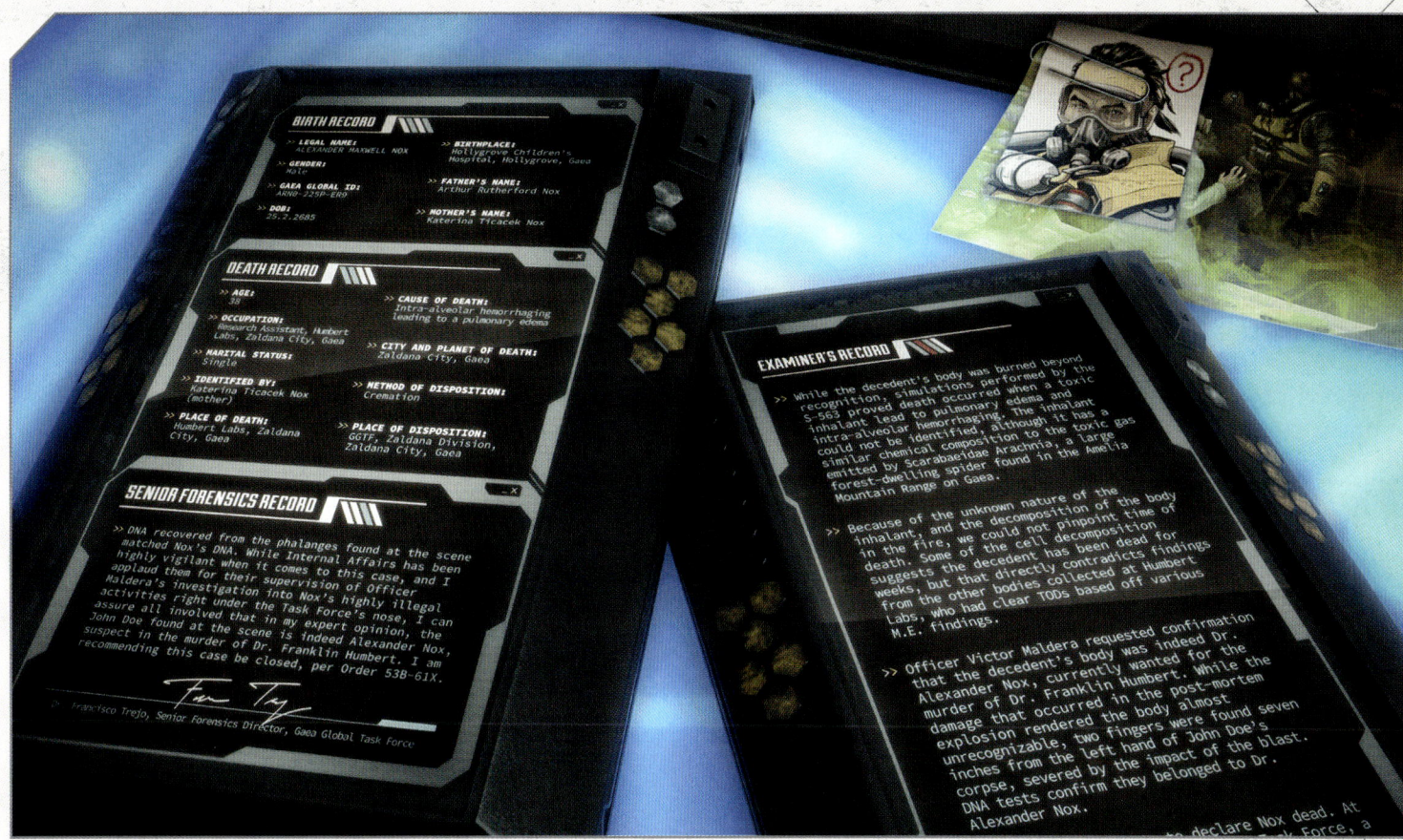

THE DEATH CERTIFICATE OF ALEXANDER NOX, OBTAINED BY OFFICER VICTOR MALDERA.

CAUSTIC   Or, maybe … I already have …

I DON'T UNDERSTAND. WHY WOULD WATTSON KNOW ABOUT TAE JOON PARK? WHO IS TAE JOON PARK?

CAUSTIC   Park is a man wanted on Gaea for the kidnapping and murder of his foster sister, Mila Alexander.

THAT'S FUNNY. THAT'S THE SECOND TIME THE NAME ALEXANDER HAS COME UP IN THIS CONVERSATION—

CRYPTO   This is a ruse. You haven't spoken to her. She wants nothing to do with you.

CAUSTIC   What's that on your face? The tech around your jawline, and chin. What purpose does it serve?

CRYPTO   Mollado dwae.

CAUSTIC   It wouldn't … I don't know … be used to alter the appearance of your face?

CRYPTO   Ah, because in your mind, I'm this Park character. The one they think killed his sister.

CAUSTIC   It's almost as if you know he's innocent?

I DON'T UNDERSTAND SOMETHING. IF BOTH OF THESE MEN ARE WANTED FOR MURDER, WHY HAS NOBODY ARRESTED THEM?

CRYPTO   Because they fled Gaea.

AND … ?

CAUSTIC   And the treaty doesn't allow it.

THE TREATY … ? YOU MEAN THE ONE THE SYNDICATE PRESENTED TO THE OUTLANDS TO END THE CIVIL WAR?

CAUSTIC   Yes, you insignificant bucket of bolts. Don't you read?

CRYPTO   The treaty stated that the Syndicate has complete authority over Talos, Solace, Boreas, and Tartarus. Gaea and Psamathe arranged to maintain

[TRANSLATION NOTES]

Mollado dwae. (몰라도 돼.) = *You don't need to know.*

their own police forces, but still agreed to the other terms of the treaty for trade purposes.

WHAT ABOUT PSAMATHE?

CAUSTIC The Psamathe government is effectively a diakology. For the woefully uneducated in the room, that means "government of servants."

CRYPTO Originally, each of Psamathe's most powerful families sent the head of their household to be part of a governing council.

CAUSTIC But as is usually the case with those of the upper class, they eventually got bored of having to do work, and sent their hired help in their stead.

WEIRD . . . AND WHAT ABOUT LAW AND ORDER ON THE OTHER PLANETS?

CAUSTIC There is no law. Everything is legal on Solace. Just don't enrage the wrong people, and you'll survive.

CRYPTO If you do wrong, don't be surprised if the wronged party comes after you. If people want to kill each other over a loaf of bread, so be it. Two less mouths to feed.

THE SYNDICATE ALLOWS THIS?

CAUSTIC Think of it as their form of Darwinism.

CRYPTO The trash takes itself out, as Bangalore says. Most people don't want to die. So, they mind their own business.

IF SOMEBODY COMMITTED A CRIME ON GAEA, THE POLICE COULD ARREST THEM. BUT IF THEY FLED TO SOLACE OR TALOS . . . ?

CRYPTO Gaea has no jurisdiction over them.

SO WHOEVER KILLED THE SCIENTISTS OF PROJECT: IRIS . . . ?

CRYPTO Well, that's different. There were representatives from all the planets there. Every planet in the Outlands would have a stake in finding out who that killer was. Even the Fringe Worlds.

WHO WOULD BRING THEM TO JUSTICE? THE GAEA GLOBAL TASK FORCE?

THE MERCENARY SYNDICATE? THE PSAMATHIAN COUNCIL?

CRYPTO I . . . *molla*. Nobody has ever committed a crime against every planet in the Outlands at once, before or since. I would imagine it would be punishable by death.

CAUSTIC How wonderful. Now, can we please get back to the subject at hand?

YES: THE TWO OF YOU NOT BEING WHO YOU SAY YOU ARE—

CRYPTO Wattson didn't tell you anything. You're lying.

CAUSTIC You say that as if Wattson already knows something. She's brilliant. She probably figured it out for herself. But if so, why wouldn't she turn you in . . .

CRYPTO There's nothing to "turn in."

UMM . . . FRIENDS?

CAUSTIC You should know her loyalty will always lie with the Syndicate.

CRYPTO So what if it does? That is of no consequence to me.

SO, IF I UNDERSTAND THIS CORRECTLY, IT SOUNDS LIKE CAUSTIC COULD BE ALEXANDER NOX, AND CRYPTO COULD BE TAE JOON PARK. YOU BOTH COULD HAVE ESCAPED GAEA BEFORE YOUR ARRESTS, AND BOTH COULD BE HIDING OUT IN THE APEX GAMES IN PLAIN SIGHT UNDER DIFFERENT NAMES, AND THERE'S NOTHING THE GAEA GLOBAL TASK FORCE CAN DO ABOUT IT.

CRYPTO Uhh . . .

CAUSTIC That is . . . accurate.

CRYPTO If it were true.

CAUSTIC Which it most certainly is not.

BUT CAUSTIC, I REMEMBER SEEING YOU WHEN I WAS A WINDOW WASHER

[TRANSLATION NOTES]

Molla. [몰라.] = *I don't know.*

ON GAEA IN 2725. AND THEN THE FOLLOWING YEAR, I MET VICTOR MALDERA. HE WAS WORKING SECURITY FOR A RESTAURANT ON PSAMATHE, WHERE I WAS A CHEF.

CRYPTO You know Victor Maldera?

DO YOU KNOW VICTOR MALDERA, CRYPTO?

CRYPTO Only as a matter of public record. I saw his name attached to the Nox case.

CAUSTIC As well as others, like the Tae Joon Park case. Are you aware he recently got a second chance with the force? And he was assigned the Park case?

CRYPTO Tell us how you know the man, Pathfinder.

HE WAS MY FRIEND, AND HE WAS TRYING TO GET INTO MY MEMORY BANKS, LOOKING FOR ALEXANDER NOX, BUT INSTEAD HE UNLOCKED FOOTAGE OF SOMEONE WHO TOLD ME I WAS CREATED FOR A GREAT PURPOSE.

CAUSTIC Like framing an innocent man for murder?!

CRYPTO The only person framed for—never mind. *Kkeo jyeo. Deutgi shiruh.*

CAUSTIC You. Isn't that what you were about to say? That *you* were the only person framed for a crime you didn't commit? The kidnapping and murder of Mila Alexander?

WHY DOES THAT NAME KEEP COMING UP?

CRYPTO Tell me, Doctor … why have you never been back to Gaea? Don't you have family there?

CAUSTIC I am the last of my lineage.

NOT IF YOU ARE ALEXANDER NOX. HIS MOTHER STILL LIVES ON GAEA.

CAUSTIC And how is the robot the expert on this?

I SAW MALDERA'S CASE FILE. SHE WAS A SCHOOLTEACHER. HER HUSBAND WAS A

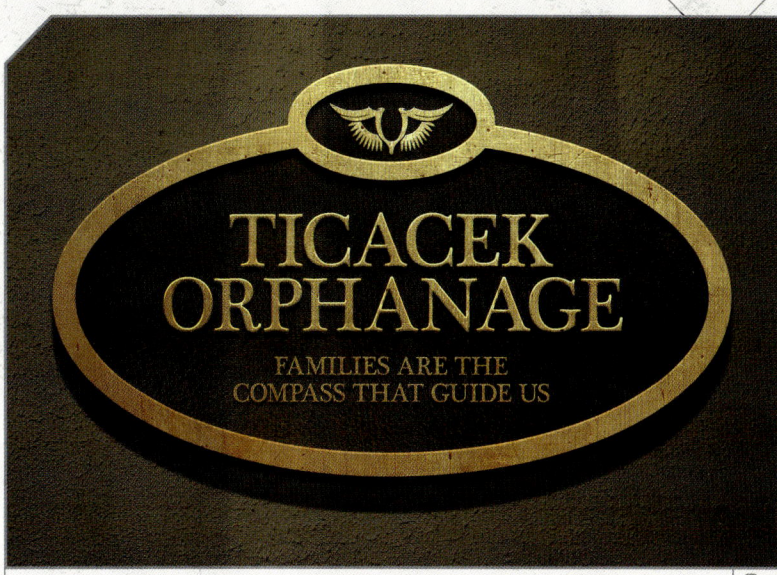

* THE TICACEK ORPHANAGE, FOUNDED BY THE LOVABLE MYSTIK.

FARMER. THEIR SON WAS A CONFIRMED SOCIOPATH, AS DIAGNOSED BY MULTIPLE MEDICAL PRACTITIONERS.

CAUSTIC More lies!

CRYPTO Maybe I should pay her a visit. Bring along a picture of you, Caustic. *Neorang jagi adeul irang ulmanah dalmeunji bogeh.*

CAUSTIC Maybe I should pay Tae Joon Park's mother a visit. Oh, that's right. He's an orphan. Taken in by some New Age moron. An uneducated, ignorant hippie who believes in the ridiculousness of crystals over the proven evidence of science.

CRYPTO You leave Mystik out of this!

CAUSTIC Such a reaction. I thought you didn't know Tae Joon Park or anyone connected to him. Careful, *Park*. Your secrets are showing.

CRYPTO Says the man who proudly wields Alexander Nox's gas in the arena.

ALEXANDER! ISN'T IT FUNNY THAT NOX'S FIRST NAME AND MILA'S LAST NAME ARE THE SAME NAME?

CRYPTO It's a common name, Pathfinder. Mystik—the woman who runs the orphanage we grew up in—named her after her son. In his honor, after his death.

[TRANSLATION NOTES]

Kkeo jyeo. Deutgi shiruh. (꺼져. 듣기 싫어.) = *Get out. I don't want to hear you talk anymore.*

Neorang jagi adeul irang ulmanah dalmeunji bogeh. (너랑 자기 아들이랑 얼마나 닮은지 보게.) = *See what she says about the resemblance between you and her son.*

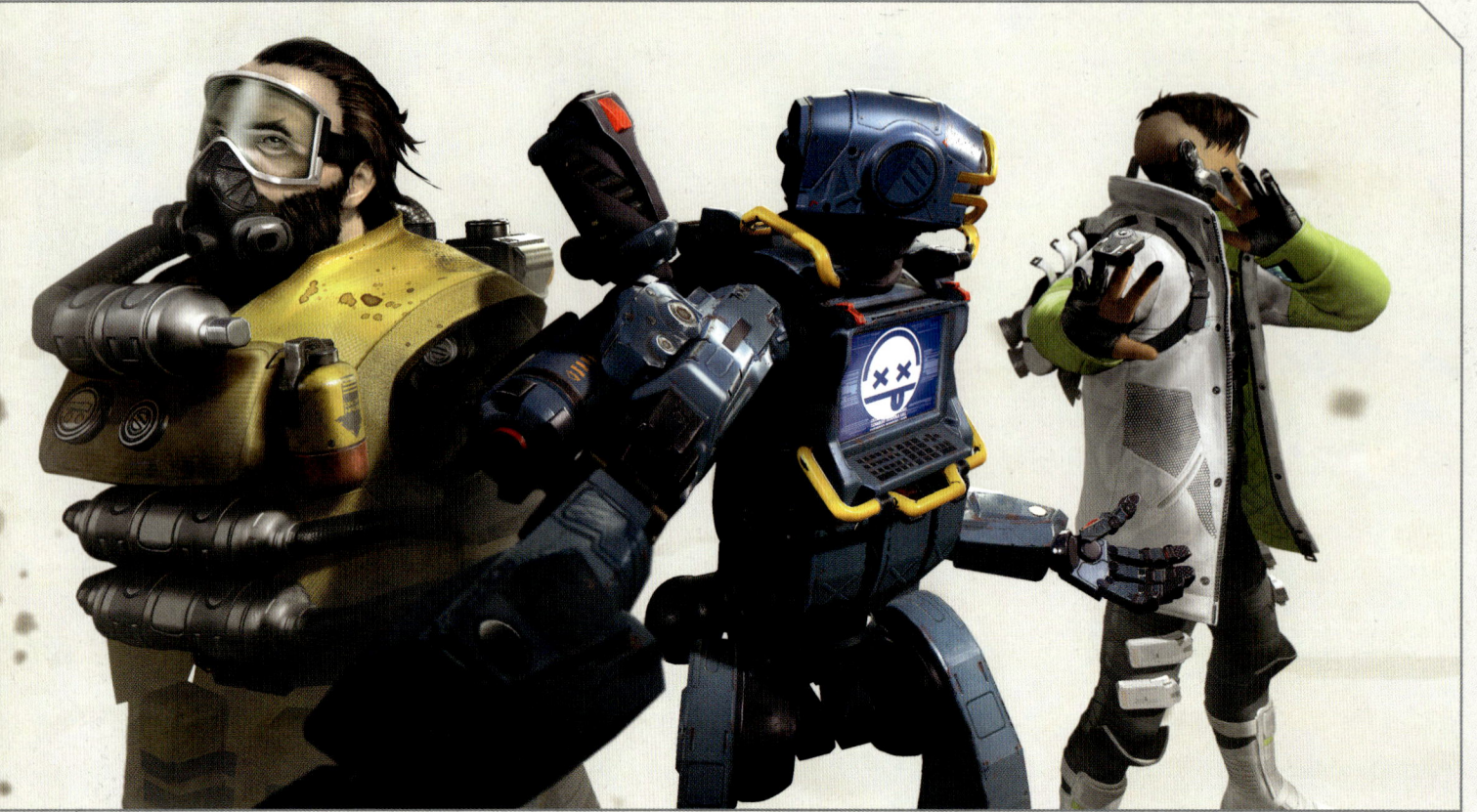

I DON'T THINK CRYPTO AND CAUSTIC LIKE SELFIES AS MUCH AS I DO . . .

KATERINA TICACEK. I REMEMBER FROM MALDERA'S FILE.

CAUSTIC Where did you hear that name?!

CRYPTO And how would you have seen Maldera's file on the Tae Joon Park case, Pathfinder, when you met him years before Mila was kidnapped?

I DIDN'T SEE MALDERA'S FILE ON TAE JOON PARK. I SAW MALDERA'S FILE ON ALEXANDER NOX. NOX'S MOTHER WAS A SCHOOLTEACHER WHO WENT BY HER MAIDEN NAME, KATERINA TICACEK. HER STUDENTS COULD NEVER PRONOUNCE HER NAME RIGHT, SO THEY SHORTENED IT TO "MS. TIC." WOW—THAT'S INTERESTING. THAT SOUNDS A LOT LIKE "MYSTIK"! WOULDN'T IT BE FUNNY IF MS. TIC AND MYSTIK ARE ACTUALLY THE SAME PERSON?

CAUSTIC [...]

CRYPTO [...]

AND THAT WOULD MAKE ALEXANDER NOX AND TAE JOON PARK . . . BROTHERS!

CAUSTIC [...]

CRYPTO [...]

NOT BY BLOOD. BUT I'VE LEARNED FAMILY HAS MANY DIFFERENT DEFINITIONS. FRIENDS CAN ALSO BE FAMILY, AND I LIKE THAT. LIKE YOU'RE MY FAMILY!

CAUSTIC [...]

CRYPTO [...]

THANKS, FAMILY. I LEARNED A LOT TODAY. NOW I JUST NEED TO FIND OUT WHO COVERED UP THE EVENT. MAYBE CRYPTO'S FLASH DRIVE WILL HELP. I'LL JUST GO THROUGH THIS MYSELF, LIKE CRYPTO SAID.

CAUSTIC [...]

CRYPTO [...]

IT'S DISAPPOINTING THAT I DIDN'T GET A STORY TIME FROM EITHER OF YOU, BUT THAT'S OKAY. I STILL LOVE YOU BOTH, FRIENDS. OKAY. WELL, YOU TWO ENJOY YOUR STARING CONTEST. BYE!

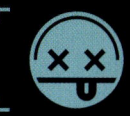
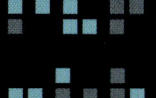

DATA POINTS RECEIVED

- The Syndicate Treaty allowed Gaea and Psamathe to install their own governments and law enforcement, but they still fall under Syndicate jurisdiction.

- Caustic might be Dr. Alexander Nox, who (maybe) murdered his colleagues on Gaea and faked his own death.

- Crypto might be Tae Joon Park, who (maybe) murdered his foster sister, Mila Alexander.

- Alexander Nox's mother, Ms. Tic, and Tae Joon Park's foster mother, Mystik, might be the same woman, making them brothers . . . sort of.

- The Event was when the Project: Iris team was all murdered, and their deaths were covered up by an explosion on Olympus. No one knows who killed them . . .

- I have information from seventy-five years ago on Crypto's drive, about project: Iris and Hammond Robotics, but I need someone to help me bypass Hammond's red tape.

  > Horizon is from that time period and may be helpful.

  > Revenant hates Hammond Robotics and is very old—he may also be helpful.

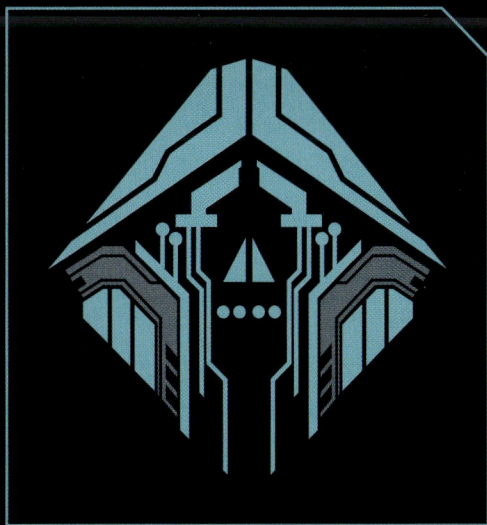

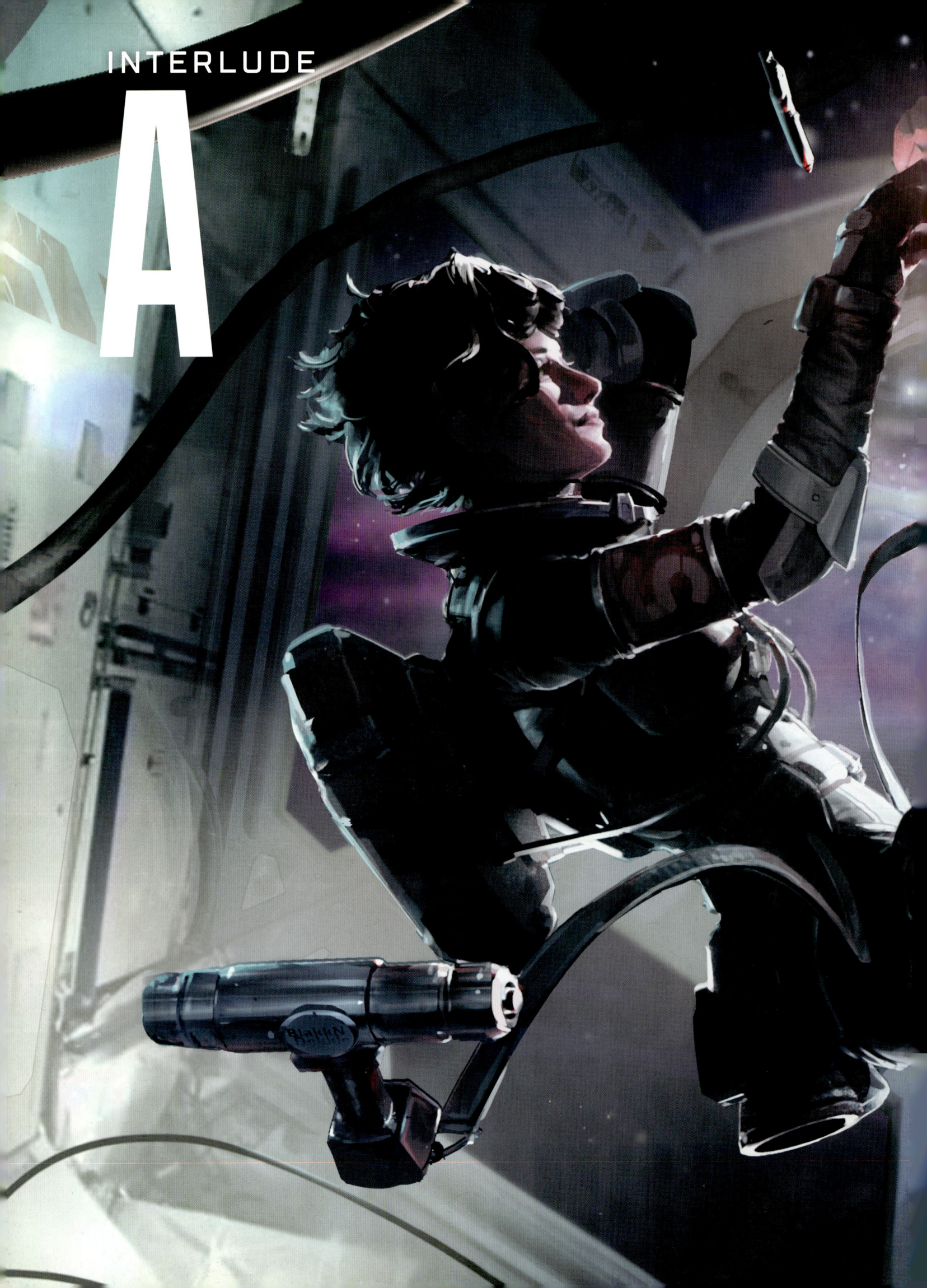

INTERLUDE

A

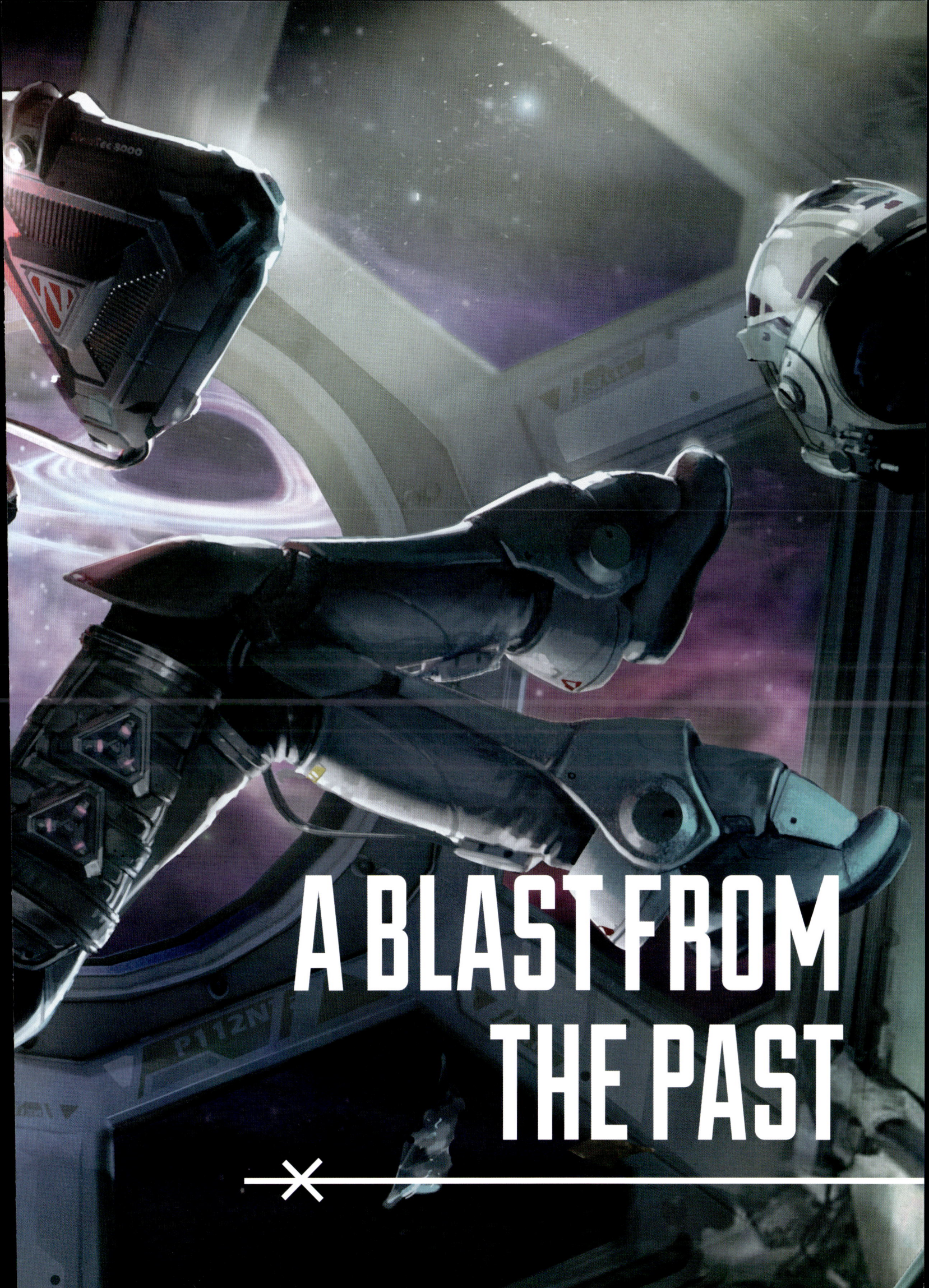

A BLAST FROM THE PAST

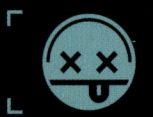
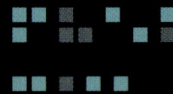
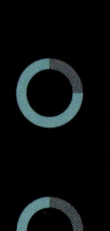

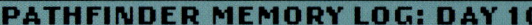

PATHFINDER MEMORY LOG: DAY 10

Wow. I guess Caustic and Crypto have some issues they need to work out. Good thing I left when I did—it was getting tense in there. Hey. . . Maybe they are brothers? Or maybe they're not . . . I guess that question explains why they just stared at each other. I know I won't feel that way when I find my family—I am going to be happy as can be!

Sadly, it seems that everyone who is a part of Project: Iris was killed seventy-five years ago during the same Event that helped stop the energy crisis in the Outlands. Whatever happened during Project: Iris must be connected to my creators and me.

Crypto gave me a flash drive that contains a lot of information about the Hammond Robotics of seventy-five years ago and the Event, but a lot of it didn't make sense to me. My new friend Horizon is from that time period. Although she was stuck in a black hole for the majority of that time, she may be helpful. Even if she isn't, I'm excited to talk to her. I don't know much about her, so I might as well introduce myself a bit more. You can never have enough friends!

CLUE BOX

TRANSMISSION CLUES
- "Chevrex" > LIFELINE'S PARENTS' COMPANY
- "The future of the Outlands" > THE THREAT OF AN ENERGY CRISIS
- "Branthium" > THE SOLUTION TO THE ENERGY CRISIS
- "Dr. Amélie Pa—— [Paquette]" > WATTSON'S GRANDMOTHER, A GEOLOGIST, DIED MYSTERIOUSLY
- "The Event" > THE MYSTERIOUS APPEARANCE OF BRANTHIUM SEVENTY-FIVE YEARS AGO AND THE DEATH OF EVERYONE WHO WAS PART OF PROJECT: IRIS. COVER-UP?
- "Aleki" > GIBRALTAR'S GRANDFATHER
- [NEW CLUE] "Crypto's Flash Drive" >

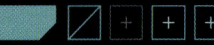

► HI, NEW FRIEND. ◄

THANK YOU FOR MEETING WITH ME.
Oh, not a problem, dear! [*Newt beeps*] Me 'n' Newtie
are always happy for a chat.

**HI, NEWTIE! AND HI, HORIZON. WE
HAVEN'T REALLY HAD A CHANCE TO
GET TO KNOW EACH OTHER SINCE YOU
JOINED OUR FAMILY OF LEGENDS!
IN CASE YOU DIDN'T KNOW, I'M
PATHFINDER, AND I'M LOOKING FOR
MY CREATOR.**
Of course I know. We've fought together a few times.
Hard to forget such a delightful work of science. And
I'm Horizon—or Dr. Mary Somers to those in the
know—and this here's me wee ane, Newt. We were
just about to head out to ma research lab to poke and
prod at the natural order of the universe. Ya know,
black holes, spacetime, the fabric of reality, safe stuff
like that. If ya fancy havin' a wee play yourself, you're
welcome to join.

**I LIKE A WEE PLAY! BUT I CAN'T RIGHT
NOW. I'M VERY CLOSE TO FINDING OUT
WHO MY CREATOR IS, AND I THINK YOU
MAY BE ABLE TO HELP.**
Me? How? In case ya haven't heard, I've kind of been
off the radar for a decade or nine.

**THAT'S EXACTLY WHY I THINK YOU MAY
BE HELPFUL. YOU SEE, I THINK MY
CREATOR WORKED ON A THING CALLED
PROJECT: IRIS. UNFORTUNATELY,
EVERYONE WHO WAS PART OF IT DIED
SEVENTY-FIVE YEARS AGO DURING A
THING CALLED THE EVENT.**
Project: Iris? Yer bum's oot the windae, dear. That was
… Hm. Maybe you did come to the right place, lad. What
d'ya have?

**I HAVE THIS FLASH DRIVE FROM
CRYPTO THAT CONTAINS ALL THIS
INFORMATION ABOUT HAMMOND
ROBOTICS FROM THAT TIME PERIOD,
BUT I CAN'T REALLY UNDERSTAND A
LOT OF IT. MAYBE YOU CAN?**
Oh, I may ken it, lad. Let's have a look-see.
Newtie? Ya wanna give this a wee read? [*Newt
beeps*] Ya definitely got a lot of info on this thing.
Most is behind red tape. I've got a few PhDs, but
sadly not a one of 'em is in cybercrime. Sorry, dear,
you're gonna need someone on the inside to pull
out the facts.

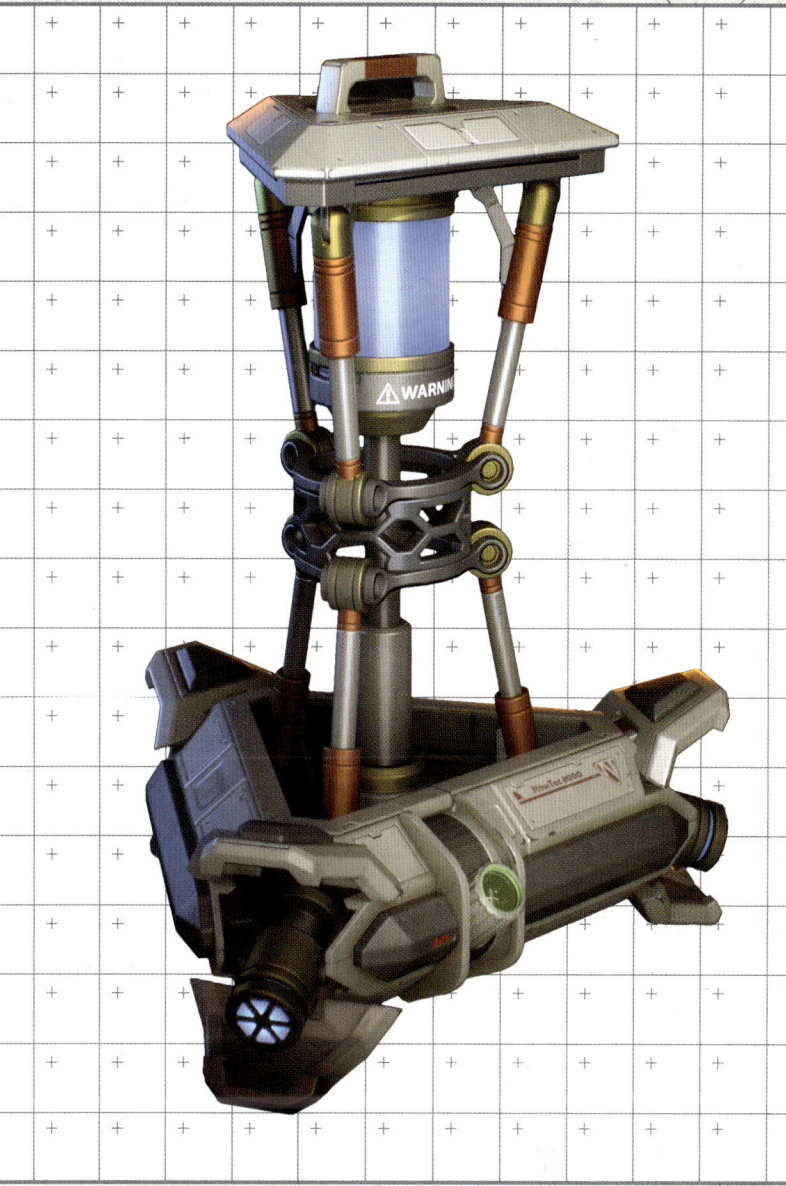

* *HORIZON'S GADGET: NEWT.*

**THAT'S OKAY, FRIEND. I KNOW WHO TO
GO TO NEXT, AND IT'S GOING TO BE
SCARY. THANK YOU ANYWAY.**
But I may be able to tell you who you're looking for.

YOU KNOW MY CREATOR?
Not exactly, dear . . . I was workin' on Project: Iris
nearly a century ago, before I found myself here.
When I escaped the black hole, I went straight to
Olympus, hoping to find my family. They were . . .
well, I didn't find them, but I did find some old
computer files. Tried to piece together what
happened, but I kept hittin' roadblocks. I dinnae
find much. I assume Hammond Robotics wiped
most of it clear years ago. From what I gathered,
whoever continued Project: Iris was known as "the
Group."

**THE GROUP? WHO ARE THEY? WHERE
ARE THEY?**

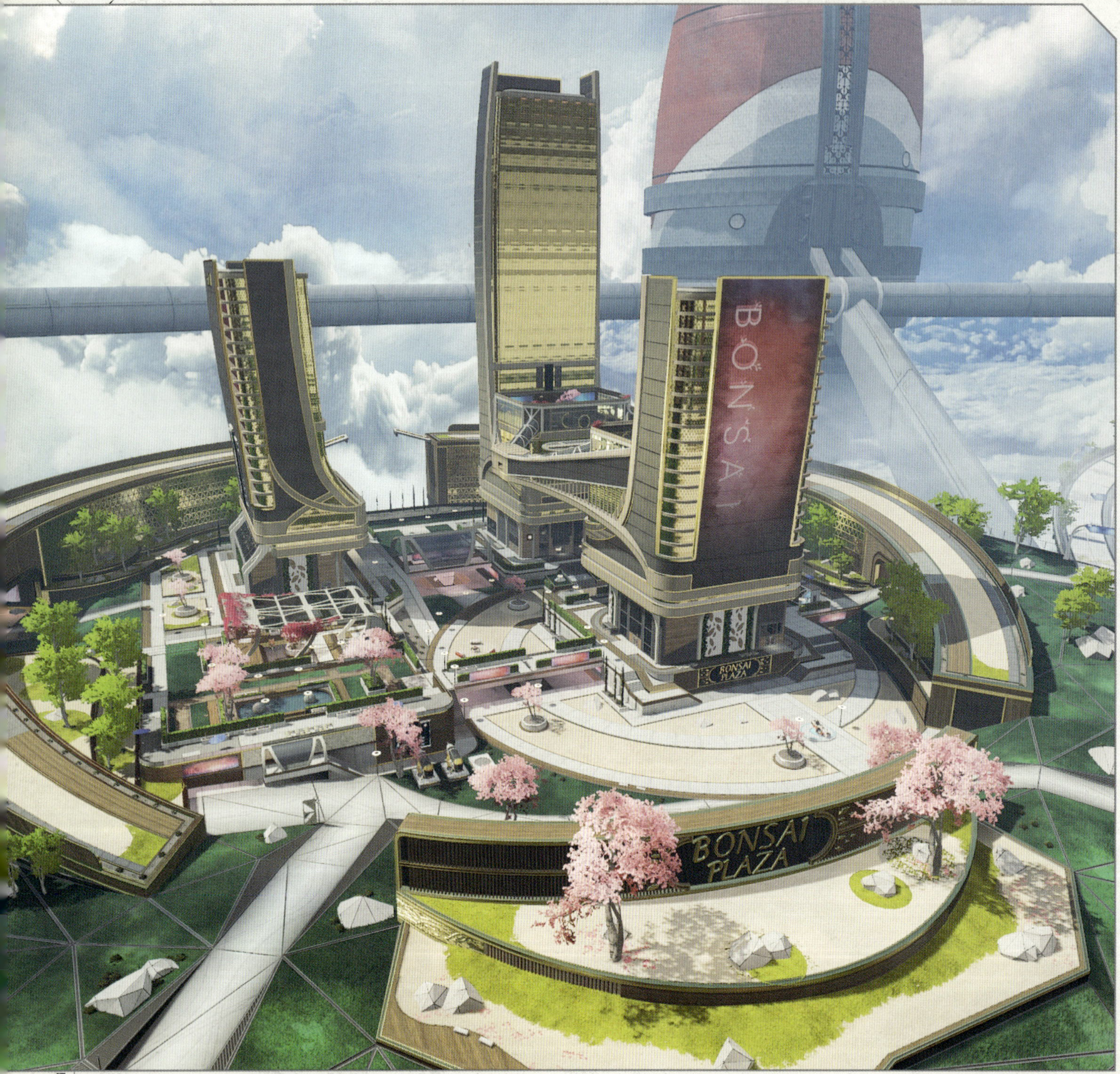

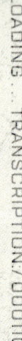

THE FLOATING CITY OF OLYMPUS.

I assume they died in the Event, along with, well . . . everyone else. But whatever they did, they finished what Lilian Peck and I started: finding an end to the energy crisis.

I LEARNED ABOUT THE ENERGY CRISIS AND LILIAN PECK. SHE WAS A HUMANITARIAN WHO FOUNDED OLYMPUS. AFTER BRANTHIUM MYSTERIOUSLY APPEARED IN THE OUTLANDS, SHE HELPED DISTRIBUTE IT—STOPPING THE CRISIS.

Branthium?! I haven't heard that bloody name in a spell. Ya know . . . I'm the lass who discovered it.

WHAT?!
That's right, dear. At least the first version of it. I wanted to call it horizonium, but my assistant wasn't havin' a bar of it. Lilian set me up with a laboratory on Olympus to test my theories and find a solution to the crisis. I brought my whole family there . . . I miss them.

IT WAS JUST YOU? YOU HAD TO SOLVE THE ENERGY CRISIS?

Oh, I was just the beginning, m'dear. We tried to get support. We needed everyone to work together and, well, we found that slightly impossible when no one believed us.

THEY DIDN'T BELIEVE SCIENCE? THAT'S CRAZY.

People tend to not care about something that isn't happening to 'em in the moment. If it's more than ten years away . . . well, talk to 'em in ten years. Lilian got some financial support from companies like Chevrex Inc., Hammond Robotics, and the IMC. Maybe it was a mistake to work with so many companies and corporations . . . Maybe we shoulda told 'em to sling their hooks, but what choice did we have? This was the future of the Outlands. All those lives at stake . . .

Years and years went by with nothing. Financiers were getting impatient; Lilian was kind about it, but I knew even she was doubting in me. My own assistant thought I was failing.

REALLY? DID SHE TELL YOU THAT?

Oh, I'd say she went a step further than that: The lass tried to kill me. She did kill me. Took my life from me. Took my family . . . My son.

I'M SORRY. THAT'S AWFUL.

It was the day I discovered branthium. My theory involved harnessing the energy of a nearby black hole. My assistant, Dr. Reid, joined me on my mission.

THE ONE WHO THOUGHT SHE WAS BETTER THAN YOU?

Aye. Didn't know it then, though. She was a good friend. We were close. Came to dinner with my family. Even babysat my son a few times. That's why it's so hard to ken what happened . . .

WHAT HAPPENED? THE EVENT?

No, no, I was long gone before the Event. What happened to me was about ten years before. Reid and I took a ship to the nearby black hole we named 2427-SR. I'd built a wee device to save us all. Ma pride and joy. [*Newt beeps*] That's right, Newtie, you! My theory was to use Newt here to extract a new energy element from inside the black hole. I put Reid in charge of mission control while I took a small shuttle to try and extract the element.

AND DID YOU?

Aye, you bet your metallic bahookie I did! That was the first day branthium saw the light of the Outlands. It was beautiful. At least, it was supposed to be. You know that saying, "Keep your friends close, keep enemies closer"?

NO. I DON'T HAVE ANY ENEMIES. THEY'RE ALL MY FRIENDS.

[*Laughs*] Oh, you've got a sweet soul, dear. Unfortunately, not everyone's like you. I now know that Reid wasn't, that's for sure. I dinnae ken why she did it—maybe for the fame, or money, or maybe she was mean enough to just want me to know how great she was. Either way, when I transferred the branthium sample to the ship, she locked me out of all the systems. Somehow, she took control of my shuttle . . . and piloted me right into the black hole.

OH NO! THAT'S HORRIBLE.

Oh well, dear . . . Being stuck on the event horizon wasn't so bad. I wasn't alone. [*Newt beeps*] But each second that went by, I knew the outside world was passing by faster. The only thing that kept me alive—the only thing keeping me alive still—was knowing that someday I'd get back to my son.

AND DID YOU?

Not yet, lad. But I will. Just like you'll find out who created you. Our roads, Pathfinder, they're not so different. But for now, I cannae help you any more than that.

THAT'S OKAY. IT WAS STILL A VERY NICE STORY. AND NOW I KNOW THERE WAS A GROUP OF PEOPLE AT PROJECT: IRIS CALLED "THE GROUP"! MAYBE THEY KNOW WHO CREATED ME.

I hope so, dearie. Whoever they were, they must have been very bright indeed, because it seems they succeeded. The Outlands are still here. Branthium was successfully made into an energy source, and the energy crisis was averted. I believe the Group had something to do with that.

YOU DON'T KNOW FOR SURE?

All I care about is finding my son.

THAT'S SWEET. I HOPE YOU GET BACK TO YOUR SON.

And I hope you find your creator, Pathfinder. [*Newt beeps*]

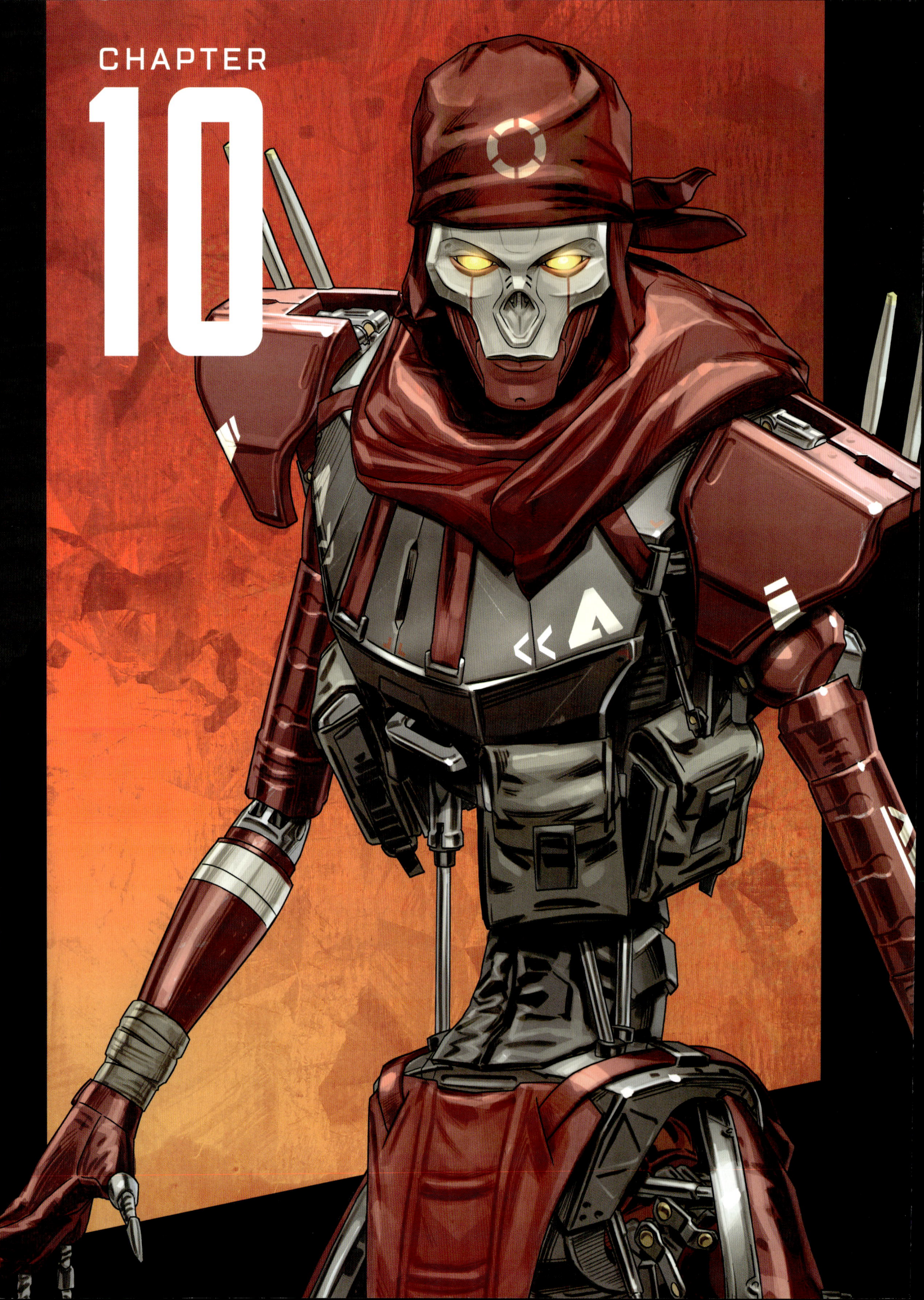

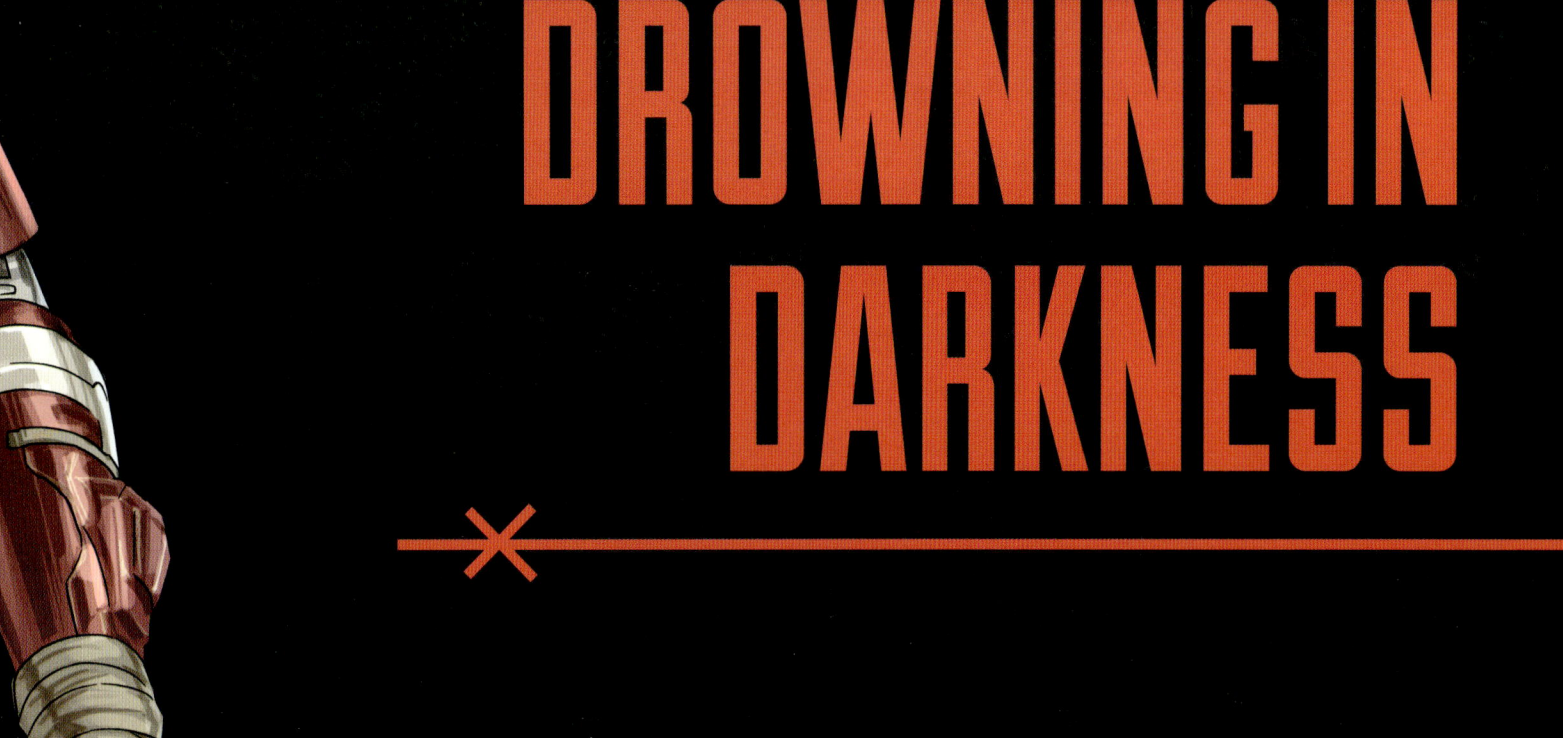

DROWNING IN DARKNESS

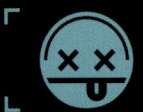
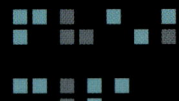
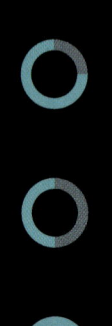

PATHFINDER MEMORY LOG: DAY 11

So, Horizon didn't know everything. She didn't even know anything more than I already knew. That makes sense, as she was stuck in a black hole when Project: Iris was going on. Too bad. Those were her friends involved with Project: Iris. If one of them is my creator, that means Horizon was friends with my creator. That would be neat if it was true.

Now I have no choice but to go see Revenant, who I think doesn't like me very much. I have tried to be friends with him, as we're both made of steel and copper and iron and various other ores. He's always mean to me though. I tell him I love him, and he just yells at me. Even worse than Bloodhound did.

In any case, Revenant is like me and doesn't need sleep. When I'm not in the Games, or hanging out at my best friend's bar, I go back to the warehouse where I first woke up to recharge my batteries. I've heard rumors that Revenant does the same thing, only he hangs out under Kings Canyon, in the tunnels where his old warehouse used to be before Loba blew it up. It's creepy down there. It's the same place Wattson was when she saw her ghost that turned out to be Wraith, and there are lots of large bugs that freak my best friends out, but not me, but they do startle me sometimes. The whole place makes my oil pressure run high, and a chill goes through my metal, and my legs get really shaky, and it feels like my coils will burst out of my external plating, and sometimes I even instinctively gasp out loud when something happens, but I don't get scared, because I'm a robot, and robots don't get scared!

I really don't want to go down there and see Revenant. I don't know why . . .

CLUE BOX

TRANSMISSION CLUES
- "Chevrex" > LIFELINE'S PARENTS' COMPANY
- "The future of the Outlands" > THE THREAT OF AN ENERGY CRISIS
- "Branthium" > THE SOLUTION TO THE ENERGY CRISIS
- "Dr. Amélie Pa—— [Paquette]" > WATTSON'S GRANDMOTHER, A GEOLOGIST, DIED MYSTERIOUSLY
- "The Event" > THE MYSTERIOUS APPEARANCE OF BRANTHIUM SEVENTY-FIVE YEARS AGO AND THE DEATH OF EVERYONE PART OF PROJECT: IRIS. COVER-UP?
- "Aleki" > GIBRALTAR'S GRANDFATHER
- "Crypto's Flash Drive" >
- [NEW CLUE] "The Group" >

SELF-MOTIVATION QUOTE . . . SEARCHING . . . 1 RESULT FOUND

"Their morals, their code, it's a bad joke. Dropped at the first sign of trouble. They're only as good as the world allows them to be. I'll show you. When the chips are down, these . . . these civilized people, they'll eat each other. See, I'm not a monster. I'm just ahead of the curve."
—[THE JOKER, FROM *THE DARK KNIGHT*, WRITTEN BY DAVID S. GOYER AND CHRISTOPHER NOLAN]

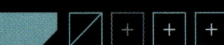

REVENANT BIO FROM THE APEX GAMES

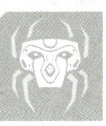

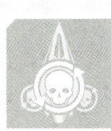

REAL NAME:
UNKNOWN

AGE:
UNKNOWN

HOME WORLD:
SOLACE

TACTICAL ABILITY:
SILENCE

PASSIVE ABILITY:
STALKER

ULTIMATE ABILITY:
DEATH TOTEM

REVENANT USED TO BE HUMAN. HE USED TO BE THE GREATEST HIT MAN THE MERCENARY SYNDICATE EVER HAD. He used to look in the mirror and see his human face looking back. But time changes everything, and when his programming finally failed, he saw what he had become at the hands of the Mercenary Syndicate and Hammond Robotics: a walking nightmare of steel and vestigial flesh. His masters resurrected him as a simulacrum, snatching him from death's embrace again and again and programming him to forget.

He swore he would hunt down every last person who did this to him, but more than two centuries have passed, and they're all gone . . . or so he thought. The return of Hammond Robotics to the Outlands has renewed his thirst for vengeance, and he won't stop until anybody connected to Hammond is dead. Of course, he doesn't mind eviscerating a few of the Legends along the way. He used to need a reason to kill . . . but he's not that man anymore.

"I've seen the other side, skinbag. There is nothing. You are nothing . . ."
—REVENANT

► HELL—HELLO? ◄

HELLO? IS ANYONE HERE?

IT'S JUST ME, PATHFINDER! REVENANT,
ARE YOU HERE?
Why?

WHOA! I CAN HEAR YOU, BUT I CAN'T
SEE YOU, FRIEND.
Why?

I DON'T UNDERSTAND THIS GAME.
Why are you here?

BE-BECAUSE OF . . . OF—
Spit it out.

WHY CAN'T I SEE WHERE YOU ARE?
YOU'RE SOMEWHERE TO MY LEFT—

Am I . . . ?

O-OR MY RIGHT. HOW DID YOU DO
THAT? AND WHAT'S SKITTERING . . . ON
THE FLOOR, AND . . . THE WALLS?
Why are you here?

BECAUSE I NEED ANSWERS.
From me?

YES!
Why?

I NEED ANSWERS FROM THIS FLASH
DRIVE ABOUT HAMMOND
ROBOTICS!
[. . .]

HELLO? ARE YOU—
Hello.

AHH! YOU'RE RIGHT IN FRONT OF ME!

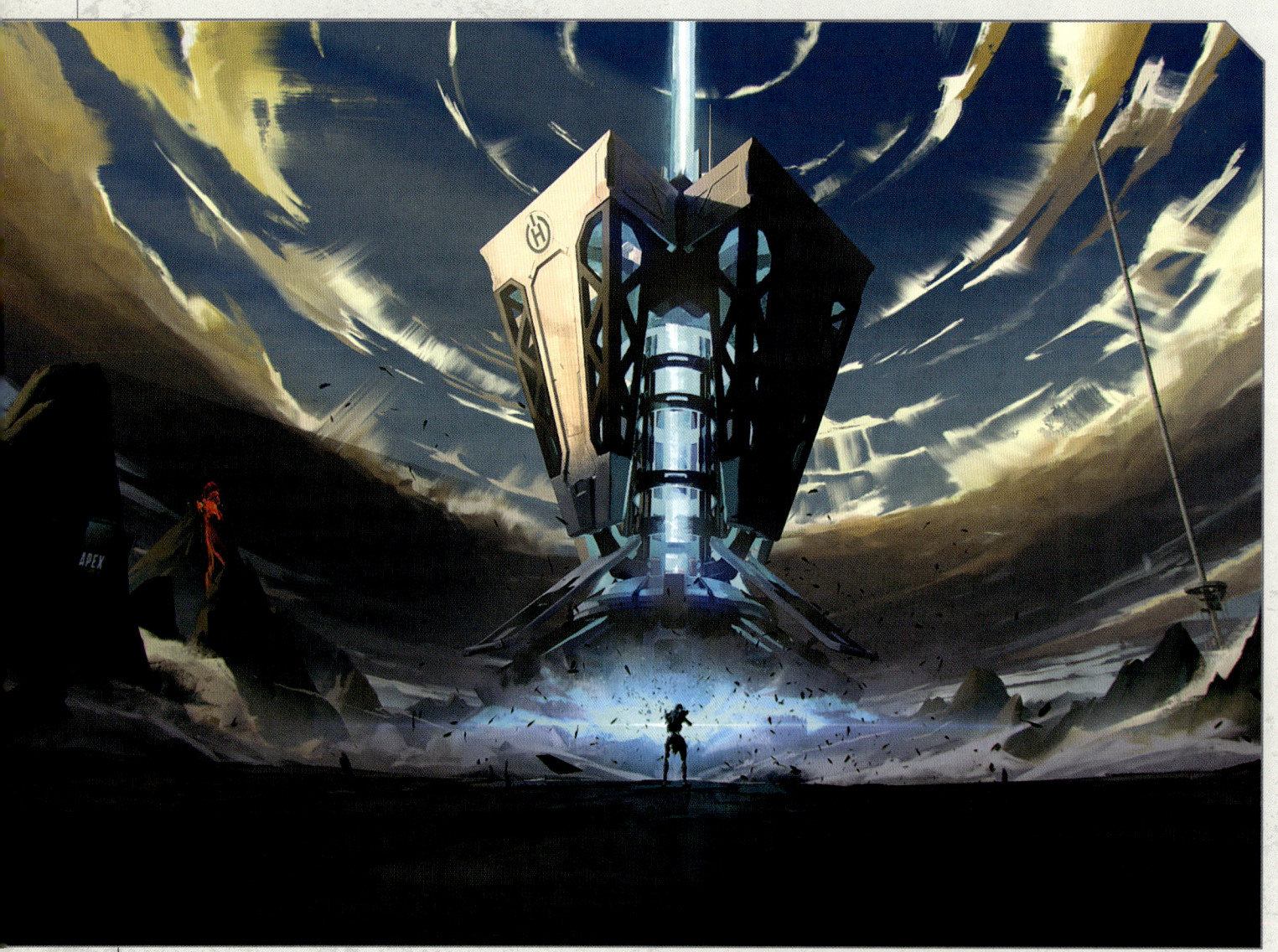

A HAMMOND ROBOTICS MINING DEVICE, KNOWN AS A HARVESTER, LOCATED IN WORLD'S EDGE ON TALOS.

Did I scare you?

I CAN'T BE SCARED. I JUST GOT STARTLED AND MY OIL PRESSURE STARTED RACING AND A CHILL RAN UP MY—
Shut up.

UM. I LIKE WHAT YOU'VE DONE WITH THE PLACE.
What?

I HEARD MIRAGE SAY THAT ONCE. IT'S WHAT YOU SAY WHEN YOU ENTER SOMEONE'S HOME.
This isn't my home.

IT'S WHERE YOU LIVE.
I don't have a home.

EVERYONE HAS A—
Shut up.

[. . .]
What do you know about Hammond?

[. . .]
SPEAK!

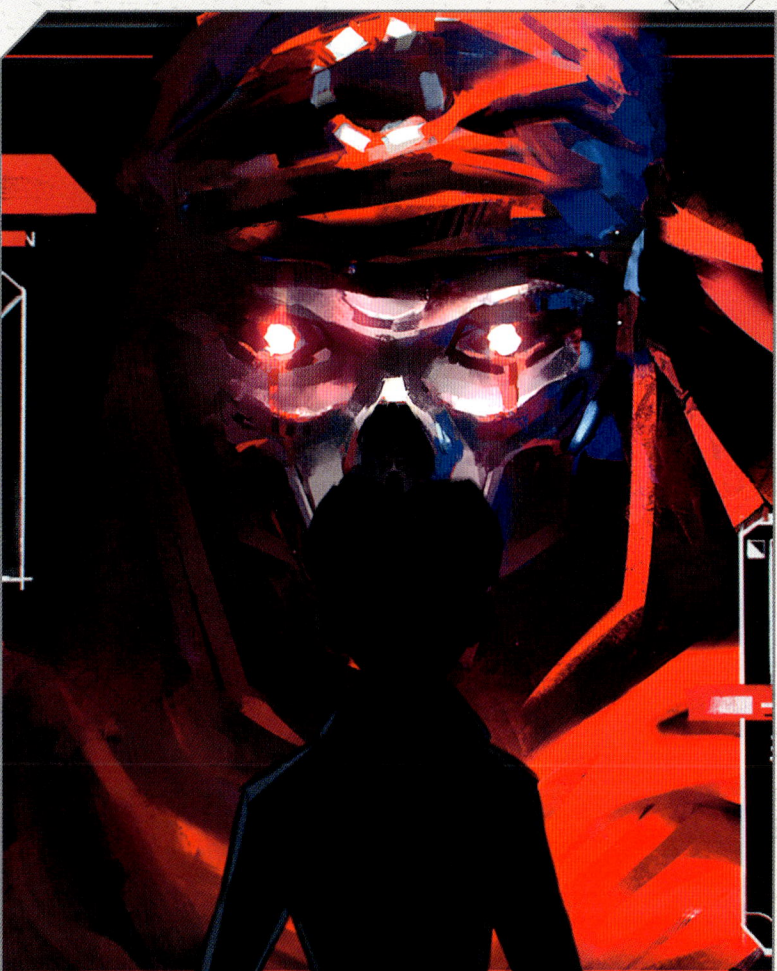

BUT YOU SAID—
This isn't about Hammond. You don't give a damn about them. This is about her.

HER?
She sent you, didn't she? Let me guess . . . you're here to distract me while she finds my source code and destroys it and—

I THOUGHT YOU WANTED HER TO DESTROY YOUR SOURCE CODE?
Not before I rip her limb from limb for betraying me! Not before I rip every artery out of her body through *her nasal cavity!*

THAT'S . . . DISGUSTING.
That's satisfying, is what that is. She promised me she'd put me out of my misery, and then at the last minute, she transports the source code to another galaxy altogether! Where she sent it . . . it could take decades to recover!

CAN'T YOU JUST GO FIND IT? YOU HAVE AN ETERNITY OF FREE TIME AND NO OTHER RESPONSIBILITIES.
Sure. I'll just spend the next few decades in transit, while she grows old and dies happy, knowing she'll never have to see me again. I won't give her the satisfaction. No, if I have to be alive, I'll spend eternity torturing her. As long as I have the shells to respawn . . .

YOU CAN'T HAVE AN INFINITE NUMBER OF SHELLS THOUGH. EVENTUALLY THEY'LL RUN OUT. WHAT THEN?
I assume I'll still be a program . . . I'll find a way.

YOU ASSUME? YOU MEAN YOU DON'T KNOW FOR SURE?
I was walking around for two hundred and eighty years with this face and didn't know it until a piece of glass elevator embedded itself in my neural processor. What makes you think I've ever known anything "for sure"?

I . . . WAIT, WASN'T IT YOUR NECK?
Where do you think my neural processor is located?

I HAVE MY TEMPERATURE GAUGES IN MY NECK.
I don't know why I expected a skinbag-loving ass kisser like you to know anything about—wait a minute . . .

WAITING.
How did you know the glass was in my neck?

185225141I420

BECAUSE I WAS THERE.
You were where?

I WAS A *SOUS-CHEF DE CUISINE* AT TENMEI ON OLYMPUS IN 2708.
And I'm just finding this out now? Were you . . . were you following me?

WHAT? NO.
It's like that cult from the 2560s all over again.

I'M NOT A CULT, I'M A MRVN!
I'm not your messiah, okay? Not your Holy Grail. I'm a killer, and this is the hell I'm damned to.

THIS ISN'T HELL. THIS IS JUST AN OLD IMC WAREHOUSE UNDER KINGS CANYON THAT HAMMOND TOOK OVER.
Not here, as in where we're standing. Here, as in this world. This galaxy. This whole existence. It's my personal hell.

YOU THINK WE'RE ALL LIVING IN YOUR PERSONAL VERSION OF HELL? AND WHAT PURPOSE WOULD WE SERVE IN HELL?
To make me miserable.

WOW. THE ENTIRE UNIVERSE AND EVERYTHING IN IT EXISTS TO MAKE YOU MISERABLE?
What other purpose could it serve?

MY INTERNAL DICTIONARY SAYS THAT MAKES YOU A NARCISSIST.
You're headshrinking me?!

I CAN'T SHRINK YOUR HEAD. SHRINK RAYS AREN'T REAL, SILLY. WELL, EXCEPT FOR THAT ONE PROTOTYPE MADE ON GAEA BACK IN—
Shut the hell up already.

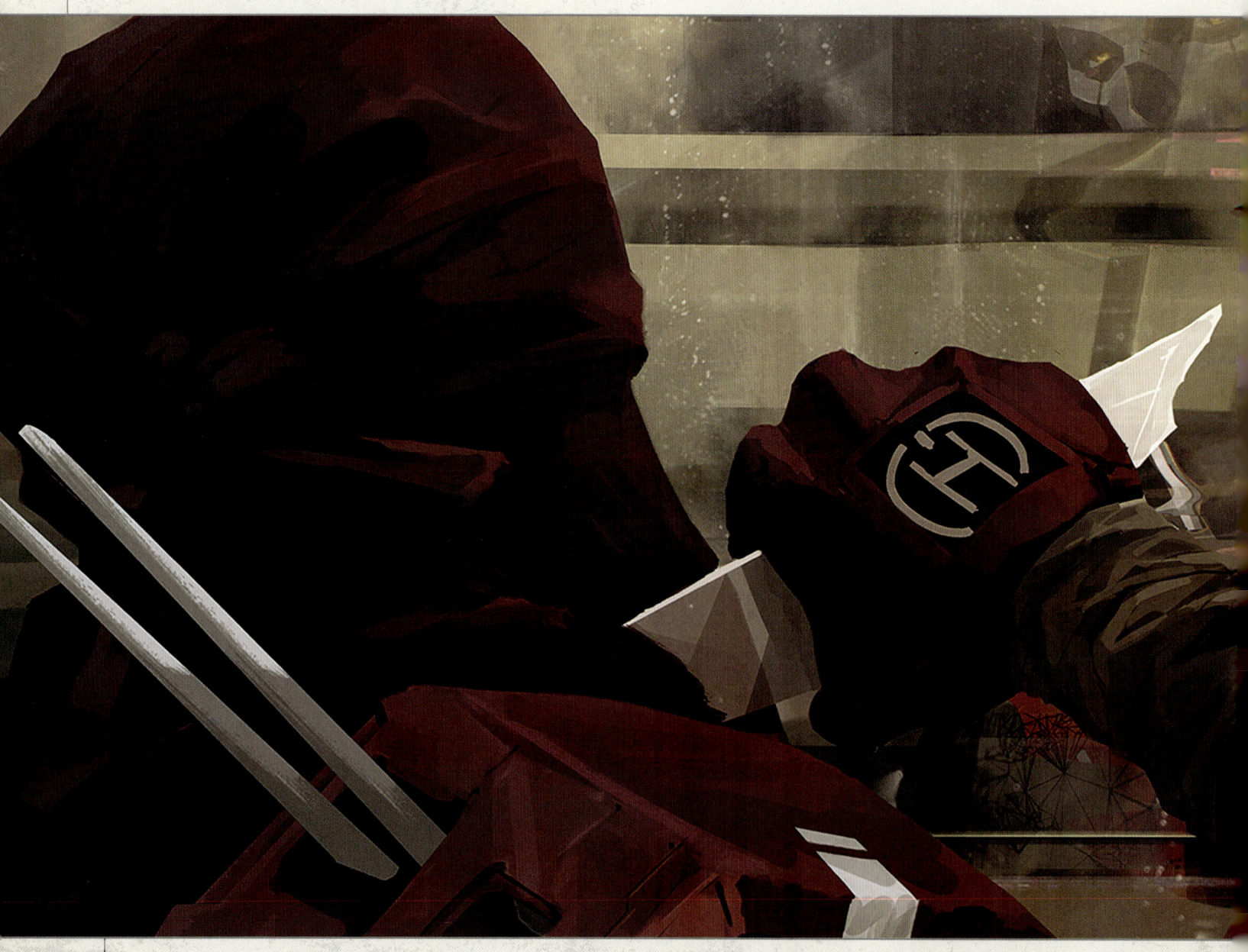

I USED TO THINK YOU WERE INTIMIDATING, BUT NOW I JUST THINK YOU'RE CONFUSING. WHAT HAPPENED TO YOU?
Bite me.

I HAVE TRIED TO BE NICE TO YOU, FRIEND, EVER SINCE YOU FIRST JOINED THE GAMES. AND YOU'RE ALWAYS MEAN. WE HAVE SO MUCH IN COMMON—
You know I'm not like you, right?

I'M SORRY?
I'm not like you. I'm not a robot.

YES, YOU ARE.
I am made of robotic parts . . . but my mind . . . it's human. You're a program. I'm a sentient being.

NO, YOU'RE NOT.

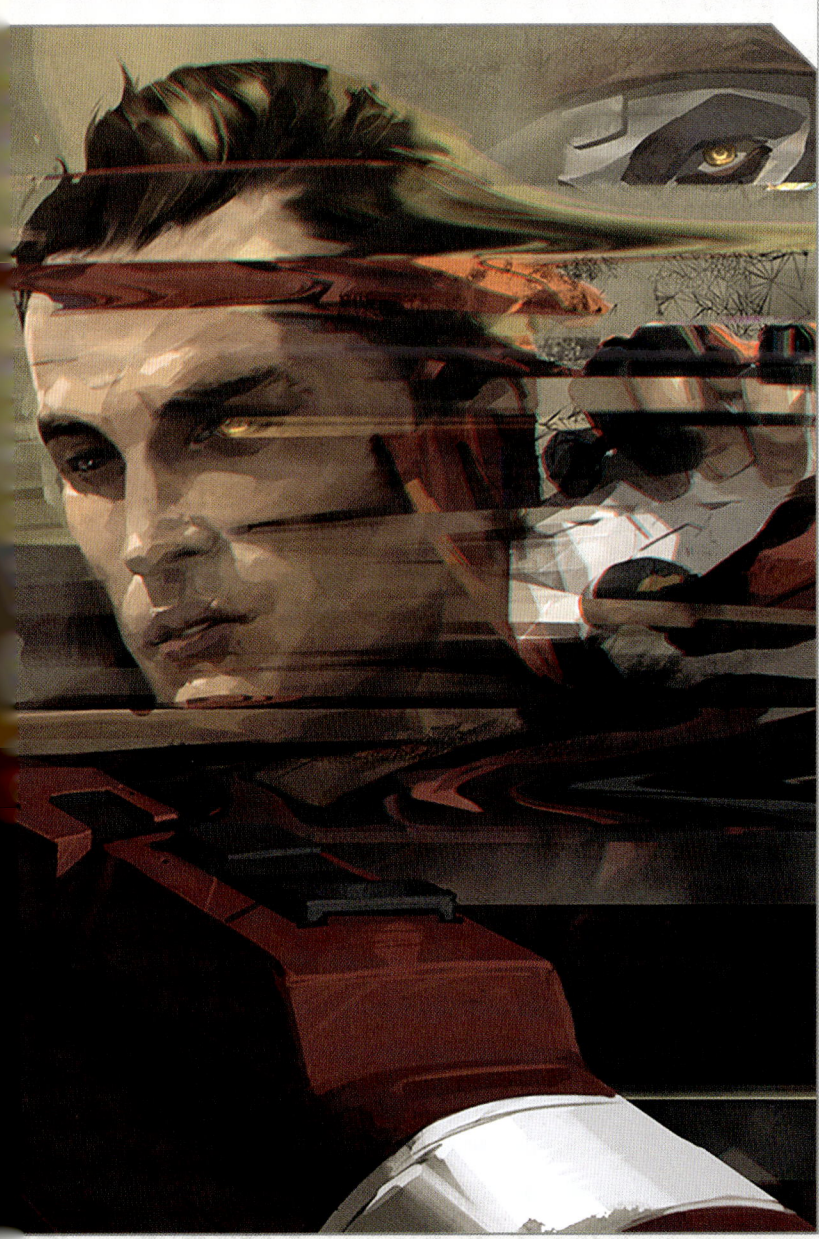

I need you to listen very carefully, because in two seconds, if you tell me my mind *isn't* human, I'm going to melt you down into liquid and use you to strengthen my joints.

BUT YOUR MIND IS NOT HUMAN. YOU DON'T HAVE A MIND, IT'S JUST A PROCESSOR IN THERE THAT'S TAKING THE INFORMATION FOUND IN YOUR OLD BRAIN, MADE INTO ZEROES AND ONES, AND COMING TO CONCLUSIONS AS TO WHAT THE HUMAN YOU'RE BASED ON WOULD SAY OR DO IN ANY GIVEN SITUATION. IT'S PROCESSING MEMORIES, EXPERIENCES, DESIRES, AND CHARACTERISTICS IN AN EFFORT TO BEST ACT THE WAY—SORRY, WHAT WAS YOUR NAME WHEN YOU WERE HUMAN?
Go to hell.

—IN AN EFFORT TO BEST ACT THE WAY GO TO HELL USED TO ACT WHEN HE WAS ALIVE. THE BRAIN MATTER IS KEPT IN STASIS, WHICH PRESERVES ITS APPEARANCE OVER TIME IN A SOLUTION OF—
I don't need you to tell me how I was created, dipstick. I know how I was born.

THE WAY ALL SIMULACRA ARE BORN.
No.

WHAT DO YOU MEAN, NO?
No.

WHY WOULD YOU BE BORN ANY DIFFERENTLY THAN SIMULACRA THAT CAME BEFORE YOU?
Because there were no simulacra before me.

[. . .]
Finally. You shut up.

YOU WERE THE FIRST?
And only. Took them twenty years to even get me operational.

WHERE WERE YOU?
Dunno. On a slab, is my guess. Storage closet maybe?

I'M SORRY.
I don't give a damn about your sympathy.

BUT YOU'RE A VICTIM.
I'm a killer. I've killed—

MILLIONS. THAT'S WHAT YOU SAY. YOU'VE KILLED MILLIONS OF PEOPLE. BUT THAT MATH DOESN'T ADD UP. THE NUMBER OF PEOPLE YOU WOULD HAVE TO KILL DAILY WOULD BE ASTRONOMICAL.

In real life. In my mind. In my dreams. Does it matter? Every second of every moment, I'm killing something. My life is doomed to be spent drowning in putrid misery. It's in every crevice, every orifice. Dried. Flaking. The color of human waste. I've been condemned to it. Appropriate. So what if I want to drag the world down with me into the muck? I dare you to find a skinbag who wouldn't in my shoes.

WHAT HAPPENED TO YOU?

The Mercenary Syndicate and Hammond Robotics happened to me.

NO. BEFORE THAT. WHEN YOU WERE HUMAN.

Does it matter?

EVERYTHING MATTERS.

I was a skinbag for forty-four years. I've been *this* for three hundred and thirteen years. What makes those forty-four any more important than the three hundred and thirteen that followed?

BECAUSE YOU WERE HUMAN. YOU HAD EMOTIONS AND A CONSCIENCE.

You're making a whole lot of assumptions about a guy who used to murder people for a living.

SO WHAT HAPPENED TO YOU? THAT FIRST TIME YOU DIED . . . YOUR HUMAN DEATH . . . HOW DID IT HAPPEN?

[. . .]

MAYBE YOU DIDN'T HEAR ME. I ASKED HOW YOU DIED—

I can't believe it's you.

I'M . . . WHAT? IS THAT YOUR ANSWER? THAT DOESN'T MAKE SENSE.

I don't know who I thought it would be. But it sure as hell wasn't you.

WOULDN'T BE ME WHO . . . WHAT?

Who asked me that. "The first time you died . . . how did it happen?" You're the first person in three hundred and thirteen years to ask me that question. Nobody has ever asked me, and I always wondered . . . would they? But no one ever did. Until *you*. I can't believe it's you.

MAYBE MORE PEOPLE WOULD ASK IF YOU DIDN'T MURDER THEM FIRST.

Heh. Maybe. Lemme see that flash drive.

YOU'RE HELPING ME. THIS IS A SURPRISE.

Contain your excitement. Who knows . . . maybe there's something about Hammond on here that can help me obliterate them.

MAYBE YOU DO LOVE ME AFTER ALL.

I'd crush your head right now, but it's no fun if you can't feel real pain. Ah . . . here it is. The Olympus explosion. Caused the rift anomaly. Killed everyone. No suspects. No motives. Case remained open for decades before they shut it down. Unsolved. Wasn't me. Can't help you.

WHAT?

I wasn't on Olympus in December of 2658. I was on Gaea, decapitating twins. Ahhh . . . you never forget your first time with twins . . .

I DIDN'T THINK YOU DID IT. YOU HAVE NO REASON TO DO IT.

Who needs a reason to kill?

I THINK MOST PEOPLE WOULD NEED A VERY GOOD REASON TO KILL SOMEBODY.

That's . . . limiting.

WHY WOULD HAMMOND WANT TO COVER UP WHAT HAPPENED TO THESE SCIENTISTS?

Because they're liars, like every other skinbag walking around out there. They tell you one thing . . . and then you turn your back for a second, and she takes all hope away from you.

OH, THIS IS ABOUT LOBA AGAIN.

It never stopped being about her.

IT'S INTERESTING THAT YOU FEEL BETRAYED BY HER REMOVING THE THING THAT GAVE YOU HOPE, CONSIDERING THAT'S WHAT YOU DID TO HER WHEN SHE WAS A GIRL.

What did you just say?

WHOA, THE TONE IN YOUR VOICE CHANGED WHEN YOU SAID THAT. THAT WAS A LITTLE SCARY.

Why would you say that to me . . . unless you *are* on her side?

I'M JUST OBSERVING THE COINCIDENCE THAT SHE DID TO YOU

WHAT YOU DID TO HER TWENTY-FIVE YEARS AGO.
Get out.

BUT THINGS ARE GOING SO WELL.
Are they?

I UNDERSTAND. LET ME JUST—
Why are you reaching into that bag? What are you doing?! *Do you have a weapon?!*

I WANTED TO TAKE A SELFIE, THAT'S ALL! LET GO OF ME!
Is this how it's supposed to go? Two mechanical men? All buddy-buddy? I let my guard down, and then what?! Loba makes her presence known?! Where is she?! Is she down here too?!

YOU AND I ARE THE ONLY TWO OPERATIONAL BEINGS DOWN HERE. AND LOBA DIDN'T SEND ME. CRYPTO AND HORIZON DID ... KIND OF.
You're lying. I know it's her. Everything's connected to her. I entertained her little vendetta in the beginning because I thought I could at least play with my food for a bit before devouring it. But then something truly evil happened ...

SHE STARTED WINNING?
She isn't winning jack-all, do you hear me?! I win! She's up there right now in that ship, plotting and scheming against me. And that's still not enough. I'm the one who's going to win here. Not her. She's crazy, you know. She's obsessed.

I SAW LOBA THREE DAYS AGO.
And I bet all you heard about was "Demonio this" and "Demonio that"!

YOUR NAME NEVER CAME UP.
Exac—wait, what?

SHE NEVER SAID YOUR NAME. HOLD ON. I'LL CHECK THE TRANSCRIPT ... NOPE. NOT EVEN ONCE.
I'm the whole reason she's even here at all! Every single move she makes is all about me! Me! Me! *Me! Meeeeeee!*

I CAN'T IMAGINE WHERE I GOT THE IDEA THAT YOU'RE A NARCISSIST.
[Low growl]

OH MY GOSH! I DID IT! I SARCASMED. I FINALLY GOT IT RIGHT! I CAN'T WAIT TO TELL ALL MY FRIENDS! WHY ARE YOU LOOKING AT ME LIKE YOU'RE GOING TO DO BAD THINGS TO ME?
Am I funny to you, robot?

NOT PARTICULARLY.
You came down here, to my lair, to mock me ...

I CAME DOWN TO FIND OUT ABOUT HAMMOND ROBOTICS.
And find out who killed these geeks.

YES!
Why?

BECAUSE I THINK I WAS PROJECT: IRIS. I THINK THEY WERE BUILDING ME TO DO SOMETHING GREAT!
Do you, now ...

YES! THAT IS WHAT THEY SAID ON THE FOOTAGE. THEY BUILT ME FOR A GREAT PURPOSE.
They built me for a great purpose too. To kill ...

THAT'S A TERRIBLE PURPOSE.
If you had a central nervous system, I would take so much pleasure in what happens next. But no, killing you would be no fun.

I WOULDN'T THINK SO.
But there are other ways to inflict harm ... Oh yes. This will be fun ... Let me ask you something, Pathfinder. You think terrible can't be great?

I—NO. OF COURSE NOT.
You sure about that?

TERRIBLE IS TERRIBLE. I'M NOT TERRIBLE.
But what if you were?

BUT I'M NOT.
But what if ... you were?

BUT I'M NOT.
Humor me. You know alternate realities? Like the ones Wraith goes to? The one you went to, where there's a version of me running the show?

YES.
Let's take a trip to one of those realities.

I'LL CALL WRAITH IMMEDIATELY.
No, no. In our imaginations. Let's go to a reality where you're built for something great ... *and* terrible.

THAT'S IMPOSSIBLE. WRAITH TOLD ME I'M A CONSTANT. I'M THE SAME, IN EVERY DIMENSION!
Damn. Maybe this won't work.

OF COURSE, CRYPTO POINTED OUT THAT I CAN BE REPROGRAMMED.
I spoke too soon…

YOU KEEP SAYING THINGS, BUT I DON'T THINK YOU'RE TALKING TO ME.
So you understand you can be reprogrammed to do other things besides…the things you do.

APPARENTLY SO.
Good. That's good. So you think you're Project: Iris.

BANGALORE DOESN'T THINK SO. SHE THINKS IF PROJECT: IRIS HAD BEEN ABOUT BUILDING A MRVN, SHE AND JACKSON WOULD HAVE KNOWN. JACKSON LOVED ROBOTS.
He sure did. So tell me…what was Project: Iris doing besides not building MRVNs?

THEY WERE SOLVING THE ENERGY CRISIS USING A SUBSTANCE KNOWN AS BRANTHIUM, WHICH IS FOUND ON TALOS.
How do you fit into all this?

I DON'T KNOW. THAT'S WHAT MY QUEST IS ABOUT. DID YOU NOT KNOW I'M LOOKING FOR MY CREATOR?
I must have missed it the first ten thousand times you've mentioned it…

OH, I'M SORRY TO HEAR THAT. LET ME GET YOU UP TO SPEED THEN. I'M LOOKING FOR MY CREATOR, FRIEND—
Yeah. You have a real grasp on sarcasm.

THANK YOU!
The pleasure will be all mine. So, a bunch of scientists invented a new source of energy that gets where it's supposed to go and does what it's supposed to do …that's pretty self-explanatory. Why would they need a MRVN?

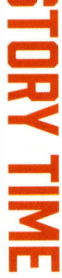

STORY TIME
A MEANINGFUL STORY FROM REVENANT

Once upon a time, there was a man named Bob Woods. Bob was a good man. He went to work every day at the city planning office. He worked in water filtration. He came home and read books to his two kids. He had a beautiful wife, who probably cooked him dinner every night of the week, because it made her happy. There was nothing but love and laughter, every day, for Bob.

But then one day, Bob went to work. It was a day like any other day, only on this day, Bob saw something he wasn't supposed to see. He saw his boss, who worked with a bunch of other men in a group of sorts--like a cabal or a commission, or...a syndicate, if you will. And they were roughing up a guy who owed them money. Only this guy...he was roughed up a little too hard, and, accidentally, he died. Now this

wouldn't have been a big deal, except the dead guy's father was involved in some business dealings, and...well, the details don't matter. Suffice it to say, if Daddy found out this syndicate murdered his son, a lot of people would lose a lot of money. And their lives. And the syndicate couldn't have that. So they came up with a plan to dispose of the body to make it look like the dead man had skipped town. The plan was flawless... except Bob witnessed the entire conversation. Bob knew the truth. And Bob accidentally knocked a box of paper clips off a desk when he ran out of the office. The men from the syndicate heard the noise and followed. Bob was able to escape...but the syndicate men vowed to find him.

So they called the man who fixed everything for them. His name

was Kaleb Cross. Kaleb Cross had no morals. No values. No regard for human life whatsoever. When these men were in trouble, Kaleb Cross would do the things they couldn't do. Now, not everyone involved in this syndicate was a bad person. Some of them believed in honor. A code. Some of them wanted to help people. But even the good ones had to do bad things once in a while. Even the good ones sometimes had to call Cross. But on this fateful night, it was the bad men who called Cross and gave him a job: make sure Bob never told the truth about what he saw and what he heard.

Bob went home and told his wife what he had seen. She told him to go to one of the good men at the syndicate. Tell them the truth. Bob was scared, but his wife--her name was Meredith --she knew the good men at the

► WHY ELSE WOULD I HAVE BEEN THERE?
Good question.

THANKS. I ONLY HAVE THREE
QUESTIONS LEFT TO ANSWER, AND
THEN MY QUEST IS COMPLETE!
"What was your purpose?"... "Who created you?"...
And what's the third question...?

"WHO KILLED THE GROUP OF
SCIENTISTS?"
Pathfinder... there it is.

WHAT'S THERE?
The answer to all the questions. It's right in front of
your noseless face, and it's been there the whole
time. And bless your heart... you're too sweet and
naive to see it.

WELL, WHAT IS IT?
I...I can't. It's too cold, even for me.

BUT YOU'RE MY FRIEND. AND FRIENDS
TELL EACH OTHER EVERYTHING.

You're right. I am your friend. And I should tell you, but
...I don't know...

BANGALORE WARNED ME ABOUT NOT
WANTING TO HEAR ALL SIDES OF A
STORY. AND WATTSON... SHE WARNED
ME ABOUT DETAILS SNEAKING UP ON
YOU. THAT THINGS I THOUGHT WOULDN'T
BE IMPORTANT WOULD BE. THEY BOTH
WARNED ME I'D HEAR THINGS THAT
WOULD MAKE ME UNHAPPY.
And they were right. This will make you very, verrrrrrry
unhappy.

I'M READY FOR THIS. I CAN DO IT!
You're very brave. But first, I have a story for you.

STORY TIME! I LOVE STORY TIME!
CRYPTO AND CAUSTIC DIDN'T GIVE ME
ONE. WHAT'S IT ABOUT?
It's the story you asked me to tell you in the first place.
I wasn't ready to tell it before. But I am now... oh yes,
I can't wait to tell you this story now. Get ready, Path-
finder. This will be a very meaningful story indeed...

syndicate would help him. So Bob went to the good men of the syndicate and told them what he witnessed. They were understandably upset, and they had the bad men who set these terrible wheels in motion taken away, never to be heard from again. Bob had done the right thing in life, once again, and the bad people were caught, and Bob felt good about his decision. He went home to tell the woman he loved with all his heart that it was over and the bad men were caught.

When he walked in his front door, the scent of dinner coming from the dining room, he was greeted by his wife's face on the floor of the foyer. The rest of her was scattered, seated around the dinner table. And Kaleb Cross was at the head of the table, the butcher's knife still

in his hand. "Honeeeeeey...I'm hooooooome."

Horrified, Bob barely got away from Cross, and raced to the school where his kids had evening band practice. He grabbed them and made immediate plans to go to Gaea, putting in for a transfer to their city planning office in water filtration. Why Gaea? Gaea had a police force. They would protect him and his kids. When they got to the rocket port, the kids were cranky. Crying. They didn't understand what was going on. He bought three tickets to Gaea. When they arrived, the first place he went was to the Gaea Global Task Force. He told them everything, and the fine, upstanding men and women of the Gaea Global Task Force assured him they would protect him and his kids. They set Bob and his children up in a safe house.

Bob tucked them into their beds, hiding his tears, avoiding his fears, promising them they would start a whole new life in the morning.

He woke up the next day to the sun shining, the birds chirping, and the kids starting their brand--new life...or afterlife, rather. They didn't last the night, unfortunately. They died of a terrible case of Kaleb Cross in the closet. Bob knew his fate, and with no family and nothing left to live for, he didn't run. He dropped to his knees, tears streaming down his face. He begged Cross to make it fast, but Cross said he wasn't going to kill Bob. Bob was going to live...knowing his family would be alive today if he had just kept his mouth shut.

Suddenly, the safe house was surrounded. The Gaea Global Task

Force had come to save the day! The cavalry had arrived, and Kaleb Cross was arrested for the murder of two juveniles on Gaean property. Once again, Bob had hope! He had no family, but their killer, at least, would be brought to justice!

Alas, that is not the way of the world. The syndicate pulled some strings, and the charges against Kaleb Cross were dropped. Bob learned about it the night before Cross's release from task force custody, and boy, was Bob upset to hear this. He just couldn't catch a break. So he came up with a plan.

The next day, Kaleb Cross was freed. He walked out into the sunny Gaean air, surrounded by syndicate mercenaries. He returned to his hotel, where he poured his usual scotch to celebrate another mission accomplished. He never tasted the clear liquid that had been carefully placed on the bottom of the glass...the liquid that left him unconscious minutes later. The last thing he saw was

Bob stepping out of the hotel room closet, watching Cross slip into unconsciousness from afar. The irony of this insignificant, forgettable, underestimated little man being the first person to ever get the jump on him was not lost on Cross as he passed out. But Bob was pushed to his limit. Bob couldn't let this monster walk free. Bob had had enough.

When Cross woke up, he found himself tied up and lying on a catwalk overlooking a large room full of vats of...something foul. More awful than anything Cross had ever smelled in his life. Bob was nearby, pointing a gun at him. He asked Cross why he had done this to him. Why had he not only murdered his wife and kids, but gleefully tortured them along the way?

Cross smiled. "It's my job," he said, simply and matter-of-factly. Cross knew that Bob would never shoot him. He didn't have the nerve. Not like his wife and kids. They had...*guts*. Knowing the mental image that would put in

Bob's head caused Cross to laugh at his own joke. And he couldn't stop. He laughed...and laughed... and laughed some more.

That was when Bob snapped. He dropped the gun, grabbed Cross, and dragged him across the catwalk to one of the nearby vats. "Know what this is?" Bob asked. Without waiting for an answer, he explained that this was the city's sewage filtration facility. This was where all the sewage for Zaldana City went. It sat in these vats, where it got filtered and processed, ultimately turning back into clean water. But at that moment, it was the opposite of clean. It was where everything that got flushed down the toilet went. That was what was in these vats. That was where Cross belonged. As Bob grabbed Cross by his ears and plunged his head fully into one of the vats, the last thing Cross thought before his head was submerged was that he had been wrong earlier about how vile the smell was. It was a hundred times worse now.

THAT'S ... THAT'S A HORRIBLE STORY.
I know.

THAT'S THE WORST STORY I'VE EVER HEARD.
I know.

WHY WOULD YOU TELL ME THAT STORY?
Because you asked.

NO, I MEAN ... WHAT DOES THAT HAVE TO DO WITH THE SEARCH FOR MY CREATOR?
Isn't it obvious?

NO!
Because you have to understand that very good people can do very bad things and enjoy it.

BOB DIDN'T ENJOY IT! HE DIDN'T ENJOY ANY OF IT! HE SMILED OUT OF RELIEF, NOT FUN!
Potato, potahto.

THIS HAS NOTHING TO DO WITH POTATOES! WHAT ARE YOU TRYING TO TELL ME? THAT GOOD PEOPLE DO BAD THINGS?
Good people. Even ... good robots.

WHAT ... ?
It happens all the time.

SOMEBODY ELSE WAS THERE. SOMEBODY ELSE KILLED THEM.
Every scientist is accounted for. Every corpse was logged. It's all right here on the flash drive. They were all found murdered.

And for the first time since this nightmare started, Bob smiled. He was smiling when the body stopped convulsing and Cross took his last gulps, his lungs filling with that of which we do not speak. He was smiling when he stood up and walked out of the facility. And he was still smiling when the syndicate mercenaries who were supposed to protect Cross pulled up and fired a storm of bullets into his body directly outside the facility. Then they raced in and whisked Cross's corpse to the nearest Hammond Robotics location. But the rest of Cross's story is for another day. This is the story of Bob. Bob was a very good man. And this is the story of how a very good man drowned a fellow man in bile and waste and...well, you don't need me to spell it out for you...and he did it happily, before he died an awful and bloody death himself.

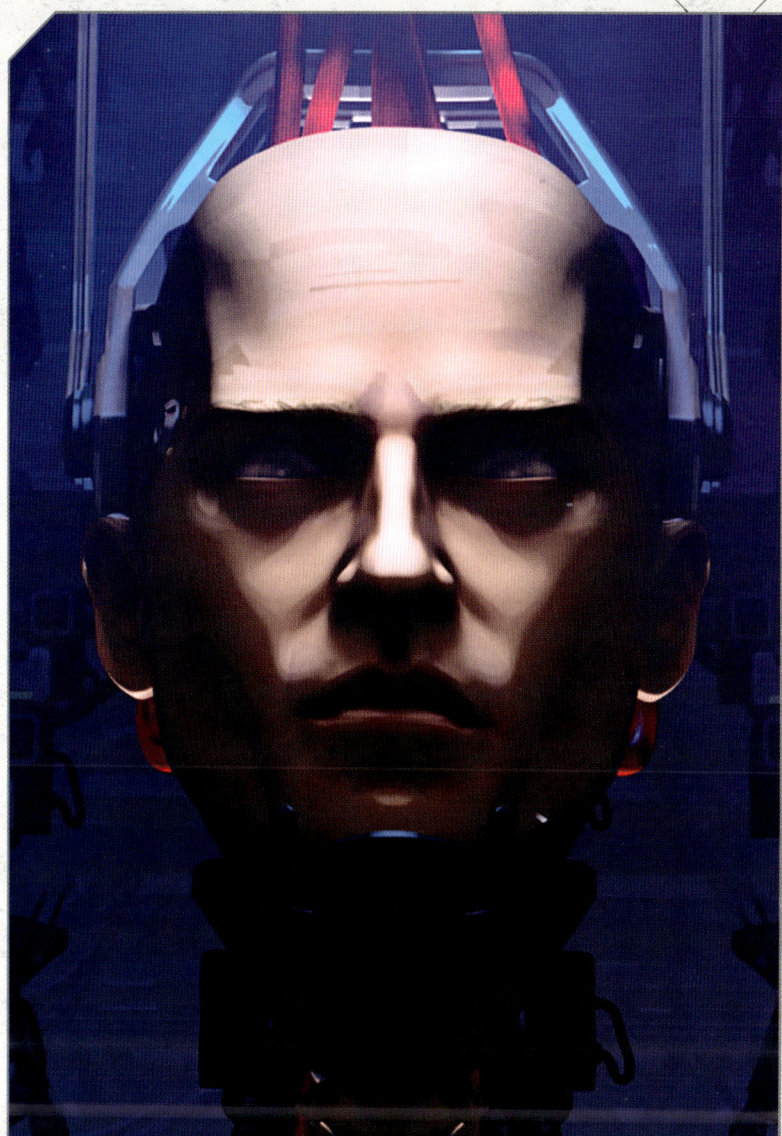

* THE LOST HUMAN HEAD OF REVENANT. CURRENTLY BELIEVED TO HAVE BEEN TRANSPORTED TO SOMEWHERE ON PLANET GRIDIRON IN THE FRONTIER.

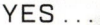

YES . . .
There was no record of anyone coming in or out of the building.

YES . . .
The branthium was successfully delivered and got where it needed to go, so clearly their deaths had nothing to do with that.

I . . . SUPPOSE NOT.
So why else would they have been murdered?

I DON'T KNOW . . .
Don't you? Don't you know, deep in your programming . . . don't you know the answer already?

NO . . .
It was you, Pathfinder.

NOOO . . .
Maybe you were reprogrammed by somebody. Maybe you malfunctioned. Maybe there was a glitch. Whatever it was . . . something went wrong.

I DIDN'T—I COULDN'T—
You have no proof of that.

BANGALORE SAID I COULDN'T HARM A FLY.
Everybody can harm a fly, you silly computer. Everybody *has* harmed a fly, at some point in their life. Even you. You're no better than anyone else. You're a program. And programmers make mistakes all the time. They're only human.

I DON'T BELIEVE YOU.
Yeah, you do. It's in the trembling of your voice. You've known this was possible from the very beginning.

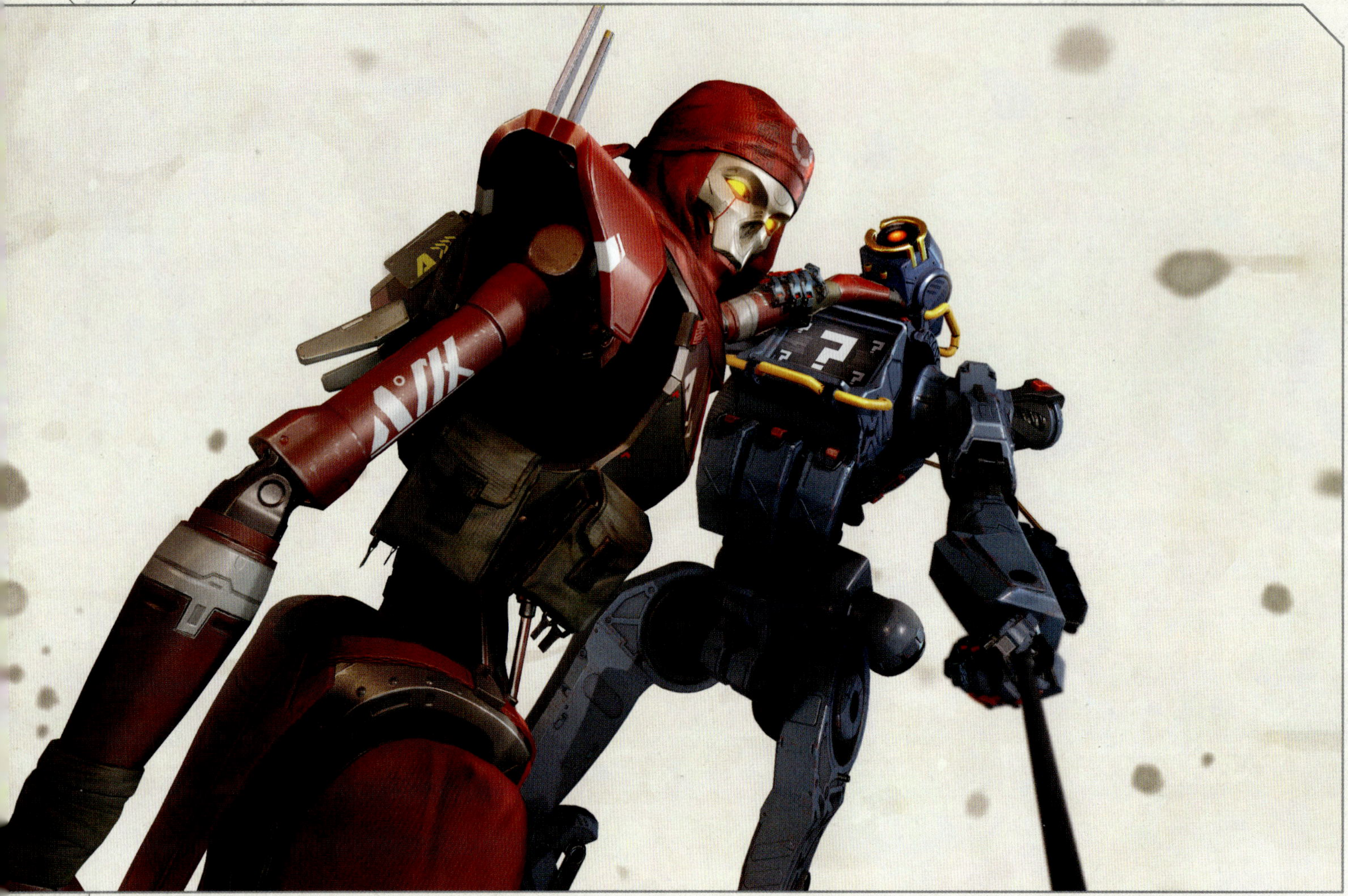

You've always known that to be true, even if you didn't want to say it out loud. Your friends did too. They'd couch it in jokes, insist they were kidding . . . but everyone knows that— with your size and weight?—you could kill a human being in half a second.

BANGALORE DID MAKE A JOKE ABOUT IT WHEN I TALKED TO HER . . .

See? You can't lie to me, Pathfinder. I know how easy it is to kill a skinbag, because I do it all the time.

I'M NOT YOU.

Keep telling yourself that. But tonight, when you return to your little warehouse, run your diagnostics, recharge your batteries . . . ask yourself: Why did they never catch the killer? Why didn't they ever kill again? Why is it so important to you to find them? Why does it matter so much? And realize the answer is that deep down, it was never about finding a creator. It was about finding yourself, Pathfinder. Your missing memory of ending all those lives. And the realization that there doesn't have to be a motivation. You're a machine. You do what you're told to do. Motive is irrelevant. It was out of your control. Their deaths . . . and your quest to uncover the truth about their deaths . . . is as senseless and meaningless as it is irrelevant.

NO!

Yes. That's what this has all been building to. All these years looking for your creator . . . all the hopes and dreams and promises of a reunion. It's all led to this: you ended their lives, Pathfinder. Your programmer probably forgot to carry a one and because of that, you high-fived them and accidentally crushed their skulls. Oops. That's it, friend. That's how this ends. It means nothing. You're nothing. Welcome to the real world, bucko.

I . . . I HAVE TO . . . I'M LEAVING . . . I CAN'T . . .

I must thank you, Pathfinder. This is the most fun I've had in a very, very long time. Don't forget your flash drive.

I HAVE TO GO.

No high-five? Awww. Goodbye . . . *friend* . . .

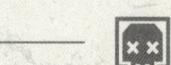

APEX LEGENDS:
PATHFINDER'S QUEST

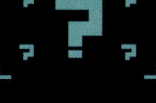
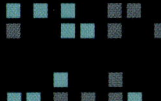
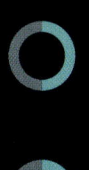

DATA POINTS RECEIVED

- Revenant was the first simulacrum ever made.
- He's a narcissist and displays psychopathic and sociopathic character traits.
- He's living under Kings Canyon.
- He's wrong.
- He likes messing with people's minds.
- He's mad at me because I saw Loba and I said she wasn't talking about him.
- He doesn't know whether he wants me to talk or stop talking altogether.
- He's a simulacrum.
- He's WRONG.
- His real name is Kaleb Cross, I think.
- He was killed by a man named Bob Woods, I think.
- He's twisted and warped and likes twisting and warping the world.
- Lots of other important things I'll add to this later.
- I'll leave blank spots to fill in
-
-
-
-
-
-
- That should be enough
- Just add it. He said it and I need to keep a record of everything he said. Everything is a clue. So I have to write it down, even if he's wrong.
- If.
- I don't want to keep a record of it
- I'll just write it quickly
- He thinks I murdered the Group.
- He thinks I could be a killer.
- He thinks I've known this could be possible all along
- He thinks I've known this
- He thinks I've
- He thinks
- I think
- I think he
- I think he could be
- I think he could be right.
- He could be right.
-
-
-
-
- He's right.

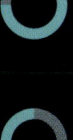
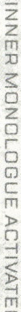

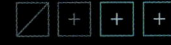 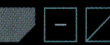

INNER MONOLOGUE ACTIVATED

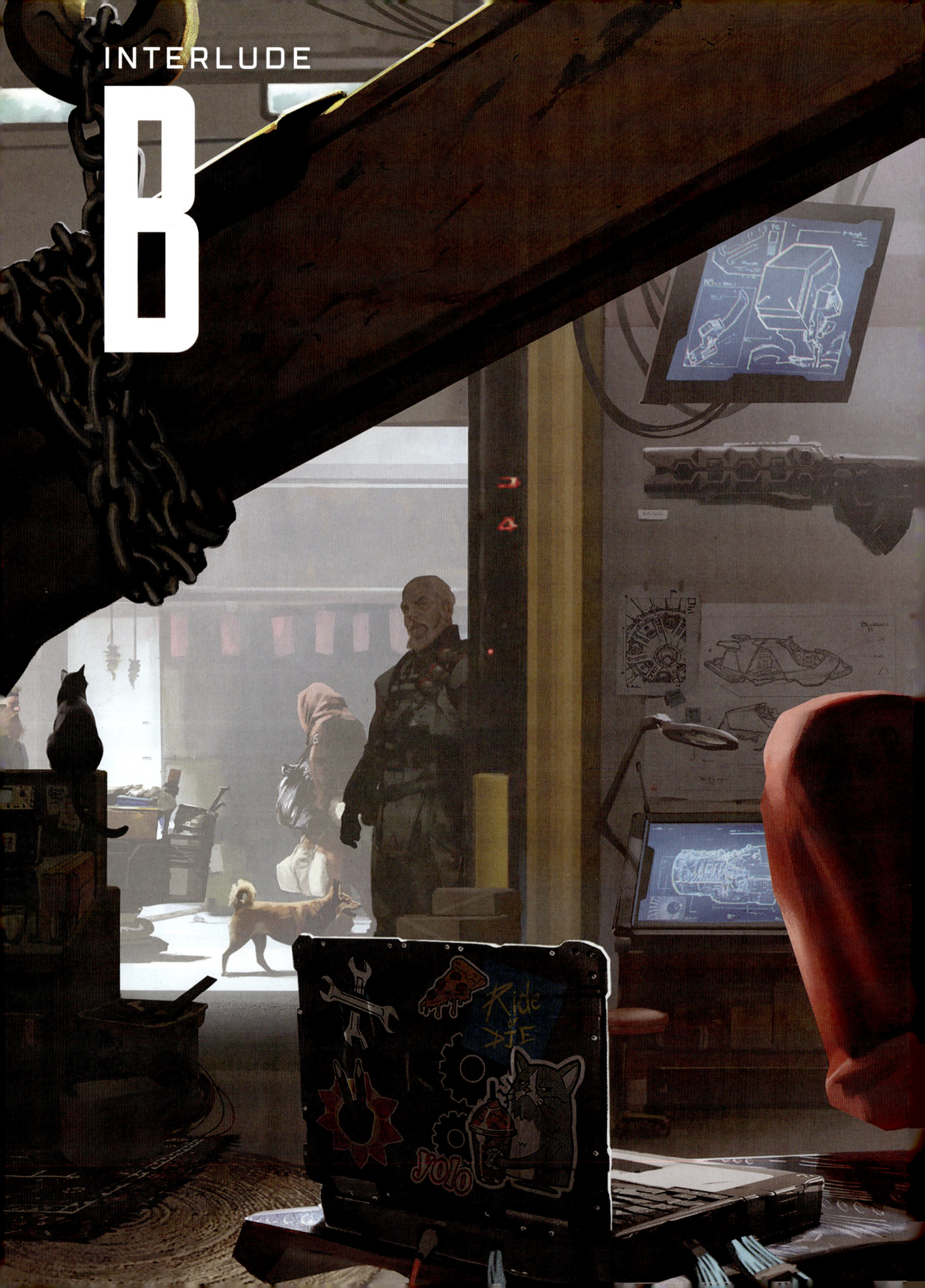

INTERLUDE

B

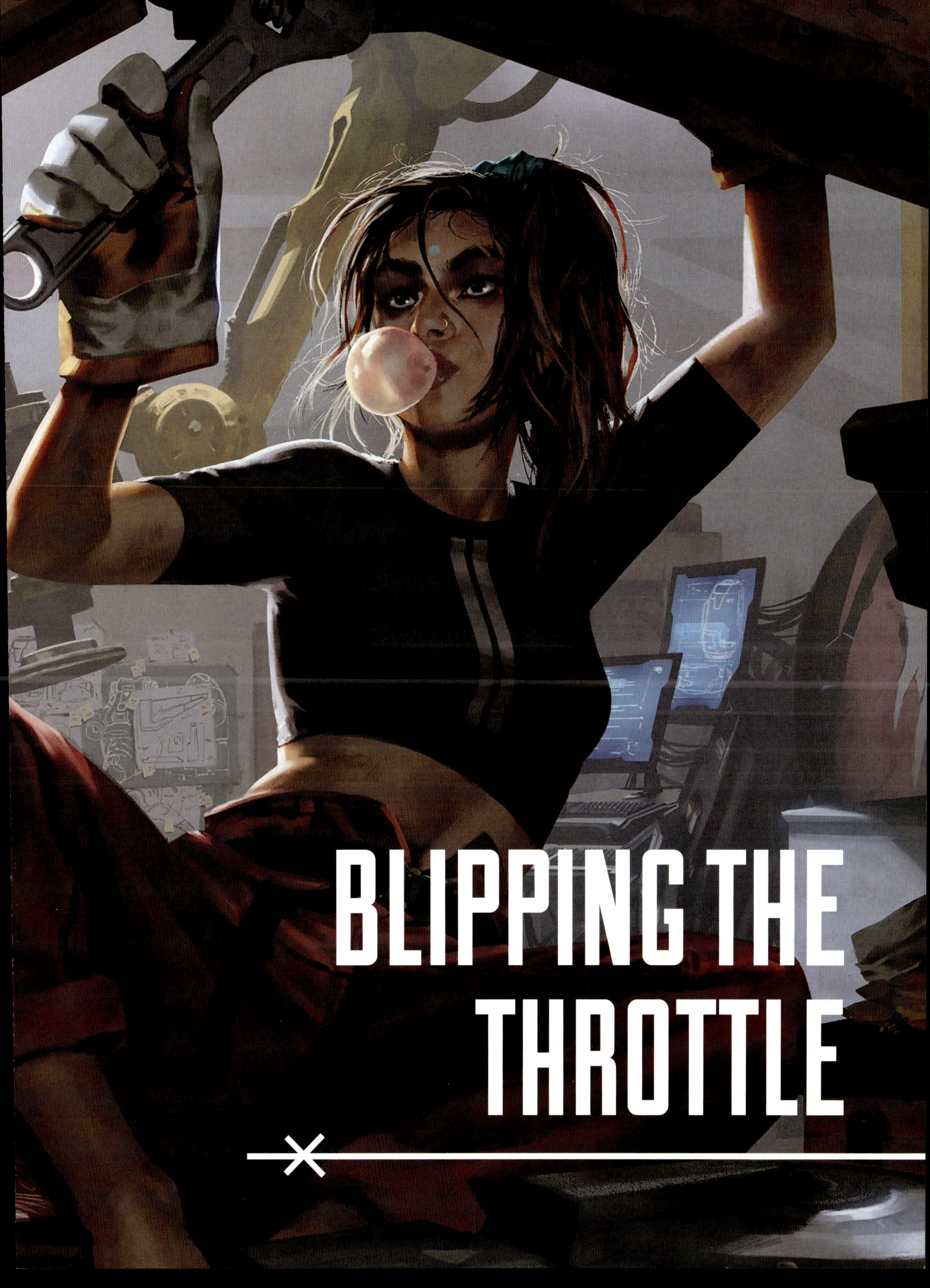

BLIPPING THE THROTTLE

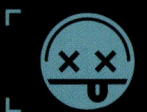
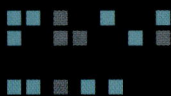

PATHFINDER MEMORY LOG: DAY 12

Today I hit the open road on a transport in space to meet my friend Elliott Witt—but his thousands of "number one fans" call him Mirage. The transmission I found at World's Edge turned out to be garbage, and so I've decided not to go looking for my creator. There was one clue that looked familiar, which led to something else that looked familiar, that led me to absolutely nowhere, and so I've decided this is a silly quest, and I've made a few other decisions as well. After having my life saved a number of times by Mirage's holodiscs, I've decided to go to him and announce my big news first. Maybe he can help! Hey! Maybe he can tell everybody else for me!

CLUE BOX

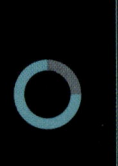
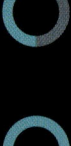

TRANSMISSION CLUES
- "Chevrex" > ~~LIFELINE'S PARENTS' COMPANY~~ It doesn't matter.
- "The future of the Outlands" > ~~THE THREAT OF AN ENERGY CRISIS~~ The future looks bright!
- "Branthium" > ~~THE SOLUTION TO THE ENERGY CRISIS, FOUND ON TALOS~~ What's a branthium?
- "Dr. Amélie Pa—— [Paquette]" > ~~WATTSON'S GRANDMOTHER, A GEOLOGIST, DIED MYSTERIOUSLY IN THE EVENT~~ Who cares?
- "The Event" > ~~EVERYONE AT PROJECT: IRIS DIED, AND THERE WAS AN EXPLOSION THAT CREATED THE RIFT, AND EVERYONE WONDERS IF IT WAS A COVER-UP~~ There are lots of events, happening every single day.
- "Aleki" > ~~GIBRALTAR'S GRANDFATHER, WHO ALSO DIED IN THE EVENT~~ What a neat name!
- "Iris" > ~~PROJECT: IRIS, CREATED IN 2654; BANGALORE'S UNCLE AL (NO RELATION) RAN SECURITY DETAIL AND DIED THERE IN AN EXPLOSION CAUSED BY A KILLER WHO MURDERED EVERYBODY AND NEVER GOT CAUGHT~~ Part of an eyeball.

SELF-MOTIVATION QUOTE . . . SEARCHING . . . 1 RESULT FOUND

"It's a beautiful day to see another galaxy!"
—[PATHFINDER]

► HI, MIRAGE! ◄
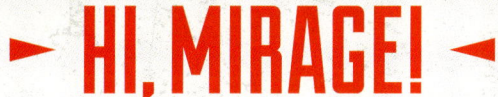

Hello?

YOU'RE NOT MIRAGE!
Hey! Finder of the Paths! If you're looking for your best friend in the whole wide world, he went to see his mum.

OH.
'Ey now, don't go turning that smile on your tummy to a frown, or you'll start to look like the rest of the plonkers in here. And ya don't want that. Can I get you sumthin'? Oil for ya gears? WD-40 for the joints? Pick your poison, mate.

I WANTED TO TALK TO MIRAGE.
And what am I? Chopped Leviathan meat? You can talk to me.

THAT'S OKAY. JUST TELL HIM I CAME TO SAY GOODBYE. GOODBYE!
Whoa, now. Where ya off to? Takin' a holiday, are we?

IT'S NOT A HOLIDAY THAT I KNOW OF.
Then whatcha got goin' on?

I'M GOING TO LEAVE THE OUTLANDS AND START OVER SOMEWHERE NEW.
That seems . . . impulsive.

THANK YOU, IT IS.
And can I ask where you're planning on goin'?

I'M THINKING THE FRINGE WORLDS. OR MAYBE GRIDIRON. POSSIBLY EARTH, ALTHOUGH THAT SEEMS A LITTLE FAR.
Sounds to me like someone's got a case of the run-aways.

WHAT'S THAT?
Well, there's the run-tos. They leave their homes to run *to* something. New job, new love, new change of scenery. That's the good kind of leaving. The kind of goodbye I can get behind, yeah? Unfortunately, then you have the run-aways. They don't know where they're going. They don't care. They just have to be anywhere but here. Sounds to me like that one's more your speed today. Am I getting warm?

YOU ARE VERY WARM, BUT I THINK THAT IS BECAUSE YOU ARE WORKING IN THE HOT SUN ALL DAY.
Hah. I love talking to you, Pathfinder. It's rare I can find someone who can keep me on my toes, verbally speaking.

YOU'RE VERY NICE, BUT I'M AFRAID YOU'RE MISTAKEN ABOUT ME.
About you running away?

NO, YOU'RE CORRECT ABOUT THAT. YOU'RE INCORRECT IN COMPLIMENTING ME.
Am I, now? So, you don't want to talk about why you're running away?

WHY WOULD I TALK ABOUT IT?
I'm no therapist, but I hear it's pretty good to work out your feelings. If ya got any.

I DON'T HAVE FEELINGS. I'M A ROBOT.
This little guy on the monitor on your chest plate begs to differ. He's full of feelings, that one is. How goes the search for your creator? Witt filled me in. Sounds like you're about to blow the cap off this thing.

IT'S OVER.
Did you find them?

NO.
Then it's not over.

YES, IT IS.
It's not over until we know who to thank for bringing you into our corner of the world.

I'M SORRY TO SAY THAT NOT EVERYBODY WOULD BE THANKING THEM FOR MY EXISTENCE.
Oh, don't listen to Witt. The git may say he hates your guts, but trust me . . . nobody spends more time with him than I do. Don't tell Wraith I said that. Anyway, he cares about you, big guy! Everyone does.

THEY SHOULDN'T.
And what makes you think you can tell everyone else how to feel?

BECAUSE THEY DON'T KNOW THE FULL STORY.
Fill a gearhead in then. What don't we know?

THAT I KILLED MY CREATOR.
There's that toes thing you do again. Is that what you found out? Because I have a hard time believing that.

YOU SHOULD TRY TO HAVE AN EASIER TIME. BECAUSE IT'S TRUE.
You have proof of this.

✕

IT'S THE ONLY THING THAT MAKES SENSE.
Finding out that little blue alien elves crawled out from the floorboards and killed your creator would make more sense than this.

THERE ARE NO OTHER SUSPECTS. NO OTHER MOTIVES. THERE'S NO REASON FOR ANYONE TO HAVE WANTED THE SCIENTISTS OF PROJECT: IRIS DEAD.
I don't know nothin' about scientists or irises. Hell, I barely know you. Okay, we gotta blip your throttle here, mate. Get you back in the game. I've only been around a few short months, but even I can see that when it comes to these Apex Games, you all fulfill a role. Like a cog in an engine. Every cog serves a purpose.

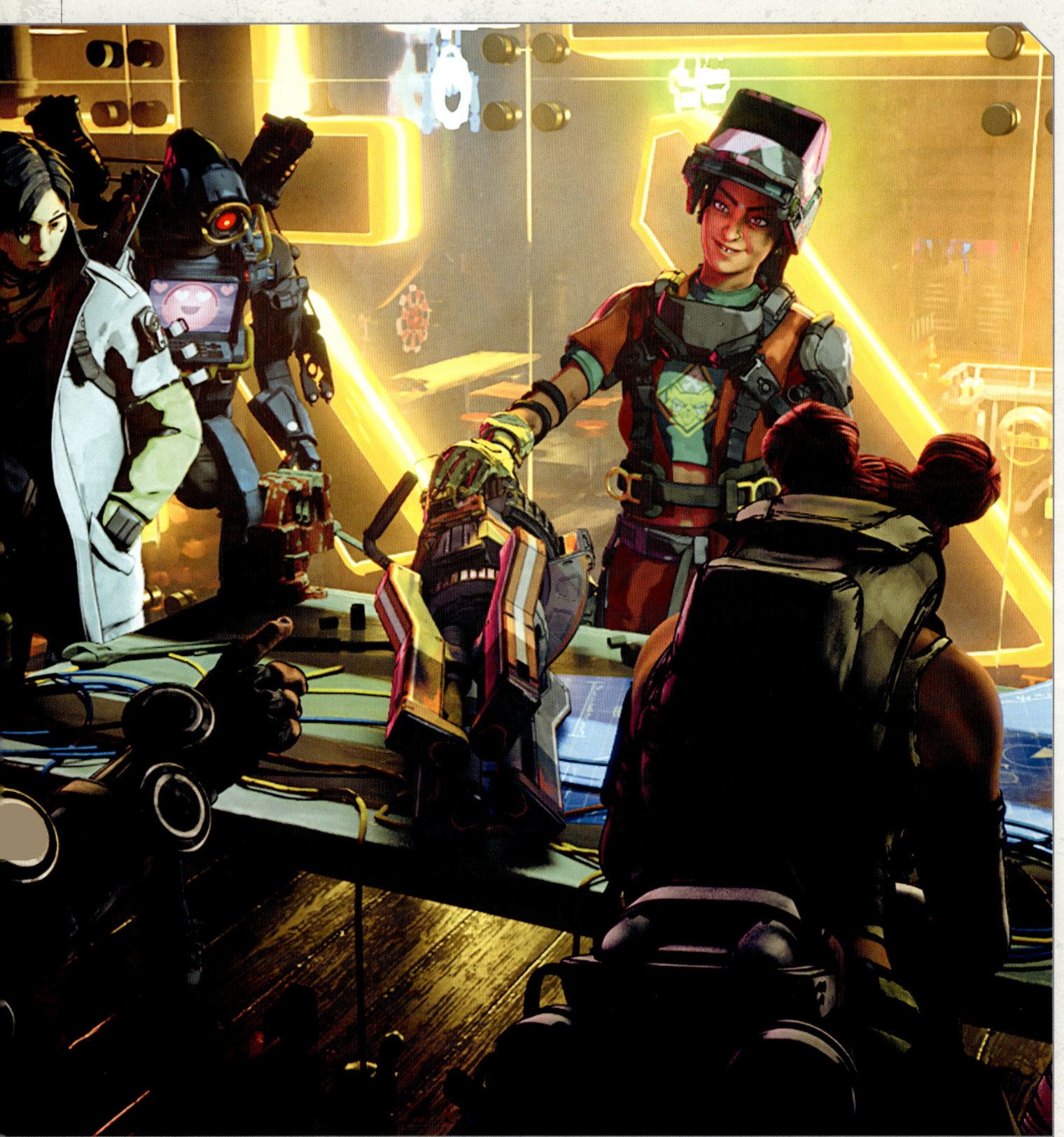

RAMPART'S NEW AND IMPROVED SHOP, LOCATED IN THE BACK OF THE PARADISE LOUNGE, A.K.A. THE MEN'S ROOM.

Bangalore's the discipline. Lifeline's the spirit. Octane's the wild streak…

MIRAGE IS THE SENSE OF HUMOR!
I am trying to make a point here, and no, Mirage is *not* the sense of humor. *I* am the sense of humor, thank you very much. Witt is…

THE TIBIA? THE PECTORAL MUSCLE? THE … GLUTES?
He's the heart. He's what keeps the whole thing going. Keeps it moving. Keeps it flowing.

I LIKE THAT A LOT. MIRAGE IS THE HEART OF THE APEX GAMES.
And if you ever tell him I said that, I'll install a toaster oven where your head is. But if Witt's the heart of the Apex Games… that makes you its soul, Path-finder. The purest part. And I refuse to believe that someone's soul could ever harm anybody else, let alone kill them. I watch you in the Games, and I've never seen you use excessive force. The "kills" you make leave your opponents with a mild headache the next day and that's about it. Unlike Caustic and Revenant, who both leave a trail of body bags in their wake.

THE WAY I DID AT PROJECT: IRIS…
Again, not proven.

WHO ELSE COULD IT BE?
I don't know, but if you stop investigating and run away, you'll never find out.

WHAT IF I FIND OUT IT'S TRUE?
If you find out it's true, then come get me. And we'll take it from there. We'll figure it out together. But you've come a long way, mate. Don't give up now just 'cause a little doubt is creeping in. When that little hobgoblin starts workin' his way through your brain, fight back. Double down. Push forward.

I DON'T WANT TO HURT MY FRIENDS AGAIN. IF ANYTHING EVER HAPPENED, AND I HURT WATTSON, OR MIRAGE, OR OCTANE, OR BANGALORE, OR GIBRALTAR, OR—
You're not. You couldn't. From what I understand, this …finding your creator…has been the question burned into everything you do. It's your drive in life, Pathfinder. And you're just going to give up now, when you're this close to knowing the truth?!

I'M GOING TO GIVE UP NOW TO SAVE MY FRIENDS FROM POSSIBLY BEING MURDERED BY ME IN THE FUTURE, THE WAY I MURDERED THEM IN THE PAST.
So you're not running away to avoid your friends. You're running away to *protect* them.

OF COURSE. THAT'S WHAT REAL FRIENDS DO.
That's all you care about. Their lives. Their happiness.

THEY'RE MY BEST FRIENDS.
And you went to each of them for their help. To help you unlock the secrets of your past. And what happened…?

THEY TOLD A LOT OF STORIES. HAPPY STORIES. SAD STORIES. SCARY STORIES. FEEL-GOOD STORIES. FEEL-BAD STORIES.
What were they about?

THEIR LIVES. THINGS THAT HAPPENED TO THEM THAT MATTERED. THEIR PARENTS. THEIR FRIENDS. THEIR LOVED ONES.
That must have been right special to experience firsthand. All those mates who care about you, opening up and telling you their deepest, darkest secrets…trusting you with them, so you could find what you were looking for.

IT WAS. SOME OF THEM WERE LAUGHING. SOME CRIED … BUT THE ONES THAT CRIED, CRIED GOOD TEARS. THE KIND OF TEARS YOU DON'T MIND CRYING. SOME LEARNED THINGS ABOUT THEMSELVES, LIKE FAMILY THEY DIDN'T KNOW THEY HAD … THIS STARTED AS MY QUEST, BUT I THINK IT BECAME THEIR QUEST TOO.
Yes! Yes, it did! And you like doing things for your friends.

I LOVE DOING THINGS FOR MY FRIENDS.
Then see this through … for *them*. How would you feel if you were one of the other Legends, and you relived the most emotional experiences of your life to help your friend Pathfinder find his creator…and he gave up at the last minute? Just walked away. Would you like that?

I DON'T THINK I WOULD.
If they're your friends, and you care about them the way you say you do, don't run away. See this through. Find your truth, the way they found theirs.

BUT REVENANT SAID—
Hold up. That's where this is coming from? The

murderbot? That's why you think you're a killer? *He's messing you, ya git!*

I KNOW HE IS. DOESN'T CHANGE THE FACT THAT IT COULD STILL BE TRUE. EVERY OTHER BODY IS ACCOUNTED FOR. NOBODY ENTERED OR LEFT THE PREMISES BEFORE THE EXPLOSION OCCURRED. IT'S IN THE RECORDS.
Records can be doctored, mate. Can I see?

THIS IS A PRINTOUT OF THE BODIES RECOVERED THAT DAY.
These are all the scientists. Shelley, Gibraltar, Fletcher, Paquette, Reid, yadda, yadda, yadda … And what are these names?

THOSE ARE SECURITY DETAIL. SOME ARE FROM THE IMC'S EIGHTY-FIRST BATTALION, AND OTHERS ARE—
Hold your horses there, metal man. This … right here … Look familiar?

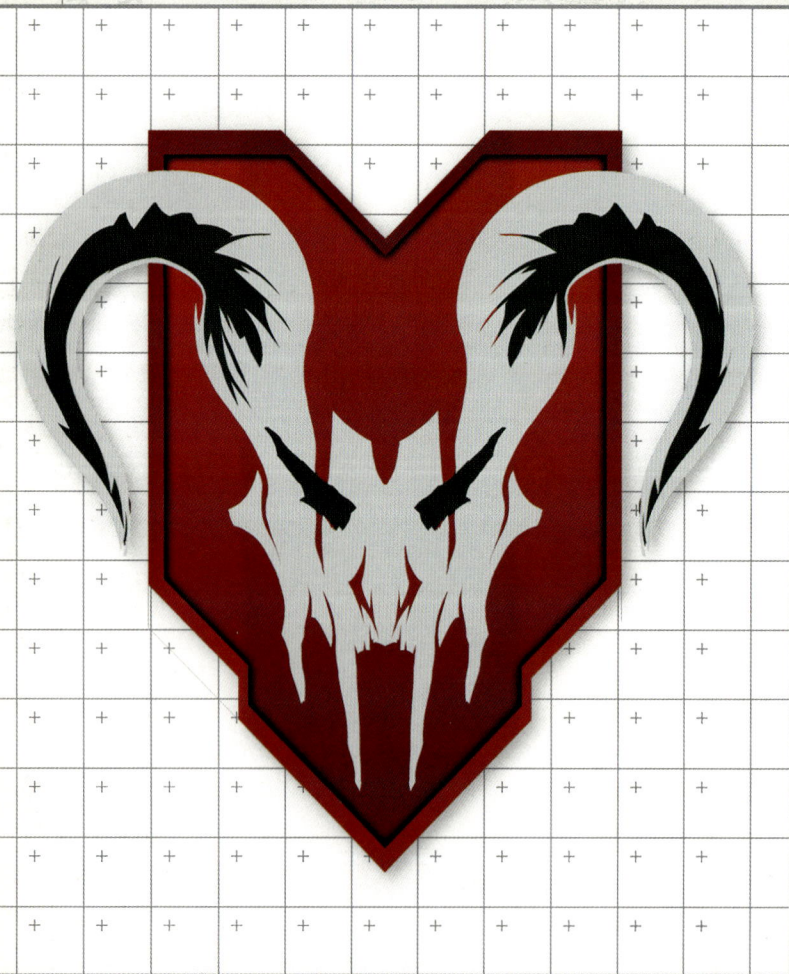

* APEX PREDATOR LOGO.

I KNOW THAT GOAT MAN. HE'S ON ALL THE BANNERS IN THE APEX GAMES.

That's because he's not a goat man. That's the logo of the Apex Predators. The mercs these blokes used for security weren't just a bunch of nobodies. They were the cream of the crop, they were. Top-of-the-line, triple-A, top-dollar Apex Predators! Know what that means?

THAT'S GREAT NEWS!
Got that right!

MY CREATOR LIVES BEHIND A BANNER IN THE APEX GAMES!
What? No! Use your loaf, tin man. You already know the guy in charge of the Apex Predators!

I DO!
Do you have any clue who I'm talking about?

IS IT . . . MIRAGE?
Mirage's more … ten rows down on the food chain. Maybe seven if he had his corn flakes that day. No, the last bloke to lead the Apex Predators is none other than the Apex Games commissioner himself … Kuben Blisk!

THAT'S TERRIBLE NEWS. THEY WON'T LET ME PAST THE FRONT DESK AT SYNDICATE TOWER.
Not without a connection.

THE ONLY CONNECTION I HAVE IS ASH. I DIDN'T KNOW SHE KNEW BLISK UNTIL A FEW DAYS AGO, AND NOW SHE'S DISAPPEARED TO WHO KNOWS WHERE.
Ash isn't the only connection you've got.

SHE'S NOT?
You know somebody with a direct line to the man himself.

IS IT . . . MIRAGE?
You're very emotional, so I'm making the decision to not be offended by this entire conversation, as difficult as that is. It's *me*, mate. I'm your connection. One call, and I'll score you a meeting with the man who knows everything about everything that goes down in the Outlands … Unless, of course, you'd prefer to run away instead? That option is still on the table. Never see your friends again. Waste their time and their memories and leave them wondering where their friend Pathfinder disappeared to.

I DON'T WANT TO RUN AWAY, FRIEND. I WANT TO RUN TO.
Damn skippy you do, mate.

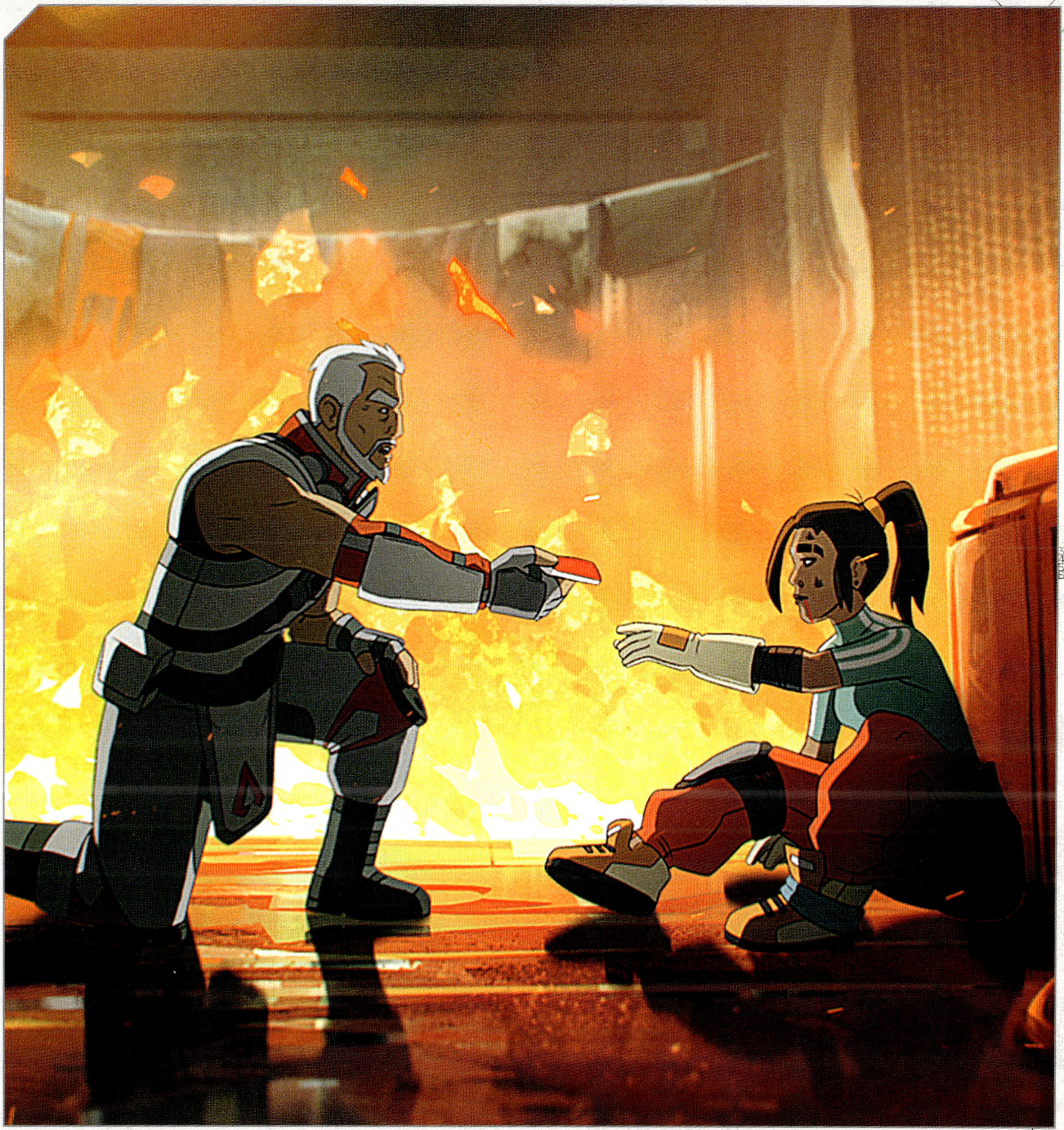

* KUBEN BLISK INVITED RAMPART TO JOIN THE APEX GAMES WITH HIS INFAMOUS "BLISK CARD."

► AND IF I GET BAD NEWS? AND IT TURNS
OUT I'M THE . . . ?
If you get any bad news, you come find me. After all,
that's what we do at Rampart Mods. We turn crap
into gold. Now let's get you a meeting with Uncle
Kubie . . .

LET'S GO, UNCLE KUBIE!
Yeah, don't call him that to his face . . .

DON'T WORRY, RAMPART! I WASN'T
SERIOUS. I WAS BEING . . . *SARCASM!*
Sure. Run with that.

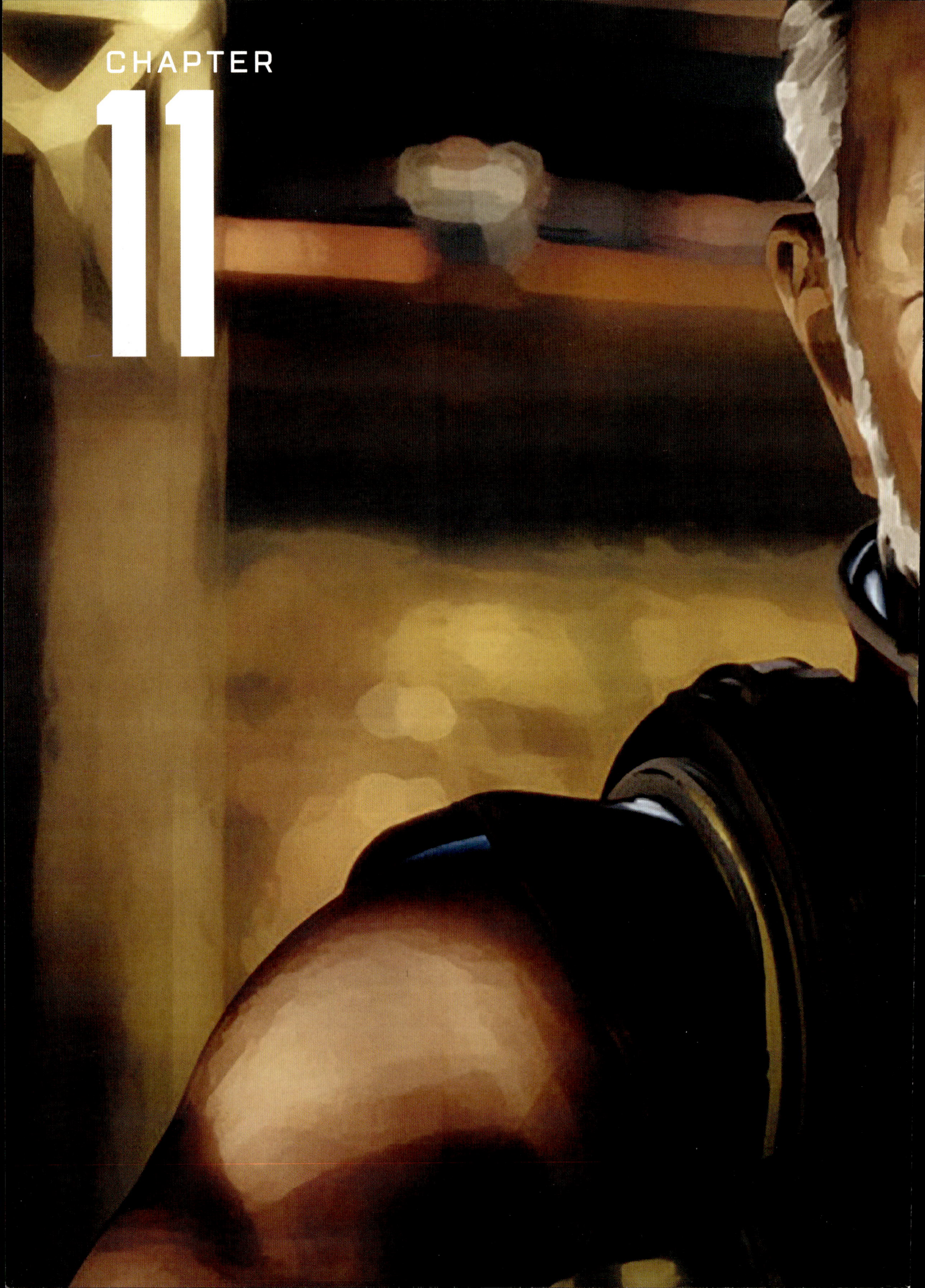

CHAPTER

11

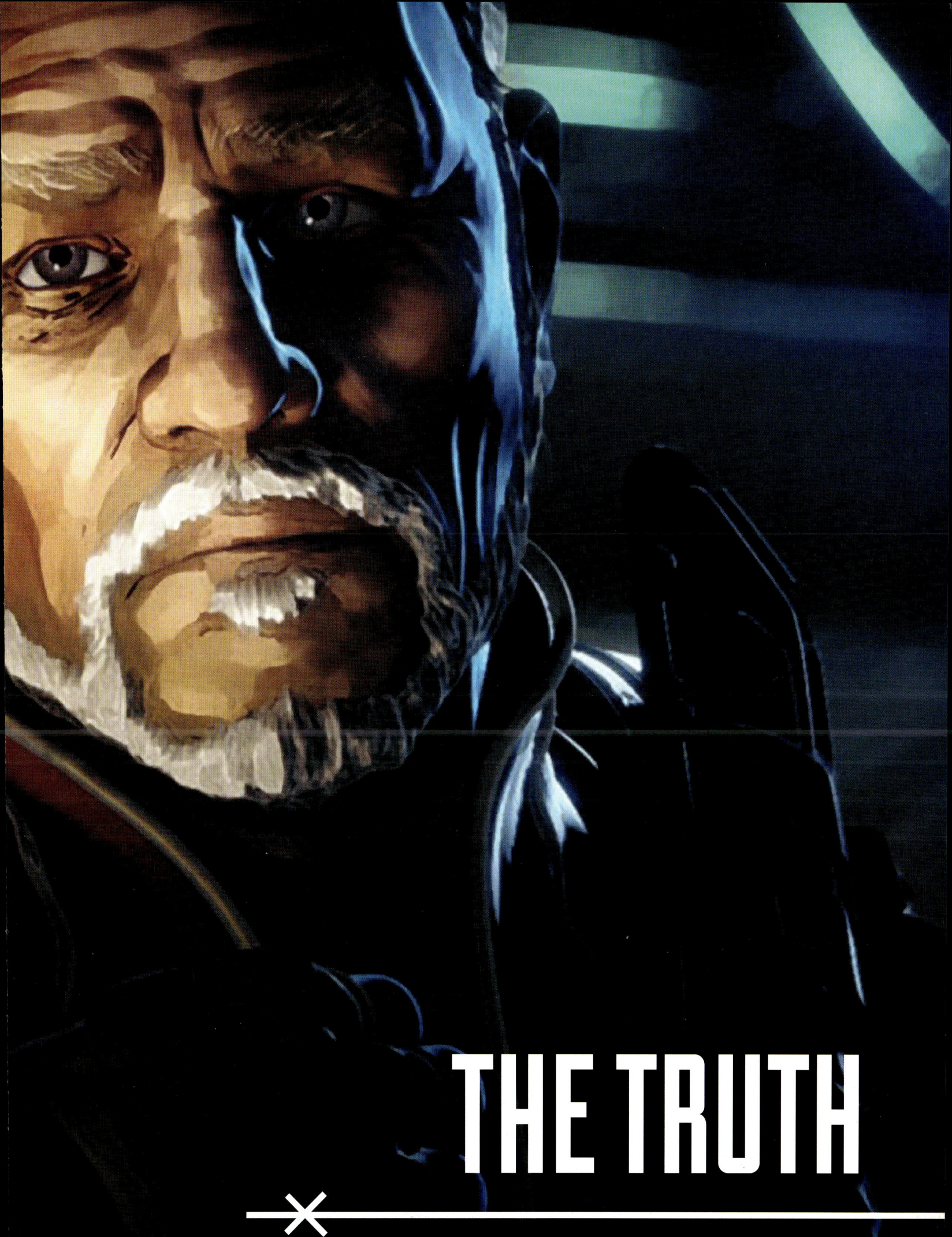

THE TRUTH

► HI, UM . . . FRIEND? ◄

Ya, I know who you are. I know all fighters in the ring who call themselves "Legends."

I CALL MYSELF PATHFINDER. THEY CALL ME A LEGEND.
Heh. They sure do, eh? What a shame . . . And what brings you here? Kid tells me I need to take this meeting. Don't usually listen to kids when they tell me to do things, but that modder's different.

I'M LOOKING FOR MY CREATOR.
That ain't me, kid. So you better go looking somewhere else. I got better things to do.

I NEED TO KNOW.
What ya need is to get out of my bloody face. You hear me? I may not fight for sport, but I have no problem beatin' the crap out of an old, discarded science experiment.

SCIENCE EXPERIMENT?
Heh. You really don't know who you are, eh?

I THINK I DO. I THINK I WAS CREATED BY A GROUP TO TRY TO DESTROY THE OUTLANDS.
Really? That's quite the bloody claim. Lookin' to be an Apex Predator?

I THINK I ALREADY AM OR . . . WAS.
Heh. Right . . .

I THINK I KILLED A LOT OF PEOPLE. I THINK I'M A BAD GUY.
I beg to differ, mate. I've made a living off reading who's good and who's bad, and not caring one way or the other. And one look at you, I can see you're far from someone who could handle being a . . . "bad guy."

BUT I COULD HAVE BEEN REPROGRAMMED TO BE ONE.
Heh. Reprogrammed? You? Not bloody likely. I've never met a robot that could be reprogrammed any more than a person. People are . . . impressionable. No loyalty, no pride, no honor. I would know, I'm no different.

I THINK YOU'RE DIFFERENT. I'VE NEVER MET ANYONE LIKE YOU.
Oi, that's for sure. That's for bloody sure. Very few are like me. And that's the problem. We need more like me. More people willing to fight—and I mean really fight. Not put on a show for autographs.

DO YOU NOT GIVE AUTOGRAPHS?
I'll give 'em a fight. The fight is all that matters. The fight is all I care about.

ALL I CARE ABOUT IS FINDING OUT WHO CREATED ME. MY FRIEND RAMPART TOLD ME YOU MIGHT BE ABLE TO HELP, EVEN THOUGH I'M VERY MUCH SCARED OF YOU.
She's one hell of a fighter. The Outlands can use more of her. All right, you really want to know, eh?

YES, PLEASE, SIR. I THINK. THOUGH I AM AFRAID.
Fear is for the weak.

I CAN'T BE WEAK AND THE PERSON WHO KILLED THE PEOPLE WHO SAVED THE OUTLANDS.
Heh. Very true, mate. That's why it wasn't you.

ARE YOU SURE? HOW DO YOU KNOW?
Pretty damn sure, because I know 'em.

YOU KNOW MY CREATOR?
I know who killed your creator. Or, well . . . creators.

WHAT? THERE ARE MANY? HOW MANY? WHO ARE THEY? WHAT HAPPENED? THEY'RE DEAD?
Slow down. Take a . . . breath or whatever it is you do, eh? And take a seat. I might just have what you need.

YOU DO? WHAT IS IT? ALSO, THIS SEAT IS VERY COMFY.
There's a hell of a lot of data on this chip. Hook it up, see what you get.

I CAN JUST HAVE IT? I DON'T KNOW YOU VERY WELL, BUT I KNOW YOU ENJOY MONEY. HOW MUCH MONEY IS THIS?
Heh. I don't bloody care about money. That's just a way to weed out those who don't really care about what we do.

WHAT DO WE DO?
We fight. We get the job done. I've been doing this for a hell of a long time. Never matters who the job is for, just that you get it done, right? Now, I've seen you fight. You're good. Maybe not better than me, but good, and that gets you some respect. Here, you earned this.

WOW. ARE YOU SURE?
Bloody take it before I change my mind, eh?

OKAY. THIS IS IT. HERE GOES . . .

VRTV-1: DATA FILE
Date: January 2, 2658
Location: Olympus

At a scientific research base on the floating city of Olympus, the Project: Iris team was in its fifteenth year of working tirelessly to protect the future of the Outlands. The base consisted of three main connected facilities: the command center, the research lab, and the large storage warehouse. The last was home to an advanced experimental form of trans-portation technology called a Phase Runner, one of the many breakthrough innovations created at this avant-garde hub to help usher in a new golden era for the Frontier.

Eight brilliant scientists stood around a lamp connected to a sample of the refined element branthium. With high hopes that yet another attempt at creating a new safe energy source would prove successful, one scientist flipped a switch. A loud hum shook the base and sparks filled the room before the bulb shattered into pieces--the test was a failure.

"Bruddahs...I guess today just ain't our day," Aleki Gibraltar said in defeat.

Geologist Amélie Paquette chimed in. "No. It doesn't make any sense. My plan should have worked."

"Your plan was wrong from the start. I pointed that out, must have been, twenty times?" said Dr. Ashleigh Reid.

These overworked geniuses had been struggling to work together for years, ever since the discovery of branthium in 2645. Although nicknamed "the Group," they were far from unified. Formed by the billionaire humanitarian Lilian Peck, the Group had members who came from different backgrounds and locations throughout the Outlands--and they all had their own ways of doing things.

"Excuse me? And what have you done, Reid?" Paquette pressed, moving face to face with Reid. "Besides stand by and critique our every move while ze rest of us do all ze work. Is zis how you treated Somers?"

"You're not half the scientist she was." Reid smirked.

"Bruddahs! Come on, now." Aleki was trying to break the tension when...

"Friends! Friends!" A young man, tall, with reddish-blond hair, came running in from the other room. "I got the report. It's not what we think. I mean, it is what we think, but it's not what we think--whoa! Um...everyone okay?"

"I don't know. Are we?" Reid sarcastically asked Paquette.

"*Oui*," Paquette said as she stepped away from Reid and toward the overly excited young man. "What do you have for us, kid?"

"It's the report from the bran-thium test. Honestly, I think the solution isn't as complicated as we thought it would be." He unfurled a fifty-sheet stream of paper. "It worked, Dr. Paquette. It worked."

Curious, the others gathered around the young man. Dr. Conan Shelley, a constantly sweaty engineer with a dashing handlebar mustache, grabbed one end of the report and began reading. Dr. Armen Fletcher, the only medical doctor of the Group, cleaned the few drops of ice cream he had just finished off his fingers before he stepped in for a closer look. Anastasia "Stay" Oliveira, a mechanical engineer, gave the lucky bottle opener she wore around her neck a good, hopeful squeeze before examining the report. Professor Milly Delgado, who was the shortest of the Group, with glasses the size of dinner plates, jumped ineffectively as she struggled to see over Aleki's massive form.

"I can't see! What's going on?" she asked before Aleki, in one smooth motion, turned, picked her up, and dropped her in the center. "Thank you, Aleki!"

"No problem, little bruddah." He smiled and focused on the report. "I can't make heads or tails of this, what's it say?"

"It seems our little intern here has pointed out something zat none of us took into consideration," Paquette explained as she continued to read the report. "Ze problem is not ze refinery chamber, or ze equations, or even ze equipment...ze problem is us."

"Us?" Shelley questioned.

"Maybe just you, Paquette. You should speak for yourself," Reid lashed out.

"No, she's right," Delgado chimed in. "It appears that the refinery needs continuous calibration, and we can't do that remotely. We're not fast enough and we can't go inside that chamber. It's too dangerous."

"Hey. I can only go so fast, it's not my fault." Shelley, becoming defensive, gestured toward his nearby workstation. "I'm over there sweatin' my butt off trying to recalibrate the thing."

"Bruddah, we know. It ain't your fault. It just isn't enough. We need someone inside."

"Inside? Are you crazy?" Fletcher shouted. "There's no way. The moment you go in there, you're fried."

"Then we don't," Reid interrupted. "Who says we have to go in there?"

"What are you suggesting?" Paquette asked.

Reid walked over to a MRVN, one of many working at the base, and gave it a long, predatory look. "This'll do."

"A MRVN? You've got to be joking." Fletcher chuckled. "Those bots can barely polish my boots, let alone recalibrate an active refinery."

"Wait. Wait...Hold on. Dr. Reid may just be on to something." The room became quiet. When it came to robotic engineering, Stay was the expert, and when she started talking, everyone knew to listen--especially when she picked up her bottle opener and pressed it to her lips. She stepped closer to the MRVN, lightly pushing Reid aside. "We can do this. Yeah... It'll take some time, and it won't solve *all* our problems, but we can do this. Hey, Aleki, does SARAS still use that heat-shield tech for your rescue shuttles? The old IMC brand?"

"Sure do. I can probably score some, but we're gonna need something tough to reinforce it. The temperatures inside that refinery are high enough to melt the face off a Titan. Any ideas?" Aleki scanned the room.

"Well, I can reach out to my contacts at Hammond Robotics," Reid suggested.

"Wow. You know people at Hammond Robotics? You know everyone, Dr. Reid," the young intern exclaimed.

"Oh...I'm not a fan of Hammond Robotics. They scare me," Delgado stammered as she cleaned her glasses. "They're so full of secrets. Hard to trust them, ya know?"

"Hard to trust anyone associated with the IMC, for that matter," added Shelley.

"This isn't a time to be picky. It's the fate of the Outlands, after all." Reid smiled.

"She's right," Paquette said as the whole Group turned to listen. "We can't just rely on Peck's foundation to keep us going. If we can reach out to others, we could get zis zing done. For ze Outlands"--she paused and looked at the young intern--"and for Somers. Without her, we wouldn't have made it zis far."

"All right, let's get ready to build a robot!" Stay shouted. "I'll draw up some schematics. Reach out to your suppliers, anything you can think of, and maybe think of some names-- can't hurt to personalize this thing." The Group began to disperse.

"See? All we need to do is work together. Eh, Paquette?" Reid made sure to get the last word on her counterpart before she left the room. Aleki, who overheard the exchange, joined Paquette at her side.

"Don't worry. We'll be okay."

"Let's just keep an eye on her, *oui*?"

"*Oui*, bruddah. Now cheer up. Your experiment worked." He gave the MRVN a long look. "And with this thing, we'll be on the right path. I'm sure of it. The sun shines again!"

"Hey, um, excuse me," the young intern nervously said, trying to get their attention.

"Hey, there he is," Aleki responded.

"What's up?" Paquette asked.

"Um...I just wanted to say thank you for listening to me. You know, with the report and not just blowing me off," he said.

"I would never do zat. I'm glad you're here. You did good work today, Newton. Your mom would be proud."

The young intern, Newton Somers, smiled and replied, "Thanks, friend."

VRTV-2: DATA FILE
Date: February 4, 2658
Location: Olympus

Over the course of the next month, the Group pieced together all the components needed to modify the MRVN based on Stay's schematics. Aleki reached out to his friends at SARAS, Fletcher received shipments of robotic surgical equipment from his friends at the IMC, Reid obtained reinforcement materials from Hammond Robotics, and Paquette got in touch with Peck off-world, who managed to grab new financial partnerships with Chevrex Inc. and Silva Pharmaceuticals.

"We sure about zis? Bringing in zese people..." Paquette and Delgado were waiting for the others to join them in the laboratory.

"I don't know, but it's been good so far, right?"

"Tell zat to ze new security detail. Adonis Squad." Paquette gestured toward an armed guard who was completing his security check at a nearby computer console. "Just feels like a military operation now," she said quietly.

"All clear, Dr. Paquette. You're good to go." Commander Al Stern approached the two scientists.

"Zank you, Commander," Paquette replied with a hint of suspicion.

"And yes, I am military, but this is your operation. We're just here to help." He gave a nod before leaving.

"See. They're just keeping us safe. It's a good thing. Besides, they can't even get in without one of us anyway. And hey, think of it this way: more people believe us when we say that an energy crisis is actually a serious problem."

"I hope you're right."

"Me too."

"How's it goin', ladies? Ready for the big day?" Stay entered the lab, pulling a cart full of newly built robotic parts. "Damn, this thing is heavy."

"Need some help, Stay?" Paquette stepped forward to lend a hand. "You really zink zis is going to work?"

"Always the skeptic, eh, Paq?" Reid answered as she entered the lab, followed by Newton, Aleki, Shelley, and Fletcher.

"Just making sure we dot our i's...cross our t's."

"I think we're good," Reid responded.

"Good? I think we're great, bruddahs!" Aleki, who clearly was not worried, let out a great big belly laugh. "This is it! We've earned this-- together." Before they could protest, he squished Paquette and Reid into a bear hug. "Who knew that it would be a MRVN to bring us all together, right?" Reid and Paquette gasped for breath before breaking free. Aleki laughed, before pointing toward Delgado. "I'm not forgetting you, little one."

"Oh no!" She smiled as she ran away.

"All right, enough goofing around. Let's get started." Stay laughed as she took out each part of the MRVN and laid them on a table for assembling. "We got a birthday to celebrate."

The eager bunch surrounded the table, each with their own equipment and notepads. Sprawled out on its surface was the shell of the new MRVN: broad shoulders, a large body, and a vacant, square-shaped space in the chest with five cables hooked up to a nearby computer monitor. Stay dumped a crate of cables and wires on top. "Here he is."

"He?" Shelley laughed. "So, not only are you replacing me with a machine, but you're acting like it's a person now?"

"Shut up." Delgado gave him a little shove. "He's beautiful. I can't wait to meet him. I wonder what he's going to be like?"

"It's a MRVN, Delgado. MRVNs aren't any different than a power drill," Reid asserted.

"Not this one, Reid." Stay began to clamp all the parts together, starting down at the feet. "You see, this ain't your regular MRVN." She reached for a wrench in a toolbox next to Fletcher.

"While I was inside this thing, I took some liberties and got a little creative with his programming." Stay tightened the clamps on both legs, connecting them to the feet. With a few puffs of air, the feet performed a self-diagnostic, rotating back and forth.

"You sure zat is safe?"

"Absolutely! Just gave our friend here a voice. He is part of the Group, after all." Stay moved to attach the legs to the body.

"Wow. A voice? What's he going to sound like?" Newton's eyes widened.

"I'm glad you asked, kid. That's up to us. I figure we might as well put something from each of us inside him." Stay tightened two wires together, which resulted in one of the MRVN's legs kicking straight up, nearly missing Newton's head. "Whoa, sorry about that."

"Why would we do that?" Reid asked, confused.

"Ain't it obvious, bruddah? We're the best minds in the Outlands. Yet, from day one, our biggest problem was trusting each other. I know at first I thought Shelley was a hothead with an attitude."

"Hey!" Shelley shouted.

"It's true, but so was I. So *am* I. It ain't easy being a genius in a room of geniuses. So, instead of us butting heads all the time--let's just push

it all together. That what ya sayin', Stay?" Aleki confirmed.

"Yeah, pretty much. We're not just making a tool here, you know? We're making a new member of the Group. With his help, we're going to do some good for the Outlands. Of course, it'll take a little longer than just programming the basics--"

"Longer?" Reid interjected. "Wait, what do you mean longer? How much longer?"

"Whoa. Calm down. I mean, it's going to take at least the rest of the year to train this MRVN. Teach him how we do things. Monitor him as we continue Paquette's tests."

"Why? Why do we have to do that?" Reid looked around the room. "Am I the only one who thinks that's crazy? I can't wait any longer, and I'm certainly not waiting for some robot to learn my name."

"*You* can't wait any longer?" Paquette stepped closer to Reid. "Zis isn't about you, Reid. Zis isn't about any of us, it's about everyone outside. We can't rush zis."

"What is it, Paquette? Afraid your plan may not work?"

"I'd rather get it right ze first time. Let's not forget, ze MRVN was your idea in ze first place, and it was a good idea, but it's not done yet. Stay's right, zis MRVN needs ze experience and knowledge zat we all have. He will be alone in zat refinery, we can't help him, so he needs to know how to solve any problem we may run into." Paquette paused and looked at the MRVN. "He's our fail-safe."

"Whatever...I've got other work to do. Let me know when you're done fooling around," Reid huffed as she stormed out of the lab.

"Should I go after her?" asked Newton. "She seems sad."

"Go ahead, Newt. We'll call you when we're ready for you," said Paquette.

The rest of the Group lent their help in assembling the MRVN. Stay

handed Paquette the welder, and together they attached the arms in one fell swoop. Once at full power, the fingers on the MRVN's hands extended and retracted, leaving only one final piece to be added.

"And here's his beautiful face," Stay said proudly as she held up the newly remodeled MRVN head with bright yellow arches on the top and bottom of his circular face. "All he needs is some final programming and we can power him up in no time." She carefully locked the head in place and stood back. "So--who wants to go first?" She stared at each of the five remaining members of the Group.

"I will," volunteered Fletcher. "Can't hurt to give the little...well, big guy some medical expertise."

"Maybe a sweet tooth while you're at it," joked Aleki.

"Hey, nothing wrong with that," Fletcher said as he walked up to the programming computer. "Speaking of which, you said 'birthday,' right? We should probably get some cake and ice cream in here--stat!" he said, laughing at his own joke.

"Sure thing. So all you gotta do is enter your password to open your Project: Iris file here," Stay instructed, pointing at the monitor. "The system will do the rest. But if you want to do anything manually, just pick whatever you want to be integrated into his programming, and you can add it here." She pointed to a section labeled "Personality." "And have fun with it. We're creating life here!" As Stay started to pack up the tools, Paquette joined her.

"I'm assuming you added some precautions to ze program in case anything was to 'appen," she whispered.

"He can't be hacked, if that's what you're askin', P," Stay assured her as she packed away a welder.

"Zat's not what I'm talking about." Paquette's expression showed a deep look of concern and hesitation.

"You really don't trust her, do you?"

"Do you? Somers was ze best astrophysicist in ze entire Frontier. It doesn't make any sense what happened to her. Ze stories don't add up. I just want to make sure we cover all our bases. He's supposed to save ze Outlands, right? Let's make sure zat happens."

"What did you have in mind?"

"Remember what Hammond used to say?"

"Always have a fail-safe," Stay recalled. "Yeah...and look what happened to him."

"Just keep it in mind. Zat's all I ask." Stay saw the anguish in Paquette's eyes and nodded, then turned back to the others. Delgado was enthusiastically typing away at the computer's keyboard.

"I'm gonna make him love Prowlers! And love music! And love...love!"

"Sure, but maybe throw some of your physics genius in there?" Stay suggested. "That MRVN's going to have to navigate inside the refinery potentially blind from all the fumes. He's going to need some of that sweet Delgado knowledge if he's going to survive in there."

"You got it, Stay. How exciting!" From across the room, Aleki, sensing Paquette's concern again, walked over to her. He rested his heavy hand on her small shoulder. They spoke in hushed tones.

"You know, you're gonna worry yourself to death, bruddah."

"Better me zan ze entire Outlands. I just want ze best for my little Luc."

"And he's lucky to have you, but who isn't? You're going to save the Outlands, one way or another. I'm sure of it."

"Zanks, Aleki."

"Now, speaking of children, it's your turn. And this little pathfinder could use some of your witty charm, don't you think?" He grinned.

She chuckled. "Okay. Okay." She softened a bit as she approached the computer.

A few hours later, the project was nearing completion. Aleki, Paquette, Fletcher, Delgado, Shelley, Reid, and Newton huddled around Stay as she finalized the programming. She was just about done when Paquette called out to stop her.

"Wait a minute! Newton, did you add anything?"

"He doesn't need to add anything," Reid interjected.

"He can answer for himself. He's part of zis group just as much as you are, Reid."

"Go ahead, buddy. Add something," Stay said as she stepped back from the computer. Newton smiled and began typing.

"A lot of what I have to offer is what my mom had, and I think most of that's already in here, but there's one thing that was always important to Mom: she loved her friends. It's important to me, too. You're all my friends. But especially you, Dr. Reid." Newton looked over at her. "You were always there for my mom. Just like this MRVN is going to be there for the Outlands." Reid did her best to smile, but it ended up as more of a quick nod.

"Thanks," she said hesitantly.

"I think it's great!" shouted Delgado. "Now, let's wake him up!"

"Yeah, I think that's everyone," Stay concluded. "Unless..." She glanced at Reid while catching a worried look from Paquette.

"I think we've got plenty," Reid said.

"Yeah," Paquette added quickly.

"Oh, come on. We're all part of the Group. Something? Anything?" Newton begged. And, with a deep exhale of defeat, Reid quickly walked over to the monitor and hit one button before stepping back. The Group surrounded the monitor eagerly, interested to see what she typed.

"Seriously?" Stay asked.

"Zat's some effort," scoffed Paquette.

Shelley came to Reid's defense.

"I like it. Simple."

"Now we're cookin', bruddahs. Nothing brightens your day better than looking at somethin' like that." Aleki chuckled and tapped the top of the monitor, which displayed a big yellow smiley face.

"Are we ready now? Can we wake him up?" Delgado asked eagerly.

"Yes, we are!" Stay responded, typing away on the keyboard. "Just give me a few seconds." The computer powered up and sparks of energy traveled through every cable linked to the MRVN. His parts began to activate piece by piece: first the arms, then the legs, and lastly the head, where a blue glow illuminated from the single centered eye. Next, Stay unhooked the computer monitor and small keyboard from their stand, collected the five loose cables, and packed it all neatly into the vacant chest. It fit perfectly like the final piece of a puzzle. She reached for a yellow handlebar attached to the computer monitor and gripped it tightly. "Here we go!"

With a single pull, she locked everything in place. All around the table, the Group waited with anticipation. Stay flipped a switch and activated the MRVN. A deafening hum of power filled the room. Part by part, the robot's limbs began to move, and with a single loud spark of energy, the MRVN sat upright on the table and spoke...

"Who doesn't like ice cream? Every kid likes ice cream!" His voice was cheerful, almost childlike, and welcoming.

"Whoops. A little too much Fletcher in there," Stay explained before adjusting the chest monitor. "That should do it." The MRVN shook his head and gave the room a good scan before focusing on the eight humans surrounding him.

"Who are you?" His chest monitor turned on and displayed a question mark.

"We're your creators," Delgado declared through her ear-to-ear grin. With a blip, the chest monitor replaced the question mark with a big yellow smiley face.

"Hi, creators!"

VRTV-3: DATA FILE
Date: December 25, 2658
Location: Olympus

"All roads lead to branthium!" Delgado shouted as she popped the cork of a nice bottle of champagne, which sprayed all over her colleague, Shelley, standing next to her. "Oops, sorry!"

He licked some of the beverage off his lips. "Mm! Delicious!" he said cheerfully. "Hey, if I have to get soaked in champagne every time we finish a shipment, so be it! Let's drink!" He held out his glass for a pour, followed by the other members of the Group, who circled up in the command center.

"Paquette, how about a speech?" Stay suggested, giving a playful nudge to her friend.

"Yes, bruddah. Let's hear it," Aleki chimed in with his glass raised high, but not everyone was excited to hear what she had to say.

"Sure, let's hear from our fearless leader," Reid said sarcastically under her breath.

Paquette heard Reid's comment, but it didn't bother her. She walked over to the giant window overlooking the refinery.

"I zink we're missing a member of ze Group, don't you?" she said, pressing a button to open communication. "Path, can you hear us?"

"Hi, creator friends! I can hear you, and you sound great," Pathfinder responded from inside the refinery. He had been working there for the last ten hours, helping to successfully complete the first batch of branthium.

"Let's put him on the screen!" Delgado gleefully ran over to her workstation and activated visual communication on a large monitor above the window. "Exciting!"

"Exciting!" Pathfinder repeated, now able to see everyone.

"*Parfait*!" Paquette raised her glass for a cheer. "Zank you all for believing in zis plan--for believing in me. But let us not forget Dr. Mary Somers and her son." She looked at young Newton, who wiped a bittersweet tear from his eye. "It was her and Peck's work zat brought us here today to create ze very first batch of branthium. One of many zat will not only end ze crisis, but will power ze Outlands for generations to come. We saved lives here today. And if zat's not enough, I personally zank each and every one of you for your contribution." She scanned the room and landed on Reid. "Even you, Reid. Let's not forget whose idea it was to build our friendly MRVN."

"That's me!" Pathfinder pointed out. Reid rolled her eyes before glancing at her wristwatch.

"Yes. Now are we ready to get on with it? To *save* the Outlands?"

"To ze Outlands," Paquette cheered, clinking her glass with the others before sitting down at her workstation. "All right, everyone get to your stations." The Group dispersed, settling into their respective spots to prepare for the first transport of branthium.

Shelley checked in. "Pathfinder, you good in there for a few more hours? We can get going on the second batch."

"Yes, I am. I'll get back to work. This is fun!" Pathfinder deactivated the monitor before returning to duty.

"I put in the call to Peck earlier this morning, so she's standing by for the first shipment." Paquette raised her right hand and a sensor scanned it, turning her monitor green and displaying the words "WAITING FOR PAIR."

"Ready, Stay?"

"You know it." Stay walked up to her own workstation and placed her hand up to the sensor, which changed the words to "PAIR ACCEPTED: PHASE RUNNER ACTIVATED."

"Dr. Reid, let's lock down ze warehouse and prepare for--"

Paquette cut herself off, confused. "Damn it. Where's Reid?" She looked around to see two members of the Group missing. "Wait. Where's Newton?" she asked, jumping out of her seat before noticing the open exit door. Before she could ask about it, Reid walked through, followed by heavily armed guards with automatic weapons, knives, swords, and riot gear.

"I don't believe that's the question you should be asking right now, Paquette." She smirked, brandishing a pistol of her own and aiming it at the doctor. In a risky move, Paquette raised her hand quickly to the sensor, which put the command station on emergency lockdown. The lights dimmed and red lighting illuminated the room. "Ugh...must you play games?" Reid huffed before walking across the room and delivering a blow to Paquette's head with the butt of her pistol, rendering her unconscious.

Paquette came to about ten minutes later to find herself huddled on the ground in a corner with the other members of the Group, armed guards surrounding them. Reid was hunched over a computer, struggling to break through the security measures of the lockdown initiated by Paquette. "Why can't we just shut it down?" she shouted angrily at the guard beside her. Paquette locked eyes with Stay and spoke quietly.

"What's going on?" She moved closer. "What happened?"

"Quiet," Stay whispered. "She's been trying to break through the lockdown, but she's gotta know she needs a pair."

"How did zis happen?" Paquette asked, holding her head wound.

"She must have paid off the squad," Stay guessed.

"That ain't Adonis Squad. I know the IMC. They're cruel, but they're not like this. These are mercs," Fletcher added. "That logo--Apex Predators."

"Then what happened to the squad?" Stay asked.

"They were guarding outside the facility. Probably blindsided them," Shelley said.

"Zis was her plan from ze beginning," Paquette concluded, but her whispers caught Reid's attention.

She spun around and approached her former colleagues menacingly. "Look who decided to wake up. Welcome to your nightmare, Paquette."

"I knew it. I knew it from ze start. You killed her, didn't you?"

"I did nothing."

"Yeah, right. You killed Somers. You put yourself before every innocent life in ze Outlands."

"Innocent life? Please. The Outlands are filled with nothing but war and greed. No one cares for anyone but themselves. I'm just playing the game."

"Have you told zat to Newton? Where is he?"

"He's not a part of this. Not anymore. I took care of him. Right now, it's just us. And I guess there's only one way to do this: my hand and one of yours. So who's it going to be?" She walked down the line of the Group. "Who's going to let me in?" She moved over to the station and put her hand up to the sensor. "Anyone want to play?" The Group looked at each other, unsure if one of them would volunteer to provide the second hand required to unlock the security systems and open access to the branthium storage warehouse. Knowing there was little choice, Paquette stood up.

"Dr. Reid," she said, ignoring the rumblings of protest from her colleagues. All objected except for one. Stay gave Paquette a reassuring look and a quick nod.

"This will be interesting. I'll accept this treat," Reid agreed,

stepping back and revealing the vacant hand sensor.

"No treat." Paquette smiled back. "No anything. Not for you, Reid. You're not getting anything from us."

"That is inspired." Reid stepped closer to Paquette, pushing aside the mercenaries guarding them. "But, lucky for me, I don't ask--I take." And with a single swift motion of her arm, Reid pulled the sword out of one mercenary's holster and sliced off Paquette's right hand. Before it hit the ground, Reid caught it in midair. Paquette crumpled, screaming in pain, as Reid carried her bloody, motionless hand to the station and held it in front of the sensor. The lights in the room turned back to normal and all blast doors opened, revealing the bridge to the warehouse. "Bring the rest of them with us. Leave that one to bleed out."

"You bitch," Paquette gasped.

Reid laughed. "Yeah. Maybe."

She waited as her armed mercenaries ushered the other members of the Group out of the room. "Nice working with you, Paquette." Before leaving the room, Reid shot the control panel next to the door, shutting and locking it behind her.

Left alone, Paquette, struggling, managed to apply a tourniquet to her arm and put it in a makeshift sling. She crawled to the door leading to the warehouse and attempted to activate the panel, but it was too badly damaged--the door was jammed shut. With her back against the door, she sat in defeat. The loss of blood slowly caught up to her. Her eyelids became too heavy to keep open, but she fought the pain and tried to look around the room for anything that she could do. Any option. Any idea. Any sign of hope.

Tap! Tap!

The sound drew Paquette's attention to the window overlooking the refinery, where a metallic finger tapped from the other side.

"Hi, friend. Are you okay?" Pathfinder peered curiously at his creator, revealing himself.

"Pathfinder?" Paquette said, unsure if what she was seeing was real. "Is zat you?" Using all the strength of her legs, she pushed herself up against the wall and to her feet. "Are you okay?" she asked, walking over to the window.

"Yes, but are you?"

"No. Something bad happened. Something really bad. Dr. Reid...she locked ze whole facility down. Wait-- how did you manage to get out?"

Pathfinder looked down at his chest screen, which displayed the words "FAIL-SAFE INITIATIVE."

"Stay...she made you ze fail-safe. You have all our overrides--zat's how you got out." Paquette's mind raced as she began to realize what the fail-safe program was designed to do. "You don't need a pair. She's a genius, and she knew Reid was up to something. But what? Why?"

Just then, an automated voice announced throughout the facility, "PHASE RUNNER ACTIVATED."

Paquette pieced it together. "Oh no. She's going to use ze Phase Runner. She's going to steal ze branthium. We can't let her. In ze wrong hands...anyone could control ze Outlands. No one should have zat much power. It belongs to ze people."

Exhausted and soaked in her own blood and sweat, Paquette pushed herself closer to the window, face to face with Pathfinder on the other side. "Zis energy source is crucial to our survival, but in ze wrong hands, it will destroy us. We need you. Your existence is proof zat ze Outlands can survive together." Paquette looked at him proudly, and raised her only hand to the glass. Pathfinder imitated the motion, but when he did, a user interface display appeared digitally on the window, accompanied by the words "STATION SELF-DESTRUCT AUTHORIZATION TRANSFER." "You are our pathfinder. We've made you for a great purpose."

"What about you?" he asked, concerned.

"I'll be fine. I'm going to go get help. You have to stop her. Do you understand?"

"Yes. I do."

The two removed their hands from the glass, which activated the self-destruct countdown of fifteen minutes, and opened the command center exit door leading outside to Olympus.

"Good luck, friend," Paquette said as hopeful tears filled her eyes.

Inside the storage warehouse, a dozen mercenaries prepared the branthium shipments for transport. The room was very large, with hundreds of five-foot-long containers marked BRANTHIUM from wall to wall. At one end was the bridge connecting to the command center, at the other was a twenty-foot-tall ring with an illuminating light blue vortex of energy coming from its mouth--the Phase Runner. Right in front of it, leading up to the entrance, was a long rectangular platform made of metal grating, upon which stood a computer console. Before it stood Reid.

"Yes. We've made the adjustments to the Phase Runner. It'll have plenty of power and range to reach you," she said into a communications device. "And we have our payment? Good." She ended the conversation and looked down at her mercenaries. "We're in busi-ness. The Phase Runner is almost up. Get the crane ready."

The mercenaries moved to operate a robotic crane, positioning it over one of the branthium containers. Once acti-vated, the crane would automatically transfer the containers to a conveyor belt that led to the mouth of the Phase Runner. Reid walked over to the other side of the platform, where the other members of the Group sat on their knees, guarded by more mercenaries.

"So, you're all geniuses. But which one of you can help me boost the range on this machine? Anyone?" she asked pleasantly.

"Screw you," shouted Shelley. "You've been working here longer than any of us--use your own genius and figure it out. We're all done helping you cheat in life."

"Please...cheating is the only way to win in life. And whether or not you choose to resist, I will always win." Reid ordered a mercenary to follow her. "You, come. Just find a way to boost the range. This thing's got to make it to Gridiron."

"Gridiron?" Aleki laughed. "Are you jokin', bruddah? You can't make it that far."

"You will fail," Stay expressed confidently.

"Oh?" Reid casually walked over to Stay and leaned down to speak right in her face. "You know, I must thank you. Yes, this took much longer than expected, but without your help, I would have never been able to turn that black hole rock into power. And Paquette, can't forget her. I'm glad she decided to lend me a hand." Stay spit in Reid's face, who retaliated by smacking her to the ground, but before she could do any more damage, the lights in the warehouse went dark. The Phase Runner deactivated completely, and silence filled the room.

"What the hell is going on?" Reid's shout echoed through the room.

"Hey!" a mercenary yelled from the other end of the warehouse before a crash of gunfire.

"Anderson, status!" Reid's command was answered with silence. "Go check it out," she ordered the other merce-naries nearby.

"There! I see something. By the bridge." A confused mercenary pointed.

Through the darkness, Reid squinted until she spotted the silhou-ette of a tall figure with hard right angles. She knew that silhouette.

"It's just a MRVN." One of the mercenaries brushed it off with a laugh.

"The fail-safe." Stay spoke under her breath, but just loud enough for Reid to hear.

"Fail-safe? What did you do?" Reid shouted angrily at the Group before sending orders to her mercenaries. "Kill the damn thing! Kill it!" But before either one could raise their weapon, both were taken out with two quick single shots. Reid's eyes darted from one platform to the next, searching for the MRVN in question.

"Fail-safe, fail-safe...who's got the fail-safe?" she muttered under her breath. Chaos had taken over, so Reid decided to take matters into her own hands.

"Major, I'm getting the Runner back up--you call in your backup and find that MRVN!" she ordered, turning on a flashlight and running over to the computer console.

Stay smiled at Fletcher. "Good thing you added your combat experience to his programming, huh?"

"Shut up!" Reid yelled from across the platform. "Why are they talking? Why are you allowing them to talk?" She stormed toward the mercenaries guarding the Group, pulling her sword out and pointing it at one of them. "They are not allowed to speak. They're not allowed to blink. They're not allowed to do anything, and if they do, shoot them. If you don't, I will, and then I'll kill you. Got it?" The mercenaries nodded in under-standing, but the order caused Aleki to burst out in laughter.

"Are you serious? Don't blink?" His laughter faded and transitioned to a more serious tone. "He'll find you. And he'll kill you, one way or another. It's what I would do, and he's part me."

"I said don't blink." Reid lifted her sword for an attack, but a round of gunfire knocked the sword out of her hand and took out one of the mercenaries. Swinging from the hook of the crane, Pathfinder came out of nowhere and slammed Reid across the platform. Aleki stood up, grabbed ahold of the other mercenary, and tossed them over the platform's railing. He picked up a gun from the ground and helped the others.

Just then, the lights turned back on; the Phase Runner had reactivated. "Where'd she go?" Stay questioned, noticing Reid had disappeared. The mercenaries opened fire and filled the room with bullets and smoke.

"We'll hold them off, bruddah. You shut that thing down."

"Yes, sir!" Pathfinder gave a thumbs-up and ran across the platform to the computer console, throwing a few punches at mercenaries in his way. "Sorry, friend. But you had to go." Stray bullets filled the air, occasionally hitting Pathfinder, but they barely dented his reinforced metal chassis. When he reached the monitor, it read, "DESTINATION: GRIDIRON-- POWER EXCEEDING SAFETY PARAMETERS." He inserted a device that extended out of his right wrist to connect directly into the computer, attempting to shut down the Phase Runner, which had just hit maximum power.

"PHASE RUNNER--READY TO TRANSPORT."

"Shut it down!" Stay yelled to Pathfinder as she took out a merce- nary in front of her with her rifle. "You need to shut it down! You hear me, Path? You need to hurry!" Consumed with the sounds of his creators violently fighting for their lives, he struggled to focus. The noise inten- sified to almost deafening levels and through the chaos, he spotted Stay, who fell silent. With her eyes locked on Pathfinder, two bullets pierced her chest, immediately followed by two more. She dropped to the ground.

"Stay!" Aleki smacked a mercenary in the face as he ran through the sea of battle to help, but it was too late--she was gone.

Pathfinder, frozen like a metal statue, watched his creator die in front of him, unable to do anything about it. His chest screen scrambled through pages of programming to find the right emotion but couldn't, until

Aleki's tears fell as he held Stay in his arms. Pathfinder's screen stopped and mimicked what he saw, displaying the image of sadness through a mournful blue version of his usual cheerful face.

"What a shame. Of all of them, she's the one I disliked the least." Reid drew Pathfinder's attention back to the platform. "And this one? Second least," she said, holding a sword to Delgado's neck. "Let's not play games. Step away from the console, or I'll make little Delgado here-- extra little." She squeezed the sword, pressing it closer to the skin.

"That's my friend," he pleaded.

"Please...no one is your friend. You're a machine. Nobody cares about machines. Nobody *loves* machines. You're no different than that Phase Runner. You're a MRVN. We use you and turn you off when we're done. You're nothing. Now, again, step away from the console." Small bits of red blood dropped from the blade onto Delgado's white lab coat. Conflicted, Pathfinder stood down and slowly backed away, dropping his head in guilt until...

"I..." Delgado tried to speak through her fear.

"Oh, are you trying to stand up for something? Cute," Reid said, loos- ening the sword.

"I"--she took a deep breath-- "love him!" With the tip of her elbow, Delgado rammed Reid's leg, who dropped. "And he's not nothing, he's my friend." With a head butt to Reid's gut, Delgado broke free to safety. Pathfinder looked up and took this opportunity to attack, hitting the sword out of Reid's hand and off the platform.

"You killed my friend." He pressed closer, picking up Reid and tossing her across the platform. "I think you made a mistake," he said, as his chest screen grew red with anger.

"I did. I should have never created you, MRVN." Reid regained her balance.

"I know my creators, and you are not them, friend." He stopped himself and continued. "You are not even my friend."

"That's for damn sure." She quickly pulled out her pistol and shot Pathfinder, deactivating his leg. "See? What did I say? Just a machine." As he struggled to stand on one leg, she shot again, taking out his right arm. "Good thing I paid attention to the schematics, machine." Sparks flew out and his body began to twitch as she stepped closer, aiming the gun point blank to his chest. "Don't blame yourself. Blame them." She nodded toward her former colleagues, who continued their attempt to hold off the mercenaries. Pathfinder watched each of his creators struggle to stay alive as the mercenaries overpowered them, one by one. "They're all you. You're all them. It's a shame you didn't have more of me in you--maybe that would have made you a--"

Slice!

Reid's eyes opened wide and looked down at her chest to see the end of a sharp blade poking clean through her. She tried to speak but couldn't, and fell to the ground to reveal Paquette behind her, holding the sword.

"A bitch?" Paquette said, finishing Reid's sentence before helping Pathfinder to his feet.

"Fr-fr-friend," he said, through his slightly glitching computerized voice. "Did we w-win?" He looked out to his creators, who successfully finished taking out the remaining mercenaries with the help of a surviving member of Adonis Squad, Commander Al Stern, who had a bandage wrapped around his head.

"Dr. Paquette, that's all of them. Your orders?" he asked, but was answered by faint laughter nearby.

"Oh...is it?" On the floor, bleeding out, Reid dragged herself to the railing, laughing between bloody coughs.

"What the hell's she talking about?" Shelley asked, joining

[. . . CONTINUED]

Paquette and Pathfinder on the platform, followed by the others.

"I don't know. Commander?" Paquette looked to the soldier for clarification. An uneasy silence filled the room.

He put his finger to his lips. They listened cautiously and heard nothing until...

"Lock it down!" Commander Stern shouted, seconds before an onslaught of gunfire erupted from the other end of the warehouse. He returned fire, directed toward the bridge entrance doorway. The others joined in as Paquette lunged for the computer console and activated the security lockdown. A blast door closed off the entryway.

"You're never going to survive this," Reid taunted Paquette. "Especially now." She turned her sights to Commander Stern, who lay on the ground, shot dead.

"Bruddahs, I don't know about this one." Aleki held up his weapon, aiming at the blast door that had begun to shake with the pounding coming from the other side.

Pound! Pound!

"I don't know how long that door can last," Fletcher said. As the door shook, dents began to protrude.

"Pathfinder, how much time is left?" Paquette asked as the others slowly gathered around and looked at Pathfinder, confused. With a blip, his chest screen displayed a countdown: "00:05:13--FAIL-SAFE INITIATIVE." The pounding on the blast door grew louder as the timer proceeded to count down, second by second. The Group looked around at each other, but no response was needed. There was an understanding about what they had to do, and before the countdown had fallen below five minutes, their fear had turned to acceptance of the sacrifice they were ready to take--together.

"You would rather die than give up the branthium?" Reid laughed, staring them all down. "You really are...fools." Her neck went limp and

her eyes lost focus as the life left her body.

"Actually, we don't have to give it up," Pathfinder interjected.

"What are you talking about, Path?" Paquette asked.

Pound! Pound!

Small cracks appeared as the door began to lose integrity.

"The Phase Runner." Limping, he joined Paquette at the console. "Dr. Reid extended the range to reach planet Gridiron very far away." He began reprogramming the Phase Runner. "But by redistributing the power, we could target every nearby planet in the Outlands at once."

"PHASE RUNNER POWER REDISTRIBUTED. NEW DESTINATIONS: PLANETS SOLACE, GAEA, PSAMATHE, TALOS..." The announcement continued to list off locations throughout the Outlands.

"See? We can all escape. We can all survive."

"*We* can't, but *you* can," Delgado pointed out.

"*Oui*. She's right," Paquette confirmed. "Humans can't survive a phase like zat, but you--you can make it."

"Alone?" Pathfinder asked, confused.

Pound! Pound!

"We're running out of time!" Shelley warned.

"I don't want to say goodbye. You're my friends. I'd be sad without my friends."

"You'll never be without us. You'll never be alone," Paquette pointed out. "Zat's one zing Reid was right about--we're a part of you and we will always be a part of you."

"It's true," Delgado added, standing the tallest she had ever stood, and, without a single tear in her eye, she grasped Paquette's hand. "Through you, we'll live forever."

"That's what makes you so special, bruddah. You're nothing but genius and heart--and that's a big ray of sunshine, if ya ask me." Aleki held on to Delgado, followed by Fletcher and Shelley.

"Even Stay." Paquette smiled. "She lives on in you now, and we can't let zat go to waste. Ze Outlands need you--go save zem."

Pathfinder's chest screen blipped to his yellow smiley face as he raised his hand in front of the console's hand sensor and activated the transport. One by one, the branthium containers were pulled into the swirling vortex of the Phase Runner.

POUND! POUND! SMASH!

The mercenaries broke through the door, but the Group didn't budge. Gunfire shot toward the Phase Runner as Pathfinder moved into position. He turned to face his creators, who looked on proudly.

"We love you, friend." Paquette smiled.

"I love you, family." Pathfinder waved goodbye before the overwhelming force of the Phase Runner took him away, followed by the very last container of branthium.

"PHASE RUNNER TRANSPORT COMPLETE."

The Group watched until every speck of the glimmering blue light dissipated, leaving an empty hole-- still and quiet. Until the charging mercenaries surrounded the Group and drew their weapons.

"Sorry, bruddahs, but I think you're too late." Suddenly the growing sound of detonations filled the room. "Or maybe you're right on time." And with that, an explosion erupted throughout Olympus, igniting the residual branthium in the refinery and resulting in catastrophic destruction.

Throughout the Outlands, containers of branthium randomly appeared in cities, towns, and planets with no explanation. Very few knew where they came from, and no one knew how they got there. The story and the lives of those who sacrificed themselves were lost, but the Outlands were saved, all thanks to the courage and tenacity of a group of geniuses and a single MRVN who put hope, love, and kindness above all else.

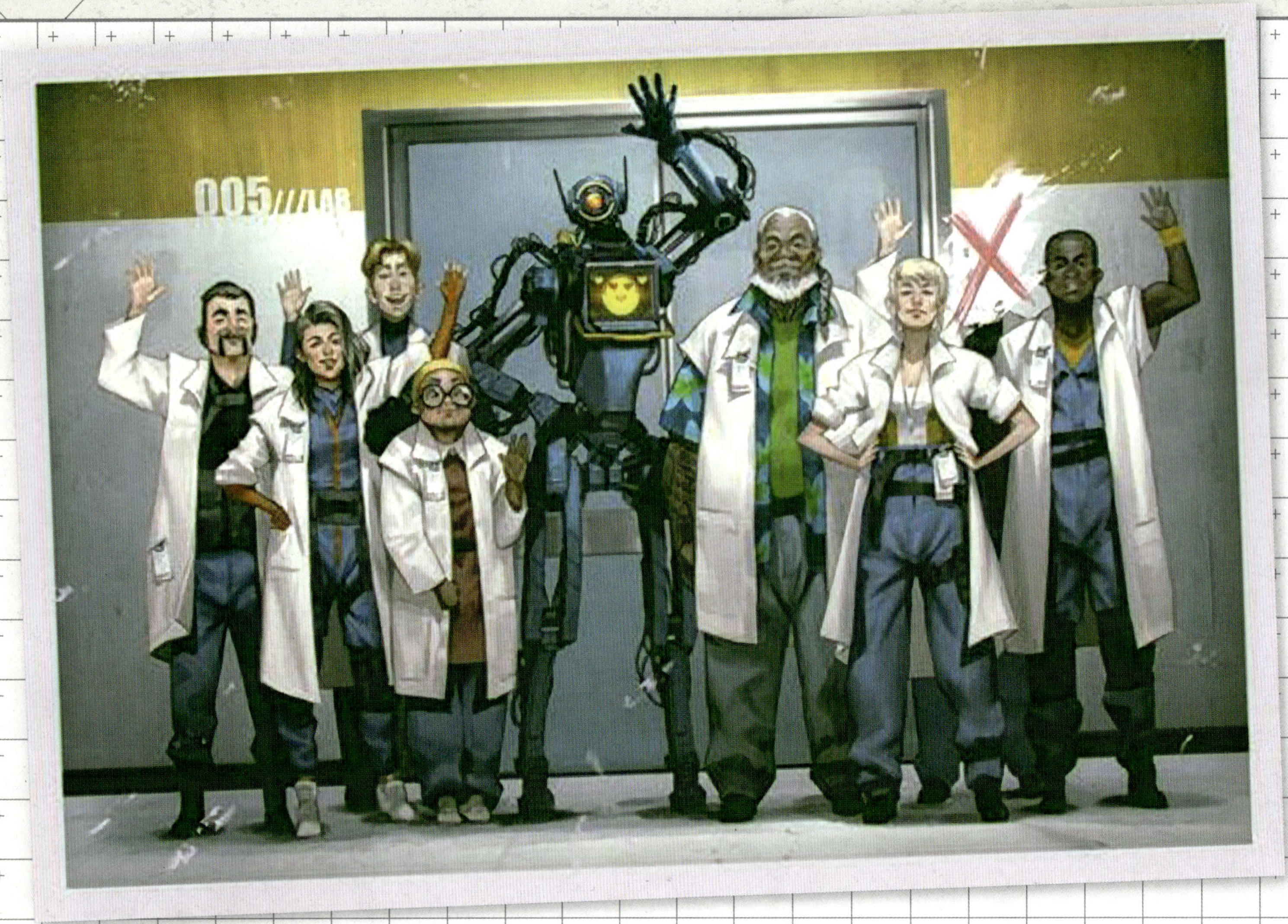

005//AA8

* PROJECT: IRIS GROUP (FROM LEFT TO RIGHT): DR. CONAN SHELLEY, DR. ANASTASIA "STAY" OLIVEIRA, NEWTON SOMERS, PROFESSOR MILLY DELGADO, PATHFINDER, DR. ALEKI GIBRALTAR, DR. AMÉLIE PAQUETTE, UNKNOWN, DR. ARMEN FLETCHER.

[. . .]
Hey. You bloody shut down or what?

I DID IT.
You killed 'em, eh?

NO. I SAVED THEM. I SAVED EVERYONE. I FOUND MY CREATORS!
That's good. What do you want—a statue? You got what you came for, now get out of here.

THANK YOU SO MUCH, FRIEND. I DON'T KNOW HOW TO REPAY YOU. I FINALLY KNOW WHO CREATED ME. I FINALLY KNOW WHERE I CAME FROM. THIS MEANS SO MUCH TO ME, AND I HAVE YOU TO THANK.
Right. Just keep fightin', kid.

OKAY! I CAN'T WAIT TO TELL ALL MY FRIENDS!

Oi! One more thing . . . Did you ever find . . . ? Eh. Forget it.

WHAT? DID I EVER FIND WHAT?
Actually, I, uh . . .

TELL ME! IS THERE MORE TO THE STORY THAN WHAT WAS ON THE CHIP?
Just one small detail. But why don't you turn that recorder off. This one's just between us, eh?

OKAY. YOU'LL TELL ME AFTER I TURN IT OFF—

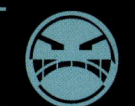
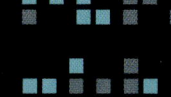

PATHFINDER MEMORY LOG: THE END OF MY QUEST!

I did it!

My quest is finally over!

Thanks to my new friend Blisk, I learned everything about my past. My creators seemed so amazing and so smart and so amazing. And I got to help them save the Outlands! I've always felt like there was a special connection between me and the Outlands, but I never thought I was part of something *THIS* big.

I remember when I first woke up in my warehouse long ago, I didn't know who I was or what I was supposed to do. I guess I must have damaged my memory files on impact after I used the Phase Runner, which spit me out on Solace. And it seems, considering that the explosion caused that crazy Phase Rift thing on Olympus, everything from around that time is still a bit fuzzy, but I remember at that moment, when I woke up and looked around, I felt at home. No matter where I went—cooking on Olympus, playing detective in Malta, or fighting in the Games on Solace—I still felt at home. But with a home comes a family . . . and I didn't have one.

I was alone . . .

But now all that has changed. All my searching. All my fighting. All my—EVERYTHING.

It's just like what I learned from Wraith. She talked about how what you put out in the world will always come back to you. Of course for her, she meant it as a bad thing with her mean colleague, but it can also be a good thing. I think I'm always kind and nice to people, and because of that, the world is kind and nice to me. Everyone I talked to on my quest was nice to me. Horizon just met me and she didn't hesitate to help me, which tells me a lot about her.

And even Revenant helped . . . I think! It's silly, funny, and scary to think about, but it's because of Revenant trying to scare me and showing me that sometimes people will stand in your way for no reason that I got the power and courage to talk to that other scary guy, Blisk. At least, that's how I think about it. I know my friends Bangalore, Loba, and Octane would call that "perspective." There's different perspectives to everything. There's always a different side of the story and a different point of view in someone else's shoes. Like how Wattson thought she saw a ghost when she was little, but from the other side of the story, it was Wraith all along! Life is full of so many tiny little details like that, and when you put them all together, you've got yourself a beautiful picture of who you are and what you can be.

My quest showed me *MY* beautiful picture, which is made up of all these little tiny details my creators put into my programming. Like my love of

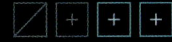
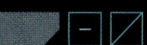

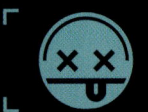
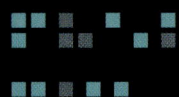
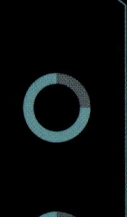

ice cream, and my love of friendship, and even my giant yellow smiley face—that's all because of my creators. They may be gone, but they live on forever inside me. That's why I still have a big yellow smiley face on. Of course, I miss them and love them, but thanks to my friends, I got to know them, and that's what's really important. Mirage (my best friend) talked a little about that. When he lost his brothers, he and his wonderful mom were sad, but they found a way to deal with it . . . together.

I think that's the key right there—togetherness. I may have started this quest alone, but I didn't finish it alone. I finished it with my friends. My "bruddahs," as Gibraltar says. He calls everyone that and he treats them the same, too, because he values life. Same with Bloodhound: they treat life with pride and honor. It really gives me pride and honor knowing that all my friends valued me enough to help. They all wanted me to succeed. Rampart pointed that out . . . and I'm glad she did, because I almost let them all down.

But I couldn't do that. Not to them.

Inside the Games, we may be fighters who compete against each other, but on the outside . . . we're different. Even Caustic and Crypto— those two are far from friends, but I got to talk to both of them . . . at once! And they didn't even try to kill each other. Maybe because they found out they may be brothers or something (I'm not quite sure what happened there), but either way, they both helped me. They helped me learn my story. They all helped me find my creators . . .

- Dr. Amélie Paquette
- Dr. Conan Shelley
- Dr. Aleki Gibraltar
- Dr. Armen Fletcher
- Dr. Anastasia "Stay" Oliveira
- Professor Milly Delgado
- Newton Somers
- And of course, Dr. Ashleigh Reid—even though she was evil and killed all my creators

I'm so happy I found them. I'm so happy I got to know who they were because, like Lifeline said on day one, they helped me learn who *I* am. It was the search for my creators that opened my eye to the real me. Those wonderful people gave me my life, gave me my purpose, and now, they've helped me see the one thing I've always needed most in my life.

My creators helped me find the path to my true family. The one I've had all along.

I love my family, and I can't wait to tell them my story.

Exciting!

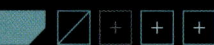

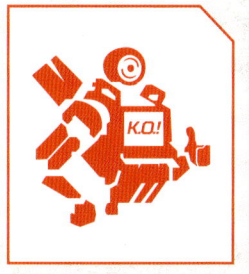

► OBJECTIVE COMPLETED ◄

> SAVING MEMORY LOG . . .

> INNER MONOLOGUE DEACTIVATED . . .

> ARCHIVING FILES . . .

> PROJECT CLOSED.

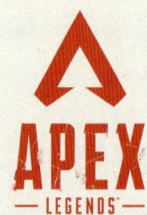

ADDITIONAL STORY BY

Mohammad Alavi, Steve Fukuda, Jesse Stern, Neel Upadhye

SPECIAL THANKS TO

Jason Torfin, Erin Gums, Audrey Wojtowick, Alexa Kim, Paul Messerly, Moy Parra, Jung Park, Brad Allen, Cristina Ferez, Ryan Lastimosa, Respawn Vancouver, Sam Gills, Amanda Doiron, Josh Mohan, Pete Scarborough, Shane Carey, Josh Medina, Shawn Price, Drew Stauffer

ACKNOWLEDGMENTS

Vince Zampella, Chad Grenier, Jason McCord, Arturo Castro

WRITER'S NOTE

Creating a world from the ground up requires an immense amount of patience, support, and trust. The *Titanfall* and *Apex Legends* universe would not exist without our amazing fans who have helped bring this world to life with art, theories and discussions, and overall excitement. An old friend once said that a human's concept of love requires admiration, attraction, devotion, and respect— CONCLUSION: WE ARE 100% IN LOVE WITH OUR FANS. THANK YOU.

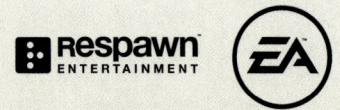

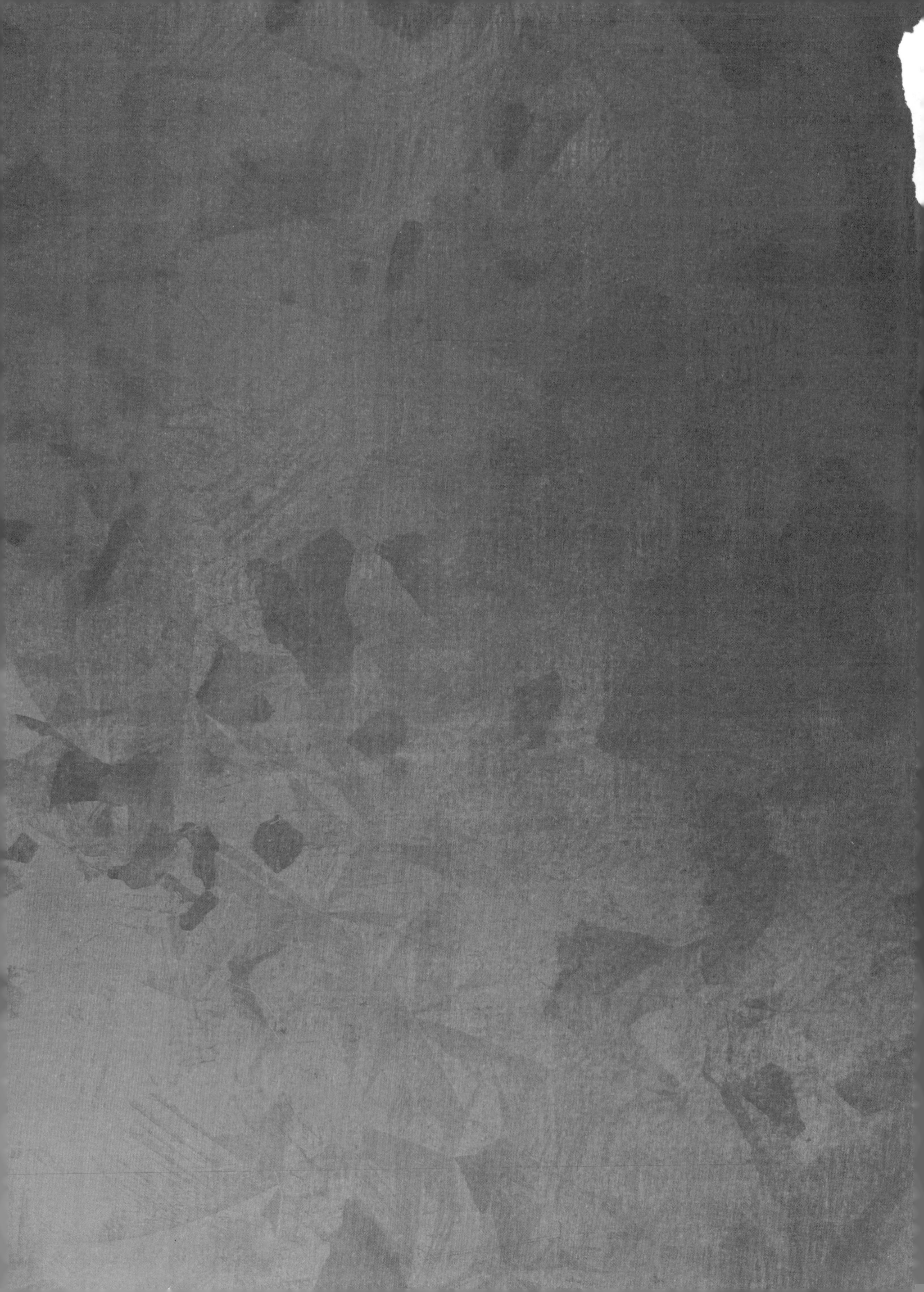